Ways of
Understanding
Religion

Ways of Understanding Religion

Walter H. Capps

The Macmillan Company, New York

The Macmillan Company
866 Third Avenue, New York, New York 10022

COLLIER-MACMILLAN CANADA, LTD., TORONTO, ONTARIO

Library of Congress catalog card number: 77-151166

FIRST PRINTING

For Doug and Liz,
Whose outlook refreshes

Preface

A book of readings makes its point in its selection of materials and the schema by which they are arranged. The point of this book is that religious study is a *subject field* before it is anything more discrete than that. In both design and content, this book gives evidence that the study of religion has many subjects, employs many disciplines, manifests many intentions, and gains insights from many sources. At the same time, it also illustrates that these subjects, disciplines, intentions, and insights can be distinguished on the basis of certain implicit "logics." Thus, the materials of the book have been selected to illustrate some of the more obvious and recurrent scholarly approaches to the study of religion. And, in the design of the book, those materials are arranged according to fundamental methodological habits and tendencies. The book itself is presented as a kind of grammar—a grammar with casebook examples—of prominent and tested, although not necessarily proven, ways of bringing religious phenomena to understanding.

The occasion for the book is partly occupational and partly convictional. Those of us with teaching positions in religious studies in colleges and universities have come to recognize that our starting point is not a matter that can be taken for granted. We also know that this matter is crucial if the goal of teaching is not simply the titillation of students but also the inspiration of scholarly excellence and the provocation of deep-seated self-knowledge. The starting point is conceived, then, as the first moment in a measured sequence, to be judged on the grounds of its resourcefulness and durability. It serves as an invitation to courtship, but it must also give any elicited romance something to feed upon. Consequently, some of us begin by referring to the major religious traditions of Western and Eastern cultures, thus attempting to bring order and depth to the subject field by focusing on *religions*. Others commence by drawing on the selected perspectives on religion that are available in other disciplines in the university curricula, joining those disciplines to religion by means of the connectors *of* or *and*. Thus, there is sociology *of* religion, philosophy *of* religion, history *of* religion, and psychology *of* religion, to name the more prominent; by the same rationale, there can also be an anthropology *of* religion, a literature *of* religion, a language *of* religion, an art *of* religion, a theology *of* religion, and several different forms of the science *of* religion. Similarly, there are also courses in psychology *and* religion, or religion *and* science, religion *and* literature, religion *and* society, religion *and* the humanities, and so on. In both of these forms, the chapters and sections in the course outline are supplied by other fields and disciplines, whereas in the world religions (or comparative religion) approach the segments in the course outline make reference to historical-cultural religious traditions. Still others focus on *history* and from there operate in one of two fundamental directions. On the one hand, they attempt to do a "history of religion"—that is, a tracing of the occurrence of religion from the earliest to more recent times. And because that task lends itself to pattern-tracing, motif-researching, and the other forms of thematic analyses that also belong to intellectual history, "history of religion" often resembles structural description and is often called "phenomenology of religion." On the other hand, the focus on history is also directed toward the large and constantly expanding body of information that has been supplied by scholarly research in religion. The materials that scholars in the field have uncovered and the tracking and collating of those materials are then joined together to provide a "history of the history of religion." Furthermore, in addition to starting points that attempt to be comprehensive, there are also those that are deliberately partial. These, too, vary widely. Sometimes they are designed to give prominence to a particular culture (as, for example, "Western religious traditions"), sometimes to a chosen focus ("religious men" or "religious institutions"), sometimes to a particular human faculty ("the religious imagination," for example), and sometimes to topics whose principal recommendation is the particular expertise of the instructor of the course.

Unlike other approaches to religious studies, this book is not partial to any of the aforementioned means of effecting rapprochement. Its primary interest is not in making the subject field more discrete; instead, it is directed toward sorting out starting points. It attempts to distinguish starting points, and to come to terms with them, by focusing on two key methodological factors that are implicit in all of them. First, it looks for a *focal object*, namely that which forms the subject or is the topic under discussion. Sometimes this is religion *per se*, sometimes religions, sometimes religious aspects of something else, and sometimes a vast array of subjects which carry ramifications regarding an interpretation and understanding of religion. Second, it searches out the particular *formal interest* of reason that is operative in a given approach. Sometimes, for instance, the inquiry into religion is guided by an interest in uncovering a fundamental core-element (the "essence" or "nature" of religion, for example). Sometimes that interest is directed toward comparison and contrast as, for example, when differences and similarities are spotted between two religious traditions. Sometimes the interest of reason is synthetic, that is, the scholar is attempting to build bridges between phenomena and to bring diverse types of things into an agreeable or systematic grouping. A synthetic formal interest is operative, for example, when religion is taken as a component of culture, and the attempt is made to blend the components together in fitting or harmonious arrangement.

Again, instead of trying to promote a single way of understanding religion, this book focuses on the techniques men employ in trying to come to terms with it. It will not proceed from there to register the claim that the reality of the subject is locked into the technique by which the subject is approached, but it will argue for clarity regarding the use of techniques and precision in recognizing their occurrence. The book holds that focal object and formal interest are present in every disciplined approach to religion (though, of course, in a great wealth of combinations), whether they are exhibited in books, articles, or in the classroom.

A third interpretive factor, distinct from the two already mentioned in that it does not function as a formal a priori, is the *insight* that a position holds to be crucial. For example, Émile Durkheim proposed that religion has social origins. Wilhelm Schmidt argued that monotheism preceded polytheism in the history of man's religious consciousness. These, and like contentions, can be regarded as being both primary and formative, for they also tend to control the positions within which they occur in a substantive way. Without them, the approaches in question would tend to collapse. They are also prominent, visible, and easy to detect.

The overall purpose of the book, then, is twofold. Its first aim is to lend order to the large and expansive subject field called "religious studies." In this respect, the book seeks more to make that order conscious than to create it. Secondly, its purpose is to call attention to some methodological factors that regulate prominent approaches within the subject field. In this respect, too, the fulfillment of purpose depends more on analytical than on creative ability. The goal is simply to secure dispositions that are already present in the materials, so that ways of understanding religion can be traced, mapped, and eventually committed to corporate awareness.

Parenthetically, it would seem that such work is necessary before the next chapter in the story of man's attempt to come to terms with religion can be enacted. If additional directives are to be forthcoming, some disciplined attempt to place and assess the results of work already undertaken or completed is required. Decisions can then be made regarding the aspects of that work that should be continued and extended. Then there will also be tested groundwork on which other ventures can be wisely begun. Indeed, it may well be that a work on method, which sorts out techniques, assesses their respective gains, and spots their vulnerabilities, is itself testimony that work long-conceived is approaching self-consciousness. It might also be a prelude to something new, or a sign that the next chapter in that enterprise can be regulated by sensitivities of a different kind. But this is a subject that belongs to another time.

The men whose writings appear in the anthology are generally representative of two classes of scholars as far as religious studies are concerned. Some can be referred to as "classical" representatives of a given stance. Others have been selected because of their association with a key "breakthrough" in the study of religion, despite the fact that many of these men did not write with religious studies foremost in mind. The "classical" scholars established definitive and repeatable patterns of scholarship. The others, for the most part, provided innovations or new wrinkles on previously established approaches. The selection of materials, therefore, is based primarily on typological considerations. Consequently, if the book is not used this way, but is taken simply as a collection of outstanding contributions in the field of religion, it will be seen to exhibit marked omissions, some of which (Arnold van Gennep and G. van der Leeuw, for instance) are glaring. Furthermore, some of the materials included are not the first that come to mind in a particular author's case, nor would they be regarded by their writers as their most important contribution. The editor is aware of these factors, yet believes he can justify the rationale that governed the selection of both spokesmen and materials. His goal was to provide a "representative sampling" based on the occurrence of typifying characteristics. When such a choice was necessary, preference was given to criteria of form rather than content, but that preference is in keeping with the overall intent that the book be a kind of casebook grammar.

In addition to using this preface for purposes of outlining the book's point of departure, the editor wishes to record his appreciation, first to the various living authors who made their works available to him, and to Professors Van A. Harvey of the University of Pennsylvania, Jonathan Z. Smith of the University of Chicago, and William F. May of Indiana University for studying the prospectus of the book. Gratitude is expressed, too, to three students, William Darrow, M. Gerald Bradford, and E. Fred Tonsing, for helping with the preparation of the manuscript, and to the members of the faculty in Religious Studies at the University of California, Santa Barbara, for reliable counsel. Special thanks go to Hinda Elmore for typing some of the selections and the introduction to the book. He is also particularly grateful to Charles E. Smith, Religion Editor of The Macmillan Com-

pany, for encouragement, valuable suggestions, and unfailing coopera-
tion, and to Joan Delaney, efficient production editor.

The book itself was prepared during the summer of 1970, part of
which the editor spent with his family in desirable places of rest and
refreshment in the Pacific Northwest. The enthusiasm for the book
was sustained by resources of simple kinds and, of course, by the
beauty of clear water, lush hills, and big sky. Sharing this with one
who cherishes the untrammeled, trains our children to hearken after
novelty, and yet holds out for the reality of concrete things, a writer
is aware that his book has enjoyed a goodly situation.

W. H. C.

Contents

Introduction

Men sometimes view religion from the outside looking in, sometimes from the inside looking out, and sometimes from the inside looking around. Where they stand has a bearing on what they see, and what they see is instrumental in what they do. What they do influences what they discover, and how they understand has an effect upon what they understand.

A map of the interests in religion displayed by scholars and non-scholars alike would give focus to the following range of interests. It would record that men sometimes seek to explain religion. At other times they wish to isolate its component parts. Sometimes they are content to locate a place for religion within the larger worlds of discourse and endeavor, and at other times they attempt to synthesize religion with other aspects of human experience. Sometimes they try to compare and contrast religion with other disciplines or forms of experience, or one religion with another. On still other occasions men question whether religious claims can be supported, and thus try to establish the grounds upon which religions can be verified. And when they explain, isolate, locate, describe, synthesize, compare, contrast, and verify religion, they characteristically talk about religion, religions, religious traditions, religious persons, religious institutions, religious values, religious influences, religious factors, religious aspects, and religious implications. What they do makes ostensible sense, but they are looking at religion from a variety of standpoints and in a variety of ways.

It is the purpose of this volume to give attention to some of the prominent patterns of understanding that have been applied to studies of religion. It seeks to map the interests that are implicit in approaches to religion, and the techniques employed. It recognizes that religion is a vast, complex, and multiform phenomenon that no singular, one-dimensional method of access can exhaust. It also knows that the particular interest men have in religion has an influence upon what they see and discover when they look at religion. For example, if one means "religious traditions" when speaking of "religion," he will look at given or known religious traditions when examining religion. But if one means "cultural component" when looking at religion, his rendering of the subject will occur primarily in cultural-component terms. Consequently, what the scholar looks for also has a bearing on what he does when he approaches the field. When the scholar sees religion as traditions, he is in position to turn his attention to examinations of the major world religions (Buddhism, Hinduism, Judaism, Shintoism, Islam, and Christianity) in depth or in relation to one another. But if he has persons in mind when he thinks of religion, the scholar's approach to religion will come to resemble psychological inquiries. In the same manner, what the scholar sees and does has a bearing on how he interprets his findings. For example, those who see religion primarily as a component of the process of human culturation are in a position to decide whether religion should be looked upon with favor or contempt. Some have argued that religion is the prime force in the civilizing process while many others have seen religion as a burden from an outmoded time, an obstacle that the human race must outlast, overcome, and eventually forget. The interpretations vary with the perspectives through which religion is seen and the auspices under which it is approached.

It would be exceedingly difficult to supply comprehensive reasons for the variations in understanding that occur when men consider religion. If there is any reason at all, it must simply be that human attention is drawn in idiosyncratic ways. Experiences do not always register in the same way, nor do the same experiences always register. Men do not see the world in the same way, nor do men always see the same world. For a host of reasons, men simply find some things interesting, and within that interest-schema some other things are noted. As Ludwig Wittgenstein tirelessly attested, "meaning" is an odd-job word that eludes regular function. Meaning, like attention and interest—the prime factors in the cultivation of perspective—is a term for which a uniform grammar of usage cannot be drawn.

Yet, while one cannot give an account for the variations in men's ways of understanding religion, he can map and trace them. He can undertake this by isolating the prime variants in selected approaches to religion. One prime variant, for example, are the *schools* in which scholars are trained. Schools—faculties and universities—approach the subject-field in somewhat characteristic fashion. Distinctive traditions of scholarship and methodological skills have been associated, for example, with the so-called Chicago and Uppsala schools. The faculty in *religionsgeschichte* and *religionswissenschaft* at the University of Marburg, to name but another institution, has fostered a long tradition of distinctive scholarship, and much of the variety within the field of religious studies can be attributed to the specific influences of such sustaining centers of learning. Another prime variant is the assortment of *special interests* that develop within the field of religious studies. A particular way of viewing religion, for example, has grown up alongside the scholarly interest in mythology. Indeed, a special-interest group—the so-called "Myth and Ritual School"—has developed on a variety of campuses with advocates from faculties around the world. And there are a number of other special interests that develop within the field in cross-campus fashion each possessing its own ways of approaching the subject. A third prime variant has reference to the *academic fields* within the university through which different interests in religion are cultivated. The attitudes and approaches to religion that develop within the field of sociology, for example, can be distinguished from those that belong to philosophy. The psychology of religion is much different in initial focus from the history of religion. Because much of the scholarly interest in religion has come out of the several subject fields that make up the arts and sciences, many of the differences in approach can be traced to those same sources. A fourth variant are the *philosophical stances*, which have often served as carriers of religious interests. For example, the philosophical position (or school) called phenomenology was first put forward to clarify a nest of epistemological dilemmas; but, very quickly, it was also seized upon by theorists in religion. Similarly, Hegelian philosophy—which has a host of its own variants—serves as the background for many of the evolutionary theories that were applied to the history of religion in the nineteenth century. A number of living scholars in religious studies have been influenced by logical positivism, or, more recently, linguistic analysis. Often the philosophical antecedent is not a distinct way of approaching the subject but is rather a figure (Immanuel Kant and Auguste Comte for example) who has posed certain issues in a particularly decisive fashion. Consequently, many of the variations that occur among approaches to religion have reference to philosophical positions and their respective sets of interests and techniques.

The format designed for this anthology, however, emphasizes none of the previously mentioned methods of classification. Instead, it looks for differences in scholarly interests and techniques. It charts what scholars look at and what they profess they would like to be able to do. It pays attention to the subjects of their inquiries—as well as to their expectations. To do this with precision, the format focuses on two methodological factors that are implicit in every disciplined approach to religion and, at the same time, admit wide variations between themselves. The first of these is the *focal object* of the examination; and the second is the *formal interest* through which the subject is approached. The focal object specifies the subject matter under discussion; it denotes the substance of the inquiry. As previously noted, focal objects range between religions, religion, religious properties, and religious aspects of other subjects and properties. The second factor, the formal interest, refers to the particular intention under which the subject is being treated; it specifies the methodological technique. Such interests of reason vary widely. They include such diverse goals as the isolation of core elements, the comparison of characteristic features, and the synthesization of constituent parts. In every disciplined and methodical approach to religion, focal object and formal interest are present. Regardless of the particularities of the subject and the inquiry, these two methodological factors adhere together. Furthermore, both focal object and formal interest are specifiable; both can be tracked and named.

For example, many scholars have made religion their focal object, and the isolation of a core element their controlling formal interest. In their own words, their purpose is a discovery of the fundamental component of religion. Some have said that the roots of religion are in magic; others have argued that the mythological mode of apprehending the world is the primary datum of religion. Some have argued that the concept of "high God" is religion's most pervasive characteristic. Others have seized upon power, fear, or awe as religion's *sine qua non*. Sometimes core-element is construed in chronological terms; then, its primacy derives from its being first, often first in a series. Chronological primacy may simply mean beginning, but "root cause" may also be implicit in it. But, as has already been indicated, primacy need not always be chronological. Sometimes the fundamental component is a logical principle. Sometimes it is also claimed to be ontological, in which case core-element also means "essence." Sometimes the fundamental component is understood in both chronological and logical terms, but, in every instance, regardless of the manner of projection, there is a methodological assumption that the materials before one's eyes will yield a single indispensable, rudimentary norm. In all such cases, religion itself is the focal object and the discovery of a fundamental core element the controlling formal interest.

The variations on this pattern are multiple. For example, some scholars will share an interest in religion as the focal object, but will care very little about isolating a singular core element. Instead, they will move toward identifying a multiplicity (or constellation) of interdependent components of religion. Their focus is on religion, but their expectation is that the norm will be a structural pattern rather than a single entity or a simple principle. At the same time, there are many inquiries in which there is a shift not only in formal interest but also in focal object. Many scholars do not focus on religion *per se*, but on religions or religious traditions. Such inquiries can make the isolation of a rudimentary norm their controlling interest of reason, but they need not do so. More frequently, they want to spot likenesses and differences among the religions, or they may intend a structural description of a given religious tradition. Similarly, the scholar who engages in comparative studies, but who has fixed his gaze on religion as a factor in the development of personality, may be interested in working with likenesses and differences between religiously sensitive men. Alternatively, if that same scholar saw religion as a factor in the development of personality but was interested in uncovering a rudimentary norm, he might seek to isolate the distinguishing marks of religious men. Then, when the interest changes from an isolating of norms to a synthesizing of components, the scholar who is looking at religions is in a position to construct a schematic framework in which several religions can be correlated. Or, he may be interested in fixing harmony between religion and other forms of cultural endeavor. Or, to change the interest but not the focus, he may want to delimit the range of religious factors in culture. Focus-interest combinations are, obviously, numerous, and the ones referred to here are cited for illustrative purposes only. They indicate something of the vastness, magnitude, and multiplicity of the ranges of interests that are invoked when men reflect upon religion.

The strategy implicit in the format of this volume is straightforward. The goal is simply a presentation of representative essays of scholars who are regarded both as methodological catalysts and as contributors of substance to the study of religion. The essays are arranged, however, to highlight some of the patterns of approach that have been prominent in this enterprise. Each of the seven patterns—some more visibly than others, and some more recently than others—has enjoyed a distinctive place in religious studies over a significant length of time. Although there are manifest variations within each of the patterns, there is also basic agreement about the direction of the study of religion and the nest of issues that form its starting point. The writers of the first group of essays, for example, share an interest in isolating a single core element; all of them understand themselves to be focusing on religion. In the second group, time is taken as the fundamental datum, and there is interest in discovering the origin or source of religion, or, alternatively, its evolutionary or historical development. Consequently, religion is seen either as a chronological first, an antecedent, or a concomitant of time. The third group of essays represents attempts to give structural description to the components of religion. For the most part, the focus in the first three sections of the anthology is on religion, and not religions, religious traditions, aspects, factors, or implications.

But in the fourth group of essays attention shifts to religions, and the intention includes both in-depth analyses of one religion and comparison-and-contrast of several of them. In addition, there is an attempt to trace the process of institutionalization as it applies to religion. The focus throughout this section is on those coordinated patterns of belief, practice, and worship that are recognized as religions or religious traditions.

Theological considerations rule the fifth group of essays, in which religion and/or religions are approached and assessed on the bases of convictions previously accepted. From this perspective, the focus might be on a particular religion (judged to be true or special) and the attempt may be made to certify the truth or uniqueness of that religion by separating it from its rivals or competitors. Or, the focus may be religious truth—a comprehensive truth larger than any individual religion—and the interest of reason may reside in subsuming all religions to that higher vision or principle, or indicating each one's share in it. The same methodological pattern would pertain if that higher principle were a socioethical ideal—the idea of tolerance, for example, or good will among people of different ethnic or cultural backgrounds—and if theological understanding were tapped to give place to all religions without making reference to scales of superiority or inferiority.

In the next group, the focal point is the language of religion and the formal interests of reason include both the quest for rudimentary elements and the structural depictions of necessary components. The final group of essays focuses attention on the human personality, and religion is treated as a factor in motivational, attitudinal, and behavioral development. The patterns of approach derive from constellations of shared interests within which there is also general agreement regarding either—and sometimes both—the focal object and the formal interest of reason vis-à-vis the study of religion.

After the reader has become familiar with the material in this anthology, and especially after he has been able to distinguish the various perspectives that are used when men reflect about religion, a number of other questions will doubtless occur to him. He might wonder, first, if there are ways in which men who represent various attitudes and approaches—and whose work originates in a variety of academic fields—can ever communicate their findings to each other. From all appearances, religious studies is a large and conglomerate field, and a very real prospect exists that there is, in fact, no common subject around which its interests turn. What men define as "the essence of religion" is not necessarily the same as what they isolate as religion's "root cause." Nor is the "religion" that is "cultural component" necessarily identical to the "religion" that is personality quotient. Indeed, it is entirely conceivable that none of the subjects under discussion when men seek to explain, describe, isolate, synthesize, and verify "religion" are the same as any of the others.

And, by the same token, it is equally conceivable that none of the substantive distinctions in "religion"—religion as tradition, institution, cultural component, form of experience, and the like—share a common likeness. Turned the other way, it would also follow that the only definitions of religion that hold are operational ones, those whose terminology is derived from distinctive, substantive, and methodological interests. It is noteworthy, for example, that many of the definitions of religion that claim to be comprehensive tend to play upon words such as *ultimacy, sacredness,* and *transcendence,* sometimes singly, and sometimes in combination. Such words must surely have reference to the qualities and characteristics of "religion" that seem to occur in more than one operational framework. The repetition of their occurrence, however, need not imply that they are indeed properties or attributes of a common essence. Nor does it follow that "religion" itself is the product of their sum total. Furthermore, it is altogether likely that scholars in the field are not necessarily interested in the same subject when they pursue "religious studies." The words "religious studies" may simply be an extrapolated container whose expansiveness, flexibility, and imprecision can give place to the various approaches to "religion" that depend upon substantive and formal exactness. In short, religious studies is a subject field before it is anything more discrete than that. When it becomes more discrete, the definitions it gives to religion tend to multiply.

Naturally, such a recognition carries important ramifications for programs of studies in religious studies in colleges and universities. Minimally, for example, it would follow that unless such programs have the resourcefulness of a large faculty with representation in all of the substance areas, they are obligated to be partial in their capabilities and stresses. Only at certain introductory levels can they pretend to be comprehensive. It might be that several such programs or departments—each with a characteristic stress—can together make some semblance of "covering the entire field." But it would also mean that a student trained under one aspect of the field should also be taught that his is one very useful approach, alongside of which there are a variety of others, because religion is a pervasive, extensive, and multiplex phenomenon. To study religion is to be engaged in reflection and research on a constellation of subjects within which there is never any one sure and direct path to the center.

In addition, the multiplexity by which religious studies is pervaded also implies, on the one hand, that the field will be characterized by a perpetual novelty and freshness. There is no conceivable end to the range, nor extent to the richness, that derives from the interplay between focal objects and formal interests. Because the combinations of interests are multiple, the number of projects that can be undertaken are almost limitless. On the other hand, this inexhaustibility also means that no student within the field can ever be completely confident that he has said all there is to be said—not only about "religion" itself but also about more specific subjects within the field. If his own personal integrity depends upon the confidence that comes from knowing that an undertaking is absolutely finished, he might be well advised to seek his inspiration from other fields of endeavor. Similarly, if he has aspirations toward professional commitments to the field, he should be warned of its multiplex character before he closes out other potential occupations. For, just as perpetual novelty and freshness can be regarded as a positive factor when understood as a deterrent to rigidity and ossification, so also can it become a burden when men want things neat, tidy, and finished.

This also raises the significant possibility that the vastness and multiplexity of the subject range is testimony to the embryonic state in which religious studies now reside. Although evidence could be mounted to dispute this claim, there is impressive support for the thesis that the objective study of religion is a very young scholarly enterprise. In many places it is just now beginning; in other places it exists simply as a possibility on a drawing board. Where it does exist in practice, an enormous amount of attention is being given to preliminary methodological questions. In fact, on many campuses the bulk of the curriculum in religious studies is devoted to introductory courses—not simply introductions to religion itself, but also introductions to the various sides of the subject that are deemed relevant. A large proportion of the materials of the study have not been translated from the languages in which they were written. Many of the instructors in religion are teaching in subject areas for which their graduate school training did not prepare them, and a large proportion of them are self-taught in the subjects in which they are teaching. Furthermore, the curriculum in religious studies is under almost constant revision. In no two schools can one count on its being the same. Indeed, as recent studies have shown, there is wide variation not only in the kinds of courses that are offered but also in the conception of the basic objectives of a religious-studies program. Some programs attempt to acquaint students with religions other than their own whereas others include religion within those subjects entailed by the quest for "meaning." Some place religion within a historical category; some include it in philosophy, some in literature, and a few others in political science. All of this makes it very apparent that religious studies, as a subject field, is very much different from those fields that possess long traditions in substance, method, and pedagogy. In some respects, religious studies can be compared to anthropology (whose self-consciousness seems to be a somewhat recent phenomenon). In other respects, it appears more like linguistics—a field that has not yet blossomed or proliferated and, yet, has shown great promise. Religious studies is a young field, an embryonic field, whose flowering must still be projected into the future. As an embryonic field, it sometimes attempts to do more than it is able to, and, at other times, does not do nearly as much as it will. It has not yet tested out its capabilities, clarified its sustaining purposes, or formed its long-range identity. As it matures, it also tends to change rather markedly.

Against this background, it is understandable that the study of religion has progressed, perhaps, first of all, because of outstanding catalytic figures. In recalling the history of the enterprise, one immediately thinks of men such as Max Müller, Sir James Frazer, Émile Durkheim, Max Weber, Raffaele Pettazzoni, Martin Nilsson, Erwin Goodenough, Joachim Wach, Geo Widengren, Mircea Eliade, and Georges Dumézil—men of unusual capacities, enormous energies, boundless interests, and almost inconceivable versatilities. In addition, a large number of the men whose writings are included in the anthology lived extraordinarily long lives; some of them—Suzuki, Müller, Nilsson, Schmidt, Frazer—came within a decade or two of being alive for an entire century. A number of them were simply encyclopedic in their range and competence. Talcott Parson's description of Max Weber comes close to being applicable to others:

> Anyone who attempts to understand his . . . work in its completeness to any degree cannot fail to be impressed, and to a great extent bewildered, by the enormous mass of detailed historical material which Weber commanded. Indeed, so vast is this mass, and much of it so highly technical in the various fields from which it is drawn, that an ordinary human being is under very serious difficulties in any sort of critical analysis, since a real factual check on Weber's work as a whole would probably be well beyond the powers of any single living scholar. Weber's was, what is exceedingly rare in the modern age, an encyclopedic mind.[1]

E. M. Cioran's comments on his early friendship with Mircea Eliade is written in the same vein:

> Even in those early days I was already astonished that he could fathom the Sankhya (on which he had published a long essay) and take an interest in the latest novel. I have never stopped being intrigued by the spectacle of a mind so hugely and breathlessly inquisitive that in anyone but him it would be pathological. There is nothing in his composition of the monomaniac's glum obstinacy, nothing of the obsessed man who squats in some one field, dismissing everything outside as secondary and frivolous. The sole obsession I have discerned in him, his polygraphy (and even it has abated with age), is really the reverse of one, as

[1] Talcott Parsons, *The Structure of Social Action* (New York: McGraw-Hill, Inc., 1937), p. 500.

it reflects a mind led by its insatiable hunger for exploration to seize on all subjects. There was one man whom Eliade used to admire passionately—Nicolas Iorga, the Romanian historian, an extraordinary figure, fascinating and disconcerting, who had written more than a thousand works, lively in patches but generally turgid, ill-constructed, unreadable, full of intuitions clogged in the mire. And Eliade admired him the way one admires the elements, a forest, the sea, the fields, fertility for its own sake, everything that sprouts, proliferates, invades, and asserts itself.[2]

From instances such as these, one can conclude that the study of religion has been carried forward by massive individual contributions that were then given to cross-disciplinary fertilization.

Furthermore, most of the catalysts of religious studies came into the field from the outside, as it were. Most of them would have felt comfortable teaching in any number of academic departments, and some of them never taught religion in any formal or curricular sense. In fact, many of the more strategic breakthroughs in the study of religion derive from insights whose first application was to another field. Max Weber, for example, studied social organization; Erwin Goodenough studied Hellenistic culture; Émile Durkheim studied Australian tribal behavior; Ernst Cassirer studied symbolic forms; Martin Nilsson studied the Graeco-Roman world; C. G. Jung listened to people tell of their dreams and then engaged in comparative cultural analysis; J. J. Bachofen learned how to decipher inscriptions in tombs. Very few, if any, of the catalysts—and this is important—attempted to study religion directly. And, in each of them, there was a combination of historical competence, on the one hand, and an ability to apply the results of historical scholarship in resourceful and multiple ways. In varying degrees that combination of skills led to the development of new subject fields, additional subfields, and innovations in methodology.

An additional observation need be made, partly, perhaps, to give this book sanction. Almost all of the ways of understanding religion that are represented in this collection of samples employ the techniques of analysis and judgment that are implicit in reflection. Because they are discursive and reflexive, these ways of understanding religion are also partial. This observation does not carry the implica-

---

[2] E. M. Cioran, "Beginnings of a Friendship," in *Myths and Symbols. Studies in Honor of Mircea Eliade*, edited by Joseph M. Kitagawa and Charles H. Long (Chicago: University of Chicago Press, 1969), pp. 407–408.

tion that religion has some unknown "essence" that can never be "gotten at." Nor is it simply a cryptic way of covering the editor's tracks, by allowing for schematic patterns that are not represented here. (Obviously, there are many of these.) More fundamentally, the observation points to an augmentation of another kind: in addition to ways of reflecting on religion, there are other ways of looking at religion, for example, as there are also ways of hearing religion. And looking, hearing, sensing, touching, and reflecting cannot be quite the same. Indeed, it may be argued that some of the principal tensions that occur in religion are modal or dispositional in origin. That which is heard is not always confirmed by that which is seen; that which is seen often finds no adequate substitute in that which is heard; that which is seen or heard is not always ratiocinatively grasped; and that which can be reflected upon does not always correlate with that which is otherwise sensed.

Large epistemological battles have been waged as to whether sensing precedes or follows reflecting in religious matters. Most would agree, however, that hearing, looking, and reflecting are distinguishable kinds of human activity whose interdependencies are both intricate and subtle. Consequently, one should not presume that religion is exhausted when, as in the cases before us, it is made the object of reflection. To say this, once again, is neither to malign reflection nor to cast it in a pejorative light. But it is to register the proviso that the most appropriate approaches to religion are probably mundane rather than polished, and only grudgingly reflexive and discursive. But this is an impression based upon evidence of another kind. Nevertheless, if the testimony of those who have been nurtured in what Wilfred Cantwell Smith calls "cumulative traditions" means anything, religion is also "understood" through the disciplining of a religious way of life.

PART 1

Reduction to First Principles: The *Sine Qua Non* of Religion

In this first group of selections, materials are included that illustrate the quest for the elemental root part of religion. Such materials are, for the most part, reductive; that is, they show an attempt to reduce all qualities, characteristics, and aspects of religion to those components that are absolutely basic. The goal in this kind of approach is an analysis of complex entities into an unambiguous simple element. That final simple element is then also understood as being indispensable. Without it, as Anders Nygren has said, religion would not be what it is.

Rudolf Otto, for example, found religion's *sine qua non* to be the idea of the holy (or the *sensus numinus*) after first placing religion, following Friedrich Schleiermacher, in the world of feeling or sensitivity. For Otto, the idea of the holy, found in the depths of human experience, was the religious *a priori*. Using similar terminology, but varying the pattern slightly, Erwin R. Goodenough understood man's adjustment to that which he could neither know nor comprehend to be religion's prime component. According to this view, religion arises from "the universal phenomenon that we are born and live in an external universe, and with internal depth and emotions, which we neither understand nor control."[1] Paul Tillich also sought to identify the fundamental component of religion after first placing religion in a cultural context. According to Tillich, religion's *sine qua non* is the depth-dimension, or as he states it:

> without a home, without a place in which to dwell, religion suddenly realizes that it does not need such a place, that it does not need to seek for a home. It is at home everywhere, namely, in the depth of all functions of man's spiritual life. Religion is the dimension of depth in all of them. Religion is the aspect of depth in the totality of the human spirit. . . . [This] means that the religious aspect points to that which is ultimate, infinite, unconditional in man's spiritual life. Religion, in the largest and most basic sense of the word, is ultimate concern.[2]

Selections from the writings of men who do not give indication of all of the steps necessary to underscore a *sine qua non* but who nevertheless believe religion to revolve around a fundamental element are also included in this section. Wilhelm Schmidt, for example, is the chief proponent of the view that the concept of a "high God" is basic to religion. According to Schmidt, the concept of a "high God" qualifies man's religious apprehensions from the beginning and lies behind religion's monotheistic base. Indeed, as Schmidt see it, the concept of a "high God" is universal, fundamental, and owns a chronological primacy. For all of these reasons, monotheism preceded polytheism in the history of religion. The selection from the writings of Raffaele Pettazzoni, who shares Schmidt's contentions in modified form, presents a functional view of religion that attests that all religions also exhibit an underlying *élan*, a common developmental process. This developmental pattern, the impetus toward growth, or, in Pettazzoni's words, "this single aspect, this common function" is responsible for the structural likenesses and functional analogies that can be drawn between Eastern and Western religions. In the manner according to which they work themselves out historically, all religions

---

[1] Erwin R. Goodenough, "Religionswissenschaft," in *Numen*, Vol. VI (1959), p. 86.

[2] Paul Tillich, *Theology of Culture*, edited by Robert C. Kimball (New York: Oxford University Press, 1964), p. 7.

exhibit a common internal dialectic. (It is for these reasons, of course, that, in addition to his affinities with Schmidt, Pettazzoni shares much with those scholars who regard time to be the fundamental datum).

This section of the anthology also includes an essay by the late Japanese scholar, D. T. Suzuki, which treats one religion in terms of its own *sine qua non*. In basing Buddhism on the concept of enlightenment, Suzuki is more singular in his goals than other reductionist thinkers. He does not intend to reduce all religions to a single, underlying element. Rather, he seeks to point out that enlightenment is the fundamental motif of Buddhism, and, as such, that which distinguishes Buddhism from all other religions.

Religion as Numinal Experience

RUDOLF OTTO

Rudolf Otto was born September 25, 1869, in Peine, Germany. A Protestant (Lutheran), Otto was trained for a career in theology at the Universities of Erlangen and Göttingen. He was a professor at Göttingen (1897–1914), at Breslau (1914–1917), and at Marburg (1917–1929). He died in Marburg on March 6, 1937.

Otto's career covers two aspects. During his days as a student he was influenced by the works of Albrecht Ritschl and Friedrich Schleiermacher, both of whom had attempted to find a basis for religious experience that would not be threatened by the judgments against religion implicit in Immanuel Kant's Critique of Pure Reason. *From Kantian tradition, Otto had inherited an interest in discovering a "religious a priori," that is, a grounding for religion that is given with religious experience, and whose reality does not depend upon empirical investigation. It is to this range of issues that Otto addressed his* Das Heilige *(The Holy) in 1917. However, early in his career, Otto also cultivated an interest in the religions of the non-Western and non-Christian worlds. In 1911–1912 he had the opportunity to visit Africa, India, and Japan, and from that time on Otto turned his attention to the cross-cultural dimensions of man's religious experiences. The two formative interests within his career came together when Otto recognized that* das Heilige *could be given a twofold role. On the one hand, it served as a category that gave religion an independence (vis-à-vis the good, the true, and the beautiful), and at the same time,* das Heilige *was both explicit and implicit in primitive and Eastern religions, that is, in man's universal religious experience.*

In the essay that follows, Otto traces the discovery of the sensus numinus, *the basis of* das Heilige, *in the Schleiermachian tradition.*

In the long course of its history, religion has frequently known the experience of "re-discovery." In this matter it has not been distinguished from other spheres of human endeavour and achievement—the fluc-

Rudolf Otto, *Religious Essays*, translated by Brian Lunn, published by Oxford University Press, London, 1931, pp. 68–77.

tuation of taste, the vicissitudes in creative endeavour in the arts and in the sciences. These have all known the youth of intensive creation, followed by periods of disintegration and hardening in which foreign influences have intruded and almost stifled the life that was there originally. Such periods have necessitated and produced the "Renaissances," rebirths and rediscoveries of that which had been half or wholly lost with results of varying importance and of varying degrees of permanence. And these renaissances have usually been associated with and brought about by creative personalities who at the same time set in motion new impulses and ideas, so that the effect was more than a mere rediscovery. What had been rediscovered had been brought upon a higher plane of activity on which it effected new and significant combinations.

So it has been with religion, especially with our religion, Christianity. It originated indeed itself as a kind of a rediscovery of the religion of the prophets, of the psalms and of the "quiet" in the land; the incrustations of legalism, the leaven of the Pharisees had to be scrapped. The work and letters of St. Paul again were a rediscovery of the Gospel when it was being obliterated under a new eruption of Judaic traditionalism. And again the achievements of St. Augustine and St. Francis for Christianity were a sort of rediscovery. A rediscovery of the first order was Luther's reformation and as a subsequent rediscovery of a minor order we may mention pietism, as an endeavour to shake off the crippling shackles of lifeless orthodoxy and of a new scholasticism.

Pietism preceded by about a century the rediscovery with which we are here concerned, I mean the achievement of that Church Father of modern Protestantism, Schleiermacher, under the influence of which we are living even now. Religion in his time was not being depraved by those old influences, pharisaism and brooding monkishness, the institutionalism of the Church, scholasticism, nor was piety being petrified by the formulas of orthodoxy. The forces with which it had to contend in Schleiermacher's time were quite different; we may call them by the names of "intellectualism" and "moralism," we can cover both by the term rationalism; they did not expose themselves to attack as obviously as the sect of the Pharisees, or as monkishness, or as the sale of indulgences and other dispensations of the medieval church, or as the convolutions of the scholastic systems. They were in the air rather than embodied in institutions, procedure, and organization. But for that very reason they were all the more dangerous. For a century they had dominated the spirit of the age and had stamped their seal upon it. The main features of the eighteenth century had not been lacking in nobility; it had been the period of "enlightenment" and as such one of the most significant epochs in the whole history of human thought; it had been a period during which our people especially came to be a "people of thinkers." It gave birth to the classic German philosophy; and it was just before the generation of Schleiermacher that this period came to its full fruition in the critical philosophy of Kant. His two chief works represented the achievement of the two fundamental lines of speculation of the time. His *Critique of Pure Reason* examined the nature and functioning of intelligence, and his *Critique of Practical Reason* that of practical ethics. It was a great period, whose prodigious achievement persists to the present time; but it was prodigiously one-sided in its rationalistic outlook, a fact which imported indeed a serious menace to the life of deeper experience and especially to the religious life.

It is usually represented nowadays that this one-sidedness of rationalism and its threat to religion lay in the fact that it denied the "miraculous," actually or by implication. Rationalism is held to be synonymous with the denial that "miracles" occur or that they have ever occurred. This is a misleading interpretation, and as applied to many individual rationalists it is mistaken. On the contrary a "miracle" in the traditional sense of the word, meaning some "extraordinary" occurrence, an interference with the usual clear, lawful, intelligible, fixed course of nature—this kind of miracle requires as its corollary a "rationalistic" conception of the world. Only if in the ordinary course of events the world proceeds in a rationally commensurable manner, can "miracles" in this sense occur and be noticed at all. In a natural universe of which the incommensurable, the irrational, and the mysterious is itself an essential function, and which is fundamentally not susceptible of rational explanation, "miracles" would indeed be to seek, for they would be distinguished only in degree and never fundamentally from the general course of events, so that they would never impinge as miracles or extraordinary occurrences. Thus rationalism was already part of the framework of orthodoxy itself, and there were rationalists amongst those who affirmed no less than amongst those who denied miracles. Schleiermacher's achievement in religion against rationalism was indeed not that he revived the old belief in miracles, for he renounced it; his achievement was of an entirely different order.

With all its great qualities, the philosophy of "the enlightenment" was characterized by an intensely one-sided appreciation of human nature. It valued man essentially as a being thinking according to the laws of intelligence and acting according to the laws of morality, as the creature of "theoretic" and "practical" reason. It was blind to that wealth of human nature which lies outside the scope of these capacities, to the rich profundities of immediate experience of life, and nature, and history, which lie beyond rationalistic analysis and moralistic considerations. The "enlightenment" understood the culture of the mind along its regular channels and moral culture according to pattern, but it had no room for the cultivation of the "soul" In Kant such narrowness was atoned for by the sublimity of his intellectual investigation into the powers of reason and the austerity of his ethical scheme; but this was not so with the minor champions of the enlightenment. The intellectualism of the *rationalismus vulgaris* of the age was reduced to a bald matter-of-fact complacency; world, nature, history became commonplace; the desire for explanation left no mystery, nothing that was wonderful or inexpressible, no profound riddle in the universe; the hidden springs were to be sealed up; the riddles of history, present and past, were to be rationalized by the trivial explanations of a meagre pragmatism. And in ethics the impulse of the time fell short of the sublime height of Kant's "categorical imperative"; its impulse was rather to find satisfaction in a sober, common-sense and commonplace moralizing in terms of utility and the common weal. At the same time the rationalists were far from being atheistical; indeed the enlightenment prided itself on having overcome "atheism," and it is certain that no period has been at such pains to adduce proof of the existence of God and of the existence and the immortality of the soul, nor has any period been so convinced that it was in possession of these proofs.

And yet in the process the very essence of religion had evaporated. Having proved the existence of God, men were at a loss what to do with Him. They possessed the intellectual concepts of religion, but they were not possessed of religion in their hearts. Indeed, as Schleiermacher says, religion had on the one hand become metaphysics, that is, learned theological or philosophical theorizing on certain ultimate things, which were called God, the soul, the world, and such like; on the other hand it had become transmuted into moralistic and utilitarian precepts. But its essential spirit which, as any pious person feels, is something quite different from the intellectual perception of some metaphysical things or the observance of ordinances, had escaped. Religion itself was suspect, it was termed "enthusiasm" and "fanaticism." The *sensus numinis* had died out.

The reaction against rationalism, and the resulting rediscovery of religion, proceeded from a group of persons of whom anything rather than piety might have been expected. If it be true in general that God loves "strange saints" and uses strange tools, this is specially the case here. The group in which the new herald of religion, Schleiermacher, lived on the most intimate terms was that of the young "romantics," the founders of the Romantic School who were then beginning to get talked about. It was the group which met in Berlin and Jena in the years 1797, 1798, and 1799; young men not over-orderly in their conduct, effervescent with a new impulse of life, critical and aggressive, arousing amazement and righteous indignation amongst their respectable contemporaries. The group included such men as Friedrich and August Wilhelm Schlegel, Novalis, Tieck, Schelling, and their friends. Fichte, who was just being forced out of the university of Jena for his alleged atheism, was closely associated with the group; and to the special exasperation of their contemporaries the group included women and indeed Jewesses who were notoriously both beautiful and intelligent. Pre-eminent among them was the noble and lovely Henrietta Herz, the wife of Marcus Herz, Kant's favourite pupil. Then there was the tender and clever Dorothea Veit, afterwards married to Schlegel, and Rahel Levin; and the witty Caroline from Göttingen née Michaelis, the widow of Böhmer, divorced from Schlegel and finally married to Schelling. It was indeed a strange group; and yet the atmosphere in this group was more conducive to the discovery of religion than in that other group of Berlin society which gathered round such people as Nicolai and Moritz and Engel and Süssmilch . . . and those meeting in the eminent Monday Club; people who were of course far more normal and reasonable, but who had petrified in the arid spirit of the times, and who were without understanding of the new surge of longing for a fuller vision of life.

It is true that neither the romantic youths nor the intelligent Jewesses, nor indeed the whole brilliant circle, would alone have done much to further the re-birth of religion, nor would they have desired to do so. Religion will not result from the mere resistance to rationalistic petrifaction of the spirit, nor yet from natures that are primarily poetic or aesthetic. It is an experience of a peculiar kind, is rooted in very different depths of significant human experience, and if it is to be promulgated with new life it requires not a poetical but a religious genius. The importance of that whole romantic circle, therefore, as far as religion was concerned, consisted wholly in the fact that it served as a stimulus to the one man amongst them who really knew from his own experience what piety meant and who surpassed them all in the profundity of his spirit, in the maturity and effectiveness of his character, and in the understanding of the virtues and the errors of his time. This man was Schleiermacher. He had become acquainted with piety in the restricted but intimate world of the Herrnhut fraternity. In the sore and bitter spiritual conflicts of his early youth with his own orthodox father he burst the bonds of his early traditional creed, and he also shed the academic theistical notions of the rationalistic theology of his period. But the eternal essence, the true gold of his old faith, had been preserved in the depths of a loyal spirit, and when his time was come he wrote his *Addresses on Religion to the Thoughtful amongst those who Despise It*, not with a view to defending for the thousandth time what had been so often defended before, but in order to arouse his contemporaries to the understanding of that which had utterly vanished in the midst of all their reasonable apologetics, to religion itself as a spiritual experience and as a possession of the eternal.

The Addresses were published in 1789. They are truly not a last word on the nature and value of religion, but rather a first word. Schleiermacher was to devote a whole life to a fuller, deeper, and truer explanation of religion, and it is not a matter which can be exhaustively dealt with by one man, or brought to a conclusion in a single lifetime. Moreover his book was by no means unconditioned by the time when it was written, nor equally suited and intelligible to all periods. The questions formulated and the answers given are entirely conditioned by the intellectual situation of the time, a situation of a highly complicated kind that was destined neither to be permanent nor to recur. And yet the book is still of importance at the present day; it has its enthusiastic readers even now, and quite apart from that the impulse of the movement which it started still agitates varied waves of current thought. It is a strange sort of apologia, and entirely different from any that was ever written before. It is not concerned with new investigations into the concepts of God, the soul, immortality, and such like; it would even appear to be indifferent to such conceptions, and indeed it sometimes makes use of phrases in connexion therewith which may seem to our ears harsh and aggressive. It is concerned with just one fundamental question: what actually is piety?—quite apart from all traditional conceptions of the schools. He proceeds to show that 'piety' is the highest and noblest thing that can enter the spirit of man, that the man and the period which lack it are poor indeed, however much they may have progressed otherwise in reasonableness or in practical morality, and that what is wanted is to imbue oneself and one's period once more with the impulse of 'piety.'

Now what is piety, according to Schleiermacher, and wherein does its value consist? We may paraphrase his answer in phraseology somewhat less abstract than his and more adapted to our habits.

Man has been set in this world that surrounds him, with its rich and varied activities. It may be conceived by the human intelligence and formed by human action and endeavour. Schleiermacher calls this world, as opened to our reasoning understanding and to our activity, the *universum*, attaching to the word a meaning different from its usual astronomical sense. In the sense in which he so frequently uses it, it signifies that great totality of being and becoming, of nature and of history in which we ourselves are partly links and partly masters that forge the chain. Our relation to this *universum*, he continues, is manifold. Firstly it is theoretic; we are enabled to penetrate and subdue the universe with our thought, to understand it in terms of cause and effect, according to intelligible laws. Such is the function of science; and when we would discover the highest laws, and the first principles of the *universum*, it is the function of the science of metaphysics. Secondly our relation to the *universum* is "practical." We are enabled to influence it in its course through our moral and cultural, our individual and communal work, to make it an expression of our will and our aims. Thus in the second place it become the object of our will, through our action upon it, and formative material for our ideals. These two relationships had both been understood and appreciated, but the previous age had failed, in Schleiermacher's opinion, to realize that they did not exhaust man's relationship to the universe, and that what was more valuable and more profound had not yet been said. There is a third relationship to the world: this is not science of the world, neither is it action upon the world; it is *experience* of this world in its profundity, the realization of its eternal content by the feeling of a contemplative and devout mind. This is not science or metaphysics; nor is it ethics or individual effort and directive activity. It is *religion*: the immediate apprisal of the universe as the one and the whole, transcending the mere parts which science may grasp, and at the same time the profound spiritual experience of its underlying ideal essence.

The following simile may be suggestive in assisting us to an understanding of Schleiermacher's meaning. A man enters a lofty Gothic cathedral. If he be technically proficient he can establish a 'theoretic relationship' with the cathedral; he can calculate its length and breadth; he can ascertain the principles according to which it has been constructed and its special characteristics of style; he may compute its cubic content. And if he have a practical eye, faults in it will not escape him and he will consider how it could be restored, made serviceable to practical purposes, altered and adapted; he may, indeed, himself set about the work. Thus he would establish a "practical" relationship. But there is a third possibility; he may disregard any theoretical or practical relationship, and, sitting quietly in a corner, "experience" the cathedral in receptive contemplation. It may be half ruin, or it may be an unfinished building, but he will be seized of its essential idea, which in the execution may even be concealed rather than expressed; to this spirit it will be revealed in its entirety and unity, in its mystery and sublimity, in its profound symbolism— all those unspeakable impressions which escape the man of pure theory and practice, and in which alone the real inner meaning and nature of the building is manifest. If our visitor to the cathedral be innocent of this third 'relationship,' though he be a great man in the relationships of theory and of practice, he is fundamentally wanting.

"Even so is it with you," Schleiermacher would say to his rationalist and anti-religious contemporaries, "in that great cathedral which we call the universe. You are able only to calculate, to seek after causes and effects, to classify and systematize, or else to brood upon how you shall employ it to advantage, or how you shall react upon the world. Learn yet a third thing, and thereby become what you 'humanists' so much desire to be: real men. Learn devout contemplation, that you may experience in your own beings the mysterious stirrings of the universe, the divine manifestations of nature, history, and life."

Religion, thus understood, reveals to Schleiermacher two chief moments. Firstly he says:

> For understanding and for action the universe is always just your *object*; it is always something which you wish to subordinate to yourselves through your intellect or your will. A futile undertaking, prompted by arrogance if it be not based primarily upon a *sense of profound humility* towards this universe, towards that totality of being and becoming, whence all things and you yourself have originated, in which you are comprehended and insistently borne along in accordance with its holy and eternal laws.

This sense and humble consciousness of one's own dependence within the mysterious whole is the root from which, in later years, his famous definition developed: "Religion is the feeling of absolute dependence."

Secondly: the intellect is able only to link up cause and cause, to reckon, to classify; it cannot perceive the essence of things. It is like the man in the cathedral; so long as he reckoned and theorized he was but surrounded by a stone structure. It was only when he became contemplative that the inner meaning of the thing, the "church" was revealed to him. So it is with us in the world; with all our understanding we cannot perceive its essence. It is to the devoted, contemplative spirit that its secret is revealed. Such a man will become aware of the eternal ideas, the secret divine plan governing the world, and the course of events. To him the world will become, so to speak, transparent; the eternal will shine through the temporal, the infinite, which neither space nor time can comprehend, will be revealed in the finite forms of time and space. Not in such a manner as to be reducible to a sober formula, nor will it be possible to penetrate the essence of the infinite in its own nature apart from its revelation in the finite; but it will reveal itself to the spirit with a genuine and profound experience and as a most vital reality. And hereby Schleiermacher not only rediscovered the *sensus numinus* in a vague and general way but he opened for his age a new door to old and forgotten ideas: to divine marvel instead of supernaturalistic miracle, to living revelation instead of instilled doctrine, to the manifestation of the divinely infinite in event, person, and history, and especially to a new understanding and valuation of biblical history as divine revelation. Without falling back again into the trammels of a primitive supernaturalism he prepared the way to a rediscovery not only of religion but of Christian religion and to a new interpretation of Christian religion, which was better and more modern than the old orthodox or rationalistic theology could give.

Selected Bibliography

The Idea of the Holy (New York: Oxford University Press, 1923).
Mysticism East and West (New York: Macmillan, 1932).
Naturalism and Religion (New York: G. P. Putnam's Sons, 1907).
Religious Essays (London: Oxford University Press, 1931).

Religion as Belief in the High God

WILHELM SCHMIDT

Wilhelm Schmidt, anthropologist, historian of religion, and Roman Catholic priest, was born in Hörde, Westphalia, on February 16, 1868. He was educated in Holland, Berlin, and Vienna, and taught in Germany, Austria, and Switzerland. Interested in his early career in linguistics, Schmidt took advantage of the many reports that members of the Society of the Divine Word sent back about their discoveries at the missionary posts in the South Seas and Australia. Schmidt became an expert in the languages of these areas. He then shifted his interests to cultural anthropology, a field in which he very vigorously challenged the evolutionistic theories of such scholars as E. B. Tylor and Herbert Spencer. Against the idea that religion has evolved through the ages, Schmidt argued that the earliest peoples believed in a supreme being in a monotheistic sense. He attempted to document this view in his twelve-volume work, Der Ursprung der Gottesidee (The Origin of the Idea of God), *on which he worked for over forty years. Schmidt fled from Germany to Switzerland in 1938, and died in Fribourg on February 10, 1954.*

We have already shown that the goal of all work on the lines of the historical method is not to set up theories or hypotheses, but to arrive at scientific certainty. Here we mean by "scientific certainty" the facts which make up our picture of primitive religion, not indeed as separate atoms, but as an organic and mutually interdependent whole.

If we apply that criterion to the abundant mass of data which we can now produce regarding the primitive Supreme Being, the first thing to notice is that the total sum of the facts is of a nature to satisfy the total sum of human needs. Man needs to find a rational cause; this is satisfied by the concept of a Supreme Being who created the world and those that dwell therein. He had social needs; these

Wilhelm Schmidt, *The Origin and Growth of Religion*, translated by H. J. Rose (New York: The Dial Press, Inc., 1931), pp. 283–284.

find their support in belief in a Supreme Being who is also the Father of mankind, who founded the family and to whom, therefore, man and wife, parents and children, brothers and sisters and kinsfolk owe allegiance. Man has moral needs; and these too find their stay and support in a Supreme Being who is lawgiver, overseer and judge of the good and the bad, and is himself free from all moral taint. Man's emotional wants, trust, love, thankfulness, are satisfied by such a being, a Father from whom comes all good and nothing but good. Man needs a protector to whom he can resign himself; this need is supplied in this Being, who is supreme and great above all others. Thus in all these attributes this exalted figure furnished primitive man with the ability and the power to live and to love, to trust and to work, the prospect of becoming the master of the world and not its slave, and the aspiration to attain to yet higher, supra-mundane goals beyond. Only through this conception of deity can we explain the power of our earliest ancestors to struggle onwards; and the most precious of human energies—labour, responsibility, aspirations upward, feeling for the unity of all mankind—still trace their origin to those primeval days. We thus find, among a whole series of primitive races, a notable religion, many-branched and thoroughly effective.

The second unity into which all the individual traits of the primitive Supreme Being combine and, as it were, stand shoulder to shoulder, is that of time; for he fills all time. From his eternal heaven he invades Nothingness, and begins the time-series with his creative activity. Throughout all the periods of creation and all successive periods he is lord of man's history, although he does not always actively interpose. He stands, moreover, at the beginning of each human life, accompanies it through all its length of days, awaits its appearance before his tribunal and determines the nature of its eternity. For such a unity as this primitive man has no model and no corroboration in what he sees and experiences in his own time.

The third unity, which also combines all the separate facts concerning the primitive Supreme Being, is that of space; for he dominates all space. There is but one Supreme Being, and he fills this universe; there is but one sovereign and one power extending over these distances and joining them one to another. For the God of these primitive men is not the god merely of one tribe and its environment; if only because he is the creator of the whole world and of all men, he has no neighbour whose realm could limit his. The thoughts and feelings of these men have no room for more than one Supreme Being. The personal experience of primitive man did not show him unity of time; still less did he find unity of space therein, and least of all in his social conditions.

Primitive monotheism is founded upon the sovereignty over these two unities; this high god is so great that he alone suffices for everything and for all—for all men and all times, all ideals, longings and needs. And therefore he has no peer, for his greatness knows no bounds and thus leaves no room for any neighbour.

Selected Bibliography

The Culture-historical Method of Ethnology (New York: Fortuny's, 1939).

High Gods in North America (Oxford: Clarendon Press, 1933).

The Origin and Growth of Religion (London: Methuen, 1931).

On Common Religious Impulses

Raffaele Pettazzoni

Raffaele Pettazzoni was born in Italy in 1883, and was educated at the University of Bologna and Rome. He was trained in Greek religion, and his scholarly career was launched with two studies, one on Zoroastrianism and the other a history of religion in Greek antiquity. (The latter was published in a revised edition in 1953.) He became a professor of the history of religions at the University of Rome in 1924, and retained that position throughout his career. Pettazzoni always exercised leadership in coordinating the work of scholars in the field of the history of religions. He was president of the International Association for the History of Religions from 1951 to his death in 1959.

Pettazzoni is perhaps best known for his studies of the concept of the "high God." He objected to Wilhelm Schmidt's term "original monotheism," although he shared with Schmidt the conviction that belief in the "high God" belonged to man's earliest religious apprehensions. He went on to examine the powers ascribed to the "high God" and singled out omniscience as a divine attribute of central significance. The investigation of divine omniscience is the subject of his book The All-Knowing God, *published in 1956.*

Christianity, Buddhism and Islam are the three chief religions into which the majority of mankind is distributed. Very different in beliefs, doctrines and dogmas, they have, nevertheless, some features in common: each of them has a founder from who it originated, each aims at the salvation of man, each practices proselytism, each addresses itself to every man of every country, of every nationality and of every culture. Even Zoroastrianism, which has but few followers today, and Manichaeism, now a dead religion, have the same characters.

All these religions, characterized as they are by the presence of a founder, by a soteriological ideal, by proselytism, by supernationalism, belong therefore to the same well-defined type which we may call "modern," especially on account of the fact that among the religions

Raffaele Pettazzoni, "A Functional View of Religions," in *The Review of Religion*, Vol. I, No. 3 (1937), pp. 225–229, Columbia University Press.

of this type are, as we have said, the three great *actual* religions of mankind. It is true that among them is even a dead religion, *i.e.*, Manichaeism. On the other hand, chronologically speaking, Buddhism is five hundred years earlier than Christianity, while Zoroastrianism is generally believed to be some centuries older than Buddhism. Therefore, these religions are "modern," not in a chronological or existential sense, but in a purely typological one, particularly in regard to other religions belonging to another type which we may rightly call "ancient."

Religions of the latter type are those of the Romans, Greeks, Egyptians, Babylonians, Hittites, Persians, Indians, Chinese, Japanese, Aztecs, etc. These religions had no founder; their origins are lost in obscurity with those of their respective peoples. They bind *all* and *only* the members of a given nation or state. They aim at the preservation and growth of their respective national and political communities rather than at the salvation of each individual in the life to come. They do not practise proselytism, nor do they tend to impose themselves on other peoples and countries. These religions are therefore *negatively* characterized by the absence of those characters appertaining to the religions of the "modern" type. *Positively* their more salient specific trait is the civic, national, public, political, more or less official character common to them all.

This religious type, so radically different from the modern, is the ancient type of religion. Of course, the term ancient has here a merely typological sense. As a matter of fact this was the type that prevailed in the ancient world, both classic and oriental, but, as among the religions of the modern type there are some no longer in existence today, not all the religions of the ancient type have now ceased to exist. The official religion of China in the form given it and systematized by Confucius about 500 B.C. lasted, at least, until the revolution of 1912, and cannot be said to have entirely died out. Shintoism, the national religion of Japan, is also a religion of the ancient type, but it still lives and offers an exceptional interest for students of religions, because it *actually* represents an archaic religious type, practically extinct.

Typology is necessarily abstract, but not so the method which goes beyond the structural or static traits in order to find dynamic traits or *functional* analogies. Christianity and Buddhism have in common such static characters as belong to the "modern" type of religion, namely supernationalism, proselytism, etc. Generally speaking, *Buddhism represents in the Far East that transition from the "ancient type" of national religion to the "modern" one of supernational religion which is represented by Christianity in the West.* This chief *functional* similarity is all the more notable since Buddhism and Christianity are, as above said, radically different in doctrinal and ideological respects. It shows once more that religion develops on a plan which is not precisely, or at least not only, that of belief or doctrine or dogma. This single aspect, this common function both of Buddhism and Christianity beyond all doctrinal divergence, establishes a dynamic, organic and therefore truly historical parallel between the religious history of the East and that of the West. We shall now follow this parallel more closely.

Christianity, born in Palestine, issued from its birthplace to conquer the West; Buddhism, born in India, started from that country to conquer the East. The expansion of both Christianity and Buddhism took place successively in two different areas, in two different periods and in two different ways.

The first immense field for the penetration of Christianity was the Roman Empire; analogously that of Buddhism was the Chinese Empire. The propagation happened to begin about the same time, but here it is not synchronism, but cultural parallelism that matters. China, an enormous empire of ancient and advanced civilisation corresponds in a certain way in the East to what the Roman Empire was in the West. The diffusion of Christianity in the Graeco-Roman world is mainly due to the religious propaganda which was carried on in the beginning among the lower classes of the population and *then* extended to the higher. Likewise in China, Buddhism found favour among the lowest classes, while it was (together with Taoism) opposed by the highest, the representatives of the official religion (Confucianism).

Buddhism came from China across Korea to Japan in the sixth century A.D. Japan was, at that time, a country of "barbaric civilisation largely exposed to the influence of the superior Chinese civilisation.

There was between China and Japan an inequality of historic-cultural level corresponding to that existing between Roman or Romanized Europe and the rest of Europe beyond the confines of the Empire: Celtic, Germanic and Slav. A corresponding change in the manner of propagation, a corresponding curve in the long parallel lines of their functions was created in both Buddhism and Christianity by this change of cultural milieu. The conversion of "barbarians" to Christianity entered into the complex process of their acculturation within the orbit of Roman (or Byzantine) civilisation, just as the introduction of Buddhism into Japan is one of the many aspects of the penetration of Chinese civilisation. In the previous period the diffusion of Christianity into the Roman world, like that of Buddhism into the Chinese, was the fruit of the spontaneous impulse of an enthusiastic faith, of an apostolic spirit, namely, of purely religious energies. In this second period, on the contrary, secular, cultural and political factors prevailed. The expansive movement did not proceed from the low to the high, but from the high to the low. In barbaric Europe it was generally the rulers and princes who first embraced the religion of Rome (or Byzantium), and their example, or rather, their orders were followed by mass conversions of the population. Similarly in Japan Buddhism made its first proselytes in court circles while most of the people continued for a long time to ignore the new religion.

Nevertheless there is a great difference within the general *functional* parallel we have traced. Buddhism and Christianity have, as is said, the same historico-religious *function*, which is that of creating, respectively in the East and in the West, the new type of supernational religion. But this common task was carried out in different ways by the two religions. In Japan, not only did the people ignore Buddhism for a long time, but also those among the upper classes who embraced the new religion did not repudiate the ancient Shintō, the Japanese national religion, continued to exist alongside Buddhism. And if, since the ninth century, Buddhism finally penetrated among the masses, it was only through a systematic Shintō-Buddhistic syncretism founded on the principle that the *kami* (Shintō deities) were the incarnations of as many Buddhist *hotoke* (Buddhas and Bodhisattvas). Thus Shintoism was able to come down to our time and it was restored in the *Meiji* epoch to the form of the "pure Shintō," *i.e.*, to its genuine form, free from its traditional Buddhist incrustations and superstructures. Analogously in China, Buddhism did not succeed in, nor did it aim at, doing away with Taoism or Confucianism, rather it entered into a special relationship with these religions thus rendering it possible for the Chinese to participate in all three together.

The process was quite different in the West. There Christianity conducted a struggle without quarter against all religions it encountered in its path, against the Graeco-Roman paganism as well as against the barbarian. Syncretistic tendencies sporadically made their appearance in the history of Christianity, but they were always finally overcome by the totalitarian and exclusive spirit of that religion. In short, it may be said that while *Buddhism in the East allowed the national religions of the various countries wherein it was diffused to* survive, *Christianity in the West did not permit the various national paganisms to exist as such.* This *functional* difference is for the historian far more important than the doctrinal differences, however profound they may be, between the two religions. Thus the religious history of the East, though sharing the general development of religion from the national (ancient) type to the supernational (modern) type, differs substantially from the religious history of the West.

Selected Bibliography

The All-Knowing God, trans. by H. J. Rose (London: Methuen, 1956).

"Confession of Sins in Primitive Religions," *Proceedings of the Jubilee Congress of the Folklore Society* (1928). London: 1930, pp. 176–181.

Essays on the History of Religions, trans. by H. J. Rose (Leiden: E. J. Brill, 1954).

"The Supreme Being: Phenomenological Structure and Historical Development," *The History of Religions. Essays in Methodology,* Mircea Eliade and Joseph M. Kitagawa, eds. (Chicago: University of Chicago Press, 1959), pp. 59–66.

In addition, Pettazzoni has written many books in Italian that have not been translated into English. See the larger bibliography of Pettazzoni's works as compiled by Mario Gandini in *Studi et Materiali di Storia delle Religioni,* 31 (1960), pp. 3–31.

Enlightenment

DAISETZ TEITARO SUZUKI

Recognized as the foremost interpreter of Zen Buddhism in the West, Daisetz Teitaro Suzuki was born on October 18, 1870, in Kanazawa, Japan. Suzuki's forefathers belonged to the samurai (or warrior) class, and by longstanding tradition had trained as physicians. Suzuki's father died when Teitaro was young, however; he was subsequently unable to meet the costs of medical training. For a while he taught in a fishing village and then took courses at the Imperial University in Tokyo, but he spent most of his time at the Zen monastery in Kamakura, near Tokyo, undergoing the discipline of a novice. Suzuki was a convinced follower of Zen Buddhism throughout his life. He came to the United States in 1897 after having secured a position as a translator for the Open Court Publishing Company. This led to other translation and publishing ventures as well as the writing of his own book, Outlines of Mahayana Buddhism. *When Suzuki returned to Japan in 1909, he was called as professor of English at the Imperial University in Tokyo. From 1921 to 1940 he was professor of English and Buddhist philosophy in Otani University in Kyoto. During World War II he was under suspicion for his opposition to militarism, but after the war he was made a member of the Japan Academy and was decorated by the Japanese government. Following the war, he traveled and lectured extensively throughout Europe, India, and the United States. Under invitation from the Rockefeller Foundation, he made his last extensive lecture tour in America at the age of eighty. His interests ranged over wide areas— from Ralph Waldo Emerson and Emanuel Swedenborg to classical Chinese and Indian philosophy. He died on October 18, 1966.*

According to my way of interpreting Buddhism, it revolves around Buddha's enlightenment experience. *Buddha* means "the enlightened one," and "enlightenment" is *bodhi*. Both *Buddha* and *bodhi* come from the same root, *budh*, "to wake," "to become aware of," etc.

Daisetz Teitaro Suzuki, "Enlightenment," in *The Review of Religion*. Vol. XVIII, Nos. 3–4 (1954), pp. 133–144, Columbia University Press.

Buddha is an awakened one, one who is awakened from a life of relativity or conditionality. What he teaches is *bodhi*, "enlightenment," or *sambodhi*, "the perfect enlightenment that knows no equal."

Buddha's doctrine is based on his enlightenment, and its purpose to make every one of us attain this enlightenment, so that Buddhism would not remain as something which stands outside oneself and does not concern one personally. Buddha was a consistent personalist and strongly urged his followers to value their personal experience and not merely to rely on authority or a superior personality. Each was exhorted to exert himself for his own emancipation. We read in the *Dhammapada*:

> By oneself, indeed, is evil done; by oneself is one injured.
> By oneself is evil left undone; by oneself is one purified.
> Purity and impurity belong to oneself. No one purifies
> another (v. 165).[1]

This may be considered altogether too individualistic, but, after all, you have to sip your own glass of water when you are thirsty. You cannot get any proxy to do your work in Heaven or Hell. Enlightenment must be personally experienced. Buddhism does not, therefore, consist in Buddha's teaching based on his enlightenment which his followers are told just to swallow even before they can taste it, each by his own personal experience. For this reason, to study Buddhism we must, above all, find out what the perfect enlightenment is.

Let us first enquire then how Buddha came to his enlightenment experience. How did he achieve it? Like all other Indian saints or philosophers, his foremost concern was to be emancipated from the bondage of birth and death, to be liberated from the shackles of existence. As far as existence is conditioned, it always binds us to something, and the binding means tension. This is the human situation in which we all are. And there is something in every one of us who reflects at all on the actualities of existence which constantly urges us to transcend them. We long for immortality, for eternal life, for absolute freedom, for liberation. Buddha was exceptionally sensitive in this respect. He wanted to be liberated from the bondage of existence by all possible means.

This longing, or desire, or urge is quite human and comes from our being able to reflect on our own situation, to become conscious of

[1] *The Dhammapada*, tr. by S. Radhakrishnan (London, 1950), p. 114.

our surroundings, inner as well as outer, and to detach ourselves from the life we live. This longing, when translated into metaphysical terms, is our probing into the ultimate significance of reality. This probing presents itself in the form of the following questions: Is life worth living? What is the meaning of life? Whence do we come and whither do we go? What is this self who raises all these questions? Is there any outside agent who handles this universe to satisfy his whims? And so on.

All these and many other questions of a similar nature, however varied they may appear, all issue from one and the same fundamental source. They are all inquiries concerning the ultimate destiny of life, the significance of reality. So we can resolve all these questions into one and say: What is reality? Philosophers and so-called religious-minded people may have their own approach to this final question. And Buddhists, especially Zen Buddhists, have theirs too, which is different from that of philosophers and also from that of the religious-minded. Most of those people try to solve the problem as it is presented to them, that is, objectively. They would take up the problem as it is asked and try to answer it in the way it is given to them.

Buddhists, on the other hand, strive to reach the source or origin itself from whence the problem issues and to see how it came to be asked at all. When the question "What is reality?" is given, instead of taking up the question as such, they go to the questioner himself. The question therefore ceases to be an abstract one; the person, the living person, is brought in. He is full of life, and so is the question, which now is no longer abstract and impersonal but vitally concerns the questioner himself. When a disciple asks, "What is the Buddha-nature or reality?" the master would counter-question and demand, "Who are you?" or "Where do you get the question?" Sometimes the master may call the questioner's name, and when the monk responds, "Yes, master," the master may remain silent for a while and ask, "Do you understand?" The monk would confess his inability to understand. The master's verdict then would be, "A good-for-nothing fellow!"

The Buddhist idea is that the question is never to be separated from the questioner. So long as they are kept separate, there will be no solution coming the way of the questioner.

How did the question ever come to be asked? How did the questioner ever take it into his head to ask the question? The questioning is possible only when the questioner separates himself from reality.

He stands outside of it, he detaches himself from it, looks at it and asks the question, "What is this?" This is the privilege allowed only to us humans; the animals have nothing of the sort; they just live reality. There is no question whatever for them. They are neither happy nor unhappy. They just take things as they come. But it is different with us. We know how to put ourselves outside actualities, and reflect upon them, and ask all kinds of questions about them. And thereby we torment ourselves or sometimes amuse ourselves. However, when the question is of vital concern to us, we are far from being amused. It is, indeed, our privilege to be tormented, and therefore it must also be our privilege to be blessed. This can never be so with the animals.

A monk asked Nansen (Nan-ch'üan), "I am told that all the Buddhas of the past, present, and future do not know that 'it' is there while the cat and the ox do know. How is this possible?" The master said, "Before the Buddha entered the Deer Park he knew something of 'it.' " The monk asked, "How about the animals knowing 'it'?" Nansen retorted, "How could you suspect them?"

The idea is that whatever we may mean by "it," "it" is no longer there when we ask about "it" as if "it" were something which can be sought outside ourselves. Every one of us lives "it," and, when we separate ourselves from "it" by asking about it, the result is that we now go out of ourselves and get lost. This is like the centipede which was unable to move any more, because it reflected upon itself to find out how it managed all its legs, one after another, without being hampered or confused. The trouble comes from this separation of questioner and question.

However, the separation of the question from the questioner is quite a natural thing with human beings, for we are so constituted as to have to ask questions everywhere and at every moment of our lives. But, at the same time, this constant questioning is the source of the most agonizing situation into which we so deeply put ourselves. The Buddhist contention is that the solution can never come out of this separation. The separation is needed to ask the question, but the separation is not the key to the solution. On the contrary, it keeps one away from the solution.

To solve the question is to be one with it. When this oneness takes place in its deepest sense, the solution comes out of the identity by itself, without the questioner's trying to solve the question. The question solves itself then. This is the position taken by Buddhists towards the solution of the question, "What is reality?" That is to say, when the questioner ceases to be outside the question, when they are one, when they return to the original situation in which they were. That is, when they return to the very beginning of things when there was yet no dichotomy of subject and object—the time before the separation took place, before there was the creation of the world—this is the time the solution is possible in one's actual experience, and not in the form of a logical demonstration.

When I say this, the reader may ask: When you say "before the dichotomization of subject and object" or "before God created the world," that means "before we were born" or "before any question comes out of ourselves." If this be the case, we have no questions to ask, hence no solution of any kind. Not only this, the enlightenment itself ceases to have any meaning whatever, for all is reduced to absolute emptiness where there was yet no God, no creation, no ourselves, and therefore no questions. This is not a solution but an annihilation.

The trouble is that I have been inadvertently leading the reader in the wrong direction, that is, I have been misleading him and putting him into the very maze out of which my object was to rescue him. For the reader here is preparing for his own funeral rites. What I wanted to do was to take him out of any sort of questioning, arguing, reasoning, etc., so that he would be absolutely free—free from all analytical disputations. This is possible only when the questioner is identified with the question, or when his whole being turns into a great question mark which covers the beginning of the world to its end. This is a matter of experience and not of argumentation. This is the point Buddha reached after six years of hard thinking and strenuous ascetic discipline. My point will become clearer as we go on.

In any event, Buddhists strongly emphasize the experience of enlightenment, only out of which comes the solution of all problems. As long as there is an intellectual separation going on in one form or another, the question will never be answered. Whatever answer we may have will be no answer in the true sense of the word, for it will come as postulate and not as an actual answer. The basic answer which touches, or rather, threatens the very existence of ourselves is no idle one.

The separation of subject and object means the raising of the question, and it is answered not intellectually but experientially, for it is in the nature of the intellect that its answer always calls forth a further series of questions and so can never be final. Besides, an intellectual solution, if it can ever be had, always remains intellectual and never touches one's own being. The intellect is peripheral and dichotomous. In one sense, we can say that the question of reality is answered already even before it is asked, but this will not be understood on the intellectual plane, for this goes beyond it.

While the question and the separation are inseparably linked together, the questioning really means that reality wishes to know itself, and to know itself it was necessary for reality to divide itself into questioner and question. This being the case, the answer must come out of reality itself before the separation took place. This means that the answer lies where the questioner and the question were still one. The question came after the separation; there was no question before the separation. Therefore, when we go where the question has never been raised, there is naturally no question, and where there is no question, there is naturally no answer. This realm of no questioning and answering is where there is a final solution. Hence a Zen philosopher's declaration that the answer is given even before the question is asked.

The question is asked, "What is God?" and the Zen master will say, "Who are you?"

Q. "Can or will Christ save me?"

A. "You are not yet saved."

Q. "Is Buddha really enlightened?" Or "What is enlightenment?"

A. "You are not enlightened."

Q. "What message did Bodhi-Dharma bring from India?"

A. "Where are you this moment?"

There was a high government officer in ancient China who was interested in Zen. He once said to a Zen master.

"A man kept a young goose in a jar. It grew bigger and the jar became too small for it. Now the problem is, How can it be safely extricated without breaking the jar?"

The master called the officer by his name, and the officer replied, "Yes, master."

Immediately then the master said, "There, the goose is out!"

The fact is that the answer always goes along with the question, for the questioning is the answering. But, at the same time, we must remember that unless the question is asked no answer will be forthcoming.

Joshu (Chao-chou) once asked Nansen (Nan-ch'üan), "What is the Tao?" (The Tao here we may take as standing for reality.)

Nansen: "Your everyday mind [2] is the Tao."

Joshu: "Does it need any specific disciplinary orientation?" [3]

Nansen: "No, when you try to orient yourself, you turn against it."

Joshu: "But if one does not, how does one know it to be Tao?"

Nansen: "The Tao does not belong to knowledge, nor does it belong to not-knowing. To know is delusion, not to know is indifference (*wu-chi, avyākṛita*). When you attain the Tao which is beyond all shadow of doubt, you will realize that it is like the great void so limitlessly expanding, so vastly empty, and no more room is left there for right and wrong."

The Tao is the perfect enlightenment, and what we can state about the Tao will also apply to the enlightenment. When you turn towards it, that is, when a question is asked about it, it is no longer there where the questioner looks. But if you do not search for it, if you do not specifically direct your attention towards it in order to locate it, it will never come within your grasp. The Tao is beyond the reach of logical comprehension, beyond the ken of intellection. All this means that the enlightenment will never be attained as long as you are on this side of the stream.

This I would call the logic of enlightenment. It is when this "logic" is understood that we can, more intelligently than before, approach the question of the enlightenment experience Buddha had, from which Buddhism with all its later developments not only in India but in China starts.

It was for this reason that Buddha could never solve his problem so long as he grappled with it at the level of a dichotomous separation, so long as the questioner was kept apart from the question itself. This meant that Buddha always saw his question dangling before him, of

---

[2] "Everyday mind" is in Chinese *p'ing-ch'ang hsin*. *P'ing-ch'ang* means "usual," "ordinary," "everyday," and *hsin* is "mind," "heart," "thought," or "consciousness." The combination is, therefore, "a state of mind in which one ordinarily is." The Buddhist scholars may designate this as "a state of suchness," "reality as it is," or simply "as-it-is-ness." When a monk asked a master, "What is meant by one's everyday thought (or consciousness)?" the master answered, "I eat when hungry; I drink when thirsty." This is a kind of instinctive unconscious life where there is no intellectual or reflective calculation. If we stop here, there will be no human life whose characteristic feature is a highly developed consciousness. To be conscious and yet to be unconscious—this then is "one's everyday mind."

[3] *Ch'ü-hsiang* in Chinese. Literally, it means "turning towards," "intentional direction." The above translation may sound too modern, but the idea is there.

which he wished somehow to make a satisfactory disposition. The story of Buddha is a typical example of what man's quest after reality or truth goes through before he can arrive at a final solution.

In the quest of truth we generally start with the study of philosophy, for the unfolding of our reasoning powers is synchronous with our reflection on reality. We first study the history of thought and see what all those ancient wise men had to say about the problem, which also troubled them immensely. Buddha followed a similar procedure. What he did first, after leaving his home life, was to go to the forest and see the most learned men of his day. This, however, failed to be satisfactory. Philosophy, by its nature, is unable to take us back to where the question has not yet been asked, for this is demanding too much of philosophy, which has its own limitations. It may give us a distant and not at all clarified view of reality itself, but it is possible that the nearer we approach the further it fades away. It is simply tantalizing. It was quite natural for Buddha that he had finally to leave his teachers.

He now tried ascetic discipline. Most of us somehow think that by curbing the claims of the flesh the mind is purified and ready to see the truth as it is. But self-mortification treats the self, the questioner, as a kind of enemy who is to be defeated and crushed. The enemy always stands before the questioner. However desperately the questioner may struggle in this deadly battle, the enemy will never be vanquished; for, so long as the self or the questioner is alive, he will create a new enemy and have to fight him. The killing of the enemy does not mean the saving of the self or the answering of the question. The self is maintained only when there is a not-self which is an enemy. The self is the creator of the enemy. The questioner is always a questioner, a question-creator.

In ascetic training the questioner is the self. The self is then made to face what is not the self, that is, the enemy, and this enemy is to be disposed of by any means. But the enemy can never be conquered so long as there is the self. The self is never left alone; it always wants something against which it can assert itself, to prove its power, to show itself as something of all-importance. The self loses its selfhood when there are no other selves over which it must demonstrate itself. Asceticism is a form of pride or self-assertion.

Ascetic discipline or moral training can never go beyond the self, but, unless we go beyond the self, there is no chance to get the solution of the problem with which we started our quest for reality. The self must be thoroughly forsaken and emptied of everything that savors of selfhood, that is, of the opposition of self and not-self.

Buddha found this in the most practical way. One day, he wished to stand up from his seat and failed because, from lack of proper nourishment, he was too feeble to support himself. He had been trying to subsist on a minimum amount of food so that his body would be too weak to assert itself. The end was attained, for the body became too weak and could not maintain itself. But the problem of reality and truth remained unsolved just as before; torturing the flesh was not the way to the solution. He then thought, "If he has to die, the questioner dies away with the question still unsolved."

He began to take food and recover his former health and strength, so that he could carry on his inquiries into the all-absorbing question. But how should he proceed now? The intellect failed to give him an answer, and the ascetic mortification was not of much avail. He did not know what to do. He was at a complete loss, but the urge to get a solution to his question was stronger than ever. If his had been a lesser and weaker mind, it might have collapsed under the weight of the situation. Cornered, as it were, into this situation, his whole being reacted against it. He now felt that he had no question to solve, no self to stand up against an enemy. His self, his intellect, indeed, his whole being was poured into the question. That is to say, he now became the question itself. The differentiation of questioner and question, of self and not-self, disappeared, and there was just one undivided *unknown*. He was buried in this *unknown*.

There was then, as we may picture to ourselves, no Shakyamuni the questioner, no ego-conscious self, no question set before his intellect and threatening his existence, and along with them no heavens sheltering him, no earth supporting him. If we could have stood beside Buddha at that time and looked into his being, we might have detected there nothing but one big question-mark occupying the entire universe. This was the state of his mind, if we can say that he then had any kind of mind. He had been in this state for some little time, when he happened to look up and see the morning star. The beams of light emanating from the star struck his eyes, and it was this incident that brought his entire consciousness back to its ordinary key. The question that had troubled him so persistently and so harassingly now disappeared altogether. Everything acquired a new significance. The whole world now appeared to him in a new light. The following is said to have been his utterance:

Thro' many a birth in Samsara wandered I,
Seeking but not finding, the builder of this house.
Sorrowful is repeated birth.

O house-builder! you are seen. You shall build no house again.
All your rafters are broken, your ridge-pole is shattered.
To dissolution goes the mind.
The end of craving have I attained.[4]

What makes a man feel that he has been going through many a cycle of births and deaths is due to his clinging to the idea of an individual ego-substance (*ātman*). When this idea is dispelled as he sees into its nature, which is unreal, transient, and conditional, and not at all self-existing, he will no longer be attached to it; for all its rafters, beams, and ridge-pole are now completely destroyed and will never be reconstructed. They were all the products of a dualistic way of thinking. This vanishing of dualism is "dissolution" which is "emptiness" (*śūnyatā*). "Dissolution," however, may not be a good term for *visaṅkhāra* means the "disappearance of things conditionally existing" (*saṅkhāra*). According to Buddhist scholars, this phenomenal world is an "aggregate" existence made up of conditions, and not a self-existing reality (*ātman*). When the mind is said to have attained "dissolution," it means that the mind has entered into a state of "absolute emptiness" (*śūnyatā*), that it is completely free from all conditionalities, that it is "Transcendence." [5] In other words, the mind gains its ultimate reality, being now above birth and death, self and not-self, good and evil. "I am absolute conqueror." This idea is asserted in the following verse (*gātha*), which is also regarded as Buddha's utterance at the time of his enlightenment:

All-vanquishing, all-knowing, lo! am I,
from all wrong thinking wholly purged and free.

All things discarded, cravings rooted out,
—whom should I follow?—I have found out all.

No teacher's mine, no equal. Counterpart
to me there's none throughout the whole wide world.

[4] *The Dhammapada*, tr. by Narada Thera (Colombo, 1946), p. 26, vv. 153–154.

[5] This is a term used by Karl Jaspers for Being-in-itself. The *citta* (mind) free from the Aggregates (*skandha*) is the "Transcendence of the world."

The Arhat am I, teacher supreme,
utter Enlightenment is mine alone;
unfever'd calm is mine, Nirvana's peace.[6]

The "all-vanquishing" or "all-conquering" one is never to be conquered by anybody. He is absolute. He knows no defeat, because he
is above all forms of opposition. He is altogether unique. Then he is
"all-knowing." This does not mean that he knows things individually,
singly, one after another. This is the ordinary knowledge we have at
the level of relativity and finitude. The knowledge possessed by the
all-knowing one is what I call "*prajñā*-intuition," a knowledge of all
things in their totality and unity, the knowledge that lies at the
foundation of all individual knowledge. It is that which makes our
relative knowledge possible; therefore, it is wholly purged and free
from "all wrong thoughts." This kind of knowledge is possessed only
by the one in whom there is no division between questioner and
question, that is, by Buddha, the enlightened one.

It is for this reason that the Mahayanist tells of Buddha as having
uttered the following at the time of his birth—biological or metaphysical as you may choose: "Above the heavens, below the heavens,
I alone am the most honored one!"

Ummon (Yün-men), a Zen master of the early Five Dynasties
period, had this to say once when he was commemorating Buddha's
birthday: "If I saw him when he made this utterance as he came out
of his mother's body, I would strike him down with one blow of my
stick and give the corpse to the dogs." Ummon in his Zen way really
echoes the spirit of Buddha's utterance itself.

We must realize that without this enlightenment experience, as I
have tried to relate it, as the greatest event in the life of Buddha,
there could never have been a religion known as Buddhism. Everything, then, that we connect with the name of Buddhism must go
back to this experience of Buddha's, and whenever we encounter any
difficulty in the study and understanding of Buddhist teachings we
must seek its ultimate solution in Buddha's enlightenment experience. A Buddha is no Buddha without his enlightenment. So is
Buddhism no Buddhism without basing itself on the meaning of
Buddha's "perfect enlightenment." Thus we can see in what way
Buddhism distinguishes itself from all other religions.

That the enlightenment is the very foundation of Buddhism,

[6] *Further Dialogues of Buddha*, Part I, tr. by Lord Chalmers, p. 121.

regardless of its wide range of ramifications as it spread out all over Asia, is seen from the fact that even in the Pure Land doctrine, which calls itself the teaching based on "the other-power" and is apparently against the spirit of "the self-power" doctrine as promulgated by the founder of Buddhism, the enlightenment idea nevertheless forms its basis. Because the Pure Land became possible by Amida's first attaining the *anuttara-samyak-sambodhi*, "incomparable supreme enlightenment," and all that follows from its establishment is no more than the inner unfolding of the enlightenment experience of Amida. While we have to elucidate in more detail what is meant by "the other-power," the main purpose of our rebirth into the Pure Land is the attainment of the perfect enlightenment in this blessed realm where all conditions are most favorably arranged for it. From this we can see that even the Pure Land doctrine, which is generally considered so remote from the "original" teaching of Buddha, is also, after all, the doctrine of enlightenment. Those who find it difficult to attain enlightenment here and now are persuaded to get or, rather, assured of getting it in their next life by being born into Amida's land.

We now know, I hope, what it was that was experienced by Buddha under the Bodhi tree on the bank of the Nairanjañā about twenty-five centuries ago. The next step in the study of Buddhism will be to find out what the contents of the perfect enlightenment are which makes us "all-conquering" as well as "all-knowing."

Selected Bibliography

A *Brief History of Early Chinese Philosophy* (London: Probsthain, 1914).

Buddhist Philosophy and Its Effects on the Life and Thought of the Japanese People (Tokyo: The Society for International Cultural Relations, 1936).

Essays in Zen Buddhism (New York: Grove Press, Inc., 1961).

Mysticism: Christian and Buddhist: The Eastern and Western Way (New York: Macmillan, 1969).

On Indian Mahāyāna Buddhism. Edited with Introduction by Edward Conze (New York: Harper & Row, Publishers, Inc., 1968).

Outlines of Mahāyāna Buddhism. Introduction by Alan Watts (New York: Schocken Books, Inc., 1963).

The Training of the Zen Buddhist Monk (New Hyde Park, N.Y.: University Books, 1965).

Religion, as Man's Adjustment to the Tremendum

ERWIN R. GOODENOUGH

Erwin R. Goodenough was born in Brooklyn, New York, on October 24, 1893. He studied at Harvard and Oxford Universities, and received a Doctor of Philosophy degree from the latter institution in 1923. From 1923 to 1962 Goodenough was on the faculty of Yale University as a historian of the religions of the Graeco-Roman era with special emphasis on Judaism and the rise of Christianity during this period. As he states in the preface to his thirteen-volume work, Jewish Symbols in the Graeco-Roman Period, *his purpose in undertaking that enormous project was "to discover the religious attitudes of Jews in the Graeco-Roman world." In addition to his work with symbols and texts, Goodenough also addressed himself to some of the methodological issues involved in the study of religion. At the same time, he pursued an interest in examining religious experience as a psychological phenomenon, an interest that formed the book* The Psychology of Religious Experiences *and registers in the book* Toward a Mature Faith.*

As a historian (and philosopher and psychologist) of religion, Goodenough tended to interpret the religious experience of men of the ancient world in terms of the concept of the* tremendum, *or, as he defines it, "that which must be feared." He views men in all ages pretending to an understanding of the* tremendum *by means of creeds and mythological, philosophical, and theological systems. But he finds all this to be illusory, because the* tremendum *resists rational comprehension. Men cannot control the universe, according to Goodenough. Hence, without power to overcome the* tremendum, *man finds in religion an "adjustment," but an adjustment of which he can be psychologically and emotionally aware. This interpretation of religion (and the view of theology as an instance of a systematic attempt to penetrate the* tremendum) *is an ingredient in the reading*

Excerpted from Chapter 1 of *The Psychology of Religious Experiences* by Erwin R. Goodenough, © 1965 by Erwin Ramsdell Goodenough, Basic Books, Inc., Publishers, New York.

selection that follows. Goodenough died on March. 20, 1965, after completing the twelfth volume of his thirteen-volume work.

Like most people, I am not a natural scientist, and so the scientific accounts as I finally understand them and the implications I draw of how the forces of nature operate are all ridiculously mythological from the point of view of pure science. I accept with utter credulity the latest theories of medicine, nervous energy, the origin and organization of the universe—which are . . . [the] primitive questions in abstract form. I am neither a vitalist nor a nonvitalist because scientists themselves do not agree on the subject, but am ready to go either way when they decide, whether I myself understand them or not. Meanwhile, of course, I live in a mythical world in which "dead" and "alive" are absolute opposites, and I find for my purposes that that myth serves very well. I use my pseudo-scientific myths of nature for two reasons: first, to have a rough and ready understanding with which I can meet the problems of life, and, second, to have a sense that I am not lost and helpless in a meaningless tremendum. And, as we shall see, my structure as a parent, moral person, and citizen is based entirely on myths of "right" and "wrong." Ancient myths and creeds served all these purposes.

Individuals have rarely dared to face the fact that they live in an unknown world, about them and within, and no society has tried to face it. "Agnosticism" is an unpopular word, and agnostics are suspect individuals because they challenge the presence of man's beliefs and throw men back on their ignorance and helplessness, which, by their myths and rituals, they are trying to conceal from their own horrified eyes. To live in awareness of their ignorance would crush the vast majority of human spirits. So between themselves and the incomprehensible-uncontrollable they have dropped curtains and projected upon them their myths, codes, rites, and beliefs to give themselves the illusion that they understand the nature of the universe and how to control it and themselves in it for their benefit and security.

The projected God or gods, stories of creation and afterlife, rules of ethics, rituals of expiation and appeasement help as they become vivid like dreams, become actual to us through faith. The designs or codes we thus project upon the curtains, fulfill, like dreams, our desires, but unlike dreams they become permanently stamped or painted on the curtains in which we wrap ourselves. In dreams, we project fleeting cinemas of wish-fulfilling symbolism. In religion, the projections become fixed, painted on the curtains, the designs so fixed, indeed, the curtains so firmly woven that we can pass them on to our children as we "bring them up in the faith" or "indoctrinate" them. Whole civilizations may be so oriented to them that they are ready to kill those who challenge their claim to represent the nature of the tremendum adequately.

In this way, we get the secure illusion that we live, not in the universe of natural forces which are as far from pity as a tornado or bolt of lightning, but in a universe ruled by love or kindness or by a God who has special favors for our selves, our sect, or our people, however he may blast the others. We ourselves need not face the vast deep of the tremendum.

Scholars have taken such notions as *mana* or "the idea of the holy" in contrast to the profane to be the basis of mankind's religious life. But none of them prove to be universal, and each has been challenged by other scholars. They are themselves specific, if widely found, patterns for curtains. The common element is no one design, but the insecurity and universal anxiety which various peoples and individuals all experience, along with the equally universal craving for explanation and control which prompts them everywhere to project or repeat primitive or elaborate myths, rites, creeds, and faiths, to make painted curtains about them. The vast majority of men get these curtains and their designs ready-made from their societies, whether from dogmas given by professional religious groups; from the "old men" or "old women" of the tribe; or, often today, from party leaders, journalistic reports, or college courses that introduce us to the fringes of scientific theory and give us the illusion of understanding. Religion accepts such stories as truths, not hypotheses, and makes men pattern their lives on them. Not the truth of an account, but its basic acceptance as truth and one's commitment to it, constitutes religion. True or false, the stories become the basis of our religion when they are accepted as describing our universe, the reality in which we live, and when they actually make the unformed tremendum seem something we can consider formed and manageable.

I write this in humility, for I know myself as a religious man. In very few aspects of my own life do I really have evidence for the validity of what I am living by. Yet my life would indeed have been chaos if I had not taken certain "truths to be self-evident," beginning with the very dubious truths announced by that phrase of the Declaration of Independence. In writing this book, I am myself painting a curtain. Insofar as any man lives by the ideas and conceptions which give his life meaning, he is living within a painted curtain, is being religious. Life has meaning only as we give it meaning. Accordingly, all men are religious, whether in the illusory terms of a traditional creed or code, in the equally illusory conception of the Enlightenment that man is a rational being who can live by reason, in the world of Mammon, or some other. For all men must live by a set of values, however unconsciously and however the values may contradict one another. That is why religion is universal in history and anthropology and must be so.

Selected Bibliography

By Light, Light: The Mystic Gospel of Hellenistic Judaism (Amsterdam: Philo Press, 1969).

The Church in the Roman Empire (New York: Holt and Company, 1931).

"The Inspiration of New Testament Research" (Presidential Address, Society of Biblical Literature and Exegesis), *Journal of Biblical Literature*, LXXI (1952), pp. 1–9.

An Introduction to Philo Judaeus (New Haven: Yale University Press, 1940).

Jewish Symbols in the Graeco-Roman World. Vols. 1–12 (New York: Pantheon Books, Inc., 1953–1965).

"Kingship in Early Israel," *Journal of Biblical Literature*, XLVIII (1929), pp. 169–205.

"Philo on Immortality," *Harvard Theological Review*, XXXIX (1946), pp. 85–108.

Psychology of Religious Experiences (New York: Basic Books, Inc., 1965).

Religious Tradition and Myth (New Haven: Yale University Press, 1937).

The Theology of Justin Martyr (Amsterdam: Philo Press, 1968).

Toward a Mature Faith (New Haven: Yale University Press, 1961).

See also the bibliography of Goodenough's writings in *Religions in Antiquity* (Festschrift for Erwin R. Goodenough), edited by Jacob Neusner (Leiden: E. J. Brill, 1968), pp. 621–632.

Religion as the Depth Dimension in Culture

PAUL TILLICH

Paul Johannes Tillich was born on August 20, 1886, in Germany, the son of a Prussian minister. He attended a number of German universities and earned the Ph.D. degree from Breslau in 1911 and a degree in theology from Halle in 1912. During the war, from 1914 to 1918, Tillich was a chaplain in the German army. After the war he began teaching and became professor of philosophy at the University of Frankfurt in 1929. Ousted from that position by the Nazis, Tillich journeyed to America in 1933 to become a member of the faculty of Union Theological Seminary in New York. He eventually also taught at Yale, Harvard, the University of California at Santa Barbara, and the University of Chicago. He died in Chicago on October 22, 1965.

One of the purposes of Tillich's intellectual endeavors was to restore to man a sense of harmony in his relationships with nature, culture, and the Judaeo-Christian religious traditions. That harmony, Tillich thought, had been broken by the passing of an earlier life-view or world outlook. The evidence of its passing was reflected in man's inability to effect any of these three relationships in personally satisfying ways. Tillich's efforts to restore order, harmony, and meaning led him to a full-scale symbolic recasting of nature, culture, and the Christian tradition by a recovery of "the dimension of 'depth.'" He addressed himself to this subject in the following selection.

When we say that religion is an aspect of the human spirit, we are saying that if we look at the human spirit from a special point of view, it presents itself to us as religious. What is this view? It is the point of view from which we can look into the depth of man's spiritual life. Religion is not a special function of man's spiritual life, but it is the dimension of depth in all of its functions. The assertion has far-reach-

Paul Tillich, *Theology of Culture*, edited by Robert C. Kimball (New York: Oxford University Press, 1959), pp. 5–9. Reprinted by permission of The Estate of Paul Tillich.

ing consequences for the interpretation of religion, and it needs comment on each of the terms used in it.

Religion is not a special function of the human spirit! History tells us the story of how religion goes from one spiritual function to the other to find a home, and is either rejected or swallowed by them. Religion comes to the moral function and knocks at its door, certain that it will be received. Is not the ethical the nearest relative of the religious? How could it be rejected? Indeed, it is not rejected; it is taken in. But it is taken in as a "poor relation" and asked to earn its place in the moral realm by serving morality. It is admitted as long as it helps to create good citizens, good husbands and children, good employees, officials, and soldiers. But the moment in which religion makes claims of its own, it is either silenced or thrown out as superfluous or dangerous for morals.

So religion must look around for another function of man's spiritual life, and it is attracted by the cognitive function. Religion as a special way of knowledge, as mythological imagination or as mystical intuition—this seems to give a home to religion. Again religion is admitted, but as subordinate to pure knowledge, and only for a brief time. Pure knowledge, strengthened by the tremendous success of its scientific work, soon recants its half-hearted acceptance of religion and declares that religion has nothing whatsoever to do with knowledge.

Once more religion is without a home within man's spiritual life. It looks around for another spiritual function to join. And it finds one, namely, the aesthetic function. Why not try to find a place within the artistic creativity of man? religion asks itself, through the mouths of the philosophers of religion. And the artistic realm answers, through the mouths of many artists, past and present, with an enthusiastic affirmative, and invites religion not only to join with it but also to acknowledge that art *is* religion. But now religion hesitates. Does not art express reality, while religion transforms reality? Is there not an element of unreality even in the greatest work of art? Religion remembers that it has old relations to the moral and the cognitive realms, to the good and to the true, and it resists the temptation to dissolve itself into art.

But now where shall religion turn? The whole field of man's spiritual life is taken, and no section of it is ready to give religion an adequate place. So religion turns to something that accompanies every activity of man and every function of man's spiritual life. We call it feeling. Religion is a feeling: this seems to be the end of the wanderings of religion, and this end is strongly acclaimed by all those who want to have the realms of knowledge and morals free from any religious interference. Religion, if banished to the realm of mere feeling, has ceased to be dangerous for any rational and practical human enterprise. But, we must add, it also has lost its seriousness, its truth, and its ultimate meaning. In the atmosphere of mere subjectivity of feeling without a definite object of emotion, without an ultimate content, religion dies. This also is not the answer to the question of religion as an aspect of the human spirit.

In this situation, without a home, without a place in which to dwell, religion suddenly realizes that it does not need such a place, that it does not need to seek for a home. It is at home everywhere, namely, in the depth of all functions of man's spiritual life. Religion is the dimension of depth in all of them. Religion is the aspect of depth in the totality of the human spirit.

What does the metaphor *depth* mean? It means that the religious aspect points to that which is ultimate, infinite, unconditional in man's spiritual life. Religion, in the largest and most basic sense of the word, is ultimate concern. And ultimate concern is manifest in all creative functions of the human spirit. It is manifest in the moral sphere as the unconditional seriousness of the moral demand. Therefore, if someone rejects religion in the name of the moral function of the human spirit, he rejects religion in the name of religion. Ultimate concern is manifest in the realm of knowledge as the passionate longing for ultimate reality. Therefore, if anyone rejects religion in the name of the cognitive function of the human spirit, he rejects religion in the name of religion. Ultimate concern is manifest in the aesthetic function of the human spirit as the infinite desire to express ultimate meaning. Therefore, if anyone rejects religion in the name of the aesthetic function of the human spirit, he rejects religion in the name of religion. You cannot reject religion with ultimate seriousness, because ultimate seriousness, or the state of being ultimately concerned, is itself religion. Religion is the substance, the ground, and the depth of man's spiritual life. This is the religious aspect of the human spirit.

But now the question arises, what about religion in the narrower and customary sense of the word, be it institutional religion or the religion of personal piety? If religion is present in all functions of the spiritual life, why has mankind developed religion as a special sphere among others, in myth, cult, devotion, and ecclesiastical institutions? The answer is, because of the tragic estrangement of man's spiritual life from its own ground and depth. According to the visionary who has written the last book of the Bible, there will be no temple in the heavenly Jerusalem, for God will be all in all. There will be no secular realm, and for this very reason there will be no religious realm. Religion will be again what it is essentially, the all-determining ground and substance of man's spiritual life.

Religion opens up the depth of man's spiritual life which is usually covered by the dust of our daily life and the noise of our secular work. It gives us the experience of the Holy, of something which is untouchable, awe-inspiring, an ultimate meaning, the source of ultimate courage. This is the glory of what we call religion. But beside its glory lies its shame. It makes itself the ultimate and despises the secular realm. It makes its myths and doctrines, its rites and laws into ultimates and persecutes those who do not subject themselves to it. It forgets that its own existence is a result of man's tragic estrangement from his true being. It forgets its own emergency character.

This is the reason for the passionate reaction of the secular world against religion, a reaction which has tragic consequences for the secular realm itself. For the religious and the secular realm are in the same predicament. Neither of them should be in separation from the other, and both should realize that their very existence as separated is an emergency, that both of them are rooted in religion in the larger sense of the word, in the experience of ultimate concern. To the degree in which this is realized the conflicts between the religious and the secular are overcome, and religion has rediscovered its true place in man's spiritual life, namely, in its depth, out of which it gives substance, ultimate meaning, judgment, and creative courage to all functions of the human spirit.

Selected Bibliography

Biblical Religion and the Search for Ultimate Reality (Chicago: University of Chicago Press, 1955).

The Courage to Be (New Haven: Yale University Press, 1952).

Dynamics of Faith (New York: Harper & Row, Publishers, Inc., 1957).

The Future of Religions, edited by Jerald C. Brauer (New York: Harper & Row, Publishers, Inc., 1966).

The New Being (New York: Charles Scribner's Sons, Inc., 1955).

The Protestant Era (Chicago: University of Chicago Press, 1948).

Systematic Theology, 3 vols. (Chicago: University of Chicago Press, 1951–1963).

See also:

D. Mackenzie Brown, *Ultimate Concern: Tillich in Dialogue* (New York: Harper & Row, Publishers, Inc., 1965).

Charles W. Kegley and Robert W. Bretall, eds., *The Theology of Paul Tillich* (New York: Macmillan, 1952).

Walter Leibrecht, ed., *Religion and Culture: Essays in Honor of Paul Tillich* (New York: Harper & Row, Publishers, Inc., 1959).

"Symposium on Tillich's Theology," *Theology Today*, Vol. XV (April 1958), pp. 36–83.

PART 2

Origin and Development: The Attempt to Recover Religion's *Primordium*

This section consists of writings that employ the passage of time as the framework for understanding the place, function, and significance of religion. Materially, this pattern of approach always invokes a chronicle that, in turn, usually includes the recognition that religion was born early in the history of the human race. But from there methodological activity runs in many directions. Some scholars use the chronicle as the base from which they search for the origins of religion. For many of them, religion is associated with primal beginnings, or with whatever is first in the chronological series. Sometimes religion is referred to as that which precedes time and history. Consequently, much attention is given to the genetic ties between religion and mythology, and to the modes of interpretation by which earliest man comprehended his experience. Detailed research has also been conducted on the arrangement of social patterns of ancient peoples. However, other scholars are more concerned to work out the manner and extent of deviation between the prime time and present time. They are aware, of course, that the mental perspective in which religion was spawned has been transcended in the subsequent history of man's understanding and depiction of the world. For them, the question of religion's ability to abide the passage of time is large. But some of them answer the charge that religion is obsolete by attempting to demonstrate that the developmental process itself, rather than the time of primal origin, is normative. From this vantage point, religion is understood to have received some of its life from the chronicle itself, and not simply from that which precedes the chronicle or is designated as a chronological first. Eventually, then, the discussion comes to select a point in (or before) time, or the process of time as the refined fundamental datum. If the former is the case the interest of reason is usually isolative. There is a built-in tendency to regard primal origins as the unambiguous simple. If the latter is the case, the interest is usually synthetic; and there is a tendency to write a growth factor into the fabric and dynamics of religious self-consciousness.

This section of the anthology includes essays that illustrate the several ways in which this pattern of approach can be construed. J. J. Bachofen's essay outlines the contention that the first period in human history was matriarchal rather than patriarchal. He goes on to indicate some of the ways in which this view illumines the religious situation of early man. Max Müller's discussion of savage man outlines some of the assumptions on which he operated in trying to discover the earliest religion. Sir James Frazer's treatment of the origin of man's conception of God pays particular attention to the ways in which the age of religion, as he contends, developed out of the age of magic. Lucien Lévy-Bruhl's essay is meant to correlate a theological mode of awareness with "primitive mentality." Émile Durkheim, who, like Lévy-Bruhl, was very much influenced by the historical chronicles of Auguste Comte—in which a present scientific age has supplanted previous metaphysical and religious ages—tried to determine the most primitive form of religion by examining the social structures of totemistic tribes. In point of fact, Durkheim's essay performs double duty, as it illustrates the quest to recover religion's *primordium*, the primary element that is also understood to be the essential nature of religion. Consequently, Durkheim's approach could also be included with those that are directed toward isolating religion's *sine qua non*. For Durkheim, the simplest form of religion is found in primitive societies because they are closest to the origins of social life. These five essays were written in the nineteenth century. Since that time their contentions have been challenged, and, particularly in Bachofen's, Müller's, and Frazer's cases, fundamentally discredited, or at least revised in considerable detail. Yet they stand as fundamental documents in the history of the interpretation of religion.

Four other essays are included in this section of the anthology. In the first—which is a kind of maverick in this context—Henri Bergson attempts to show that developmental processes can become guiding dispositional factors in religious sensitivity. By means of that factor, Bergson goes on to suggest a series of typological distinctions between dynamic and static religions and the ways that distinctions can be applied to given religions. The other essays are summary assessments of "evolution" or "development" as a useful category of interpretation. In recounting some of the significant conclusions to which he came after studying Greek religion for a half century, Martin Nilsson acknowledges in guarded fashion that "evolution" has indeed been helpful. He also argues that that category cannot be understood in any simplistic fashion. "Evolution" does not always imply progress or greater sophistication, according to Nilsson, for the similarities between religious phenomena must also be referred to associations of a more subtle kind. Geo Widengren's comprehensive essay approaches the issue directly, and pushes the subject back to the theories of Frazer. He demonstrates that Frazer's contentions do not have the support of more recent sociological and anthropological research. Finally, E. E. Evans-Pritchard argues that the series of attempts to recover the *primordium* can be understood as one long chapter in the study of religion. Paying particular attention to the logic implicit in that enterprise, Evans-Pritchard is critical of its methodological assumptions. Before he ends, he also provides hints of another enterprise, one more reliably based, which should replace the attempt to recover a *primordium*. Evans-Pritchard acknowledges, however, that the innovations he recommends have been suggested by the experiences of those who sought primal origins.

The Matriarchal Period of Human History

J. J. BACHOFEN

Born on December 22, 1815, in Basel, Switzerland, Johann Jakob Bachofen enjoyed a career that combined interests in anthropology, jurisprudence, and Graeco-Roman history. Born into a prominent Swiss family whose wealth had been made in the silk industry, Bachofen studied at the Universities of Basel, Berlin, Göttingen, Paris, and Cambridge. He received his doctorate in Roman Law (1840) from Basel, where he became professor of Roman Law in 1842 at the age of twenty-seven. From 1842 to 1866 Bachofen served as a judge in the criminal court of that city. He resigned from his professorship in 1844 to be able to more fully pursue his interests in anthropology and Roman antiquity.

Although he wrote essays and books in the areas of jurisprudence and legal history, Bachofen's reputation is based on his theories regarding the concept of "mutterrecht" (mother right). During his travels to Italy and Greece (1842–1843, 1848–1849, and 1851–1852), in which he developed a way of interpreting the symbolism of tombs, Bachofen gathered evidence that the first period of human history was matriarchal. For the first time the theory that the monogamous patriarchal family came first in the evolution of social institutions was challenged. In order to place that thesis within a larger frame of reference Bachofen familiarized himself with other cultures and made use of new anthropological and ethnological findings. Eventually his interests were directed to a more general history of culture, and he sought to isolate the laws that were universally exhibited in man's progress in his struggle against nature.

The selection that follows was put in its present form in 1861. It is a portion of the Introduction to Das Mutterrecht, which Bachofen subtitled "An Investigation of the Religious and Juridical Character of Matriarchy in the Ancient World."

The present work deals with a historical phenomenon which few have observed and no one has investigated in its full scope. Up until now archaeologists have had nothing to say of mother right. The term is new and the family situation it designates unknown. The subject is extremely attractive, but it also raises great difficulties. The most elementary spadework remains to be done, for the culture period to which mother right pertains has never been seriously studied. Thus we are entering upon virgin territory.

We find ourselves carried back to times antedating classical antiquity, to an older world of ideas totally different from those with which we are familiar. Leaving the nations we commonly associate with the glory of the ancient world, we find ourselves among peoples who never achieved the level of classical culture. An unknown world opens before our eyes, and the more we learn of it, the stranger it seems. Everything contrasts with the idea of a highly developed culture; everywhere we find older conceptions, an independent way of life that can only be judged according to its own fundamental law. The matriarchal organization of the family seems strange in the light not only of modern but also of classical ideas. And the more primitive way of life to which it pertains, from which it arose, and through which alone it can be explained, seems very strange beside the Hellenic. The main purpose of the following pages is to set forth the moving principle of the matriarchal age, and to give its proper place in relationship both to the lower stages of development and to the higher levels of culture. Thus the scope of this work is far broader than its title indicates. I propose to investigate all aspects of matriarchal culture, to disclose it diverse traits and the fundamental idea which unites them. In this way I hope to restore the picture of a cultural stage which was overlaid or totally destroyed by the later development of the ancient world. This is an ambitious undertaking. But it is only by broadening our horizon that we can achieve true understanding and carry scientific thinking to that clarity and completeness which are the very essence of knowledge.

And now I shall attempt a general survey of my ideas, which, I believe, will facilitate the study of the work itself.

Of all records relating and pertaining to mother right, those concerning the Lycian people are the clearest and most valuable. The Lycians,

Herodotus [1] reports, did not name their children after their fathers like the Hellenes, but exclusively after their mothers; in their genealogical records they dealt entirely with the maternal line, and the status of children was defined solely in accordance with that of the mother. Nicolaus of Damascus [2] completes this testimony by telling us that only the daughters possessed the right of inheritance, and traces this institution back to the Lycian common law, the unwritten law which, as defined by Socrates, was handed down by the godhead itself. All these customs are manifestations of one and the same basic conception. Although Herodotus regards them merely as an odd deviation from Hellenic customs, closer observation must lead to a deeper view. We find not disorder but system, not fancy but necessity. And since it is expressly denied that these customs were influenced by any positive body of legislation, the hypothesis of a meaningless anomaly loses its last shred of justification. We find, then, side by side with the Hellenic-Roman father principle, a family organization which differs diametrically both in its foundation and in its development, as a comparison of the two clearly shows. This opinion is confirmed by the discovery of related conceptions among other peoples. The limitation of the right of inheritance to the daughters among the Lycians finds a parallel in the obligation (recorded by Diodorus for Egypt) of the daughters alone to provide for aged parents. And in line with the same basic conception Strabo [3] reports that among the Cantabri the sisters provided their brothers with dowries.

All these traits join to form a single picture and lead to the conclusion that mother right is not confined to any particular people but marks a cultural stage. In view of the universal qualities of human nature, this cultural stage cannot be restricted to any particular ethnic family. And consequently what must concern us is not so much the similarities between isolated phenomena as the unity of the basic conception. Polybius' [4] passage about the matriarchal genealogy of the hundred noble families among the Epizephyrian Locrians suggests two further observations which have been confirmed in the course of our investigation: (1) mother right belongs to a cultural period preceding that of the patriarchal system; (2) it began to decline only with the victorious development of the paternal system. The matriarchal forms are observed chiefly among the pre-Hellenic peoples

[1] Herodotus 1.173.

[2] Fragment 129 (Müller, *Fragmenta Historicorum Graecorum*).

[3] Strabo 34.18.

[4] Polybius 12.5.4.

and are an essential component of this archaic culture, upon which they set their imprint as much as do patriarchal forms upon Greek culture.

The principles which we have here deduced from a few observations are confirmed in the course of our investigation by an abundance of data. The Locrians lead us to the Leleges, Carians, Aetolians, Pelasgians, Caucones, Arcadians, Epeians, Minyae, and Teleboeans, who furnish a diversified picture of mother right and the culture based on it. The prestige of womanhood among these peoples was a source of astonishment to the ancients, and gives them all, regardless of individual coloration, a character of archaic sublimity that stands in striking contrast to Hellenic culture. Here we discern the basic idea from which sprang the genealogical system set forth in the Hesiodic *Eoiai* and "Catalogues," [5] the unions of immortal mothers wedded to mortal fathers, the emphasis on maternal property and the name of the maternal line, the closeness of maternal kinship, which gave rise to the term "mother country," the appellation "motherland," the greater sanctity of female sacrifices, and the inexpiability of matricide.

In these prefatory remarks, concerned not with individual data but with general perspectives, we must stress the importance of the mythical tradition for our investigation. In view of the central position of mother right among the earliest Greek peoples, we may expect this system to be reflected in myth. And accordingly this oldest form of tradition becomes an important source for our knowledge of matriarchal institutions. The question therefore arises: What importance may we impute to this primordial form of human tradition, and what use are we justified in making of its testimony? The answer to this question is provided by a single example drawn from Lycian mythology.

The maternal transmission of inheritance is attested for this sphere not only by the purely historical account of Herodotus but also by the mythical history of the Lycian kings. Not the sons of Sarpedon, but Laodamia, his daughter, is entitled to his heritage, and she passes the kingdom on to her son, to the exclusion of his uncles. A story recorded by Eustathius [6] gives this system of inheritance a symbolic expression, disclosing the basic idea of mother right in all its sensuous sexuality. If the reports of Herodotus and of Nicolaus had been lost, those who hold the prevailing view would have attempted to dis-

[5] Poems of Hesiod, now lost except for some fragments, which dealt with the mythical and legendary genealogy of the Greek peoples.

[6] *Commentarii* (*Iliad*) 12.1. 101, 894 (Vol. 3, p. 100).

credit Eustathius' story on the ground that its authenticity could not be supported by any older, not to mention contemporaneous sources; they would have argued that its cryptic character indicated invention by some foolish mythographer. They would have said, not that the myth had formed around the fact like a shell, but on the contrary, that the fact had been abstracted from the myth. They would have set it down as worthless rubbish and relegated it to the discard pile whose steady growth marks the destructive progress of the so-called "critical" approach to mythology. But comparison of the myth and the historical account shows the fallacy of this entire method. Tested by historically established truths, the mythical tradition is seen to be an authentic, independent record of the primordial age, a record in which invention plays no part. The preference of Laodamia over her brothers must then be taken as adequate proof that mother right prevailed in Lycia.

There is scarcely a feature of the matriarchal system that cannot be documented in this way, although the parallels cannot always be taken from one and the same people. In fact, we have such parallels even for the general picture of matriarchal culture; and the reason is that mother right was preserved at least partially down to relatively recent times. Both the mythical and the strictly historical traditions present very similar pictures of the system. Products of archaic and of much later periods show such an astonishing accord that we almost forget the long interval between the times when they originated. This parallelism proves the value of the mythical tradition and shows that the attitude of present-day scholarship toward it is untenable. Precisely in regard to the most important aspect of history, namely, the knowledge of ancient ideas and institutions, the already shaky distinction between historic and prehistoric times loses its last shred of justification.

Our question has been answered: the mythical tradition may be taken as a faithful reflection of the life of those times in which historical antiquity is rooted. It is a manifestation of primordial thinking, an immediate historical revelation, and consequently a highly reliable historical source.

Eustathius declares that the favoring of Laodamia over her brothers is entirely contrary to Hellenic attitudes. His remark is all the more noteworthy in view of its recent date. Unlike modern critics, the learned Byzantine does not question, much less modify the tradition because of the anomaly he seems to find in it. Such uncritical, candid acceptance of tradition, often attacked as thoughtless copying, provides the best pledge of the reliability of our sources even when they are relatively late. Among all the ancients who wrote about the earliest times we find the same meticulous fidelity in preserving and handing down tradition, the same reluctance to tamper with the vestiges of the primordial world. It is to this attitude that we owe the possibility of discerning with any degree of certainty the essential character of the most ancient periods and of tracing the history of human ideas back to their beginnings. The less inclined he is toward critique and subjective combination, the more reliable an author will be, and the less prone to falsification.

There is still another reason why myth demonstrates the authenticity of mother right. The contrast between mythical conceptions and those of subsequent days is so marked that where more recent ideas prevailed, it would not have been possible to invent the phenomena of matriarchy. The older system represented an utter puzzle to the patriarchal mind, which consequently could not have conceived any part of it. Hellenic thought could not possibly have fabricated Laodamia's priority, for it is in diametric opposition to such a conception. The same is true of the innumerable vestiges of matriarchal form woven into the prehistory of all ancient peoples—not excluding Athens and Rome, two most resolute advocates of paternity. The thinking and literature of any period unconsciously follow the laws of its life form. So great is the power of such laws that the natural tendency is always to set the new imprint on the divergent features of former times.

The matriarchal traditions did not escape this fate. We shall encounter some very surprising phenomena produced by the impact of late conceptions on the vestiges of older views and by the weakness which led some writers to replace the incomprehensible by what was comprehensible from the standpoint of their own culture. Old features are overlaid by new ones, the venerable figures of the matriarchal past are introduced to contemporaries in forms consonant with the spirit of the new period, harsh features are presented in a softened light; institutions, attitudes, motives, passions are reappraised from a contemporary point of view. Not infrequently new and old occur together; or the same fact, the same person, may appear in two versions, one prescribed by the earlier, one by the later world; one innocent, one criminal; one full of nobility and dignity, one an object of horror and the subject of a palinode. In other cases the mother gives way to the father, the sister to the brother, who now takes her place in the legend or alternates with her, while the feminine name is replaced by a

masculine one. In a word, maternal conceptions cede to the require·
ments of patriarchal theory.

Thus, far from writing in the spirit of a surpassed, vanished culture,
the later age will endeavor to extend the rule of its own ideas to ideas
and facts that are alien to it. And this circumstance frequently guarantees the authenticity of the mythical vestiges of the matriarchal
age, lending them the force of reliable proof. But where it has succumbed to later influence myth becomes still more instructive. Since
the changes usually result from the unconscious action of the new
ideas, and only in exceptional cases from conscious hostility to the
old, the legend becomes in its transformations a living expression of
the stages in a people's development, and for the skillful observer, a
faithful reflection of all the periods in the life of that people.

These considerations, I hope, will serve to justify the use that is
made of the mythical tradition in the following. But the richness of
the results it brings can only be appreciated in the course of detailed
study. Preoccupied as they are with the facts, personalities, and institutions of particular epochs, our modern historians have drawn a
sharp distinction between historical and mythical times and prolonged
the so-called mythical era out of all proportion. Along these lines any
penetrating and coherent understanding of antiquity is impossible.
All historical institutions presuppose earlier stages of formation: nowhere in history do we find a beginning, but always a continuation,
never a cause which is not at the same time an effect. True scientific
knowledge cannot consist merely in an answer to the question, What?
It must also discover the *whence* and tie it up with the *whither*.
Knowledge becomes understanding only if it can encompass origin,
progression, and end.

Since the beginning of all development lies in myth, myth must
form the starting point for any serious investigation of ancient history.
Myth contains the origins, and myth alone can reveal them. It is the
origins which determine the subsequent development, which define
its character and direction. Without knowledge of the origins, the
science of history can come to no conclusion. A distinction between
myth and history may be justified where it refers merely to a difference in mode of expression, but it has neither meaning nor justification when it creates a hiatus in the continuity of human development. The success of our undertaking depends essentially on the
abandonment of any such distinction. The forms of family organization prevailing in the times known to us are not original forms, but
the consequences of earlier stages. Considered alone, they disclose

only themselves, not their causality; they are isolated data, elements of knowledge at most, but not of understanding. The strictness of the Roman patriarchal system points to an earlier system that had to be combatted and suppressed. And the same applies to the paternal system of Athens, the city of Athene, motherless daughter of Zeus. With all its Apollonian purity, it too represents the peak of a development, the first stages of which must have belonged to a world characterized by entirely different ideas and institutions. How then shall we understand the end if the beginnings remain a riddle to us? But where are these beginnings to be found? The answer is not in doubt. In myth, the faithful picture of the oldest era, and nowhere else.

The thirst for systematic knowledge has inspired many attempts to arrive at a picture of the origins by philosophical speculation, to fill in the great gaps in our historical records with the shadowy figures of abstract reasoning. A strange inconsistency: to reject myth as invention and to accept one's own utopias so confidently. In the following investigations we shall painstakingly avoid temptations of this sort. Cautiously, perhaps overcautiously, we shall steer our course along the solid land, following the bends and bays of the shoreline, avoiding the dangers and accidents of the high seas. Where no earlier experience is available, one must pay the closest attention to detail. Only an abundance of particulars can supply the comparisons which will enable us to distinguish the essential from the accidental, the lawful and universal from the local, and to arrive at increasingly universal principles.

It has been said that myth, like quicksand, can never provide a firm foothold. This reproach applies, not to myth itself, but only to the way it has been handled. Multiform and shifting in its outward manifestation, myth nevertheless follows fixed laws, and can provide as definite and secure results as any other source of historical knowledge. Product of a cultural period in which life had not yet broken away from the harmony of nature, it shares with nature that unconscious lawfulness which is always lacking in the works of free reflection. Everywhere there is system, everywhere cohesion; in every detail the expression of a great fundamental law whose abundant manifestations demonstrate its inner truth and natural necessity.

In the matriarchal culture the homogeneity of a dominant idea is particularly apparent. All its manifestations are of one mold, disclosing a self-contained stage in the development of the human spirit. The primacy of motherhood in the family cannot be regarded as an isolated phenomenon. It is utterly incompatible with a culture such as that of the Greek classical period. The opposition between the paternal and maternal systems is bound to permeate the entire life form surrounding them.

This homogeneity of matriarchal ideas is confirmed by the favoring of the left over the right side. The left side belongs to the passive feminine principle, the right to the active masculine principle. The role played by the left hand of Isis in matriarchal Egypt suffices to make the connection clear. But a multitude of additional data prove its importance, universality, primordiality, and freedom from the influence of philosophical speculation. Customs and practices of civil and religious life, peculiarities of clothing and headdress, and certain linguistic usages reveal the same idea, the *major honos laevarum partium* (greater honor of the left side) and its close connection with mother right. Another no less significant manifestation of the same basic law is the primacy of the night over the day which issued from its womb. The opposite relation would be in direct contradiction to matriarchal ideas. Already the ancients identified the primacy of the night with that of the left, and both of these with the primacy of the mother. And here, too, age-old customs, the reckoning of time according to nights, the choice of the night as a time for battle, for taking counsel, for meting out justice, and for practicing the cult rites, show that we are not dealing with abstract philosophical ideas of later origin, but with the reality of an original mode of life. Extension of the same idea permits us to recognize the religious preference given to the moon over the sun, of the conceiving earth over the fecundating sea, of the dark aspect of death over the luminous aspect of growth, of the dead over the living, of mourning over rejoicing, as necessary characteristics of the predominantly matriarchal age. In the course of our investigation all these traits will appear many times over and take on an increasingly profound meaning.

Already we have before us a world in which mother right no longer appears as a strange, incomprehensible form, but rather as a homogeneous phenomenon. The picture, however, still presents numerous gaps and obscurities. But it is characteristic of all profound perceptions that they quickly gather related objects into their sphere and find their way from the patent to the hidden. A gentle hint from the ancients often suffices to open up new insights. An example may be found in the favored position of the sister and of the youngest child. Both notions are aspects of the matriarchal principle and both demonstrate new ramifications of the basic idea. The significance of sisterhood among the Germanic people is disclosed by an observation of

Tacitus,[7] and a corresponding statement from Plutarch [8] about Roman customs proves that this is no accidental local notion, but a consistent and fundamental idea. The favoring of the youngest child is attested by many passages in Philostratus' *Heroicus,* a work which, though late, is extremely important for the elucidation of the oldest ideas. And vast numbers of examples, some taken from mythical tradition and others from the history of ancient or still living peoples, prove the universality and primordiality of both phenomena. It is not difficult to ascertain the aspect of the matriarchal idea they are related to. The favoring of the sister over the brother merely lends new expression to the favoring of the daughter over the son, and the preference given to the youngest child identifies the survival of the clan with the youngest scion of the maternal line, who, because he is last born, will also be last to die.

There is scarcely any need to point out what new perspectives are disclosed by these two observations. The judgment of man according to the laws of natural life, which leads to preference for the shoots of the springtime, is in perfect accord with the Lycian metaphor of the leaves of the trees; it characterizes mother right as the law of material-corporeal, not of higher spiritual life, and shows the matriarchal world as a whole to be a product of the maternal-tellurian, not of the paternal-uranian attitude toward human existence.

And it hardly seems necessary to point out how many passages in ancient writings, how many phenomena of matriarchal cultures, were illuminated and made available for this work by Tacitus' remarks about the far-reaching implications of sisterhood as the basis of the Germanic family. The greater love for the sister leads us into one of the noblest aspects of matriarchal culture. Hitherto we have stressed the juridical aspect of mother right, but now we perceive its ethical significance. Its juridical forms surprised us by their contrast with what we have become accustomed to regarding as the natural organization of the family; at first sight they seemed incomprehensible. The ethical aspect strikes a resonance in a natural sentiment which is alien to no age: we understand it almost spontaneously. At the lowest, darkest stages of human existence the love between the mother and her offspring is the bright spot in life, the only light in the moral darkness, the only joy amid profound misery. By recalling this fact to our attention, the observation of still living peoples of other continents has

[7] Tacitus. *Germania* 20.
[8] Plutarch, *Quaest. Rom.* 17.267.

clarified the mythical tradition which represents the appearance of the Φιλοπάτορες (father lovers) as an important turning point in the development of human culture. The close relation between child and father, the son's self-sacrifice for his begetter, require a far higher degree of moral development than mother love, that mysterious power which equally permeates all earthly creatures. Paternal love appears later. The relationship which stands at the origin of all culture, of every virtue, of every nobler aspect of existence, is that between mother and child; it operates in a world of violence as the divine principle of love, of union, of peace. Raising her young, the woman learns earlier than the man to extend her loving care beyond the limits of the ego to another creature, and to direct whatever gift of invention she possesses to the preservation and improvement of this other's existence. Woman at this stage is the repository of all culture, of all benevolence, of all devotion, of all concern for the living and grief for the dead.

Myth and history express this idea in any number of ways. The Cretan expressed his love for the land of his birth by the term "mother country"; origin in a common womb is regarded as the closest bond, as the true and originally the only relation of kinship; to help, to protect, and to avenge the mother is seen as the highest duty, while to threaten her life is looked upon as a crime beyond all expiation, even if it is done in the service of offended fatherhood.

There is no need of further details. These suffice to arouse our interest in the ethical character of matriarchal culture. How significant become all those examples of loyalty to mothers and sisters; of men inspired by the peril or death of a sister to undertake the gravest hardships; and, finally, of pairs of sisters who stand out as universal prototypes. Yet the love that arises from motherhood is not only more intense, but also more universal. Tacitus, who hints at this idea in his account of the Germani but speaks explicitly only of the sister relationship, can scarcely have realized its full significance and its full historical scope. Whereas the paternal principle is inherently restrictive, the maternal principle is universal; the paternal principle implies limitation to definite groups, but the maternal principle, like the life of nature, knows no barriers. The idea of motherhood produces a sense of universal fraternity among all men, which dies with the development of paternity. The family based on father right is a closed individual organism, whereas the matriarchal family bears the typically universal character that stands at the beginning of all development and distinguishes material life from higher spiritual life.

Every woman's womb, the mortal image of the earth mother Demeter, will give brothers and sisters to the children of every other woman; the homeland will know only brothers and sisters until the day when the development of the paternal system dissolves the undifferentiated unity of the mass and introduces a principle of articulation.

Selected Bibliography

For additional works by Bachofen, see the bibliography appended to *Myth, Religion, and Mother Right: Selected Writings of J. J. Bachofen*, trans. by Ralph Manheim (with a Preface by George Boas and an Introduction by Joseph Campbell) (Princeton: Princeton University Press, 1967), pp. 259–270.

Reflections on Savage Man

F. MAX MÜLLER

Max Müller, one of the chief catalysts in the field of comparative mythology and history of religion, was born in Dessau, Germany, on December 6, 1823. From 1841 to 1844 he studied Sanskrit at the University of Leipzig. Afterward, his studies branched out into the fields of comparative philology, philosophy, and comparative religion at the Universities of Berlin and Paris. In 1846 Müller went to England to edit a translation of the Rig Veda. *After completing this project he remained in England, and took a post at Oxford, although he failed to receive the professorial chair in Sanskrit. After 1860 he turned his attention more and more to the study of language and mythology. In 1868 he became professor of comparative philology at Oxford. It was his work in comparative philosophy and mythology that brought him into the field of religion. In 1873 he published his* Introduction to the Science of Religion. *In 1875 he became editor of a massive project of about fifty volumes,* Sacred Books of the East, *which consisted of translations of scriptures of Eastern religions. He spent the rest of his life at Oxford serving as a curator of the Bodleian library after 1875, at which time he stopped lecturing. His global outlook continued to expand, however. He died at Oxford on October 28, 1900, in favor in England and respected by scholars throughout the world.*

There are people in the world who are very fond of asking what they call point-blank questions. They generally profess to hate all shilly-shallying, and they are at no pains to hide their suspicion that any one who declines to say yes or no to any question which they choose to ask has either his intellect clouded by metaphysics or has not the courage of his opinions. The idea that it is often more difficult to ask a sensible question than to answer it, and that a question, however pointed it may sound, may for all that be so blunt and vague that no accurate and honest thinker would care or dare to answer it, never enters their mind; while the thought that there are realms of knowledge where indefinite language is more appropriate, and in reality

F. Max Müller, "The Savage," in *The Nineteenth Century*, Vol. XVII (1885), pp. 109–132.

more exact and more truthful than the most definite phraseology, is scouted as mere fencing and intellectual cowardice.

One of those point-blank questions which has been addressed to me by several reviewers of my books is this, "Tell us, do you hold that man began as a savage or not?" To say that man began as a savage, and that the most savage and degraded races now existing present us with the primeval type of man, seems to be the shibboleth of a certain school of thought, a school with which on many points I sympathise, so long as it keeps to an accurate and independent inquiry into facts, and to an outspoken statement of its discoveries, regardless of all consequences, but from which I totally dissent as soon as it tries to make facts subservient to theories. I am told that my own utterances on this subject have been ambiguous. Now even granting this, I could never understand why a certain hesitation in answering so difficult a question should rouse such angry feelings, till it began to dawn on me that those who do not unreservedly admit that man began as a savage are supposed to hold that man was created a perfect and almost angelic being. This would amount to denying the gospel of the day, that man was the offspring of a brute, and hence, I suppose, the Anathema.

Now I may say this, that though I have hesitated to affirm that man began as a savage, whatever that may mean, I have been even more careful not to commit myself to the opinion that man began as an angel, or as a child, or as a perfect rational being. I strongly object to such alternatives as that if man did not begin as a savage he must have begun as a child. It would be dreadful if, because there is no sufficient evidence to enable us to form a decided opinion on any given subject, we were to be driven into a corner by such alternatives, instead of preserving our freedom of judgment until we have the complete evidence before us.

But in our case the evidence is as yet extremely scanty, and, from the nature of the case, will probably always remain so. If we want to prove that man began as a child, what evidence can we produce? If we appealed to history, history is impossible before the invention of language; and what language could the primitive child have spoken, what life could it have lived, without a father and without a mother? If we give up history and appeal to our inner consciousness, our reason, nay, our very imagination, collapses when approaching the problem how such a child could have been born, how such a child could have been nourished, reared, and protected from wild animals and other dangers. We feel we have come to the end of our tether, and are running our head against a very old, but a very solid, wall.

Has Kant then written in vain; and is it still supposed that our senses or our reason can ever reach transcendent truths? Has the lesson to be taught again and again that both our senses and our reason have their limits; that we are indeed tethered, and that it is no proof of intellectual strength or suppleness to try to stand on our own shoulders? We are so made that neither can our senses perceive nor can our reason conceive the real beginning and end of anything, whether in space or in time. And yet we imagine we can form a definite conception of the true beginning of mankind.

Then what remains? There remains the humbler and yet far nobler task of studying the earliest records of man's life on earth: to go back as far as literature, language, and tools will allow us, and for the time to consider that as primitive which, whether as a tool, or as a word, or as a proverb, or as a prayer, is the last we can reach, and seems at the same time so simple, so rational, so intelligible, as to require no further antecedents. That is the true work of the historian, and of the philosopher too; and there is plenty of work left for both of them before they dive into the whirlpool of their inner consciousness to find there the primordial savage.

Instead of allowing ourselves to be driven into a corner by such a question as "Did man begin as a savage or as a child?" we have a perfect right to ask the question, What is meant by these two words, *savage* and *child*?

Has anyone ever attempted to define the meaning of savage, and to draw a sharp line between a savage and a non-savage? Has anyone ever attempted to define the meaning of child, if used in opposition to savage or brute? Have we been told whether by child is meant a suckling without a mother, or a boy who can speak, and count, and reason without a father? Lastly, are savage and child really terms that mutually exclude each other? May not a savage be a child, and may not a child be a savage?

How, then, is anyone who has given serious thought to the problem of the origin of mankind to answer such a question as "Tell me, do you hold that man began as a savage or as a child?"

When we read some of the more recent works on anthropology, the primordial savage seems to be not unlike one of those hideous india-rubber dolls that can be squeezed into every possible shape, and made to utter every possible noise. There was a time when the savage was held up to the civilised man as the inhabitant of a lost paradise

—a being of innocence, simplicity, purity, and nobility. Rousseau ascribed to his son of nature all the perfection which he looked for in vain in Paris and London. At present, when so many philosophers are on the look-out for the missing link between man and beast, the savage, even if he has established his right to the name of man, cannot be painted black enough. He must be at least a man who maltreats his women, murders his children, kills and eats his fellow-creatures, and commits crimes from which even animals would shrink.

This devil-savage, however, of the present anthropologist is as much a wild creation of scientific fancy as the angel-savage of former philosophers. The true Science of Man has no room for such speculations. . . .

Whatever other benefits a study of the science of language may confer, there is one which cannot be valued too highly—namely, that it makes us not only look *at* words, but *through* words. If we are told that a savage means an uncivilised man, then, to say that the first man was a savage is saying either nothing or what is self-evident. Civilisation consists in the accumulated wisdom of countless generations of men, and to say that the first generation of men was uncivilised is therefore pure tautology. We are far too tolerant with respect to such tautologies. How many people, for instance, have been led to imagine that such a phrase as the survival of the fittest contains the solution of the problem of the survival of certain species and the extinction of others? To the student of language the survival of the fittest is a mere tautology, meaning the survival of the fittest to survive, which is the statement of a fact, but no solution of it.

It is easy to say that the meaning of savage has been explained and defined by almost every writer on anthropology. I know these explanations and definitions, but not one of them can be considered as answering the requirements of a scientific definition.

Some anthropologists say that savage means wild and cruel. But in that case no nation would be without its savages. Others say that savages are people who wear little or no clothing. But in that case the greatest philosophers, the gymnosophists of India, would have to be classed as savages. If it means people without a settled form of government, without laws and without a religion, then, go where you like, you will not find such a race. Again, if people who have no cities and no central government are to be called savages, then the Jews would have been savages, the Hindus, the Arabs, the ancient Germans, and other of the most important races in the history of the world. In fact, whatever characteristics are brought forward as distinctive of a savage, they can always be met by counterinstances, showing that each definition would either include races whom no one dares to call savage, or exclude races whom no one dares to call civilised. It used to be imagined that the use of letters was the principal circumstance that distinguishes a civilised people from a herd of savages incapable of knowledge or reflection. Without that artificial help, to quote the words of Gibbon, "the human memory soon dissipates or corrupts the ideas committed to her charge, and the nobler faculties of the mind, no longer supplied with models or with materials, gradually forget their powers, the judgment becomes feeble and lethargic, the imagination languid or irregular." Such arguments might pass in the days of Gibbon, but after the new light that has been thrown on the ancient history of some of the principal nations of the world they are no longer tenable.

No one would call the ancient Brahmans savages, and yet writing was unknown to them before the third century B.C. Homer, quite apart from his blindness, was certainly unacquainted with writing for literary purposes. The ancient inhabitants of Germany, as described by Tacitus, were equally ignorant of the art of writing as a vehicle of literature; yet for all that we could not say, with Gibbon, that with them the nobler faculties of the mind had lost their powers, the judgment had become feeble, and the imagination languid.

And as we find that the use of letters is by no means an indispensable element of true civilisation, we should arrive at the same conclusion in examining almost every discovery which has been pointed out as a *sine quâ non* of civilised life. Every generation is apt to consider the measure of comfort which it has reached as indispensable to civilised life, but very often, in small as well as great things, what is called civilised to-day may be called barbarous to-morrow. Races who abstain from eating the flesh of animals are apt to look on carnivorous people as savages; people who abstain from intoxicating drinks naturally despise a nation in which drunkenness is prevalent. What should we say if we entered a town in which the streets were neither paved nor lighted, and in which the windows were without glass; where we saw no carriages in any of the thoroughfares, and where, inside the houses, ladies and gentlemen might be seen eating without forks and wearing garments that had never been washed? And yet even in Paris no street was paved before 1185. In London Holborn was first paved in 1417, and Smithfield in 1614, while Berlin was without paved streets far into the seventeenth century. No houses had windows of glass before the twelfth century, and as late as the fourteenth century anything might be thrown out of window at Paris, after three times calling out *"Gare l'eau!"* Shirts were an invention of the Crusades, and the fine dresses which ladies and gentlemen wore during the Middle Ages were hardly ever washed, but only refreshed from time to time with precious scents. In 1550 we are told that there existed in Paris no more than three carriages—one belonging to the Queen, the other to Diane de Poitiers, and the third to René de Laval. In England coaches (so called from the Hungarian *kossi*) date from 1580, though whirlicotes go back to the fourteenth century. So far as we know, neither Dante nor Beatrice used forks in eating, and yet we should hardly class them as savages.

It is easy to say that all these are matters of small importance. No doubt they are, but we often see them treated as matters of great importance, when we speak of races with red skins or black skins. With us civilisation, whether consisting of these small or great matters, has often become a burden, a check rather than a help to the free development of all that is noble in human nature; while many conditions of life which we are inclined to call barbarous were almost essential for the growth of the human mind during its earlier stages. Can we imagine a religion growing up in modern Paris? Would a travelling bard, such as Homer, find an audience in the streets of London? Would a Socrates be listened to by the professors of Berlin? A Panini sitting almost naked under a pippal tree and composing the rules of his marvellous grammar of Sanskrit, a Bâdârâyana with dishevelled hair, spinning out of his mind the subtle web of Vedânta philosophy, would be shunned as wild creatures by a young English officer, and yet, on the ladder that leads to the highest excellence of intellect, how many steps would the former stand above the latter! For carrying out the chief objects of our life on earth, very little of what is now called civilisation is really wanted. Many things are pleasant, without being really essential to our fulfilling our mission on earth. For laying the foundations of society, for settling the broad principles of law and morality, for discovering the deep traces of order and unity in nature, and for becoming conscious of the presence of the Divine within and without, a life in the forests, on the mountains, ay, even in the desert, is far more favourable than a lodging in Bond Street.

I have thus tried to show how untenable is the theory which would boldly identify the modern savage with primitive man, and how cautious we ought to be whenever we take even a few hints here and there from degraded tribes of the present day in order to fill out our imaginary picture of the earliest civilisation of our race.

In arguing so far, I have carefully kept to the historical point of view, though I am well aware that the principal traits in the imaginary picture of primitive man are generally taken from a very different source. We are so made that for everything that comes before us we have to postulate a cause and a beginning. We therefore postulate a cause and a beginning for man. The ethnologist is not concerned with the first cause of man, but he cannot resist the craving of his mind to know at least the beginning of man.

Most ethnologists used to hold that, as each individual begins as a child, mankind also began as a child; and they imagined that a careful observation of the modern child would give them some idea of the character of the primeval child. Much ingenuity has been spent on this subject since the days of Voltaire, and many amusing books have been the result, till it was seen at last that the modern baby and the primeval baby have nothing in common but the name, not even a mother or a nurse.

It was chiefly due to Darwin and to the new impulse which he gave to the theory of evolution that this line of argument was abandoned as hopeless. Darwin boldly asked the question whose child the primeval human baby could have been, and he answered it by representing the human baby as the child of non-human parents. Admitting even the possibility of this *transitio in aliud genus,* which the most honest of Darwin's followers strenuously deny, what should we gain by this for our purpose—namely, for knowing the primitive state of man, the earliest glimmerings of the human intellect? Our difficulties would remain exactly the same, only pushed back a little further.

Disappointing as it may sound, the fact must be faced, nevertheless, that our reasoning faculties, wonderful as they are, break down completely before all problems concerning the origin of things. We may imagine, we may believe, anything we like about the first man; we can know absolutely nothing. If we trace him back to a primeval cell, the primeval cell that could become a man is more mysterious by far than the man that was evolved from a cell. If we trace him back to a primeval pro-anthropos, the pro-anthropos is more unintelligible to us than even the protanthropos would be. If we trace back the whole solar system to a rotating nebula, that wonderful nebula which by evolution and revolution could become an inhabitable universe is, again, far more mysterious than the universe itself.

The lesson that there are limits to our knowledge is an old lesson, but it has to be taught again and again. It was taught by Buddha, it was taught by Socrates, and it was taught for the last time in the most powerful manner by Kant. Philosophy has been called the knowledge of our knowledge; it might be called more truly the knowledge of our ignorance, or, to adopt the more moderate language of Kant, the knowledge of the limits of our knowledge.

Selected Bibliography

Anthropological Religion (London: Longmans, Green and Co., Ltd., 1898).

Chips from a German Workshop (London: Longmans, Green and Co., Ltd., 1868–1875).

India: What Can It Teach Us? (London: Longmans, Green and Co., Ltd., 1896).

Introduction to the Science of Religion (London: Longmans, Green and Co., Ltd., 1873).

Lectures on the Origin and Growth of Religion as Illustrated by the Religions of India (New York: Charles Scribner's Sons, Inc., 1879).

The Origin of Man's Conception of God

Sir James George Frazer

The author of the famous The Golden Bough, Sir James George Frazer was born in Glasgow, Scotland, on January 1, 1854. He was educated in Glasgow and Cambridge in anthropology and the classics. After teaching social anthropology at Liverpool for one semester in 1907, he went to Cambridge and remained on the faculty there throughout his teaching career. His book, The Golden Bough, served two prominent functions. First, it provided a testing ground for the theory that there is an evolutionary sequence from magic to religion to science in the history of mankind. Secondly, it was the occasion for gathering together great masses of information about religion, magic, and folklore from all parts of the world. While the theory itself has been discredited, the book stands as a useful collection of materials in these fields. Like other scholars in the field, Frazer enjoyed a long life. He died at Cambridge on May 7, 1941.

If we are indeed to discover the origin of man's conception of God, it is not sufficient to analyse the ideas which the educated and enlightened portion of mankind entertain on the subject at the present day; for in great measure these ideas are traditional, they have been handed down with little or no independent reflection or inquiry from generation to generation; hence in order to detect them in their inception it becomes necessary to push our analysis far back into the past. Large materials for such an historical inquiry are provided for us in the literature of ancient nations which, though often sadly mutilated and imperfect, has survived to modern times and throws much precious light on the religious beliefs and practices of the people who created it. But the ancients themselves inherited a great part of their religion from their prehistoric ancestors, and accordingly it becomes desirable to investigate the religious notions

Sir James George Frazer, from *Man, God and Immortality* (New York: Macmillan, 1927), pp. 197, 201, 248–253. Used by permission of A. P. Watt & Son and Trinity College, Cambridge.

of these remote forefathers of mankind, since in them we may hope at last to arrive at the ultimate source, the historical origin, of the whole long development.

But how can this be done? How can we investigate the ideas of peoples who, ignorant of writing, had no means of permanently recording their beliefs? At first sight the thing seems impossible; the thread of inquiry is broken off short; it has landed us on the brink of a gulf which looks impassable. But the case is not so hopeless as it appears. True, we cannot investigate the beliefs of prehistoric ages directly, but the comparative method of research may furnish us with the means of studying them indirectly; it may hold up to us a mirror in which, if we do not see the originals, we may perhaps contemplate their reflections. For a comparative study of the various races of mankind demonstrates, or at least renders it highly probable, that humanity has everywhere started at an exceedingly low level of culture, a level far beneath that of the lowest existing savages, and that from this humble beginning all the various races of men have gradually progressed upward at different rates, some faster and some slower, till they have attained the particular stage that each of them occupies at the present time.

If this conclusion is correct, the various stages of savagery and barbarism on which many tribes and peoples now stand represent, broadly speaking, so many degrees of retarded social and intellectual development, they correspond to similar stages which the ancestors of the civilized races may be supposed to have passed through at more or less remote periods of their history. Thus when we arrange all the known peoples of the world according to the degree of their savagery or civilization in a graduated scale of culture, we obtain not merely a comparative view of their relative positions in the scale, but also in some measure an historical record of the genetic development of culture from a very early time down to the present day. Hence a study of the savage and barbarous races of mankind is of the greatest importance for a full understanding of the beliefs and practices, whether religious, social, moral, or political, of the most civilized races, including our own, since it is practically certain that a large part of these beliefs and practices originated with our savage ancestors, and has been inherited by us from them, with more or less of modification, through a long line of intermediate generations.

That is why the study of existing savages at the present day engrosses so much of the attention of civilized peoples. We see that if we are to comprehend not only our past history but our present condition, with all its many intricate and perplexing problems, we must begin at the beginning by attempting to discover the mental state of our savage forefathers, who bequeathed to us so much of the faiths, the laws, and the institutions which we still cherish; and more and more men are coming to perceive that the only way open to us of doing this effectually is to study the mental state of savages who to this day occupy a state of culture analogous to that of our rude progenitors. Through contact with civilization these savages are now rapidly disappearing, or at least losing the old habits and ideas which render them a document of priceless historical value for us. Hence we have every motive for prosecuting the study of savagery with ardour and diligence before it is too late, before the record is gone for ever. We are like an heir whose title-deeds must be scrutinized before he can take possession of the inheritance, but who finds the handwriting of the deeds so fading and evanescent that it threatens to disappear entirely before he can read the document to the end. With that keen attention, what eager haste, would he not scan the fast-vanishing characters? With the like attention and the like haste civilized men are now applying themselves to the investigation of the fast vanishing savages.

Thus if we are to trace historically man's conception of God to its origin, it is desirable, or rather essential, that we should begin by studying the most primitive ideas on the subject which are accessible to us, and the most primitive ideas are unquestionably those of the lowest savages. For a similar reason the study of inorganic chemistry naturally precedes the study of organic chemistry, because inorganic compounds are much simpler and therefore more easily analysed and investigated than organic compounds. So with the chemistry of the mind; we should analyse the comparatively simple phenomena of savage thought into its constituent elements before we attempt to perform a similar operation on the vastly more complex phenomena of civilized beliefs.

Rudimentary Notion of God Among Many Savages

Much of the controversy which has raged as to the religion of the lower races has sprung merely from a mutual misunderstanding. The savage does not understand the thoughts of the civilized man, and few civilized men understand the thoughts of the savage. When the savage uses his word for god, he has in his mind a being of a certain sort: when the civilized man uses his word for god, he has in his mind a being of a very different sort; and, if, as commonly happens, the two men are equally unable to place themselves at the other's point of view, nothing but confusion and mistakes can result from their discussions. If we civilized men insist on limiting the name of God to that particular conception of the divine nature which we ourselves have formed, then we must confess that the savage has no god at all. But we shall adhere more closely to the facts of history if we allow most of the higher savages at least to possess a rudimentary notion of certain supernatural beings who may fittingly be called gods, though not in the full sense in which we use the word. That rudimentary notion represents in all probability the germ out of which the civilized peoples have gradually evolved their own high conceptions of deity: and if we could trace the whole course of religious development, we might find that the chain which links our idea of the Godhead with that of the savage is one and unbroken. . . .

The Passage from Magic to Religion

If an Age of Religion has thus everywhere, as I venture to surmise, been preceded by an Age of Magic, it is natural that we should inquire what causes have led mankind, or rather a portion of them, to abandon magic as a principle of faith and practice and to betake themselves to religion instead. When we reflect upon the multitude, the variety, and the complexity of the facts to be explained, and the scantiness of our information regarding them, we shall be ready to acknowledge that a full and satisfactory solution of so profound a problem is hardly to be hoped for, and that the most we can do in the present state of our knowledge is to hazard a more or less plausible conjecture. With all due diffidence, then, I would suggest that a tardy recognition of the inherent falsehood and barrenness of magic set the more thoughtful part of mankind to cast about for a truer theory of nature and a more fruitful method of turning her resources to account. The shrewder intelligences must in time have come to perceive that magical ceremonies and incantations did not really effect the results which they were designed to produce, and which the majority of their simpler fellows still believed that they did actually produce. This great discovery of the inefficacy of magic must have wrought a radical though probably slow revolution in the minds of those who had sagacity to make it. The discovery amounted to this, that men for the first time recognized their inability to manipulate at pleasure certain natural forces which hitherto they had believed to be completely within their control. It was a confession of human ignorance and weakness. Man saw that he had taken for causes what were no causes, and that all his efforts to work by means of these imaginary causes had been vain. His painful toil had been wasted, his curious ingenuity had been squandered to no purpose. He had been pulling at strings to which nothing was attached; he had been marching, as he thought, straight to the goal, while in reality he had only been treading in a narrow circle. Not that the effects which he had striven so hard to produce did not continue to manifest themselves. They were still produced, but not by him. The rain still fell on the thirsty ground: the sun still pursued his daily, and the moon her nightly journey across the sky: the silent procession of the seasons still moved in light and shadow, in cloud and sunshine across the earth: men were still born to labour and sorrow and still, after a brief sojourn here, were gathered to their fathers in the long home hereafter. All things indeed went on as before, yet all seemed different to him from whose eyes the old scales had fallen. For he could no longer cherish the pleasing illusion that it was he who guided the earth and the heaven in their courses, and that they would cease to perform their great revolutions were he to take his feeble hand from the wheel. In the death of his enemies and his friends he no longer saw a proof of the resistless potency of his own or of hostile enchantments; he now knew that friends and foes alike had succumbed to á force stronger than any that he could wield, and in obedience to a destiny which he was powerless to control.

Thus cut adrift from his ancient moorings and left to toss on a troubled sea of doubt and uncertainty, his old happy confidence in himself and in his powers rudely shaken, our primitive philosopher must have been sadly perplexed and agitated till he came to rest, as in a quiet haven after a tempestuous voyage in a new system of faith and practice, which seemed to offer a solution of his harassing doubts and a substitute, however precarious, for that sovereignty over nature which he had reluctantly abdicated. If the great world went on its way without the help of him or his fellows, it must surely be because there were other beings, like himself, but far stronger, who, unseen themselves, directed its course and brought about all the varied series of events which he had hitherto believed to be dependent on his own magic. It was they, as he now believed, and not he himself, who made the stormy wind to blow, the lightning to flash, and the thunder to roll; who had laid the foundations of the solid earth and set bounds to the restless sea that it might not pass; who caused all the glorious lights of heaven to shine; who gave the fowls of the air their meat and the wild beasts of the desert their prey; who bade the fruitful land to bring forth in abundance, the high hills to be clothed with forests, the bubbling springs to rise under the rocks in the valleys, and green pastures to grow by still waters; who breathed into man's nostrils and made him live, or turned him to destruction by famine and pestilence and war. To these mighty beings, whose handiwork he traced in all the gorgeous and varied pageantry of nature, man now addressed himself, humbly confessing his dependence on their invisible power, and beseeching them of their mercy to furnish him with all good things, to defend him from the perils and dangers by which our mortal life is compassed about on every hand, and finally to bring his immortal spirit, freed from the burden of the body, to some happier world, beyond the reach of pain and sorrow, where he might rest with them and with the spirits of good men in joy and felicity for ever.

In this, or some such way as this, the deeper minds may be conceived to have made the great transition from magic to religion. But even in them the change can hardly ever have been sudden; probably it proceeded very slowly, and required long ages for its more or less perfect accomplishment. For the recognition of man's powerlessness to influence the course of nature on a grand scale must have been gradual; he cannot have been shorn of the whole of his fancied dominion at a flow. Step by step he must have been driven back from his proud position; foot by foot he must have yielded, with a sigh, the ground which he had once viewed as his own. Now it would be the wind, now the rain, now the sunshine, now the thunder, that he confessed himself unable to wield at will; and as province after province of nature thus fell from his grasp, till what had once seemed a kingdom threatened to shrink into a prison, man must have been more and more profoundly impressed with a sense of his own helplessness and the might of the invisible beings by whom he believed himself to be surrounded. Thus religion, beginning as a slight and partial acknowledgement of powers superior to man, tends with the growth of knowledge to deepen into a confession of man's entire and absolute dependence on the divine; his old free bearing is exchanged for an attitude of lowliest prostration before the mysterious powers of the unseen, and his highest virtue is to submit his will to theirs: *In la sua volontade é nostra pace.* But this deepening sense of religion, this more perfect submission to the divine will in all things, affects only those higher intelligences who have breadth of view enough to comprehend the vastness of the universe and the littleness of man. Small minds cannot grasp great ideas; to their narrow comprehension, their purblind vision, nothing seems really great and important but themselves. Such minds hardly rise into religion at all. They are, indeed, drilled by their betters into an outward conformity with its precepts and a verbal profession of its tenets; but at heart they cling to their old magical superstitions, which may be discountenanced and forbidden, but cannot be eradicated by religion, so long as they have their roots deep down in the mental framework and constitution of the great majority of mankind.

Selected Bibliography

The Belief in Immortality and the Worship of the Dead (London: Dawsons of Pall Mall, 1968).

Creation and Evolution in Primitive Cosmogonies (Freeport, New York: Books for Libraries Press, 1967).

Folk-lore in the Old Testament (New York: Macmillan, 1923).

The Golden Bough, 12 vols. (New York: Macmillan, 1935).

Lectures on the Early History of the Kingship (New York: Macmillan, 1905).

The Worship of Nature (New York: Macmillan, 1926).

On Primitive Mentality

LUCIEN LÉVY-BRUHL

Lucien Lévy-Bruhl was born in Paris on April 10, 1857. He trained and taught as an anthropologist, but eventually became professor of the history of modern philosophy at the Sorbonne from 1904 until 1927. His interests were many-sided. He worked in psychology and moral philosophy, in addition to anthropology, sociology, and religious theory. As a sociologist and anthropologist he was deeply influenced by the thought of Auguste Comte and Émile Durkheim. Like Comte, who viewed human history in terms of the transitions from theological to metaphysical to scientific modes of thought, Lévy-Bruhl was trained to see discrepancies between the reasoning processes of primitive and civilized men. With Durkheim, he sought to explain human experience in social rather than in individual terms. On the supposition that various kinds of mentality exist among men, he investigated the form of thought most unlike a civilized mentality, namely that of primitive men. His contention was that the collective representations of primitive men are mystical, prelogical, and pervaded by a sense of affectational participation (by which Lévy-Bruhl meant that the data of experience tend to inhere and partake of each other rather than being regulated by cause-and-effect relationships). He also argued that there are mediating stages between the mentalities of primitive and civilized men, and that the mystical mode is never fully supplanted even in rational men. In later life, Lévy-Bruhl tended to deradicalize the differences between primitive and civilized mentalities and to underscore those aspects of primitive thought that are retained in modern religious sensitivities. He died in Paris on March 13, 1939.

The all-pervading presence of spirits, witchcrafts, and enchantments ever threatening in the background, the dead so closely connected with the life of the living—this ensemble of representations is an inexhaustible source of emotion to the primitive, and it is to this that his mental activity owes its characteristic features. It is not only mystic, that is, at all times orientated to occult forces: it is not only prelogical, that is, indifferent as a rule to the law of contradiction: it is more than this; the causality it pictures to itself is of a type differing from that familiar to us, and this third characteristic is indissolubly bound up with the other two.

As we understand it, the connection between cause and effect necessarily unites phenomena in time, and conditions them in such a way that they are arranged in a series which cannot be reversed. Moreover, the series of causes and effects are prolonged and intermingled to infinity. All the phenomena of the universe, as Kant says, have universally reciprocal influence; but however complex the system may be, the certainty we have that these phenomena are always arranged in causal series, is the very foundation, to our minds, of the order of the universe, and, in short, of experience.

The primitive's mind views the matter very differently, however. All, or nearly all that happens, is referred by him, as we have just seen, to the influence of mystic or occult powers, such as wizards, ghosts, spirits, etc. In acting thus, his mind doubtless obeys the same mental instinct as that which guides us. But instead of both cause and effect being perceptible in time and nearly always in space, as in our case, primitive mentality admits only one of the two conditions to be perceptible at one time; the other belongs to the sum-total of those entities which are invisible and imperceptible to sense.

It is true that to the primitive's mind the latter are no less real and no less directly perceptible than the former, and this very fact is one of the characteristics peculiar to his mentality; but the causal connection between these two heterogeneous conditions will differ profoundly from that which we should imagine it to be. One of these conditions—that which we call cause—has no visible link with the beings and the circumstances of the world perceived by sense. It is extra-spatial, and consequently, in one aspect at least, extra-temporal. It does undoubtedly precede its effect; it will be the resentment felt by a dead man, for instance, that will cause him to inflict such-and-such a disaster upon the survivors. But, nevertheless, the fact that .the mystic forces which are "causes," remain invisible and imperceptible to ordinary observation, makes it impossible to fix them in time and in space, and often does not allow of their being individualized. As visitants from an inaccessible region they float around, they radiate, so to speak; they surround on all sides the primitive, who finds nothing extraordinary in feeling them to be present in several places at the same time. The world of experience thus formed in the primi tive mind may appear richer than ours, as I have already remarked, not only because this experience comprises elements which ours does not contain, but also because its constitution is different. To primitive mentality these mystic elements seem to involve a supplementary dimension unknown to us, not exactly a spatial dimension, but rather a dimension of the sum-total of experience. It is this peculiar quality of experience which allows primitives to regard as quite simple and natural, forms of causation which we cannot imagine.

To prelogical mentality, cause and effect present themselves in two forms, not essentially different from one another. Sometimes the collective representations impose a definite preconnection; for example, if a certain taboo is infringed, a certain misfortune will be the result, or inversely, if such-and-such a misfortune supervenes, it is because such-and-such a taboo has been violated. Or again, the fact which is apparent may be related to a mystic cause in a general way; an epidemic is raging, and it may be due to the wrath of ancestors, or the evil work of a wizard; this can be ascertained, either by divination, or by making the persons suspected of witchcraft submit to trial by ordeal. In either case there is a direct relation between cause and effect. It admits of no intermediate links, or at any rate, if it does recognize them, it regards them as negligible, and pays no heed to them.

When we say that a death has been caused by poisoning, we imagine a number of phenomena which have followed in definite order upon the introduction of poison into the system. In the body it will have acted, for example, on a certain tissue, certain digestive organs; this action will have reacted on the nerve-centres; then the respiratory organs will have become involved, etc., until finally the whole of the physiological functioning will be found to have ceased. To the primitive mind, if the poison proves effective, it is solely because the victim has been "doomed." It is between death on the one hand and the fatal influence of witchcraft on the other that the connection is established, and all the intermediary phenomena are quite unimportant. They are only produced by the will and, above all, by the power of the magician. Had he desired it, they might have been quite different. It is not even a process that he sets in motion. The idea of such a process, which would necessarily develop from a given moment, involves a clear conception of the determinism of certain phenomena, and primitive mentality has no such conception. Its place is supplied by the representation of obedient and docile agents, such as the crocodile which carries off the victim pointed out by the witch. It is certain that the crocodile is going to carry him off, but this is not because the man has exposed himself imprudently to the animal's attack. On the contrary, according to the primitive, if the crocodile were not acting as the witch's agent, it would do the man no harm.

In the same way paralysis, acute pain, and even death produced by poisoning, are by no means the necessary effect of the poison in the body, but the means chosen by mystic powers to slay their victim.

We now perceive the fundamental reason which accounts for the primitive's indifference towards the search for secondary causes. His mind is accustomed to a type of causality which obscures, as it were, the network of such causes. While these constitute the links and chains which stretch throughout time and space, the mystic causes to which primitive mentality nearly always turns, being extra-spatial and even at times extra-temporal, exclude the very idea of such links and chains. Their influence can only be direct. Even if it be produced at a distance (as so often happens in cases of witchcraft), and if its effect is not perceived till after a certain lapse of time, it nevertheless does not fail to be represented—or, to put it more accurately, to be felt—as producing itself without any intermediary.

The connection (which is altogether mystic) and most frequently we must add, the preconnection, links the occult power to the effect produced, however distant this may be. The question *how* it does this, hardly ever presents itself to a mind of this kind. At the same time, the direct nature of mystic causality equals, and even goes beyond, what we call evidence, whether it be of the senses, or rational or intuitive. The very essence of a preconnection is to be unquestioned and incontestable. When natives find Europeans refusing to believe in it, they pity them, or else they recognize that what means a good deal to themselves means nothing to white people. A very sound conclusion, but not in the sense in which they mean it.

The predominance of this kind of mystic and direct causality in their minds helps to give their mentality as a whole, the characteristics which make it so difficult for us to enter into their thought. For evidently time and space are not exactly the same to them as they are to us—I mean to us in daily life, and not in philosophic or scientific thought. Can we imagine what our familiar idea of time would be if we were not accustomed to consider phenomena as bound together in the relation of cause and effect?

It is because to us these phenomena are arranged, without our having to think about them at all, in series which cannot be reversed, with definite and measurable intervals between them; it is because effects and causes appear to us as if arranged in order in surrounding space, that time, too, seems to us to be a homogeneous quantum, divisible into parts which are identical with each other, and which succeed each other with perfect regularity. But how is time represented in minds which disregard these regular series of phenomena in space, and which pay no attention, at least deliberate attention, to the unalterable succession of cause and effect? Having no support, it can but be indistinct and ill-defined. It rather resembles a subjective feeling of duration, not wholly unlike the *durée* described by Bergson. It is scarcely a representation.

Our idea of time seems to us to be a natural attribute of the human mind. But that is a delusion. Such an idea scarcely exists where primitive mentality is concerned, for that sees the direct causal relation between the given phenomenon and the extra-spatial occult power.

As Hubert has shown,[1] primitive mentality is much more conscious of time according to its qualities than it conceives of it by its objective characteristics. "The negroes who live more in the interior of the country," writes Bosman, "distinguish time in a curious way, namely as happy and unhappy. There are some districts where the long happy time lasts for nineteen days, and the little one" (for you must know that they differentiate them thus) "seven days; between these two periods they reckon seven days that are unlucky, and these really are their holidays, for then they do not travel, nor begin a campaign, nor undertake anything important, but remain quietly at home doing nothing."[2] In this we recognize the classical distinction between the *fasti* and *nefasti*. Periods and salient points of time are characterized by the manifestations of the mystic powers which occur in them; it is to them, and almost entirely to them, that primitive mentality clings. Certain investigators have expressly noticed this. Thus, "what we Europeans call the past, is linked to the present, and this in its turn is connected with the future. For, believing as these people do in a life of two existences which are continuous, merging one into the other as the human does into the spiritual, and back again as the latter does in the former, time for them has in reality no divisions as it has for us. Equally so, it has neither value nor object, and for this reason is treated with an indifference and a contempt that is altogether inexplicable to the European."[3] This remarkable passage of

[1] Hubert et Mauss: *Mélanges d'histoire des réligions*, pp. 197 ff.
[2] Bosman: *Voyage de Guinée*, p. 164 (edit. 1705).
[3] Major A. G. Leonard: *The Lower Niger and Its Tribes*, p. 181.

Major Leonard's is somewhat obscure, probably like the very representations which he desires to give an idea of. But they are the representations of minds which live as much in the world of invisible realities as in that which we call objective reality.

What has just been said of time applies equally well to space, and for the same reasons. Space which we think of as absolutely homogeneous—not the space of the geometricians alone, but the space implied in our current ideas, appears to us like a background of canvas, unconcerned with the objects which are traced upon it. Whether phenomena are produced in this or that region of space, in the north or south, above or below, on our right or on our left, makes, we think, absolutely no difference to the phenomena themselves; it merely allows us to place, and often to measure, them. But such an idea of space is possible only to minds accustomed to the consideration of a series of secondary causes, which in fact do not vary, whatever the region in space wherein they appear. Let us imagine minds quite differently orientated, engaged primarily and almost entirely with occult forces and mystic powers whose agency is manifested in a direct way. These minds will not picture space as a uniform and immaterial quantum. On the contrary, to them it will appear burdened with qualities; its regions will have virtues peculiar to themselves; they will share in the mystic powers which are revealed therein. Space will not be so much imagined, as *felt*, and its various directions and positions will be qualitatively differentiated from one another.

In spite of appearances, homogeneous space is no more a natural datum of the human mind than homogeneous time. Undoubtedly the primitive moves in space exactly as we do; undoubtedly when he desires to throw his projectiles or to reach a distant goal, he knows as we do, and sometimes better than we do, how to calculate distances rapidly, to retrace a path, and so on. But action in space is one thing, and the idea of space quite another. It is the same thing here as in causation. Primitives constantly make use of the actual relation of cause to effect. In their construction of implements, for instance, or of traps, they often make proof of an ingenuity which implies a very careful observance of this relation. Does it follow that their idea of causation is like ours? To arrive at such a conclusion we should have to admit that the possession of a means of activity is the same as being able to analyse it, and as a reasoned knowledge of the mental or physiological processes which accompany it. We have but to formulate such an assumption to see that it is untenable.

When we describe the experience of primitive mentality as being different from our own, it is a question of the world formed for them by their collective representations. From the point of view of action, they move in space as we, and as the animals, do; they attain their ends by means of instruments, the use of which involves the actual connection between cause and effect, and if they did not conform to this objective connection, they, like ourselves (and like the animals), would immediately perish. But what actually makes them human beings is that the social group does not rest satisfied to act in order to live. Every individual member has a representation of the reality in which he is living and acting, absolutely in accordance with the constitution of this group. In fact, their minds cling to it above all for other reasons than the objective relations upon which practical activity and industry are established.

Thus it is that in primitive mentality, which is wholly mystic and prelogical, not only the data, but even the limits of experience fail to coincide with our own. Bergson's well-known theory which requires us to conceive of time as a homogeneous quantum by fusing living duration and space, which is such a quantum, does not seem applicable to primitive mentality. It is only in races which are already somewhat developed, when the mystic preconnections become weak and tend to be dissociated, when the habit of paying attention to second causes and their effects is growing stronger, that space becomes homogeneous in the representations, and time tends to become so too. Thus the limits of our experience are sketched little by little, are strengthened and become fixed. Much later, when reflection leads us to make these ideas our own, we are tempted to believe that they are its constituent elements—innate, as the philosophers used to say. The observation and analysis of the collective representations of inferior races are far from confirming this hypothesis.

Selected Bibliography

The History of Modern Philosophy in France (Chicago: Open Court Publishing Company, 1924).

How Natives Think (New York: Washington Square Press, Inc., 1926).

Primitive Mentality (New York: Macmillan, 1923).

The "Soul" of the Primitive (New York: Frederick Praeger, Inc., 1966).

The Elementary Forms of Religious Life

Émile Durkheim

Often credited as the founder of the science of sociology, Émile Durkheim was born in Alsace on April 15, 1858, of Jewish parentage. Most of his academic training was in philosophy, although even during his days as a student he was interested in social and political subjects. In 1887, after he had studied in Germany for a year, Durkheim was appointed as the first professor of sociology in France—although the chair was in sociology and education—at Bordeaux. In that capacity he laid the groundwork for a comprehensive analysis of social systems. He eventually became professor of sociology at the Sorbonne. He died in Paris on November 15, 1917.

In terms of sociological theory, Durkheim is perhaps known best for his concept of collective representation (conscience collective). *By this, Durkheim had reference to ideas and symbols that carried force in society because they were collectively created. In ascribing a social origin and function to religion, Durkheim was able to extend this concept. For him, religion too had a collective source. It was established to support and preserve group goals, and it functioned to give such goals sanctity and authority. In his book* The Elementary Forms of the Religious Life *(1912), from whose introduction the following reading selection is taken, Durkheim provided a detailed account of the datum of religion as projected through social experience. In basing his comments on studies of Australian tribes, he contended that the functional origin of religion can also be given chronological confirmation.*

In this book we propose to study the most primitive and simple religion which is actually known, to make an analysis of it, and to attempt an explanation of it. A religious system may be said to be the most primitive which we can observe when it fulfils the two following conditions: in the first place, when it is found in a society whose organization is surpassed by no others in simplicity;[1] and secondly, when it is possible to explain it without making use of any element borrowed from a previous religion.

We shall set ourselves to describe the organization of this system with all the exactness and fidelity that an ethnographer or an historian could give. But our task will not be limited to that: sociology raises other problems than history or ethnography. It does not seek to know the past forms of civilization with the sole end of knowing them and reconstructing them. But rather, like very positive science, it has as its object the explanation of some actual reality which is near to us, and which consequently is capable of affecting our ideas and our acts: this reality is man, and more precisely, the man of today, for there is nothing which we are more interested in knowing. Then we are not going to study a very archaic religion simply for the pleasure of telling its peculiarities and its singularities. If we have taken it as the subject of our research, it is because it has seemed to us better adapted than any other to lead to an understanding of the religious nature of man, that is to say, to show us an essential and permanent aspect of humanity.

But this proposition is not accepted before the raising of strong objections. It seems very strange that one must turn back, and be transported to the very beginnings of history, in order to arrive at an understanding of humanity as it is at present. This manner of procedure seems particularly paradoxical in the question which concerns us. In fact, the various religions generally pass as being quite unequal in value and dignity; it is said that they do not all contain the same quota of truth. Then it seems as though one could not compare the highest forms of religious thought with the lowest, without reducing the first to the level of the second. If we admit that the crude cults of the Australian tribes can help us to understand Christianity, for example, is that not supposing that this latter religion proceeds from the same mentality as the former, that it is made up of the same superstitions and rests upon the same errors? This is how the theoretical importance which has sometimes been attributed to primitive religions has come to pass as a sign of a systematic hostility to all religion, which, by prejudging the results of the study, vitiates them in advance.

---

[1] In the same way, we shall say of these societies that they are primitive, and we shall call the men of these societies primitives. Undoubtedly, the expression lacks precision, but that is hardly evitable, and besides, when we have taken pains to fix the meaning, it is not inconvenient.

There is no occasion for asking here whether or not there are scholars who have merited this reproach, and who have made religious history and ethnology a weapon against religion. In any case, a sociologist cannot hold such a point of view. In fact, it is an essential postulate of sociology that a human institution cannot rest upon an error and a lie, with out which it could not exist. If it were not founded in the nature of things, it would have encountered in the facts a resistance over which it could never have triumphed. So when we commence the study of primitive religions, it is with the assurance that they hold to reality and express it; this principle will be seen to re-enter again and again in the course of the analyses and discussions which follow, and the reproach which we make against the schools from which we have separated ourselves is that they have ignored it. When only the letter of the formulae is considered, these religious beliefs and practices undoubtedly seem disconcerting at times, and one is tempted to attribute them to some sort of a deep-rooted error. But one must know how to go underneath the symbol to the reality which it represents and which gives it its meaning. The most barbarous and the most fantastic rites and the strangest myths translate some human need, some aspect of life, either individual or social. The reasons with which the faithful justify them may be, and generally are, erroneous; but the true reasons do not cease to exist, and it is the duty of science to discover them.

In reality, then, there are religions which are false. All are true in their own fashion; all answer, though in different ways, to the given conditions of human existence. It is undeniably possible to arrange them in a hierarchy. Some can be called superior to others, in the sense that they call into play higher mental functions, that they are richer in ideas and sentiments, that they contain more concepts with fewer sensations and images, and that their arrangement is wiser. But howsoever real this greater complexity and this higher ideality may be, they are not sufficient to place the corresponding religions in different classes. All are religions equally, just as all living beings are equally alive, from the most humble plastids up to man. So when we turn to primitive religions it is not with the idea of depreciating religion in general, for these religions are no less respectable than the others. They respond to the same needs, they play the same role, they depend upon the same causes; they can also well serve to show the nature of the religious life, and consequently to resolve the problem which we wish to study.

If it is useful to know what a certain particular religion consists in, it is still more important to know what religion in general is. This is the problem which has aroused the interest of philosophers in all times; and not without reason, for it is of interest to all humanity. Unfortunately, the method which they generally employ is purely dialectic: they confine themselves to analysing the idea which they make for themselves of religion, except as they illustrate the results of this mental analysis by examples borrowed from the religions which best realize their ideal. But even if this method ought to be abandoned, the problem remains intact, and the great service of philosophy is to have prevented its being suppressed by the disdain of scholars. Now it is possible to attack it in a different way. Since all religions can be compared to each other, and since all are species of the same class, there are necessarily many elements which are common to all. We do not mean to speak simply of the outward and visible characteristics which they all have equally, and which make it possible to give them a provisional definition from the very outset of our researches; the discovery of these apparent signs is relatively easy, for the observation which it demands does not go beneath the surface of things. But these external resemblances suppose others which are profound. At the foundation of all systems of beliefs and of all cults there ought necessarily to be a certain number of fundamental representations or conceptions and of ritual attitudes which, in spite of the diversity of forms which they have taken, have the same objective significance and fulfil the same functions everywhere. These are the permanent elements which constitute that which is permanent and human in religion; they form all the objective contents of the idea which is expressed when one speaks of *religion* in general. How is it possible to pick them out?

Surely it is not by observing the complex religions which appear in the course of history. Every one of these is made up of such a variety of elements that it is very difficult to distinguish what is secondary from what is principal, the essential from the accessory. Suppose that the religion considered is like that of Egypt, India or the classical antiquity. It is a confused mass of many cults, varying according to the locality, the temples, the generations, the dynasties, the invasions, etc. Popular superstitions are there confused with the purest dogmas. Neither the thought nor the activity of the religion is evenly distributed among the believers; according to the men, the environment, and the circumstances, the beliefs as well as the rites are thought of in different ways. Here they are priests, there they are monks, else-where they are laymen; there are mystics and rationalists, theologians and prophets, etc. In these conditions it is difficult to see what is common to all. In one or another of these systems it is quite possible to find the means of making a profitable study of some particular fact which is specially developed there, such as sacrifice or prophecy, monasticism or the mysteries; but how is it possible to find the com-mon foundation of the religious life underneath the luxuriant vegeta-tion which covers it? How is it possible to find, underneath the dis-putes of theology, the variations of ritual, the multiplicity of groups and the diversity of individuals, the fundamental states characteristic of religious mentality in general?

Things are quite different in the lower societies. The slighter de-velopment of individuality, the small extension of the group, the homogeneity of external circumstances, all contribute to reducing the differences and variations to a minimum. The group has an in-tellectual and moral conformity of which we find but rare examples in the more advanced societies. Everything is common to all. Move-ments are stereotyped; everybody performs the same ones in the same circumstances, and this conformity of conduct only translates the conformity of thought. Every mind being drawn into the same eddy, the individual type nearly confounds itself with that of the race. And while all is uniform, all is simple as well. Nothing is deformed like these myths, all composed of one and the same theme which is end-lessly repeated, or like these rites made up of a small number of gestures repeated again and again. Neither the popular imagination nor that of the priests has had either the time or the means of refining and transforming the original substance of the religious ideas and practices; these are shown, in all their nudity, and offer themselves to an examination, it requiring only the slightest effort to lay them open. That which is accessory or secondary, the development of luxury, has not yet come to hide the principal elements.[2] All is reduced to that which is indispensable, to that without which there could be no re-ligion. But that which is indispensable is also that which is essential, that is to say, that which we must know before all else.

Primitive civilizations offer privileged cases, then, because they are

---

[2] But that is not equivalent to saying that all luxury is lacking to the primitive cults. On the contrary, we shall see that in every religion there are beliefs and practices which do not aim at strictly utilitarian ends (Bk. III, ch. iv. 2). This luxury is indispensable to the religious life; it is at its very heart. But it is much more rudimentary in the inferior religions than in the others, so we are better able to determine its reason for existence here.

simple cases. That is why, in all fields of human activity, the observations of ethnologists have frequently been veritable revelations, which have renewed the study of human institutions. For example, before the middle of the nineteenth century, everybody was convinced that the father was the essential element of the family; no one had dreamed that there could be a family organization of which the paternal authority was not the keystone. But the discovery of Bachofen came and upset this old conception. Up to very recent times it was regarded as evident that the moral and legal relations of kindred were only another aspect of the psychological relations which result from a common descent; Bachofen and his successors, MacLennan, Morgan and many others still laboured under this misunderstanding. But since we have become acquainted with the nature of the primitive clan, we know that, on the contrary, relationships cannot be explained by consanguinity. To return to religions, the study of only the most familiar ones had led men to believe for a long time that the idea of god was characteristic of everything that is religious. Now the religion which we are going to study presently is, in a large part, foreign to all idea of divinity; the forces to which the rites are there addressed are very different from those which occupy the leading place in our modern religions, yet they aid us in understanding these latter forces. So nothing is more unjust than the disdain with which too many historians still regard the work of ethnographers. Indeed, it is certain that ethnology has frequently brought about the most fruitful revolutions in the different branches of sociology. It is for this same reason that the discovery of unicellular beings, of which we just spoke, has transformed the current idea of life. Since in these very simple beings, life is reduced to its essential traits, these are less easily misunderstood.

But primitive religions do not merely aid us in disengaging the constituent elements of religion; they also have the great advantage that they facilitate the explanation of it. Since the facts there are simpler, the relations with which men account for their acts have not yet been elaborated and denatured by studied reflection; they are nearer and more closely related to the motives which have really determined these acts. In order to understand an hallucination perfectly, and give it its most appropriate treatment, a physician must know its original point of departure. Now this event is proportionately easier to find if he can observe it near its beginnings. The longer the disease is allowed to develop, the more it evades observation; that is because all sorts of interpretations have intervened as it advanced, which tend to force the original state into the background, and across which it is frequently difficult to find the initial one. Between a systematized hallucination and the first impressions which gave it birth, the distance is often considerable. It is the same thing with religious thought. In proportion as it progresses in history, the causes which called it into existence, though remaining active, are no longer perceived, except across a vast scheme of interpretations which quite transform them. Popular mythologies and subtle theologies have done their work: they have superimposed upon the primitive sentiments others which are quite different, and which, though holding to the first, of which they are an elaborated form, only allow their true nature to appear very imperfectly. The psychological gap between the cause and the effect, between the apparent cause and the effective cause, has become more considerable and more difficult for the mind to leap. The remainder of this book will be an illustration and a verification of this remark on method. It will be seen how, in the primitive religions, the religious fact still visibly carries the mark of its origins: it would have been well-nigh impossible to infer them merely from the study of the more developed religions.

The study which we are undertaking is therefore a way of taking up again, *but under new conditions*, the old problem of the origin of religion. To be sure, if by origin we are to understand the very first beginning, the question has nothing scientific about it, and should be resolutely discarded. There was no given moment when religion began to exist, and there is consequently no need of finding a means of transporting ourselves thither in thought. Like every human institution, religion did not commence anywhere. Therefore, all speculations of this sort are justly discredited; they can only consist in subjective and arbitrary constructions which are subject to no sort of control. But the problem which we raise is quite another one. What we want to do is to find a means of discerning the ever-present causes upon which the most essential forms of religious thought and practice depend. Now for the reasons which were just set forth, these causes are proportionately more easily observable as the societies where they are observed are less complicated. That is why we try to get as near as possible to the origins.[3] It is not that we ascribe particular virtues to the lower religions. On the contrary, they are rudimentary and gross; we cannot make of them a sort of model which later religions

[3] It is seen that we give a wholly relative sense to this word "origins," just as to the word "primitive." By it we do not mean an absolute beginning, but the most simple social condition that is actually known or that beyond which we cannot go at present. When we speak of the origins or of the commencement of religious history or thought, it is in this sense that our statements should be understood.

only have to reproduce. But even their grossness makes them instructive, for they thus become convenient for experiments, as in them, the facts and their relations are easily seen. In order to discover the laws of the phenomena which he studies, the physicist tries to simplify these latter and rid them of their secondary characteristics. For that which concerns institutions, nature spontaneously makes the same sort of simplification at the beginning of history. We merely wish to put these to profit. Undoubtedly we can only touch very elementary facts by this method. When we shall have accounted for them as far as possible, the novelties of every sort which have been produced in the course of evolution will not yet be explained. But while we do not dream of denying the importance of the problems thus raised, we think that they will profit by being treated in their turn and that it is important to take them up only after those of which we are going to undertake the study at present.

But our study is not of interest merely for the science of religion. In fact, every religion has one side by which it overlaps the circle of properly religious ideas, and there, the study of religious phenomena gives a means of renewing the problems which, up to the present, have only been discussed among philosophers.

For a long time it has been known that the first systems of representations with which men have pictured to themselves the world and themselves were of religious origin. There is no religion that is not a cosmology at the same time that it is a speculation upon divine things. If philosophy and the sciences were born of religion, it is because religion began by taking the place of the sciences and philosophy. But it has been less frequently noticed that religion has not confined itself to enriching the human intellect, formed beforehand, with a certain number of ideas; it has contributed to forming the intellect itself. Men owe to it not only a good part of the substance of their knowledge, but also the form in which this knowledge has been elaborated.

At the roots of all our judgments there are a certain number of essential ideas which dominate all our intellectual life; they are what philosophers since Aristotle have called the categories of the understanding: ideas of time, space,[4] class, number, cause substance, personality, etc. They correspond to the most universal properties of

[4] We say that time and space are categories because there is no difference between the role played by these ideas in the intellectual life and that which falls to the ideas of class or cause (on this point see, Hamelin, *Essai sur les éléments principaux de la représentation*, pp. 63, 76).

things. They are like the solid frame which encloses all thought; this does not seem to be able to liberate itself from them without destroying itself, for it seems that we cannot think of objects that are not in time and space, which have no number, etc. Other ideas are contingent and unsteady; we can conceive of their being unknown to a man, a society or an epoch; but these others appear to be nearly inseparable from the normal working of the intellect. They are like the framework of the intelligence. Now when primitive religious beliefs are systematically analysed, the principal categories are naturally found. They are born in religion and of religion; they are a product of religious thought. This is a statement that we are going to have occasion to make many times in the course of this work.

This remark has some interest of itself already; but here is what gives it its real importance.

The general conclusion of the book which the reader has before him is that religion is something eminently social. Religious representations are collective representations which express collective realities; the rites are a manner of acting which take rise in the midst of the assembled groups and which are destined to excite, maintain or recreate certain mental states in these groups. So if the categories are of religious origin, they ought to participate in this nature common to all religious facts; they too should be social affairs and the product of collective thought. At least—for in the actual condition of our knowledge of these matters, one should be careful to avoid all radical and exclusive statements—it is allowable to suppose that they are rich in social elements.

Even at present, these can be imperfectly seen in some of them. For example, try to represent what the notion of time would be without the processes by which we divide it, measure it or express it with objective signs, a time which is not a succession of years, months, weeks, days and hours! This is something nearly unthinkable. We cannot conceive of time, except on condition of distinguishing its different moments. Now what is the origin of this differentiation? Undoubtedly, the states of consciousness which we have already experienced can be reproduced in us in the same order in which they passed in the first place; thus portions of our past become present again, though being clearly distinguished from the present. But howsoever important this distinction may be for our private experience, it is far from being enough to constitute the notion or category of time. This does not consist merely in a commemoration, either partial or integral, of our past life. It is an abstract and impersonal frame which surrounds, not only our individual existence, but that of all humanity. It is like an endless chart, where all duration is spread out before the mind, and upon which all possible events can be located in relation to fixed and determined guide lines. It is not *my time* that is thus arranged; it is time in general, such as it is objectively thought of by everybody in a single civilization. That alone is enough to give us a hint that such an arrangement ought to be collective. And in reality, observation proves that these indispensable guide lines, in relation to which all things are temporally located, are taken from social life. The divisions into days, weeks, months, years, etc., correspond to the periodical recurrence of rites, feasts, and public ceremonies.[5] A calendar expresses the rhythm of the collective activities, while at the same time its function is to assure their regularity.[6]

It is the same thing with space. As Hamelin has shown, space is not the vague and indetermined medium which Kant imagined; if purely and absolutely homogeneous, it would be of no use, and could not be grasped by the mind. Spatial representation consists essentially in a primary co-ordination of the data of sensuous experience. But this co-ordination would be impossible if the parts of space were qualitatively equivalent and if they were really interchangeable. To dispose things spatially there must be a possibility of placing them differently, of putting some at the right, others at the left, these above, those below, at the north of or at the south of, east or west, etc., etc., just as to dispose states of consciousness temporally there must be a possibility of localizing them at determined dates. That is to say that space could not be what it is if it were not, like time, divided and differentiated. But whence come these divisions which are so essential? By themselves, there are neither right nor left, up nor down, north nor south, etc. All these distinctions evidently come from the fact that different sympathetic values have been attributed to various regions. Since all the men of a single civilization represent space in the same way, it is clearly necessary that these sympathetic values, and the distinctions which depend upon them, should be equally universal, and that almost necessarily implies that they be of social origin.

[5] See the support given this assertion in Hubert and Mauss, Melanges d'Histoire des Religions (*Travaux de l'Année Sociologique*), chapter on *La Représentation du Temps dans la Religion.*

[6] Thus we see all the difference which exists between the group of sensations and images which serve to locate us in time, and the category of time expresses a time common to the group, a social time, so to speak. In itself it is a veritable social institution. Also, it is peculiar to man; animals have no representations of this sort.

Besides that, there are cases where this social character is made manifest. There are societies in Australia and North America where space is conceived in the form of an immense circle, because the camp has a circular form; and this spatial circle is divided up exactly like the tribal circle, and is in its image. There are as many regions distinguished as there are clans in the tribe, and it is the place occupied by the clans inside the encampment which has determined the orientation of these regions. Each region is defined by the totem of the clan to which it is assigned. Among the Zuni, for example, the pueblo contains seven quarters; each of these is a group of clans which has had a unity: in all probability it was originally a single clan which was later subdivided. Now their space also contains seven quarters, and each of these seven quarters of the world is in intimate connection with a quarter of the pueblo, that is to say with a group of clans. "Thus," says Cushing, "one division is thought to be in relation with the north, another represents the west, another the south," etc. Each quarter of the pueblo has its characteristic colour, which is exactly the same as that of the corresponding quarter. In the course of history the number of fundamental clans has varied; the number of the fundamental regions of space has varied with them. Thus the social organization has been the model for the spatial organization and a reproduction of it. It is thus even up to the distinction between right and left which, far from being inherent in the nature of man in general, is very probably the product of representations which are religious and therefore collective.

Analogous proofs will be found presently in regard to the ideas of class, force, personality, and efficacy. It is even possible to ask if the idea of contradiction does not also depend upon social conditions. What makes one tend to believe this is that the empire which the idea has exercised over human thought has varied with times and societies. To-day the principle of identity dominates scientific thought; but there are vast systems of representations which have played a considerable role in the history of ideas where it has frequently been set aside: these are the mythologies, from the grossest up to the most reasonable.[7] There, we are continually coming upon beings which

[7] We do not mean to say that mythological thought ignores it, but that it contradicts it more frequently and openly than scientific thought does. Inversely, we shall show that science cannot escape violating it, though it holds to it far more scrupulously than religion does. On this subject, as on many others, there are only differences of degree between science and religion; but if these differences should not be exaggerated, they must be noted, for they are significant.

have the most contradictory attributes simultaneously, who are at the same time one and many, material and spiritual, who can divide themselves up indefinitely without losing anything of their constitution; in mythology it is an axiom that the part is worth the whole. These variations through which the rules which seem to govern our present logic have passed prove that, far from being engraven through all eternity upon the mental constitution of men, they depend, at least in part, upon factors that are historical and consequently social. We do not know exactly what they are, but we may presume that they exist.

Selected Bibliography

The Division of Labor in Society (New York: The Free Press, 1949).

Education and Sociology (New York: The Free Press, 1956).

The Elementary Forms of the Religious Life (New York: The Free Press, 1965).

Essays on Sociology and Philosophy (New York: Harper & Row, Publishers, Inc., 1960).

The Rules of the Sociological Method (New York: The Free Press, 1938).

Socialism (New York: Macmillan, 1958).

Suicide (New York: The Free Press, 1951).

Sociology and Philosophy (New York: The Free Press, 1953).

With Marcel Mauss, *Primitive Classification* (Chicago: University of Chicago Press, 1963).

See also P. M. Worsley, "Emile Durkheim's Theory of Knowledge," in *Sociological Review*, Vol. IV (1956), pp. 47–62.

Dynamic vs. Static Religion

HENRI BERGSON

In the strict sense, Henri Bergson (who was born October 18, 1859, in Paris) was neither a historian of religion nor a philosopher of religion but a philosopher who focused his attention on the nature of time. For Bergson, who was influenced by Charles Darwin, Herbert Spencer, and Maine de Biran, among others, reality was shaped by an élan vital (a vital impetus or "flow"), which could also be directly intuited as a primary inner experience. This view led Bergson to make a number of contrasts, as, for example, between determinism and freedom, and between intellect and intuition, as well as between two kinds of time, two kinds of memory, two kinds of morality, and two forms of religion. Dynamic religion, on the one hand, is pervaded by the vital process; it is open, antidogmatic, and sensitive to mystical intuition. Static religion, by contrast, tends to resist the vital impulse; it is closed, self-centered, and presents an obstacle to man's evolution. Thus, for the purposes of this anthology, Bergson stands as one who was deeply committed to time and evolutionary process as the fundamental datum of reality and who then, quite typically, defined religion in correspondingly open, processlike, evolutionary terms.

Bergson was professor of philosophy at the Collège de France. During World War I he served in various diplomatic missions, and later worked with the League of Nations' Committee on Intellectual Co-operation. Bergson received the Nobel Prize for Literature in 1927 and died in Paris on January 4, 1941.

Let us cast a glance backward at Life, this life which we had previously followed in its development up to the point where religion was destined to emerge from it. A great current of creative energy is precipitated into matter, to wrest from it what it can. At most points, remember, it came to a stop; these stops are equivalent, in our eyes, to the phenomena of so many living species, that is to say, of organisms in which our perception, being essentially analytical and synthetic, distinguishes a multitude of elements combining to fulfil a multitude of functions; yet the work of organization was but the step itself, a simple act, like the making of a footprint, which instantly causes a myriad grains of sand to cohere and form a pattern. We might have thought that along one of these lines where it had succeeded in going furthest, this vital energy would carry the best of itself with it and would go straight on; but it swerved inward, and the whole circle re-formed: certain creatures emerged whose activity ran indefinitely in the same circle, whose organs were ready-made instruments and left no room for the ceaselessly renewed invention of tools, whose consciousness lapsed into the somnambulism of instinct instead of bracing itself and revitalizing itself into reflective thought. Such is the condition of the individual in those insect societies where organization is highly perfected, but the effect of it is sheer automatism.

The creative effort progressed successfully only along that line of evolution which ended in man. In its passage through matter, consciousness assumed in that case, as it were from a mould, the shape of tool-making intelligence. And invention, which carries reflection with it, was at liberty to develop.

But intelligence was not without its dangers. Up to that point, all living creatures had drunk greedily of the cup of life. They lapped up with relish the honey which nature had smeared on the rim; they were prepared to gulp down the rest blindly. Not so intelligence, which peered into the bottom of the cup. For the intelligent being was not living in the present alone; there can be no reflexion without foreknowledge, no foreknowledge without inquietude, no inquietude without a momentary slackening of the attachment to life. Above all, there is no humanity without society, and society demands of the individual an abnegation which the insect, in its automatism, carries to the point of an utter obliviousness of self. Reflexion cannot be relied upon to keep up this selflessness. Intelligence, except it be that of a subtle utilitarian philosopher, would more likely counsel egoism. Thus, from two directions it called for a counterpoise. Or rather it was already provided with one, for nature, we repeat, does not make her creatures piecemeal; what is multiple in its manifestation may well be simple in its genesis. A new species coming on to the scene brings with it, in the indivisibility of the act creating it, all the elements that impart life to it. The very check of the creative impetus which has expressed itself in the creation of our species has provided, along with intelligence, within human intelligence, the myth-making function that contrives the pattern of religions. That then is the office, that is the significance of the religion we have called static or natural. Religion is that element which, in beings endowed with reason, is called upon to make good any deficiency of attachment to life.

It is true that the possibility of another solution at once occurs to the mind. Static religion, such as we find it when it stands alone, attaches man to life, and consequently the individual to society, by telling him tales on a par with those with which we lull children to sleep. Of course they are not like other stories. Being produced by the myth-making function in response to an actual need and not for mere pleasure, they counterfeit reality as actually perceived, to the point of making us act accordingly: other creations of the imagination have this same tendency, but they do not demand our compliance; they can remain just ideas; whereas the former are ideo-motory. They are none the less myths, which critical minds, as we have seen, often accept in fact, but which they should, by rights, reject. The active, moving principle, whose mere stopping at an extreme point has expressed itself in mankind, doubtless requires of all created species that they cling to life. But, as we have previously shown, if this principle produces all species in their entirety, as a tree thrusts out on every side branches which end in buds, it is the act of placing in matter a freely creative energy, it is man, or some other being of like significance—we do not say of like form—which is the purpose of the entire process of evolution. The whole might have been vastly superior to what it is, and this is probably what happens in worlds where the current rushes through matter less refractory than ours: just as the current might never have found a free outlet—even to this inadequate extent—in which case the quality and quantity of creative energy represented by the human species would never have been released at all on our planet. But whichever way we look at it, life is a thing at least as desirable, even more desirable, to man than to the other species, since the latter receive it as the effect, produced in passing, by the creative energy, whereas in man life is that successful effort itself, however precarious and incomplete this success may be. This being so, why should man not recover the confidence he lacks, or which has perhaps been undermined by reflexion, by turning back for fresh impetus, in the direction whence that impetus came? Not through intelligence, at least not through intelligence alone, could he do so: intelligence would be more likely to proceed in the opposite direction; it was provided for a definite object, and when it attempts speculation on a higher plane, it enables us, at the most, to conceive possibilities, it does not attain any reality. But we know that all around intelligence there lingers still a fringe of intuition, vague and evanescent. Can we not fasten upon it, intensify it, and above all, consummate it in action, for it has become pure contemplation only through a weakening in its principle, and, if we may put it so, by an abstraction practised on itself?

A soul strong enough, noble enough to make this effort would not stop to ask whether the principle with which it is now in touch is the transcendant cause of all things or merely its earthly delegate. It would be content to feel itself pervaded, though retaining its own personality, by a being immeasurably mightier than itself, just as an iron is pervaded by the fire which makes it glow. Its attachment to life would henceforth be its inseparability from this principle, joy in joy, love of that which is all love. In addition it would give itself to society, but to a society comprising all humanity, loved in the love of the principle underlying it. The confidence which static religion brought to man would thus be transfigured: no more thought for the morrow, no more anxious heart-searching; materially the object would no longer be worth while, and morally would take on too high a significance. Now detachment from each particular thing would become attachment to life in general. But should we, in such a case, still speak of religion? Or were we right to have used the word before for all the preceding argument? Are not the two things so different as to exclude each other, and to make it impossible to call them by the same name?

Yet there are many reasons for using the word religion in both cases. In the first place mysticism—for that is what we have in mind—may, it is true, lift the soul to another plane: it none the less ensures for the soul, to a pre-eminent degree, the security and the serenity which it is the function of static religion to provide. But we must above all bear in mind that pure mysticism is a rare essence, that it is generally found in a diluted form, that even then it still gives to the substance with which it mingles its colour and fragrance, and that it must be taken together with the substance, to be regarded as practically inseparable from it, if it is to be observed in its active state—since it was in this state that it finally imposed its sway upon the world. Looking at it from this angle, we should perceive a series of transitions, and, as it were, differences of degree, whereas really there is a radical difference of nature. Let us go back briefly over each of these points.

In defining mysticism by its relation to the vital impetus, we have implicitly admitted that true mysticism is rare. We shall deal presently with its significance and its value. Let us confine ourselves for the moment to noting that it lies, according to the above, at a point which the spiritual current, in its passage through matter, probably desired to reach but could not. For it makes light of obstacles with which nature has had to come to terms, and, on the other hand, we can understand the evolution of life, setting aside any bypaths it has been compelled to follow, only if we view it as seeking for something beyond its reach, something to which the great mystic attains. If all men, if any large number of men, could have soared as high as this privileged man, nature would not have stopped at the human species, for such a one is in fact more than a man. The same can be said of other forms of genius: they are all equally rare. It is not by chance, then, it is by reason of its very essence that true mysticism is exceptional.

But when it does call, there is in the innermost being of most men the whisper of an echo. Mysticism reveals, or rather would reveal to us, if we actually willed it, a marvellous prospect: we do not, and in most cases we could not, will it; we should collapse under the strain. Yet the spell has worked; and just as when an artist of genius has produced a work which is beyond us, the spirit of which we cannot grasp, but which makes us feel how commonplace were the things we used to admire, in the same way static religion, though it may still be there, is no longer what it was, above all it no longer dares to assert itself, when truly great mysticism comes on the scene. To static religion, mainly at any rate, humanity will still turn for the support of which it is in need; it will leave the myth-making function, remoulding it as best it can, to go on with its work; in a word, man's confidence in life will remain much the same as was ordained by nature. But he will sincerely believe that he has sought and even to some extent found that contact with the very principle of nature which expresses itself in quite a different attachment to life, in a transfigured confidence. Incapable of rising to these heights, he will go through the motions, assume the appropriate attitudes and in his speech reserve the foremost place for certain formulae which he can never see filled with their whole meaning, the whole operation being reminiscent of some ceremony where certain chairs, reserved for high dignitaries, are standing empty. Thus may arise a mixed religion, implying a new direction given to the old, a more or less marked aspiration for the ancient god who emanated from the myth-making function to be merged into the God Who effectively reveals Himself, Who illuminates and warms privileged souls with His presence. Thus do we find interposed, as we were suggesting, transitions and differences, ostensibly of degree, between two things which are as a matter of fact radically different in nature and which, at first sight, we can hardly believe deserve the same name. The contrast is striking in many cases, as for instance when nations at war each declare that they have God on their side, the deity in question thus becoming the national god of paganism, whereas the God they imagine they are evoking is a God common to all mankind, the mere vision of Whom, could all men but attain it, would mean the immediate abolition of war. And yet we should not, on the strength of this contrast, disparage religions born of mysticism, which have generalized the use of its formulae and yet have been unable to pervade all humanity with the full measure of its spirit. It sometimes happens that well-nigh empty formulae, the veriest magical incantations, contrive to summon up here and there the spirit capable of imparting substance to them. An indifferent schoolmaster, mechanically teaching a science created by men of genius, may awaken in one of his pupils the vocation he himself has never possessed, and change him unconsciously into an emulator of those great men, who are invisible and present in the message he is handing on.

Yet there is a difference between the two cases, and if we take it into account, we shall notice, in the matter of religion, a gradual disappearance of the contrast between the static and the dynamic, on which we have just insisted in order to bring out the characteristics of the two religions. The great majority of men may very well know practically nothing about mathematics and yet admire the genius of a Descartes or a Newton. But those who have, from afar off, bowed their heads to the mystic word, because they heard a faint echo of it within themselves, will not remain indifferent to its message. If they already have their different faiths, from which they will not or cannot break away, they will persuade themselves that they are effecting a transformation of them, as indeed they are: the same elements will subsist, but they will be magnetized and by this very magnetizing process be diverted into another direction. A religious historian will have no difficulty in discovering in the material form of a vaguely mystic belief, which has spread far and wide among mankind, some mythical and even magic elements. He will prove thereby that there exists a static religion, natural to man, and that human nature is unchanging. But, if he stops at that, he will have overlooked something, and perhaps the essential. At any rate he will, unwittingly perhaps, have bridged the gulf between the static and the dynamic, and justified the use of the same word in such widely different instances. One will indeed be still dealing with a religion, but with a new one.

We shall be still more convinced of this, we shall see from another angle how these two religions are antagonistic and yet come together, if we take into consideration the attempts of the second to lodge within the first, preparatory to supplanting it. As a matter of fact, it is we who convert them into attempts by an act of retrospection. They were, when they occurred, complete and self-sufficient actions, and they have assumed the guise of initial preparatory efforts only since the day when ultimate success transformed them into partial failures, by virtue of the mysterious power which the present exerts over the past. They will none the less serve us to mark the intervening stages, to analyse into its virtual elements the indivisible act by which dynamic religion is posited, and at the same time to show, by the manifest unity of direction of all those efforts which now prove to have been unsuccessful, that the sudden leap which marked final achievement was in no way fortuitous. . . .

Selected Bibliography

Creative Evolution (New York: The Modern Library, 1944).
Creative Mind (Totowa, New Jersey: Littlefield Adams, 1965).
Duration and Simultaneity (Indianapolis: Bobbs-Merrill, Inc., 1912).
Matter and Memory (New York: Macmillan, 1950).
The Philosophy of Poetry (New York: Philosophical Library, Inc., 1959).
Time and Free Will (New York: Harper & Row, Publishers, Inc., 1912).
Two Sources of Morality and Religion (New York: Doubleday & Company, Inc., 1935).
World of Dreams (New York: Philosophical Library, Inc., 1958).

A Modified Evolutionary View

MARTIN P. NILSSON

Martin P. Nilsson was born in Sweden on July 12, 1874, and was educated at the Universities of Lund, Basel, and Berlin. He received his doctorate in classical archaeology and ancient history in 1899 at Lund, at which institution he began studying the history of Greek religions before such a subject was listed in the university's curriculum. He became professor at Lund in 1909 and "rector magnificus" of the university in 1939. After 1939 he taught in the United States for a time, chiefly at the University of California, Berkeley, but then returned to his home in Lund. His biographer, Einar Gjerstad, has written:

> *As professor at the University of Lund, Martin Nilsson was a scholar who laid a firm foundation for his learning by making a great many special investigations. He had an infallible and clear sense of realities. Facts, interest in reality, and his own experience were his guiding stars. He abstained from aesthetics and philosophy. His structure was historical reality; he put together the architectural groundwork methodically and then raised the vaults of his ideas on these firm foundations. Not infrequently the vaults were boldly constructed. The scholar Martin Nilsson, and the man, were cast in the same mould. In his youth, like most people, he had been seized with poetic inspiration. But shortly both poetry and literary prose were discarded. Sound judgment and manly self-control were his ideals. The true farmer does not show his feelings. He conceals his pain. He does not laugh outright, a gleam in the eye is enough, or, at most, a smile, often sceptical, perhaps malicious.*

From 1899 on, Nilsson was a prolific writer. A list of his works runs well over one hundred pages. By 1921 he had finished a multivolumed history of Greek religion, but he also continued his work in other aspects of classical studies. During his career the courses he

Martin P. Nilsson, "Letter to Professor Arthur D. Nock on Some Fundamental Concepts in the Science of Religion," in *Harvard Theological Review*, Vol. XLII, (1949), pp. 345–382. Reprinted by permission.

111

taught ranged from Greek language and epigraphy to Greek vase-painting.

In terms of theory, Nilsson stood between those who advocated the concept of the "high God" and those who were thoroughgoing evolutionists. Although he shared certain affinities with both, he could totally agree with neither. On the question of evolution in religion, we have his statement. Regarding the "high God," Nilsson has written: "Moreover the notion of the High God as being a Cosmic God has receded. We do not think of the Cosmic God when we pray: 'Our Father in Heaven.' This is my last word in studies to which I have devoted a long life." He died on April 7, 1967, three months before his ninety-third birthday.

Lund, May 15, 1947

My dear Nock:

I wrote down these considerations, not for publication but for myself, in order to clear up matters, to test old ideas and new opinions and to coordinate them. But as you take an interest in them I send them to you for your own edification and, I hope, as an occasion for a stimulating correspondence. In my early days I was intensely interested in primitive religion and anthropology and I wrote a book on primitive religion and another on primitive culture (in Swedish), but in the early twenties I began my extensive work in Greek Religion; (my book on Homer and Mycenae belongs also to this series, for the study of religion drove me to try to fill up the gap between the prehistoric and the historical age of Greece). Thus my reading of anthropological literature has necessarily been limited. . . . My age would prevent me from a long and exhaustive study, but certain new tendencies among the young scholars of the science of religion in my country have made me reconsider my views.

These young scholars would imply that, in the light of more recent research, the work of an older generation is fit only for the wastepaper basket, but this is not true. The putting of the questions, the results achieved, the terminology of an older generation are more enduring than a younger generation is willing to admit. The battle against evolutionism is in part a tilting against windmills. There is always a development, always an evolution. That it is lacking among primitive peoples is an illusion due to the fact that we know but a brief space of their existence. Evolution may go in either direction to higher or lower forms, the latter is called degeneration. Take for example Gnosticism which began as a kind of philosophy with a strain of myth and ended in gross mythology and magic. Higher or lower is a value-judgment, subjective, the outcome of the individual's own personal viewpoint (which is itself not necessarily devoid of logic). On the whole evolution goes from what are, in regard to formalities and concepts, more elementary forms to purer and more complicated forms, just as material evolution does. It would be strange if spiritual and religious evolution did not show any progress; after all, material evolution and techniques do so. . . .

Anti-evolutionism would, however, not have taken so strong a hold, if it did not have some justification. Let us look at the common series: power, taboo, magic, daemons, gods, religion. It is very often taken to be an evolutional series: preanimism, dynamism, animatism, animism, polydaemonism, polytheism, monotheism; that is, it is thought to be an historical evolution.

I have long been opposed to this taking of one thing for another, to this taking a logical for an historical series, but I think I should still be called an evolutionist. For I acknowledge the logical series, going from lower to higher ideas, but as conceptual, not as historical. . . . My views were greatly determined by my experience during a fairly extensive work with anthropological materials when I wrote my book on Primitive Time-Reckoning.[1] In this field conditions are fairly simple, some simple facts are the basis. The simplest ideas are the same everywhere: determining the time of the day by the position of the sun, the time of the year by the change of the seasons, the rising of the stars, the phases of the moon and their connection with the seasons, the naming of years from events. Evolution varies and is different in certain parts of the world, these do not agree with the *Kulturkreise*. Survivals of primitive time-reckoning are found among all civilized peoples.

Associations: More than thirty years ago I asked for something which I called *eine primitive Erkenntnisslehre*. What I had in mind will appear from the following. This desire seemed to be met by a large work of Lévy-Bruhl, primitive mentality, but it is not satisfactory. Lévy-Bruhl was hampered by his desire *à tout prix* to say something absolutely new. He is criticized and rightly. . . .

The faculty of thought in primitive man does not differ essentially from that of civilized man, but I cannot agree with the opinion of

---

[1] Nilsson is referring to his book, *Primitive Time Reckoning* (Lund: C. W. K. Gleerup, 1920). Editor's note.

certain anthropologists that they are absolutely identical; a development from lower to higher forms has taken place. The beginning is the same, but there is a difference like that between the jingling of a musical child and the playing of a virtuoso. Like everything the faculty of thought can and must be exercised and trained, let us say developed. This is the difference. I should say with you that primitive (you say prelogical) mentality is a fairly good description of the mental behavior of most people today except in their technical or consciously intellectual activities.

The materials with which the faculty of thought works are supplied by associations. I avoid the common expression 'association of ideas' because the word 'idea' seems to imply something reasonable, but the associations may be as arbitrary and non-logical as possible. Moreover one of the members is often not an idea but a sense perception. Associations are of central importance for the understanding of primitive mentality and I must dwell upon them, not only with regard to the mentality of savage and barbarous peoples, but also with regard to the like mentality among civilized people. . . . I am not competent and I do not wish to say anything about the philosophical discussion concerning the association of ideas, I take them empirically. The importance which I ascribe to them does not commit me either way as to the assertion that consciousness comes into being through mental chemistry, nor concerning the great problem of the *Gestaltpsychologie*.

Here something of great importance must be pointed out. Civilized people think chiefly in words, primitive people in imagery. Language is the instrument of thought and some knowledge of primitive languages, of their vocabulary as well as of their grammar, is helpful to understand the modes and lines of thought of primitive peoples. Primitive languages are very concrete and poor in abstract expressions. This is not to be confused with any lack of general representations. I come back to this later on.

An association is a coupling of two components. One which calls forth the association can be a sense perception or a representation in mind, the other which is coupled with the former is a representation in mind or a remembrance. A representation may rise to the level of consciousness without calling forth an association. Many years ago the name Kirsopp Lake came into my mind and I began to cast about in my mind as to whether it meant a man or a lake. Much later I learned that it was the name of a very well known scholar. We shall see that this is of certain importance in regard to the associations. More commonly a representation is called forth through a sense perception or another representation which is coupled with it. It is superfluous to dwell upon this, but it should be noted that the sense perception or representation which calls forth the association may be subconscious. One evening I had laid aside the papers on my writing desk and was staring unthinkingly at the blotting paper, beside which there was a calendar of the month. Suddenly I was astonished to find that Professor Wrangel came into my mind. After a while I glanced at the calendar and behold the name Evert—the Christian name of Professor Wrangel. Associations may be as fortuitous and arbitrary as possible and this is the reason why I do not like to add 'of ideas.' Another example throws light on a point which, moreover, is very important in my opinion, the tendency of an association to be repeated and fixed. Long ago when bicycling on a bit of road over which I often go in the summer, a Dutch friend came into my mind. This happened the next time I went over this piece of road and soon I could not go there without thinking of van Hille. Later on, when I came there once with a son of mine I told him this. He asked: Do you think of van Hille when you go in the opposite direction too? I did not then but ever since that day I do think of him.

Modern philosophers criticize Plato's two categories of associations, similarity and contiguity, i.e., nearness in space or time. Association by contrast can, though with a certain difficulty, be subordinated to these two categories. Philosophers speak of association through interest. This may be tested. I begin with a time-honored example. In a place in New Guinea where a missionary lived, an unknown disease broke out which proved devastating as so often happens when a new disease appears among a savage people. The natives imputed it first to a sheep, an animal unknown to them, which the missionary had brought with him, and compelled him to kill it. As the disease did not abate, the natives imputed its continuance to a portrait of Queen Victoria in the missionary's study. The reason why the natives coupled these things with the disease was that they were something new, something unknown to them. To us it seems unreasonable, but the natives acted just as a scientist does who tries to find out the cause of a new phenomenon, he casts about for a new circumstance which may be the cause of it. Under ordinary circumstances, they would have cared neither for the sheep nor the portrait, but the interest, the tension caused by the epidemic, made them cast about for a cause and called forth the association. Professor von Sydow has written a paper on the importance of the unusual in belief and custom.[2] He wants to present a new category of associations of ideas which he names phantasy or emotional associations because, he says, there is nothing in itself which leads thought from the one when the other appears. This is correct, but I have stated already that an association can be as fortuitous as it is thinkable. If your mind is intensely occupied with something, it is enough that some other thing should appear, i.e., nearness in space or time, to evoke an association. I take an example of von Sydow's, the pillar pine (a very unusual and remarkable form of the pine tree) at the root of which coins were laid by the sick. When anyone was sick the very striking appearance of this tree produced an association with the disease, especially when we take into consideration the known rôle of trees and plants in popular medicine. Others of his examples are quite analogous with that adduced from New Guinea. Interest forms no new category of associations. To use a comparison from chemistry, it serves as a catalyst which calls forth a process which would otherwise not have appeared. You may also compare it with the technique of electricity and say that interest is the tension the increase of which causes the spark to pass from one pole to another. It is absolutely necessary to have a clear conception of the fortuitousness and arbitrariness of associations, because they are foreign to our logical methods of thought. I shall return to this difference.

There is another, little observed form of association which has a certain similarity with the last mentioned, a willed, purposeful association. If you want a Latin term, I may call it a voluntative association. You make a knot in your handkerchief in order to remember something. In Peru this was developed in the *quipu*. Such aids to the memory are common among primitive peoples. The Pima of Arizona make use of a tally. The year-mark is a deep notch across the stick. The records of early years are memorized, and there are a few minor notches to aid in recalling them. The year-notches are all alike, yet when a narrator is asked to recount the years, he never makes a mistake. Taking the stick in his hand, he would rake his thumb-nail across a year-notch and begin: This notch means that, etc. More on this is to be found in my book *Primitive Culture* where I pointed to the importance also of such arbitrary associations for primitive art

[2] In the Swedish periodical 'Folkminnen och Folktankar,' xiii. 1926, pp. 53 ff.

which interprets geometrical patterns as animals and objects. It is enough for a primitive man to have a certain animal in his mind when drawing a line or two or cutting a notch to connect these with a certain animal. Through repetition the associations of a geometrical design with a certain animal or object can be fixed. Similarly primitive people find men, animals, and objects in the constellations.

I fear that your psychologist may accuse me of a superannuated associationist psychology. To this I reply as follows: I speak solely of the origin of ideas. An idea arises by necessity in a single brain and vanishes with this, if it is not accepted by others. The mode of life, the lines of thought, the interests of a group of men may be so much akin that the same idea is likely to arise in the minds of several men. The same circumstances may cause an idea, proffered by an individual, to be readily accepted by his fellows. This conditions the living on of an idea, i.e., the social group is the necessary condition. An idea is formed and fixed by the social group, and this group is the bearer of the tradition by which an idea lives on. It may also modify the ideas and add new ideas. Thus, social psychology is of paramount importance.

It has been objected that associationist psychology refers only to single elements of complex ideas. This is not true. If I see an object belonging to a certain man, this may recall the whole man, his shape, his manners, his actions, etc. To take an extreme instance, the anecdote that Newton seeing an apple falling from a tree hit upon the law of gravitation: The falling apple is a complex idea, the other component is much more complex, the whole universe. Or, take the example of the sheep and the plague. The sheep is a complex idea and the plague and its consequences also.

I may be reproached for generalizing too much, and thought to "make the 'primitive' into a kind of fictitious absolute category," as says Professor Kluckhohn. To this objection I reply: my purpose is to analyze a certain mode of 'thought' which is at the bottom of the minds of unlettered people (savages, barbarians, or peasants of a bygone age), and of which traces are found frequently even in educated people of today. I adduce examples from my own experience too. I am fully aware of the variability of the culture of primitive peoples, of the fact that the elements discussed here are developed differently in different peoples. But after all, there is a common background and my aim was to find out this common background of undeveloped human thought.

Selected Bibliography

Cults, Myths, Oracles and Politics in Ancient Greece (Lund: C. W. K. Gleerup, 1951).

The Dionysiac Mysteries of the Hellenistic and Roman Age (Lund: C. W. K. Gleerup, 1957).

Greek Folk Religion (New York, Harper & Row, Publishers, Inc., 1961).

Greek Piety, trans. by H. J. Rose (New York, W. W. Norton & Co., Inc., 1969).

A *History of Greek Religion,* trans. by F. J. Fielden (Oxford, Clarendon Press, 1949).

Homer and Mycenae (New York, Cooper Square Publishers, 1968).

Imperial Rome (New York, Schocken Books, Inc., 1962).

The Mycenaen Origin of Greek Mythology (New York, W. W. Norton & Co., Inc., 1963).

For a comprehensive bibliography of Nilsson's works, see Erik J. Knudtzon and Christian Callmer, *Scripta Minora,* 1967–1968 (Lund: C. W. K. Gleerup, 1968), pp. 37–139.

An Analysis of "Evolution" as an Interpretive Principle

Geo Widengren

Born in Sweden on April 24, 1907, Geo Widengren has been professor in the history of religions at the University of Uppsala since 1940. Since 1960 he has been the president of the International Association for the History of Religions. Currently he is also dean of the faculty in theology at Uppsala University.

Trained under Professor Tor Andrae (whom he has succeeded at Uppsala) in the history of religion, and thoroughly trained in philological skills, Widengren has conducted extensive and painstaking research in a wide range of areas. His dissertation in 1936 dealt with Babylonian and Israelite religions as self-contained entities. He has also done significant work in Iranian religions, Islam, the Old Testament, and Gnostic studies. Widengren has championed sacral kingship theory, influencing Ivan Engnell, the author of Studies in Divine Kingship in the Ancient Near East. Because of the times in which he has lived, Widengren has also inherited an interest in the evolution of religion, and, more particularly, the theory of the "high God" as championed by Wilhelm Schmidt. Against Schmidt he rejects the notion of a primitive monotheism, but with Pettazzoni (whose theories he has embellished) Widengren attributes particular power to the sky-god. As an heir to the evolutionist traditions from the days of Frazer, Widengren is also a very severe critic (as the present essay shows). From another side, he also registers as a phenomenologist of religion (witness his book Religionsphänomenologie). However, if he were asked to typify his approach, Widengren might reply that he identifies most readily with those who approach religion through sound and thorough philological studies of primary textual materials, regardless of the area or the subject under scrutiny.

From Geo Widengren, "Evolutionism and the Problem of the Origin of Religion," in Ethnos, Vol. X, Nos. 2–3 (1945). Reprinted by permission of the author.

The Question of "Primitive Mentality" and Survivals

The evolutionistic tenets in the field of comparative religion are apparently based on two fundamental theories: 1. Among primitive peoples and tribes we are still able to discern the religious beliefs which have been the characteristics of early mankind.[1] The religious beliefs held by primitive peoples are supposed to go back ultimately to a "primitive mentality," in most respects differing from our own.

Let us then examine the first of these suppositions with a view to criticizing one of the principal evolutionistic trends which can easily be traced also in much work on comparative religion of later years. For if we put this tendency to a closer examination, we shall find that there is very often to be found a definite conception of "primitive religion." What is then meant by this expression? In answering this question it may be well to look for the meaning of the word "primitive" in modern Anglo-Saxon ethnological literature. In case we undertake such a rapid survey it will not be long before we discover a striking dissimilarity in the use of the word "primitive" on the side of modern anthropologists and on that of evolutionistic writers on comparative religion. In the literature of the former category we can see that the word "primitive" is used in contrast to that of "civilized." After pointing to the incomparably more advantageous situation of modern civilization in comparison with the conditions under which savage peoples are living, Boas exclaims: "Such is the contrast that presents itself to the observer. What wonder if civilized man considers himself a being of higher order as compared to primitive man . . . "! From Boas this terminology has passed to younger American ethnologists. From this use of the term "primitive" it follows that "primitive" peoples or tribes are designations used parallelly with "savages" or "natives," or to put it in other words: by "primitive" religion is intended only the religion found among uncivilized peoples. The question then arises: what peoples can be said to be void of the so-called blessings of civilization? There seems to be quite a unanimous opinion as to the answer to this question in so far that no people possessing a generally accepted and commonly used writing can be said to lack civilization. History teaches us that such "higher cultures" (in German "Hochkulturen") developed, seemingly independently, in the areas of Egypt, Mesopotamia, India-Iran, China, and Ancient America. Besides written records there are other data

[1] F. Boas, *The Mind of Primitive Man*, New York, 1929, p. 2.

which may be adduced in order to characterize the "higher cultures"; but *writing* definitely remains the decisive criterion.

In evolutionistic literature on comparative religion, on the other hand, the designation "primitive" has a much wider and, at the same time, vaguer meaning. For if we read one of the older treatises on "primitive religion," we will soon find out that the word "primitive" there covers a vast field. It does not only mean the religion of savage peoples, but also many forms of religion practised in higher cultures, both ancient and modern, e.g. in China and in the ancient high-cultures of America. This use of the term "primitive" is made possible by a very broad view concerning the notion of "survival." Many ethnologists want to make us believe that certain religious ideas and institutions found in ancient higher cultures, and even nowadays among civilized peoples, are in reality nothing but "survivals" from an earlier period in the history of mankind, still existing as isolated phenomena. The reason for this conclusion was taken from the fact that savage peoples seemed to exhibit a type of religion where such survivals were to be found in their true and coherent surroundings. From the agreement between primitive tribes and ancient and modern peoples having a high culture evolutionistic scholars concluded that, when such similarities are discovered, we are confronted with a type of religion that is "primitive" in a chronological as well as a phenomenological sense of the word. This conclusion again was founded on a fixed opinion as to the age of so-called primitive peoples. For the evolutionistic theory demanded that all the races living on a cultural level that ought to be called primitive were as numerous examples of backwardness, because these peoples were held to be still living on the stages of cultural development reached by mankind many thousands of years before the beginning of our era. When a primitive people like the Australian tribes did not know the use of metals, but were equipped with weapons and implements of stone, they were unhesitatingly spoken of as "a stone-age people." And because such peoples were looked on as being on an early level of culture, the inference, of course, seemed quite inevitable: their religious beliefs were surely those of mankind in the stone-age. If then corresponding notions and institutions were discovered among civilized peoples, they ·must be taken for survivals from an older stage of culture already passed through.

But it was not enough that certain tribes and peoples were classified as being proofs of cultural stagnation, for they were also presented as exhibiting definite traits of what is called "primitive mentality." In order to demonstrate the evolution of religious thought and institutions from "lower" and "cruder" to "loftier" and more "spiritual" stages, beginning with Frazer and onwards, the most curious modes of thinking were ascribed to the primitives as exponents of "primitive mentality." It is well known that these efforts have reached their apparent climax in the sagacious writings of Lévy-Bruhl. But consciously or unconsciously the same opinion underlies most of the theories concerning the origin of the religion advanced by evolutionistic writers on comparative religion. For all these views were apparently excellent proofs of the lack of rational power in primitive man. Let it suffice to refer the reader to the theories of Frazer on the development of religion from magic. Boas, who has devoted much care to the problem whether there really exists a "primitive mentality," after a very thorough investigation arrives at the conclusion that "the difference in the mode of thought of primitive man and that of civilized man seems to consist largely in the difference of character of the traditional material with which the new perception associates itself." The traditional material handed over from generation to generation is of quite a different order in modern society as compared with that of a primitive people. Hence, as Boas shows, the types of reasoning and association take another course than in the case of modern educated people. Still the fundamental traits are the same, as can be clearly seen from the illustrations chosen by Boas. Especially illuminating are his remarks on the mode of behaviour not in conformity with the accepted and customary manners, and the reaction against such a behaviour displayed both in savage and civilized society.[2] In this case it can without any doubt be alleged that the seemingly illogical mode of thinking found among primitive peoples is based on certain psychological reactions recurring even in modern society.

Radin has added some valuable observations on the real rôle played by magic in the life of a primitive tribe. On the surface there seems to be valid reasons for ascribing to the primitives the assumption that magic rites have secured the success of e.g. a hunting expedition. Says Radin: "They may tell you, if directly interrogated, that a poisoned arrow discharged for a short distance into a deer trail will cause the death of a deer that is to be hunted on the following day. What inference can we very well expect a person to draw from such a statement but that a magical nonrational rite has achieved a practical and all-important result? Must we not insist, then, that the mentality of

[2] *Op. cit.*, pp. 211 ff.

people who accept such a belief is different in degree and possibly in kind from our own? There seems indeed to be no escape." [3] But Radin indicates in the following that the magical rite performed by the hunter is only one part of a whole series of activities, the other acts being of a purely practical and totally rational character, namely the waiting on the trail, the pursuing and the killing of the deer. And even more, we may, as Radin states, safely assume that the hunter does not perform the magical rite except when he knows from practical experience that he has selected the most suitable time for his going out hunting.[4] As Radin puts it: "I once asked a Winnebago Indian whether the rite of shooting an arrow into a trail of which he had no knowledge would be effective, and received a prompt and amused denial.[5] The rite of discharging an arrow does not mean anything to the practical-minded man, Radin contends. Such people simply repeat mechanically what has been formulated by medicine-men and religious thinkers.

Modern ethnologists who are at the same time field-workers accordingly make the strongest reservations against any theories aiming at the acceptance of the hypothesis of a special primitive mentality. Boas, for his part, has shown concerning primitive man "that the oft-repeated contention that he has no power of attention, no originality of thought, no power of clear reasoning, could not be maintained; and that all these faculties are common to primitive man and to civilized man, although they are excited on different occasions." [6]

In the same way as modern ethnology has proved that there is no special primitive mentality, so has it also demonstrated the lack of foundation for the supposition that the existing primitive cultures reflect early stages of culture. This theory was based on the assumption that human cultures always develop from simple to complex forms. But later research has shown that this contention cannot be held to claim general validity.[7]

[3] P. Radin, *Primitive Man as Philosopher*, New York & London 1927, p. 15.

[4] *Op. cit.*, p. 16.

[5] *Op. cit.*, p. 17 f.

[6] Boas, *op. cit.*, p. 247.

[7] Cf. Boas, *op. cit.*, p. 193. Boas demonstrates "that the history of industrial development is almost throughout that of increasing complexity." He contrasts this statement by a reference to the history of primitive languages which "are, on the whole, complex. Minute differences in point of view are given expression by means of grammatical forms; and the grammatical categories of Latin, and still more so those of modern English, seem crude when compared to the complexity of psychological or logical forms which primitive languages recognize, but which in our speech are disregarded entirely" (p. 194).

And moreover, must we not say that the marriage conditions of our days are infinitely more simple in our civilized society than even among "a stone-age people," the Australian aborigines, with their marriage classes of the most complicated and intricate character requiring a most intensive and often repeated study from the scholar if he wants to be able to keep all data in mind?

But we may advance a step further. Modern research has clearly demonstrated that the so-called primitive peoples have passed through a long history. As Boas says: "Even the most primitive cultures must be considered as having had a historical development no less complex than that of civilization." [8] And again, there is an immense difference between "primitive" and "primitive" peoples. For is it not a curious thought to class as primitive and put on one and the same level the Australian savages and the subjects of an African kingdom as that of Ganda or Lunda?

Evolutionistic Theories in the Field of Comparative Religion

There is one special department of scientific research where evolutionist theories have held the field longer than in the other branches of science, viz. comparative religion, perhaps not so much among the specialists as among those scholars who did not keep close contact with advance in ethnology and sociology, e.g. writers on topics in Classical, Aryan, or Semitic religions. And the educated classes, not to speak of the general public, were surely largely dominated by evolutionist views in the domain of the history and psychology of religion. That this deplorable state of things has prevailed for so long a time is a rather astonishing fact, since the theories of the evolutionists were exposed to some keen criticisms as early as in the last decade of the nineteenth century. And in the years from 1920 and onward American ethnologists must be said to have overcome the evolutionistic hypothesis even in comparative religion. From the outset it was the great British scholar Sir James Frazer who was, so to speak, the incarnation of the evolutionistic spirit in the department of comparative religion. For his bulky volumes, packed with ethnographic data from all parts of the world, could, notwithstanding his ever changing theories, always be taken as an ideal illustration of what evolutionists meant by "the comparative method." It was Frazer's opinion of the true essence of magic, its age and its structural "primitivity" in relation to

[8] F. Boas, *Primitive Art*, p. 121.

religion that from the beginning was determined to be the centre of discussion for many years. Supplemented with the views of Marett concerning the notion of impersonal, supernatural power, *mana*, and *tabu* as the negative aspect of *mana*, the evolutionistic theories held a mighty and fascinating sway over the minds, not only of the general public but also of many scholars. Today when these theories are definitely dated they are still embraced in some parts of the scientific world with some of the devotion bestowed on the dogmas in the periods of doctrinal controversies in Christian and other churches. . . .

As early as in the beginning of this century the two French sociologists Hubert and Mauss were able to ascertain that the Frazerian theory of the development of magical ideas and institutions out of a misunderstanding of the ideas of association must be wrong. Their main objections against the hypothesis of Frazer may be summarized in two points: on one hand Frazer has not succeeded in establishing as an irrevocable fact that all magic is based on the idea of sympathetic ideas and actions, for there are incontestable magic words and actions which are not sympathetic, e.g. incantations. On the other hand it can be demonstrated with all necessary explicitness that there can be no misrepresentation of the ideas of associations of likeness when a magical rite is performed against an enemy, because there need be no similarity between the person in question and the image used in the magical rite to symbolize him. Instead of using a puppet of wax representing his foe (which, moreover, very often had not the slightest likeness to the person concerned) the magician had a free hand to introduce an object of a merely symbolical character, e.g. an onion into his manipulations, and this he pierced with a needle again and again. It goes without saying that such an object, e.g. a bird, a branch, a ring etc., could not possibly by any association of ideas of likeness direct one's thoughts to the enemy to be destroyed. . . .

And now to the argument of the uniform character of magic! Here Lowie has no difficulty in pointing to the fact that magic is not at all as uniform as Frazer contends. Besides, the famous English ethnologist is not quite fair, for, as Lowie points out, "Sir James is not comparing comparable phenomena." If religions are compared in their specific characteristics, and magical faiths only as regards their most abstract common traits, the former will of course appear diverse and the latter uniform. A fair survey, on the other hand, will bring out frequent recurrences of religious no less than of magical practice." Concluding his remarks Lowie establishes the outcome of this critical review in these words: "In short, Frazer's argument breaks down at every point, and even if we adopt his definitions there is no reason to ascribe greater antiquity to magic than to religion. . . . In the state of our knowledge, both magic and religion are best regarded as extremely ancient components of the human world-view." . . . [Similarly] Goldenweiser . . . expresses the general opinion among scholars when he characterizes "The Golden Bough" with the following words: "Negligible as theory, indispensable as a collection of material on primitive religion."

Selected Bibliography

The Accadian and Hebrew Psalms of Lamentation as Religious Documents (Stockholm: Thule, 1937).

The Ascension of the Apostle and the Heavenly Book (Uppsala: Lundequistska Bokhandeln, 1950).

The Great Vohu Manah and the Apostle of God. Studies in Iranian and Manichean Religion (Uppsala: Lundequistska Bokhandeln, 1945).

The King and the Tree of Life in Ancient Near Eastern Religion (Uppsala: Lundequistska Bokhandeln, 1951).

Literary and Psychological Aspects of the Hebrew Prophets (Uppsala: Lundequistska Bokhandeln, 1948).

Mani and Manichaeism (London: Weidenfeld and Nicolson, 1965).

Mesopotamian Elements in Manichaeism (Uppsala: Lundequistska Bokhandeln, 1946).

Muhammad, The Apostle of God, and His Ascension (Uppsala: Lundequistska Bokhandeln, 1955).

"Myth and History," *Culture in History. Essays in Honor of Paul Radin*, ed. by Stanley Diamond (New York: Columbia University Press, 1960), pp. 467–495.

"Oral Tradition and Written Literature Among the Hebrews in the Light of Arabic Evidence, with Special Regard to Prose Narratives," *Acta Orientalia*, Vol. XXIII, Nos. 3, 4 (1959), pp. 201–226.

Religionens Värld (Stockholm: Svenska Kyrkans Diakonistyrelses Bokförlag, 1953).

Religionsphänomenologie (Berlin: Walter de Gruyter, 1969).

Observations on the Search for Religion's Primordium

E. E. EVANS-PRITCHARD

E. E. Evans-Pritchard was born in England on September 21, 1902, and has been professor of social anthropology at Oxford University since 1946. From 1926 to 1929 he was involved in anthropological expeditions in central, eastern, and northern Africa, from which expeditions he derived much of the material used in his studies of the Nuer. He became professor of sociology at Egyptian University in Cairo in 1930. In 1935 he was appointed Research Lecturer at Oxford, a position he held until 1940. After the close of World War II he taught for a year at Cambridge before resuming his career at Oxford. Throughout his career Evans-Pritchard has been particularly interested in primitive peoples. In his book Theories of Primitive Religion *(from which our selection is taken), he attempted both a summary and critique of prevalent intellectual, psychological, and sociological attempts to reach the* primordium *of religious experience.*

I have given you an account, with some illustrations, of various types of theory which have been put forward to explain the religious beliefs and practices of primitive man. For the most part the theories we have been discussing are, for anthropologists at least, as dead as mutton, and today are chiefly of interest as specimens of the thought of their time. Some of the books—those, for example, of Tylor, Frazer, and Durkheim—will doubtless continue to be read as classics, but they are no longer much of a stimulus for the student. Others —for example, Lang, King, Crawley, and Marett—have more or less passed into oblivion. That these theories no longer make much appeal is due to a number of factors, a few of which I shall mention.

One reason is, I believe, that religion has ceased to occupy men's minds in the way it did at the end of last, and at the beginning of this, century. Anthropological writers then felt that they were living at a momentous crisis in the history of thought, and that they had

E. E. Evans-Pritchard, *Theories of Primitive Religion* (Oxford: Clarendon Press, 1965), pp. 100–112. Reprinted by permission.

127

their part to play in it. Max Müller remarked in 1878 that 'Every day, every week, every month, every quarter, the most widely read journals seem just now to vie with each other in telling us that the time for religion is past, that faith is a hallucination or an infantile disease, that the gods have at last been found out and exploded. . . .'[1] Crawley wrote, twenty-seven years later, in 1905, that the enemies of religion 'have developed the opposition of science and religion into a deadly struggle, and the opinion is everywhere gaining ground that religion is a mere survival from a primitive and mythopoeic age, and its extinction only a matter of time'.[2] I have discussed elsewhere[3] the part played by anthropologists in this struggle, so I do not pursue the matter any further. I mention it here only because I think that the crisis of conscience to some extent accounts for the efflorescence of books on primitive religion during this period, and also that the passing of the crisis may account in some degree for the absence among later generations of anthropologists of the passionate interest their predecessors had in the subject The last book in which one senses a feeling of urgency and conflict is S. A. Cook's *The Study of Religion*, finished and published when the calamity of 1914 had already fallen.

There were other reasons why the debate abated. Anthropology was becoming an experimental subject, and as field research developed, both in quality and in quantity, what appeared to be more in the nature of philosophical speculation on the part of scholars who had never seen a primitive people was at a discount. It was not merely that facts revealed by modern research only too often cast doubt on earlier theories, but that the theories came to be seen to have faulty construction. When anthropologists attempted to make use of them in their field studies, they found that they had little experimental value, because they were formulated in terms which seldom permitted their being broken down into problems which observation could solve, so they could not be proved either true or false. What use as a guide to field research are Tylor's and Müller's and Durkheim's theories of the genesis of religion?

It is the word genesis on which emphasis is placed. It was because explanations of religion were offered in terms of origins that these theoretical debates, once so full of life and fire, eventually subsided. To my mind, it is extraordinary that anyone could have thought it

[1] *Lectures on the Origin and Growth of Religion*, 1878, p. 218.

[2] Crawley, *The Tree of Life*, 1905, p. 8.

[3] Evans-Pritchard, "Religion and the Anthropologists," *Blackfriars*, Apr. 1960, pp. 104–118.

worth while to speculate about what might have been the origin of some custom or belief, when there is absolutely no means of discovering, in the absence of historical evidence, what was its origin. And yet this is what almost all our authors explicitly or implicitly did, whether their theses were psychological or sociological; even those most hostile to what they dubbed pseudo-history were not immune from putting forward similar explanations themselves. A long essay might be written about the appalling confusion in these discussions with regard to the ideas of evolution, development, history, progress, primitive, origin, genesis, and cause, and I do not propose to unravel it. It must suffice to say that there is little or nothing one can do with such theories.

I think that most anthropologists would today agree that it is useless to seek for a *primordium* in religion. Schleiter says, truly, 'all evolutionary schemes of religion, without exception, in the determination of the primordium and the serial stages of alleged development, proceed upon a purely arbitrary and uncontrolled basis'.[4] Also, it has been clearly established that in many primitive religions peoples' minds function in different ways at different levels and in different contexts. So a man may turn to a fetish for certain purposes, and appeal to God in other situations; and a religion can be both polytheistic and monotheistic, according to whether Spirit is thought of as more than one or as one. It is now also clear that even in the same primitive society there may be, as Radin pointed out,[5] wide differences in this respect between individuals, differences he attributes to differences of temperament. Finally, I suppose it would be agreed that the kind of cause-and-effect explanation which was implicit in so much earlier theorizing is hardly in accord with modern scientific thought in general, which seeks rather to reveal and understand constant relations.

In these theories it was assumed, taken for granted, that we were at one end of the scale of human progress and the so-called savages were at the other end, and that, because primitive men were on a rather low technological level, their thought and custom must in all respects be the antithesis of ours. We are rational, primitive peoples prelogical, living in a world of dreams and make-believe, of mystery and awe; we are capitalists, they communists; we are monogamous, they promiscuous; we are monotheists, they fetishists, animists, preanimists or what have you, and so on.

Primitive man was thus represented as childish, crude, prodigal, and

[4] F. Schleiter, *Religion and Culture*, 1919, p. 39.
[5] Radin, *Monotheism Among Primitive Peoples*, 1954 edit., pp. 24–30.

comparable to animals and imbeciles. This is no exaggeration. Herbert Spencer tells us that the mind of primitive man is 'unspeculative, uncritical, incapable of generalizing, and with scarcely any notions save those yielded by the perceptions'.[6] Then, again, he says that in the undeveloped vocabularies and grammatical structures of primitives only the simplest thoughts can be conveyed, so, according to an unnamed authority whom he quotes, the Zuni Indians 'require much facial contortion and bodily gesticulation to make their sentences perfectly intelligible'; and that the language of the Bushmen needs, according to another source, so many signs to eke it out that 'they are unintelligible in the dark', while the Arapahos, says a third authority, 'can hardly converse with one another in the dark'.[7] Max Müller quotes Sir Emerson Tennent to the effect that the Veddahs of Ceylon have no language: 'they mutually make themselves understood by signs, grimaces, and guttural sounds, which have little resemblance to definite words or language in general.' [8] In fact they speak Sinhalese (an Indo-European tongue). Then, does not Darwin, in a most unscientific passage, describe the people of Tierra del Fuego, a rather pleasant people according to better observers, as practically sub-human beasts,[9] and does not Galton, in an even more unscientific spirit, claim that his dog had more intelligence than the Damara (Herero) whom he met? [10] Many other examples could be cited. A superb collection of foolish, if not outrageous, observations of this sort may be found in the paper 'Aptitudes of Races' [11] by the Reverend Frederic W. Farrar, the author of *Eric, or Little by Little* and *The Life of Christ*. His dislike of, and hostility to, Negroes equals that of Kingsley. Fifty years of research have shown that such denigrations (the word in this context is etymologically ironical) were ill-informed misconceptions, or in other words so much rubbish.

All this fitted in very well with colonialist and other interests, and some were prepared to admit that some of the discredit must go to the American ethnologists who wanted an excuse for slavery, and some also to those who desired to find a missing link between men and monkeys. . . .

[6] Op. cit., i. 344.

[7] Op. cit., i. 149.

[8] *Selected Essays on Language, Mythology and Religion*, ii. 27.

[9] C. Darwin, *Voyage of the Beagle, 1831–36*, 1906 edit., chap. x.

[10] F: Galton, *Narrative of an Explorer in Tropical South Africa*, 1889 edit., p. 82.

[11] *Transactions of the Ethnological Society of London*, N.S., v (1867), pp. 115–26.

Such views as I have outlined would not be acceptable today. On whether they were justified by the information available at the time I will pronounce no judgement, not having carried out the laborious literary research that would be required to form one. My task is expository, but I have also to put before you what seems to me to be the fundamental weakness of the interpretations of primitive religion which at one time appeared to carry conviction. The first error was the basing of them on evolutionary assumptions for which no evidence was, or could be, adduced. The second was that, besides being theories of chronological origins, they were also theories of psychological origins; and even those we have labelled sociological could be said to rest ultimately on psychological suppositions of the 'if I were a horse' sort.[12] They could scarcely have been otherwise so far as the armchair anthropologists were concerned, those whose experience was restricted to their own culture and society, within that society to a small class, and within that class to a yet smaller group of intellectuals. I am sure that men like Avebury, Frazer, and Marett had little idea of how the ordinary English working man felt and thought, and it is not surprising that they had even less idea of how primitives, whom they had never seen, feel and think. As we have seen, their explanations of primitive religion derived from introspection. If the scholar himself believed what primitives believe, or practised what they practise, he would have been guided by a certain line of reasoning, or impelled by some emotional state, or immersed in crowd psychology, or entangled in a network of collective and mystical representations.

. . . We use the word 'supernatural' when speaking of some native belief, because that is what it would mean for us, but far from increasing our understanding of it, we are likely by the use of this word to misunderstand it. We have the concept of natural law, and the word 'supernatural' conveys to us something outside the ordinary operation of cause and effect, but it may not at all have that sense for primitive man. For instance, many peoples are convinced that deaths are caused by witchcraft. To speak of witchcraft being for these peoples a supernatural agency hardly reflects their own view of the matter, since from their point of view nothing could be more natural. They experience it through the senses in deaths and other misfortunes, and the witches are their neighbours. Indeed, for them, if a person did not die

---

[12] The author is referring to the fallacy of supposing that one can understand primitive man by inferences based on psychological introspection: if I were a horse I would do what horses do for one or another reason or feeling. Editor's note.

from witchcraft, it might be better said, at least in a certain sense, that he did not die a natural death, and that to die from witchcraft is to die from natural causes. We might here consider further the dichotomy between sacred and profane, also the meaning of *mana* [13] and similar ideas, the differences between magic and religion, and other topics which appear to me to be still in a very confused state, largely on account of failure to realize that very fundamental semantic problems confront us—or, if we prefer to say so, problems of translation; but this would require a lengthy discussion, to which I hope to give attention at another time and in another place. . . .

Here and now I have a different task to perform: to suggest what should be the procedure in investigations of primitive religions. I do not deny that peoples have reasons for their beliefs—that they are rational; I do not deny that religious rites may be accompanied by emotional experiences, that feeling may even be an important element in their performance; and I certainly do not deny that religious ideas and practices are directly associated with social groups—that religion, whatever else it may be, is a social phenomenon. What I do deny is that it is explained by any of these facts, or all of them together, and I hold that it is not sound scientific method to seek for origins, especially when they cannot be found. Science deals with relations, not with origins and essences. In so far as it can be said that the facts of primitive religions can be sociologically explained at all, it must be in relation to other facts, both those with which it forms a system of ideas and practices and other social phenomena associated with it. As an example of the first kind of partial explanation, I would instance magic. To try to understand magic as an idea in itself, what is the essence of it, as it were, is a hopeless task. It becomes more intelligible when it is viewed not only in relation to empirical activities but also in relation to other beliefs, as part of a system of thought; for it is certainly often the case that it is primarily not so much a means of controlling nature as of preventing witchcraft and other mystical forces operating against human endeavour by interfering with the empirical measures taken to attain an end. As an example of explanation in terms of the relation of religion to other social, and in themselves non-religious, facts, we might instance ancestor cults, which clearly can only be understood when

[13] "The Analysis of Mana: an Empirical Approach," *Journal of the Polynesian Society*, xlix (1940), pp. 483–610. A. Capell, "The Word 'Mana': a Linguistic Study," *Oceania*, ix (1938), pp. 89–96. Also, F. R. Lehmann, *Mana, Der Begriff des 'außerordentlich Wirkungsvollen' bei Südseevölkern*, 1922, *passim*.

they are viewed as part of a whole set of family and kin relationships. The ghosts have power over their descendants, among whom they act as sanction for conduct, seeing that they carry out their obligations to one another and punishing them if they fail to do so. Or again, in some societies God is conceived of as both the one and the many, the one as thought of in relation to all men or a total society, and the many as thought of, in the form of a variety of spirits, in relation to one or other segment of society. A knowledge of the social structure is here obviously required for the understanding of some features of religious thought. Then again, religious ritual is performed on ceremonial occasions in which the relative status of individuals and groups is affirmed or confirmed, as at birth, initiation, marriage, and death. Clearly, to understand the role of religion on these occasions one must here again have a knowledge of the social structure. I have given some very simple examples. A relational analysis of the kind suggested can be made at any point where religion is in a functional relation to any other social facts—moral, ethical, economic, juridical, aesthetic, and scientific—and when it has been made at all points, we have as full a sociological understanding of the phenomenon as we are ever likely to have.

Selected Bibliography

Anthropology and History (Manchester: Manchester University Press, 1961).

The Comparative Method in Social Anthropology (London: Athlone Press, 1963).

Essays in Social Anthropology (New York: The Free Press, 1963).

The Institutions of Primitive Society (Oxford: Basil Blackwell, 1965).

The Nuer (Oxford: Clarendon Press, 1940).

Nuer Religion (Oxford: Clarendon Press, 1956).

The Position of Women in Primitive Societies (New York: The Free Press, 1965).

Social Anthropology (New York: The Free Press, 1952).

Witchcraft, Oracles, and Magic Among the Azande (Oxford: Clarendon Press, 1937).

The Zande Trickster (Oxford: Clarendon Press, 1967).

PART 3

Structural Depictions: Perceptible Aspects of Religion

This section of the anthology includes selections from scholars whose primary interest lies neither in isolating unambiguous simples nor in recovering pristine beginnings. Their basic intention is to give a thorough and accurate description to the manner and form in which religious phenomena appear in human experience. Rather than searching for underlying causes, essences, or exhaustive explanations, they focus on the manifestable and describable features of phenomena. Their eventual goal is to provide a complete account of a thing's form, structure, and distinguishing lines. Consequently, they refer to their approach by using words such as *structure*, *description*, *morphology*, and *phenomenology*. All of them assume that within the proper manner of viewing—which combines empirical techniques with a kind of intuitive grasping of the subject—such manifestable features "stand out" for the scholar to see.

The selections in this section are preceded by two essays that serve to introduce the subject. Maurice Merleau-Ponty's piece is a preliminary description of the intention and tone of phenomenology, both as a school and as a method in philosophy. The reader should be warned, however, that a large number of so-called "phenomenologists of religion" are only indirectly dependent on the point of departure of philosophical phenomenology.[1] Next, Geo Widengren's essay portrays some of the more prominent arrangements of materials that have been inspired by phenomenological approaches to religion. As is evident from its tone, Widengren's study is meant to be expository and analytical in nature rather than the occasion for advancing the author's proposals. Following Widengren's essay, samples of the several ways in which "phenomenology" can be construed and employed in religious studies are included. C. J. Bleeker prefers the term *entelecheia*, whose roots are in Aristotelian philosophy, in giving classification to the components of religion. Mircea Eliade builds a morphology of religious experience by focusing on the contrasts between the sacred and profane dimensions of being in the world. If space were available, our sampling would include the writings of Gerardus van der Leeuw and W. Brede Kristensen.

Other variations in approach occur when one includes such "structural depictions" as those provided by Claude Lévi-Strauss and Georges Dumézil. In the strict sense, neither is a phenomenologist nor is the latter a structural analyst, yet both analyze structures. Both train their eyes, first of all, not on religion or religious factors but on social patterns. According to Lévi-Strauss, there are certain patterns of social arrangement—in primitive society, mythological imagination, and in kinship relationships—that have a formative effect upon everything included in such arrangements. Naturally, such patterns also affect religious beliefs and practices. Similarly, on the basis of a detailed, many-sided examination of the cultures of proto-Indo-European peoples, Dumézil argues that a tripartite structural arrangement is the formative morphological factor. Because of its prominence, the tripartite pattern of social stratification is also the context in which religious sensitivities are rooted. Finally, the piece by Clifford Geertz —an anthropologist who is generally regarded as the champion of the position that religion can be understood as a cultural system—addresses itself to the question of how the religious perspective of a people comes to be known and described.

---

[1] For an additional longer, but clear and informative response to the question "what is phenomenology?", particularly in its philosophical aspect, the reader is referred to Pierre Thevenaz' essay by that title. Pierre Thevenaz, *What Is Phenomenology?*, edited with an introduction by James M. Edie (Chicago: Quadrangle Books, 1962), especially pp. 37–92.

What Is Phenomenology?

Maurice Merleau-Ponty

*Born in France in 1908, Maurice Merleau-Ponty had served for eight
years as professor of philosophy at the Collège de France in Paris, the
successor of Henri Bergson and Etienne Gilson, at the time of his
death on May 4, 1961. He had also received the acclaim and esteem
of philosophers around the world for his brilliant contributions to
philosophy, and, particularly, to phenomenology. His brief remarks
on "What Is Phenomenology?" are included here because of his fa-
cility in giving description to a philosophical tendency that often resists definition and typification.*

*Founded by Edmund Husserl, phenomenology tries to investigate
the world of "lived experience" instead of worlds that are products of
theory, preconceptions, and presuppositions. Seeking to return "to the
things themselves," Husserl worked painstakingly to separate those
"things" (or phenomena) from unexamined assumptions about them.
Similarly, he wanted to shed new light on the ingredients of the
lebenswelt ("life-world") instead of abandoning that world as being
too private or subjective for scientific analysis. Just as scholars from
the time of Immanuel Kant had been trying to typify various aspects
of man's subjective awareness, Husserl, along with his disciples and
successors, attempted a "grammar" of those layers of human experience that often go unprobed in everyday living. But unlike Kant,
Husserl sought access to the whole of "lived experience" and not
simply to the faculties of cognition or intellection. For Husserl, this
was not simply a controlling personal goal, but, beyond that, a means
of giving science a firm foundation.*

*As has already been noted, philosophical "phenomenology" and the
"phenomenology" of religion are not always synonymous; nor do they
very frequently build upon the same intentions and methodological
ploys. Most frequently, "phenomenology of religion" has reference to
typological distinctions used in differentiating the materials of religion.
In the philosophical sense, there are few, if any, true phenomenologies
of religion. Yet, because the typological studies in religion that are*

From Maurice Merleau-Ponty, "What Is Phenomenology?" in *Phenomenology of
Perception* (New York: Humanities Press, Inc., 1962), pp. vii–xi. xvii–xxi.

referred to as "phenomenologies" often claim to have been prompted by insights in Husserl's (or other phenomenologist's) thought, Merleau-Ponty's "introduction" is included here as a necessary preliminary statement.

What is phenomenology? It may seem strange that this question has still to be asked half a century after the first works of Husserl. The fact remains that it has by no means been answered. Phenomenology is the study of essences; and according to it, all problems amount to finding definitions of essences: the essence of perception, or the essence of consciousness, for example. But phenomenology is also a philosophy which puts essences back into existence, and does not expect to arrive at an understanding of man and the world from any starting point other than that of their "facticity." It is a transcendental philosophy which places in abeyance the assertions arising out of the natural attitude, the better to understand them; but it is also a philosophy for which the world is always "already there" before reflection begins—as an inalienable presence; and all its efforts are concentrated upon re-achieving a direct and primitive contact with the world, and endowing that contact with a philosophical status. It is the search for a philosophy which shall be a "rigorous science," but it also offers an account of space, time and the world as we "live" them. It tries to give a direct description of our experience as it is, without taking account of its psychological origin and the causal explanations which the scientist, the historian or the sociologist may be able to provide. . . .

It is a matter of describing, not of explaining or analysing. Husserl's first directive to phenomenology, in its early stages, to be a 'descriptive psychology,' or to return to the 'things themselves,' is from the start a rejection of science. I am not the outcome or the meeting-point of numerous causal agencies which determine my bodily or psychological make-up. I cannot conceive myself as nothing but a bit of the world, a mere object of biological, psychological or sociological investigation. I cannot shut myself up within the realm of science. All my knowledge of the world, even my scientific knowledge, is gained from my own particular point of view, or from some experience of the world without which the symbols of science would be meaningless. The whole universe of science is built upon the world as directly experienced, and if we want to subject science itself to rigorous scrutiny and arrive at a precise assessment of its meaning and scope, we must begin by reawakening the basic experience of the world of which science is the second-order expresssion. Science has not and never will have, by its nature, the same significance *qua* form of being as the world which we perceive, for the simple reason that it is a rationale or explanation of that world. I am, not a 'living creature' nor even a 'man,' nor again even 'a consciousness' endowed with all the characteristics which zoology, social anatomy or inductive psychology recognize in these various products of the natural or historical process—I am the absolute source, my existence does not stem from my antecedents, from my physical and social environment; instead it moves out towards them and sustains them, for I alone bring into being for myself (and therefore into being in the only sense that the word can have for me) the tradition which I elect to carry on, or the horizon whose distance from me would be abolished—since that distance is not one of its properties—if I were not there to scan it with my gaze. Scientific points of view, according to which my existence is a moment of the world's, are always both naive and at the same time dishonest, because they take for granted, without explicitly mentioning it, the other point of view, namely that of consciousness, through which from the outset a world forms itself round me and begins to exist for me. To return to things themselves is to return to that world which precedes knowledge, of which knowledge always *speaks*, and in relation to which every scientific schematization is an abstract and derivative sign-language, as is geography in relation to the countryside in which we have learnt beforehand what a forest, a prairie or a river is. . . .

The world is there before any possible analysis of mine, and it would be artificial to make it the outcome of a series of syntheses which link, in the first place sensations, then aspects of the object corresponding to different perspectives, when both are nothing but products of analysis, with no sort of prior reality. Analytical reflection believes that it can trace back the course followed by a prior constituting act and arrive, in the 'inner man'—to use Saint Augustine's expression—at a constituting power which has always been identical with that inner self. Thus reflection itself is carried away and transplanted in an impregnable subjectivity, as yet untouched by being and time. But this is very ingenuous, or at least it is an incomplete form of reflection which loses sight of its own beginning. When I begin to reflect my reflection bears upon an unreflective experience; moreover my reflection cannot be unaware of itself as an event, and so it appears to itself in the light of a truly creative act, of a changed structure of consciousness, and yet it has to recognize, as having priority over its own operations, the world which is given to the subject, because the subject is given to himself. The real has to be described, not constructed or formed. Which means that I cannot put perception into the same category as the syntheses represented by judgements, acts or predications. My field of perception is constantly filled with a play of colours, noises and fleeting tactile sensations which I cannot relate precisely to the context of my clearly perceived world, yet which I nevertheless immediately 'place' in the world, without ever confusing them with my daydreams. Equally constantly I weave dreams round things. I imagine people and things whose presence is not incompatible with the context, yet who are not in fact involved in it: they are ahead of reality, in the realm of the imaginary. If the reality of my perception were based solely on the intrinsic coherence of 'representations,' it ought to be for ever hesitant and, being wrapped up in my conjectures on probabilities, I ought to be ceaselessly taking apart misleading syntheses, and reinstating in reality stray phenomena which I had excluded in the first place. But this does not happen. The real is a closely woven fabric. It does not await our judgement before incorporating the most surprising phenomena, or before rejecting the most plausible figments of our imagination. Perception is not a science of the world, it is not even an act, a deliberate taking up of a position; it is the background from which all acts stand out, and is presupposed by them. The world is not an object such that I have in my possession the law of its making; it is the natural setting of, and field for, all my thoughts and all my explicit perceptions. Truth does not 'inhabit' only 'the inner man,' or more accurately, there is no inner man, man is in the world, and only in the world does he know himself. When I return to myself from an excursion into the realm of dogmatic common sense or of science, I find, not a source of intrinsic truth, but a subject destined to be in the world.

Suggested Readings

Les Aventures de la dialectique (Paris: Gallimard, 1955).

Humanism and Terror, trans. by John O'Neill (Boston: The Beacon Press, 1969).

In Praise of Philosophy (Evanston: Northwestern University Press, 1963).

Phenomenology of Perception, trans. by Colin Smith (New York: Humanities Press, 1962).

The Primacy of Perception, James M. Edie, ed. (Evanston: Northwestern University Press, 1964).

Sense and Non-Sense, trans. by Hubert L. Dreyfus and Patricia Allen Dreyfus (Evanston: Northwestern University Press, 1964).

Signs, trans. by Richard C. McCleary (Evanston: Northwestern University Press, 1964).

The Structure of Behavior, trans. by Alden L. Fisher (Boston: The Beacon Press, 1963).

Themes from the Lectures at the Collège de France, 1952–1960, trans. by John O'Neill (Evanston: Northwestern University Press, 1970).

The Visible and the Invisible, trans. by Alphonso Lingis (Evanston: Northwestern University Press, 1968).

An Introduction to Phenomenology of Religion

Geo Widengren

Phenomenology as a term and a notion was created by Chantepie de la Saussaye, one of the founders of the modern study of the history of religion.[1] As an independent discipline of what was called "Comparative Religion" it developed out of the comparative study of religion as this study was practiced at the end of the last and the beginning of this century. Chantepie de la Saussaye, however, and after him E. Lehmann, clearly saw that phenomenology of religion was a discipline different from "Comparative Religion."[2] However, as treated by Lehmann and his contemporaries—with the exception of Brede Kristensen—the phenomenology of religion suffered both from the general evolutionistic presuppositions of the period and from either theological or anti-theological bias.[3]

Both defects were visible in the comprehensive work of G. van der Leeuw who in the thirties contributed vastly to the spread of the phenomenological method and whose textbook *Phänomenologie der Religion* especially in theological circles was looked upon as *le dernier cri* as far as method was concerned—and much admired.[4] Proceeding chiefly from the same presuppositions as Nathan Söderblom, F. Heiler, and Rudolf Otto[5] his book was seriously marred by the fact that its material was taken chiefly from the religions of illiterate peo-

[1] *Lehrbuch der Religionsgeschichte*, 1st ed. 1887, pp. 48 ff. "Die Phänomenologie der Religion."

[2] Cf. e.g. E. Carpenter, *Comparative Religion*, London 1913. In this book a sketch of phenomenological character was given, typically enough focused on "the lower culture" as it is called.

[3] *Lehrbuch der Religionsgeschichte*, 4th ed. 1925, I, pp. 23–130 "Erscheinungsund Ideenwelt der Religion."

[4] *Phänomenologie der Religion* (Tübingen, 1933).

[5] This has been pointed out by C. J. Bleeker, *The Phenomenological Method*, NUMEN VI/1955, reprinted in: *The Sacred Bridge*, 1963, pp. 1–15 (there p. 13). It is only fair to state that van der Leeuw shared this defect with most of his predecessors.

Geo Widengren, "Some Remarks on the Methods of the Phenomenology of Religion," in *Universitet Och Forskningen* (Festschrift for Torgny T. Segerstedt), (Uppsala: Almquist and Wiksells, 1968), pp. 250–260. Reprinted by permission of the author.

ples and by his interpretation of religious phenomena being based on outdated theories of evolutionistic origin or hypotheses much in vogue at that time, such as the theories of Lévy-Bruhl.[6] In all this he is certainly dependent on previous research along the lines of "comparative religion." His work is also deficient, in spite of his declarations, in that he evidently is much influenced by certain theological presuppositions of a non-scientific character.[7]

In spite of these defects one must concede, however, that the pioneer effort of the author does possess great merit. Even today, his book can be read with some profit. More specifically, van der Leeuw was the first to formulate two principles of great value to phenomenological research—though he has not always been true to his own principles.

One fundamental principle is the so-called *epoché*, meaning the suspension of any judgment. Phenomenology does not occupy itself with the problem of the truth of religion. We may question the usefulness of the term *epoché* but we must of course accept the principle itself.

However, it would seem that this principle of *epoché* has been rather imperfectly practiced even by scholars who proclaim their adherence to it. We have spoken of van der Leeuw's not being quite true to his own principles because he allows his scientific work to be dominated by his strong Christian feelings. That the same observation holds true, for example, Söderblom is well known. More astonishing is it to find judgements of value recommended by a modern expert in phenomenology who has pondered over the questions of method more than most scholars. In his thought-provoking essay "Some Remarks on the 'Entelecheia' of Religious Phenomena," C. J. Bleeker speaks unhesitatingly of religions "of a higher quality," of religions as having "suddenly reached higher level of self-realization," of "the religious value of various modern exotic sects," of "superstition," of "a gradual rising of the religious level," of an under-valuation of the religious quality, of "the fact that the so-called world-religions have offered humanity a new and purer conception of God," of "many cases of retrogression and of religious corruption." While perfectly agreeing with Bleeker in his general attitude in this essay—an attitude to which I shall return later—I feel bound to declare it absolutely

[6] This is conspicuous everywhere, but most of all in the first part of the book where everything is based on the mana-theories, moreover in an extremely far-fetched fashion.

[7] This trait comes to the fore in the rather unhappy typology of individual religions presented in the fifth part of the book.

impossible for phenomenology of religion to pass such judgements of value, purely subjective as they are. For what would be the objective standard according to which a branch of the science of religion were to formulate opinions of the type quoted? In a manifest way such judgements transgress the borders of objective scholarly work. Here a very strong *epoché* is surely called for.

The second principle invoked by van der Leeuw is what has been called *eidós*—by the way we observe the predilection of Greek technical terms alongside with the Latin expressions used especially by Otto—the searching for "the essentials of religious phenomena." [8] The difficulty connected with this principle is of course to ascertain what the essentials of a given phenomenon really are. The phenomenon is what "appears," *tó phainómenon*, but it is not sure at all that what appears to us really constitutes the essentials behind or within the phenomenon. Very often we must try to search behind the phenomenon in order to find the essentials. Here attention also must be paid to the context of the phenomenon. As a typical concrete illustration we may choose the Vedic sacrifice which in older literature was interpreted in a superficial way.[9] The same observation is valid in the case of the Vedic notion of "faith," *śraddhā*, which was analyzed in a highly mechanical manner.[10] The chief fault with scholars belonging to an older generation was, however, that they were far too prone to interpret religious phenomena in the light of magic. A favourite topic was to demonstrate that Christian sacraments were nothing but magical actions—an obvious misinterpretation which needs no refutation to-day.

But with the formulation of these two methodical principles we have only tackled some of the minor problems of the phenomenology of religion, minor problems because these principles are on the whole rather self-evident.

We just alluded to the views of C. J. Bleeker. His article took up for analysis a methodological topic which he had discussed and R. Pettazzoni as well. Pettazzoni, well known for his outstanding phenomenological monographs, was of the opinion that the existing text-

[8] The formulation is Prof. Bleeker's *The Sacred Bridge*, p. 3.

[9] Scholars proceeded from "the idea of reciprocal obligation" formulated in the crudest (sic) terms: dahi me, dadami te, "Give to me, I give to thee, Carpenter, op. cit., p. 142 f. A much more correct view of the sacrifice of gift was presented by J. Pedersen, *Israel*, I–II, 1940, p. 231. van der Leeuw, op. cit., p. 328 1st ed. formulated the phenomenological implications, following Grönbech who has influenced also Pedersen.

[10] Cf. I. Levi, *La doctrine du sacrifice dans les Brahmanas*, 1898, criticized by G. Dumézil, *Mitra-Varuna*, 2nd ed., 1948, p. 67 f.

books and monographs of a phenomenological character neglect the concept of development.[11] Bleeker for his part admits that by this statement "he has put the finger on the weak point." [12] "It is certainly true that the significance of religious phenomena can be clarified to a great extent if they are examined, so to say, as arrested pictures. But it should not be forgotten that they are also moving pictures i.e. that they are subject to a certain dynamic.[13] Bleeker, "in order to do justice to this element" further introduced the notion of what he calls "the entelecheia of the phenomena." [14] By this notion he was led to formulate the judgements of value, these I was unable to follow.[15] However, the problem is left: "Generally the task of the phenomenology of religion is taken as a static one," says Bleeker. With this method another problem is introduced. Given the impossibility of illustrating a religious phenomenon by presenting a full-scale inventory of all the historical contexts of various religions where the phenomenon in question is found the scholar has to be content with some representative illustrations. A critical observer has called this method a collecting of a lot of impressionistic pictures and sketches.[16] This characterization is certainly correct but we must ask in return: what would the alternative be? Well, the critic in question in his own meritorious phenomenological work has chosen another method. He has given rather detailed, partly highly abstract descriptions of what he thinks the phenomenon in a given case really is. But he has been very parsimonious in illustrating his statements by quoting the relevant material. This method too has its obvious weaknesses and has brought with it some disastrous consequences as far as the evaluation of the historical facts are concerned which in its turn led to entirely false accents in the phenomenological exposition, a regrettable fundamental fault in an otherwise original and stimulating work. It is of course to be conceded that no scholar can be a specialist in all fields and even the best method doesn't exclude material errors. But it would seem that if the author had paid less attention to his abstract, "philosophically" tinged descriptions and given more attention to a thorough and correct presentation of the material facts upon which his phenomenological conclusions must be based most of these funda-

[11] Cf. Il metodo comparativo, NUMEN VI/1955.
[12] Bleeker, *The Sacred Bridge*, p. 14.
[13] Cf. Bleeker, op. cit., p. 14.
[14] Cf. Bleeker, op. cit., pp. 16–24.
[15] Cf. Bleeker, op. cit., p. 16.
[16] Cf. K. Goldammer, *Die Formenwelt des Religiösen*, 1960, p. XXIX.

mental errors could have been avoided. We conclude therefore that in the ideal phenomenological monograph the basic material should be presented as complete as possible, but that in the phenomenological text-book we have to be content with representative illustrations, chosen as to illustrate as far as possible various religions and various culture-areas.

In this regard it has already been pointed out that van der Leeuw showed a remarkable onesidedness in his choice of material in so far as the religions of illiterate peoples were quoted out of all proportion to their real importance.[17] This was most probably a heritage from the days of the works belonging to the old "comparative religion" with its evolutionistic overestimation of what was called "primitive religion," a term and notion still very popular in some German quarters.[18] This misplacement of accents is to be discovered also in such phenomenological text-books and monographs which are not at all based upon the same presuppositions as van der Leeuw's, Goldammer's and Heiler's, e.g. those of Pettazzoni and Eliade.[19] I myself also have to confess my shortcomings in this respect but I have tried resolutely to remedy this fault in a forthcoming textbook.[20]

According to my considered opinion an overall treatment of the

[17] van der Leeuw also drew heavily on Egyptian and Greek religions among the religions of antiquity.

[18] Both Goldammer, Heiler and Bianchi without any hesitation use the misleading expression "primitive religion." But it is to the credit of both Goldammer and Heiler that in order to illustrate phenomenological observations they both quoted extensively from Christian material, Heiler also from Indian religion. In this regard Heiler's work is extremely valuable and very instructive.

[19] In Pettazzoni's fundamental work *The All-Knowing God*, 1956 the treatment of the material taken from the great religions of antiquity (except Greek religion) and the living universal religions can stand no comparison to his mastery of the religions of the illiterate peoples. Bleeker, op. cit., p. 13, has pointed out the limitations of Eliade's *Traité d'Histoire des Religions*, 1947, when giving the following statement about it: "the attention of the author is mainly directed on different forms of 'hierophanies' as they occur in the religions of illiterate peoples."

[20] In the German edition of my phenomenological work, *Die Welt der Religion*. I have considerably expanded the material taken from religions of antiquity and from universal religions, especially Islam. There is still a remarkable lack of quotations from Eastern religions. (Widengren's book, *Religionsphänomenologie*, was published in Berlin by Walter de Gruyter in 1969. Editor's note.)
To some extent the same remark holds true of the earlier work of E. O. James, *Comparative Religion*, 1938. Good examples of overall treatments are provided by more recent books of James and above all of S. G. F. Brandon, *Man and his Destiny in the Great Religions*, 1962, and *History, Time and Deity*, 1965. Prof. Bleeker in his methodological essay "The Phenomenological Method" found the book *Comparative Religion* of James and my own textbook "the best examples of an overall handbook of the phenomenology of religion." This, however, was written in 1955.

phenomenological subject should be given. But how does one evade the difficulty of presenting only a static impression of the religious phenomenon? We cannot be content with presenting only what Bleeker aptly called "arrested pictures." Pettazzoni argued for a close connection between phenomenology and history of religion. If then, we go to his own phenomenological books which are the "pièce de résistance" of his life-work as a scholar we will find in the German booklet *Der allwissende Gott* a very good and clear summary of his researches into the belief in a High-God.[21] Now, from what Pettazzoni has written about the intimate relation he wants to see established between history and phenomenology of religion we should await an approach of a character entirely different from what is the case in older phenomenological monographs and textbooks. If such are our expectations we will certainly be disappointed. The author establishes his connection between historical and phenomenological methods only by the way of a juxtaposition. After a short introduction he gives a phenomenology (here called morphology, which seems an unnecessary deviation from an established usage) of the divine omniscience and then presents a hypothetical explanation of the historical-ethnographical background of this religious idea. Last, he adds a meritorious sketch of the iconography of divine omniscience, i.e. how this idea found expression in art, and in an appendix provides some reflections on the rise of monotheism. What is especially interesting here from a methodological point of view and very valuable is the endeavour to use the monuments of art for a phenomenological purpose. This has been done in the past to a very small extent but we should proceed further along this way. In this endeavour of Pettazzoni I see a most promising innovation. On the whole art and archaeology have been far too little used in both history and phenomenology of religion.[22]

The author's phenomenological presentation of his material doesn't disclose any startling news. He starts by treating the subject of divine omniscience and here he passes without any hesitation from classical religion to the religions of illiterate peoples (p. 18 f.),[23] and then in

[21] This slender volume summarizes the results of a life-work, presented in great detail in "The All-Knowing God" and started already in 1922 with the publication of his book *Dio* (which remained a torso).

[22] It should not be left unmentioned that Brandon has acquired some merits in this regard too by using in his *History, Time and Deity* some illustrative material from very interesting and important monuments of religious art.

[23] The terminology of Pettazzoni is out of date among anthropologists of today and really misleading.

this and the next section he goes on treating of the object of divine omniscience in absolutely the same manner as most other phenomenological scholars.[24] It surely calls for notice that when dealing with some minor topic the author has no hesitation whatsoever in comparing phenomena of vastly different religions in order to elucidate a special aspect of his subject (e.g. p. 31 bottom).

In all this Pettazzoni does not deviate from other works in the same field. In his illuminating remarks (pp. 69–76) on the religious and ideological structure of divine omniscience there is to be found the same method. Jahweh, on the one hand, Tore among the pygmies of Ituri on the other hand are shown to exhibit the same characteristics, to mention but one example.

It is only in the third section (pp. 77–98) that Pettazzoni according to his own statement is passing on to another method, the historical method. He declares his intention to be to proceed backwards until he reaches the oldest stage of civilization where the notion of divine omniscience appears. This intention of his is realized in that way that he first of all treats of the Heavenly Father, then of the Mother Earth, and thirdly of the Lord of Animals. His so-called "historical" approach is, however, as such rather modest, for it is reduced to the statement that the notion of a Heavenly Father is found all over the earth among pastoral nomads (a corresponding explanation is given for the two other divine figures). But when comparing Jahweh and Tezcatlipoca (who moreover doesn't belong to a nomadic but to an agricultural people) [25] the author is driven to rather uncertain hypotheses. Not that I have anything against comparing the belief in a High-God among nomadic peoples belonging to different civiliza-

---

[24] Cf. op. cit., pp. 24–69. There he starts with the Old Testament, then proceeds back to the Egyptian religion (in spite of the fact that from a historical point of view the inverse order would have been the correct one), then goes on to Mesopotamia and Phoenicia (same observation here, and quite especially Phoenicia as furnishing the historical background of the O.T. ought to have been referred to *before* the O.T.), passes to Indo-Iranian religion, to Classical religion, to Celtic, Teutonic and Slavonic religions. The author thereafter examines the material from the peoples of Eurasia, including Chinese religion, from Indonesia and Oceanian islands, Australia, and finally ends with the illiterate peoples of Africa and America. I cannot see that on principle this treatment differs from the examination of the material that I have already in the first Swedish edition of 1945 of my *Religionens värld* when dealing with the belief in a High-God.

[25] If—with Pettazzoni (p. 82)—we assign this deity to an older people speaking a Nahuatl-language, in itself of course only a hypothesis, it calls for notice that this older people must have been a people of hunters, and not at all a pastoral nomadic people because pastoral nomadism was unknown in America at the time of the arrival of the Europeans—simply for lack of suitable animals. This is a well-known fact.

tions. Already in 1938 in my phenomenological work "Hochgottglaube im alten Iran" I presented a comparison of the ideas about a High-God among African pastoral nomads and nomadic pastoral tribes of eastern Iran in antiquity. While, for my part, I was content with a phenomenological comparison restricted to pastoral nomadic peoples in Africa and Iran, Pettazzoni extended the comparison to the whole earth, trying to find in nomadic pastoral cultures the clue to the *history* of the High-God belief. By doing so he clearly transgressed the borders of phenomenology; it is therefore difficult to see that he has given any new contribution to the methods of phenomenology.

To my mind it is self-evident that there sometimes will be an overlapping between history and phenomenology. When treating of such phenomena where the historical setting is of special importance for the phenomenological interpretation it will be necessary to present the corresponding phenomena in their own structures within a given religion. As to my own work I have found it necessary to proceed like this when dealing with faith, confession, holy scriptures, and the formation of a scriptural canon, to mention but a few striking examples.[26] The individual aspect of the phenomenon may sometimes be so sharply marked that single details cannot be taken out of the structure of totality to be treated as typical and compared to and classified with other typical phenomena.

When presenting the material for a given phenomenon in the context of the whole structure of its own religion it will be possible to give not only "arrested pictures" but also a sketch of the historical development of the phenomenon in question. This I tried to do when treating of the faith and the rise of a canon of holy scriptures, and after that trying to establish the typical phenomenological features of this phenomenon. But the historical development may also be indicated within the framework of an overall phenomenological treatment of a comparative character such as I endeavoured to present in my monograph on the connections between the garb of the monk and the dress of the harlequin. Here the historical development of a given theme was followed from most remote times of common Indo-European civilization to the period of the European society in the seventeenth and eighteenth centuries.

I just referred to the structures of religious phenomena. The

[26] This tendency of mine is much more marked in the German edition *Die Welt der Religion* than in both the Swedish editions. In this regard I think I have learned something about method in the twenty-five years that have passed since I wrote the first Swedish edition of my phenomenological work.

importance of paying due attention to these structures has been emphasized by Georges Dumézil and Bleeker. The latter actually devoted a whole essay to the special problem of structures. He concentrated his attention on four elements: constant forms, irreducible factors, points of crystallization, and types. I am not going to discuss here Bleeker's idea of structure which has its great merits. What I am interested in here is the methodological problem arising for phenomenology out of the idea of structure. For it stands to reason that a given phenomenon when taken out of its structure for phenomenological comparison will lose something of its real significance which it has only when serving as part of the total structure of the individual religion. Here, obviously, a real danger lies that a phenomenological investigation may lead to highly superficial comparisons and therefore be absolutely misleading.

I already hinted at the fact that the well-known phenomenological work of van der Leeuw suffered *inter alia* from the fact that his material was taken to an excessive extent from non-literate peoples. Above all the nearly total absence of illustrative material from the great universal religions (except to some extent Christianity) should be pointed out, there surely must be something wrong with a methodological approach to the phenomenology of religion where the greatest living religions are not asked to give their contributions to the phenomenological researches, but obscure African or Indian tribal beliefs or even modern folklore are heavily drawn upon. In this regard Heiler deserves to be praised for having extensively quoted both Christian and Indian illustrative examples. That Islam so little has been utilized for phenomenological work is very regrettable. To some extent, however, this is due to the fact that some highly important phenomena as myth, sacrifice, and confession of sins, are extremely difficult or even impossible to illustrate from Islam.[27]

Last but not least a methodological principle, emphasized by Brede Kristensen [28] and Hidding [29] among others: the scholar must for every religion accept the evaluations of its believers. As Brede Kristensen rightly notes, "the concepts, 'primitive' and 'highly developed' forms of religion, are therefore fatal for historical research."

[27] In the German edition of *Die Welt der Religion* I have tried to use more Islamic material than has been the case with other phenomenological textbooks.

[28] Cf. W. Brede Kristensen, *The Meaning of Religion*, 1960, p. 13 f.

[29] Cf. K. A. H. Hidding, *De evolutie van het godsdienstig bewustzijn*, 1965, p. 7. As far as I can see Bleeker offends his own principles by trying to ascertain —from his own point of view which is, moreover, not defined at all—what religious values and elements of truth there are to be found in a given religion.

That the investigator of religion is positively interested in his subject must be taken for granted. There must be found in him an earnest will to interpret as faithfully as possible all religions with which he is occupied, but no special personal qualifications are needed.[30] This is not a question of method, however, but of personal aptitude for using the existing methods. Thus, this sometime hotly discussed problem may here be passed over in silence.

[30] It is often urged by theologians that every scholar occupied with the study of religion must himself be a "religious" man. To this it must be objected first that the borderline between "religious" and "not-religious" is extremely difficult to draw with exactitude, and second that experience shows that such an outstanding religious personality as e.g. Söderblom was absolutely unable to do justice to Islam, whereas the certainly not-religious Nöldeke was a pioneer in Islamic studies. The decisive factor is of course to be sought elsewhere.

The "Entelecheia" of Religious Phenomena [1]

C. J. Bleeker

A Dutch scholar, trained under W. Brede Kristensen in Leiden and influenced by Gerardus van der Leeuw, C. J. Bleeker was born in 1898. In the early part of his career, he was interested primarily in the religions of ancient Egypt. But gradually, then increasingly, he turned to phenomenology and worked within the church for twenty years. For a number of years he was secretary-general of the International Association for the History of Religions, and editor of that organization's journal, Numen. *In 1969 he retired from his professorship in the history of religions at the University of Amsterdam.*

It can be said without exaggeration that the student of the history of religions can theoretically survey a period of at least five thousand years, if prehistory is left aside. The oldest civilizations, those of Egypt and Mesopotamia, appeared into the bright light of history in the fourth millennium before Christ. During these five thousand years much has happened. Religions came into existence, reached their full bloom and suffered decline. Other forms of religion underwent considerable modifications as to their structure. History is an endless process in which religious phenomena are constantly either being created or transformed or broken down.

These considerations raise the question: what is the nature of the religious development that has taken place during these five thousand years of history? Can we discover any logical idea in it? In my opinion no science is better qualified to tackle this problem than the phenomenology of religion, as it possesses at least theoretically the required familiarity with the entire field of religious phenomena, both in their historical and in their geographical dimensions.

[1] This article gives in abbreviated form part of a book written by the author in Dutch, entitled *De structuur van de godsdienst*, 1956. It has been published in Scritti in onore di Guiseppe Furlani, 1957, Part II.

From C. J. Bleeker, *The Sacred Bridge. Researches into the Nature and Structure of Religion* (Leiden: E. J. Brill, 1963), pp. 16–24.

Generally the task of the phenomenology of religion is taken as a static one. It is certainly true that the significance of religious phenomena can be clarified to a great extent if they are examined, so to say, not as moving pictures but as arrested pictures. In previous studies I myself have mainly engaged in this latter kind of research, by stating a double objective for the phenomenology of religion, viz. the inquiries into the theōria and into the logos of the phenomena. The first objective, the theōria, leads to an understanding of the religious implications of various aspects of religion which occur all over the world, such as the idea of God, sacrifice and magic art. The second objective, i.e. the study of the logos of the phenomena, uncovers the hidden structure of the different religions by showing that they are built up according to strict inner laws. This short indication must suffice within the scope of this article. We have to focus our attention here on the main question which we have raised and which arises quite naturally when the religious phenomena are examined in their historical development. Scientifically formulated the question reads: does religious development during the five thousand years of history yield any proof of the existence of an entelecheia of the religious phenomena? It should be added that entelecheia is taken here in the sense which Aristotle assigned to this work, viz. the course of events in which the essence is realised by its manifestations.

By formulating the problem in this way, three theories are eliminated by implication, viz. the theories 1) of a primordial monotheism, 2) of a gradual historical evolution, and 3) of a catastrophic end of history. A few explanatory words on each of these theories. Recent studies have elucidated that the so called High Gods have played a greater part in the oldest stage of religion than a previous generation of scholars was ready to accept. However, it would be erroneous to derive from this fact a theory of primordial monotheism, brought about by a primeval revelation of God. For several reasons. Firstly the belief in a High God is nowhere in primitive religion predominant to such an extent that it totally rules out polytheism. Secondly genuine monotheism cannot be found at the beginning of the history of humanity because it is the outcome of a prophet's preaching, as R. Pettazzoni has made clear by well-known studies. Thirdly it is evident that the history of religions by its very principles is unable to decide whether or not certain historical facts, in this case the belief in a High God, are the result of a revelation of God. Moreover this theory generally leads to an evaluation of the history of religions which followed, seen as a decline from original pure religious conceptions. This view of history, though it may have religious value, cannot be used for scientific purposes, as it is built on presuppositions which pure historical research can neither prove nor reject. An analogous observation can secondly be made on evolutionism. Influenced by Darwin's idea on the origin of species scholars have tried to trace a similar evolution in the history of religions, showing how religion evolved from a simple initial stage into the highest forms known to humanity. They even thought that all types of religion could be located somewhere on this line of gradual evolution. It needs no further argument that the theory of evolutionism is totally obsolete today in the field of historical research. Two world wars have sharpened the eye for the fact that the historical development is frequently interrupted by a tragical cultural relapse. This holds also true for the history of religions in which no unbroken line of evolution can whatsoever be discerned. Thirdly no theory of a catastrophical end of history, whether it derives from the Christian doctrine of eschatology which expects the coming of the Kingdom of God sooner or later, or is prompted by modern pessimism which considers European civilization as being worn out, can shed light on the enigmatic nature of the historical course of events. There is no convincing proof that religion after having flourished in former times is on its decline since the beginning of modern history so that a total collapse of the spiritual forces must be feared in the near future.

By asking for a possible entelecheia of the religious phenomena the student of the history of religions approaches the object of his study in an unbiased way. He knows that history is a narrative of continuous changes. The essential question therefore is whether there is any sense in this endless flux of happenings. In my opinion the phenomenology of religion is able to clarify this problem to a certain extent. To this end the question of the entelecheia should be divided into four subsidiary questions.

The first is the question regarding our knowledge of the origin of religion. Is it possible to discover at which time religion was born, as it were? People generally are very keen on knowing the origin of things and religion is quite naturally the object of the same curiosity. In order to solve this question scholars have sought guidance from two different disciplines, prehistory and primitive religion, for apparently obvious reasons. During prehistory the homo sapiens came into existence. At a certain moment religious belief must have dawned upon him. What was the character of this primeval religion? This knowledge is thought to be of primary importance because it is believed that the knowledge of the oldest form of religion will afford the best insight into its true nature. However this may be, prehistory gives only very vague informations. Sometimes we find traces of a worship of the dead, in other cases vestiges of a cult of the sun or of a female deity. But no answer is given to the question of the origin of religion. Neither does primitive religion help us in clarifying the problem. It is a fallacy to think that primitive religion represents the oldest stage of religion. Primitive religion has a history of its own though this history has nowhere been written down. This means that at the time when European explorers met primitive religion it has long ago passed the initial religious stage where religion is supposed to have come into existence.

This negative result should act as a challenge to scrutinize the question itself. Why are people interested in the origin of religion? The answer is that they hope to discover a point at which they can observe how religion arises from non-religious factors. This is another fallacy. Religion always starts by itself and cannot be deduced from non-religious elements. The conclusion is that history gives no answer to the question of the origin of religion. In order to make sense the problem should be approcahed in a psychological way, viz., how religion has arisen in the course of history and how it originates today. Much could be said about the circumstances under which religion appears. But the real reason for its origin is beyond scientific comprehension. Religion appears spontaneously. The same must have been true for primeval times.

Secondly we have to look for characteristics in the course of the history of religions which point to a certain historical logic. Under this heading the problem should be brought of religions that have died out. To this category all religions of antiquity belong. Why did they die? Apparently religions also obey the biological law of birth, growth, maturation and death as the successive stages of the life-cycle. Several reasons could even be enumerated why certain religions have disappeared: they were too intimately bound up with a type of society that had become obsolete; they were superseded by a more vigorous religion of a higher quality. In general we are used to say: their strength was spent. But these explanations are not at all satisfactory. There is something mysterious in the fact that religions which during centuries had provided their adherents with spiritual food, such as the religions of ancient Egypt and Greece, or Manicheism, have died. Their disappearance means a religious loss. This process has repeated itself many times up to the present. It cannot be doubted that in the course of history certain religious values and elements of truth are lost.

However, this loss is compensated by religious gain. New religions have appeared on the stage and have replaced the older ones. Their emergence can not be fully explained by historical considerations, since they make a completely fresh start. All will understand which type of religion is meant, viz. the religion of Zarathustra, the Jewish religion, Buddhism, Christianity and Islam, religions which are characterised by the fact that they bear the mark of their founder who by revelation or by enlightenment received the truth which he preached. It can be doubted whether these founders really made a new beginning. It is a well-known fact that Zarathustra made use of several ancient Iranian numina for his theology, that Moses went back to the faith of the Patriarchs, that the background of the teaching of Buddha is formed by certain currents in Brahmanism, that many sayings of Jesus are to be found in the rabbinical writings and that Mohammed borrowed his main ideas from Judaism and Christianity. Yet the originality of these prophets and teachers is an established fact, and for two reasons: a) they have discovered the true nature of the god whom their compatriots had known long before, or rather, they received a decisive religious truth by revelation or by enlightenment, b) they have laid down once for all the pattern of the religion which they founded, to which pattern all its adherents are bound. In my opinion the emergence of this type of religions proves the existence of the entelecheia of the religious phenomena, entelecheia understood here as a non-evolutionistic concept in which creative forces play their part. Though from the dawn of human history man had a vague notion of what religion is, men as Zarathustra, Moses, Buddha, Jesus and Mohammed added new life and fresh colours to these well-known ideas. By their work religion suddenly reached a higher level of self-realisation.

It is perhaps even possible to distinguish something of the rhythm dominating this process of the ripening of religion. H. Frick, following the footsteps of Rudolf Otto, in his booklet "Vergleichende Religionswissenschaft" has drawn up a schedule of two series of parallel religious events which occurred in Israël, Greece, China, and India. In the eighth and seventh century before Christ the first prophets appear in Israël, religion rises to a higher level in Greece, history starts in China, Brahmanism comes about in India. In the sixth to the fourth century Ezekiel and the Second Isaïah proclaim a universal monotheism, Plato and Aristotle teach their philosophies, Lau-tse and Confucius spread their wisdom, Buddha preaches his doctrine of salvation. These are striking parallels though it can not be denied that their number is scant and that Frick's schedule is somewhat arbitrary. We are on a safer ground when considering the dynamics governing the religions which owe their origin to a founder. The founder is mostly succeeded by a generation of theologians and teachers whose task it is to expound and to guard the revealed truth. They stand for orthodoxy. A class of priests is formed to whom the fostering of religion has become a profession. Tradition gains more and more in authority. Unfortunately this tradition, so carefully protected, has the effect on the one hand of stifling true faith and on the other hand of evoking vigorous protests. In the last case a reformer appears before the floodlights of history. The significance of his act of reformation is not the discovery of a completely new truth, but the reinterpretation of the fundamental principles of his religion. This is not only true of Luther, Calvin and Zwingli, the famous Christian reformers, but also of all non-Christian reformers, for instance in Japanese Buddhism. This phenomenon shows that religion never totally loses its original creative force. This power of regeneration is part of the entelecheia of the religious phenomena.

Thirdly, attention should be paid to the problem of impure religion. This is really a delicate problem. The phenomenology of religion would forgo its fundamental principle of impartiality if it made a distinction between true and false religion. For it should refrain from passing any judgment on the metaphysical truth of religion. However, it can not evade stating the difference between pure and impure religion. This means that certain phenomena must be labelled as belonging to the field of pseudo-religion. It is evident that this judgment is pertinent in those cases in which human ideas and values are exalted to the dignity of the divine. This occurs when science, art, technology or politics try to play the part of religion. The same is true of the way in which the ideologies of the Nazis and of the Communists sometimes have functioned or are still functioning, notwithstanding the fervour with which these ideas may be professed. It is more difficult to assess the religious value of various modern exotic sects which flourish thanks to the fact that a large part of our generation is spiritually uprooted. Do these forms of belief represent superstition, a substitute for religion or religious truth? A legitimate question which is not easily answered because the phenomenology of religion is lacking unequivocal criteria to test the religious validity of these phenomena. Nevertheless this problem cannot be evaded. It could even work as an incitement to make inquiries into the origin and the development of modern types of belief, thereby giving new insight into the nature and the religious quality of several products of contemporary history of religions.

It is easier to pass a judgment on the so-called Satanism. People have always existed who worshipped the devil because they considered him mightier than God. Witches are believed to have concluded a pact with the devil. There are also rumours that now and then "la messe noir" has been celebrated as a parody of the true mass. Apparently these phenomena are alien to true religion however interesting they may be from the point of the historian of religion. The belief in witches is mainly part of mass-psychology and the witch herself should be an object of psychopathological research. Satanism is a spiritual aberration which cannot be taken seriously.

To a certain extent the satanists were honest in professing their belief in evil. Several times religious people are shrewd hypocrites bearing a mask behind which unbelief is concealed. This leads to some interesting observations on the part which falsehood is playing in religion. Belief is theoretically thought to be identical with sincerity. Nevertheless the lie which permeates the whole society is also subtly intertwined with religion. It is even sometimes officially accepted, for instance in the shape of the pia fraus. Let us take the magician as a striking example. His magic art is partly a make-belief of which, curiously enough, he himself and the persons present are the victims, though they must know that they are pretending. It is deceit committed in good faith. It is hard to tell in how far the magician believes in his art and to which extent he is conscious of the fact that he is deceiving people by his manipulations and his formulae.

Pia fraus is a children's sin compared with other forms of corruption of religion which have never failed to rouse severe criticism. So it has been said that religion is nothing but ill diguised sensuality or ambition. These are the two vices which time and again rouse moral indignation. Surely, it cannot be denied that sexuality makes an important impact on religion. However it is needless to argue with people who teach that religion is the direct outcome of sexual impulses. They refute themselves by their exaggerations. This problem is only interesting to the student of the phenomenology of religion when he is confronted with types of religion in which sexual symbols and practices play a certain role, for instance the cult of the phallus and temple-prostitution. These phenomena offend the ethical conceptions of modern man. Here the phenomenology of religion shows the way out by teaching that in Antiquity people had another evaluation of sexuality than modern man. To them it was a manifestation of divine, creative energy, so that temple-prostitution for instance was no sign of deliberate debauchery. As to ambition, it is true that religion is often used to subjugate people. However, the well-known accusation against kings and priests that by a secret pact they cooperate in oppressing their subjects in the name of religion, can easily be refuted by the history of religions. Recent studies have thrown sufficient light upon the sacral king of Antiquity, for instance. We know for certain that he was no dictator, as he is often described, but a prince ruling his people according to divine commandments and therefore bearing a heavy responsibility. It is quite clear that this divine commission has not always prevented these sacral rulers from acting tyrannically. As to the priests it can not be doubted that they, generally speaking, have always performed their office with sincerity, notwithstanding the undeniable fact that sinful passions and the lust for power have corrupted a lot of them. These brief observations on the problem of impure religion must suffice. It is a complicated and much neglected subject. Its significance for our trend of argument becomes clear when we ask whether religion in the course of history has been able to purify itself from this kind of spiritual infection.

Therefore our last question must be whether the phenomenology of religion produces evidence of a gradual rising of the religious level. Does the development which the history of religions describes imply a purification of religion? It is evident that this question touches the most crucial and at the time the most vital point in the search for the entelecheia of the religious phenomena. An answer can only be given in a tentative way by the following remarks: a) A gradual change in the trend of religious thinking can be noticed and thereby an increase of the discerning power. The magical world conception has given way to a more realistic outlook. The people of Antiquity for instance believed in the interrelation and in the mutual participation of religious symbols and ideas in a way which we hardly understand any longer. They also mingled religious values with secular elements. Modern man has a clearer view of what is genuinely religious, is more able to distinguish the religious from the secular, and makes higher demands as to the quality of religion. b) It can hardly be debated that the religions which owe their origin to a founder, have made a decisive contribution to the spiritualization of religion. This does not imply an undervaluation of the religious quality of the religions of primitive people and of Antiquity. The latter are unique in themselves. Neither should it be overlooked that these religions show a slow increase of their spiritual level, marked for instance by a tendency towards heno-theism. Nevertheless it is a fact that the so-called world-religions have offered humanity a new and purer conception of God. c) In these religions a process is in operation which might be called a retarded chain-reaction. This means that from time to time a religious revival bursts out. Inspired by the original spirit of their religion the initiators of these movements plead for a new interpretation of the fundamental ideas of their belief and a better application of God's commandments to the present situation of society. Thereby they bring about a rising of the religious level.

Exploring the entelecheia of the religious phenomena is a hazard-ous undertaking. The points of support are few. Facts that seem to speak in favour of an entelecheia can easily be nullified by a broad description of the many cases of retrogression and of religious cor-ruption. Nevertheless this article has shown we hope that traces of an entelecheia can be discovered. It should only be clearly stated that this entelecheia is no evolutionistic concept. It rather operates accord-ing to the historical law formulated by A. J. Toynbee, viz. the law of challenge and response. Each relapse seems to evoke in religious people strong desire for and an attempt of restoring religion. Actually this effort results in a rising of the religious level. The phenomenology of religion teaches us that religion is man's inseparable companion. It is an invincible, creative and self-regenerating force. So there is good reason for applying the old proverb: *magna est veritas et prevalebit.*

Selected Bibliography

Egyptian Festivals (Leiden: E. J. Brill, 1967).
The Sacred Bridge (Leiden: E. J. Brill, 1963).
See also *Liber Amicorum. Studies in Honour of Professor Dr. C. J. Bleeker* (Leiden: E. J. Brill, 1969), for additional bibliography.

Tripartitism in Indo-European Mythology

C. Scott Littleton on Georges Dumézil

Georges Dumézil, who was born in 1898 and now teaches in Paris, has become well known for two reasons. First, he is widely recognized as the world's leading authority on the religion and culture of proto-Indo-European peoples. Second, he is the author of the theory of "tripartitism," which has been gaining respect among anthropologists, ethnologists, folklorists, cultural historians, and historians of religion. According to this theory, the religious behavior and expressions of a large number of peoples—not simply those of Indo-European culture—exhibit the same basic tripartite social and cultural pattern. In commenting on this, Mircea Eliade has listed some examples: ". . . Dumézil has convincingly shown that the Indian mind elaborated the original scheme in cosmological terms while the Romans have 'historicized' the mythological data, so that the most archaic, and the only genuine, Roman mythology is to be deciphered in the 'historical' personages and events described by Titus Livius in the first book of his Histories" *(Mircea Eliade,* The Quest *(Chicago: University of Chicago Press, 1969), p. 33). C. Scott Littleton provides an outline for Dumézil's proposals in the reading selection that follows.*

Perhaps the best way to introduce Professor Dumézil's system is to consider it in context.[1] Let us begin, as he often begins, with the ancient I-E speaking communities of northern India.

As is well known, classical Indian social organization was composed of four main castes: the *Brahmans,* or priests, the *Kṣatriyas* (Rajputs), or warriors, the *Vaiśyas,* or cultivators, and the *Śūdras,* or those whose obligation was to serve all the rest. Of these castes, only the first three

---

[1] For a more detailed discussion of Dumezil's theories, see Littleton's book, *The New Comparative Mythology: An Anthropological Assessment of the Theories of Georges Dumezil* (Berkeley: University of California Press, 1966).

From C. Scott Littleton, "The Comparative Indo-European Mythology of Georges Dumézil," in *Journal of the Folklore Institute* (Indiana University). Vol. I (1964), pp. 149–162.

were defined as *Arya*, a description which, like the word "Navajo," seems originally to have meant simply people or 'human beings';[2] the *Śūdras*, thus were "out-castes" in the best sense of the term and in theory, at least, included the conquered, indigenous population. In its broad outlines, this system still obtains, despite the proliferation of sub-castes within each major group and the fact that today the line between *Vaiśya* and *Śūdra* is by no means clearly defined in many regions, especially in South India.

If one analyzes the ancient Sanskrit religious literature, Dumézil claims, one can see that the earliest Indian pantheon reflected this stratified social organization, especially the three *Arya* castes. Even in the oldest of all Indian texts, the *Rig Veda*,[3] there can be found three hierarchically ranked, functionally differentiated strata of gods—a pattern that appears over and over again in the later *Vedas* and *Brāhmaṇas*, and indeed persists, in a somewhat altered form, in the great Indian epic, the *Mahābārata*.

At the highest of these three divine levels appear the sovereign gods, Mitra and Varuṇa. The characteristics of these two deities are such that in Dumézil's opinion they are projections—or collective representations—of the *Brahman* caste which, of course, in the mortal scheme of things, is at the apex of the social system. Moreover, Dumézil has concluded that there exists between the two gods in question a definite division of supernatural labor as regards the management of the universe. On the one hand, Mitra is concerned with the rational and legal aspects of sovereignty; indeed, Meillet, as early as 1907, had suggested that Mitra might be the personification of the idea of 'Contract.' Varuṇa, on the other hand, represents the awesome and sometimes terrible magico-religious aspects of sovereignty. Thus, respectively, Mitra and Varuṇa reflect the two basic functions of the *Brahman*: (1) to serve as an arbiter of legal and contractual disputes, and (2) to serve as a magical and religious practitioner, conducting sacrifices, divining, performing marriages, etc. Here, then, is an example of what Dumézil has labeled the "first function": the relationship or correspondence between Mitra and Varuṇa, together with

[2] Dumézil and Paul Thieme have engaged in a long running debate over the meaning of the Skt. root *ari-*. The latter has suggested that it means 'foreigner' or 'stranger,' while the former has maintained that it is simply an ethnic self-identification term, like 'Navajo.'

[3] The hymns of the *Rig Veda* do not present a fully developed picture of the classical Indian castes or *varna*, although the roots of the words later used as caste designations (e.g. *Brahman*, from *brah-*) are indeed present; see Dumézil, *Jupiter, Mars, Quirinus* (Paris, 1941), pp. 20–30; *Mitra-Varuṇa, essai sur deux représentations indoeuropéennes de la souveraineté*, 2nd ed. Paris, 1948.

their celestial "assistants," so to speak (a set of lesser deities who share certain aspects of the sovereignty: e.g., Bhaga, Aryaman) and the priestly caste or class (as it appears to have been in the earliest period). In summarizing the nature of the "first function," Dumézil claims that it is concerned with " . . . *l'administration à la fois mysterieuse et réguliére du monde.*"

At the second supernatural level one finds a set of young, virile, warlike gods (i.e., the *Maruts*), dominated by the imposing figure of Indra, who is the personification of the warrior ideal. It is Indra who fights monsters (e.g., Vṛta), leads armies, and, unlike Mitra and Varuṇa, generally gains his ends through the exercise of physical strength. Indra, thus, is a collective representation of the *Kṣatriya* caste, whose prime function is to protect the society against the threat or actuality of armed invasion. This relationship, then, between the warrior caste or class and its personifications constitutes the "second function."

Finally, at the lowest level, there appear a number of deities whose principal function is to maintain and promote plant and animal fertility, to assure bountiful harvests, and generally to preside over matters of human physical well-being and comfort. Chief among these are the *Aśvins*, of 'Divine Twins.' Also included here (and elsewhere, as we shall see) is a female figure, the goddess Sarasvatī. This lowest divine stratum, the occupants of which are seen as collectively representing the food-producing class, constitutes the "third function," which is defined as " . . . *la fécondité, avec beaucoup de consequences et de resonances, telles que la santé, la longue vie, la tranquillité, la volupté, le 'nombre'.*"

Thus, in brief, is the picture Dumézil draws of ancient Indian myth and society: three functionally integrated strata of men and gods, dominated by the conception of a joint or dual sovereignty shared by a pair of gods representing, respectively, juridical and magico-religious processes. Together, these strata, or "functions," form an integrated social and supernatural whole.

If the foregoing system were limited to Vedic India, it would be difficult to generalize it as I-E. But as noted earlier, Dumézil has attempted to demonstrate the presence of these same three functions, as well as the concept of joint sovereignty, in the myths and social structures of most of the ancient I-E speaking communities. Outside of India, his best evidence so far comes from the rest of the Indo-Iranian speaking region, as well as from those regions historically associated with Italic, Germanic, and Celtic speaking peoples.

As far as Iran itself is concerned, it is in the theological reforms of Zoroaster (seventh-sixth centuries B.C.) that Dumézil sees the clearest expression of the I-E system. In attempting to substitute an ethical and metaphysical dualism for the ancient Iranian polytheism—a polytheism which appears to have been broadly similar to that of Vedic India—Zoroaster conceived of a series of more or less abstract beings as part of the retinue, so to speak, of the Good Principle (Ahura Mazda). These beings, labeled *Ameša Spentas* ("Immortal Beneficent Ones"), remarkably parallel the Indic gods previously discussed: *Aša* ("Order") and *Vohu Manah* ("Good Thought"), respectively, correspond to Varuna and Mitra and can thus be viewed as representatives of the first function; *Xšathra* ("Dominion") parallels Indra and represents the second function; the pair *Haurvatāt* ("Health") and *Ameretāt* ("Immortality") parallel the *Ašvins* and relate to the third function, as does the female figure *Armāiti* ("Pious Thought"), a Zoroastrian version of the archaic Iranian goddess Anahita and a counterpart of the previously mentioned *Sarasvatī*.

Turning our attention to the West, Dumézil claims to have uncovered some excellent examples of social and supernatural tripartition in early Rome. And here, in my opinion, he has made a most important contribution to scholarship, whatever may prove to be the fate of his over-all system.

At first glance, Rome appears to have possessed a culture characterized by an abundance of ritual and a paucity of myth. There is Virgil; there is Ovid; there are numerous identifications between Roman and Greek divinities; but on the surface, at least, there seems to be little in the way of native Roman myth. However, after an exhaustive examination of the admittedly legendary early history of the city, as found in the first books of Livy and elsewhere, Dumézil has concluded that Rome's myths had indeed become euphemerized. In a brilliant series of works devoted to the subject (1941–1948), he finds in the persons of Romulus, Numa, and the warlike Tullus Hostilius, the three earliest kings of Rome, the characteristic gods of the joint sovereignty (Romulus equaling Varuna and Numa Mitra), as well as that of the second function (Tullus Hostilius equaling Indra). The third function is less clearly evident, although Dumézil feels it was represented by the Sabines, who were traditionally viewed as devotees of luxury. . . .

Among the Celts, although Dumézil and his students have uncovered a number of tripartitions which do seem to relate to the three assumed I-E functions—for example, the traditions surrounding the three Machas of Ulster, one of whom was a prophetess, the wife of Nemed the Sacred, the second a female warrior who fought her way to the throne, and the third the beautiful wife of a farmer, to whom she brought additional riches and presented twins—no over-all division of either the Irish, Brythonic, or Gallic pantheons has yet been made with any degree of certainty. This, of course, is in large part due to our imperfect knowledge of these pantheons, especially that of ancient Gaul. As far as the latter is concerned, more often than not we are forced to rely upon the *interpretatio romana*, which, it would appear, was in many cases quite arbitrary and based upon political expediency. For reasons too detailed to enumerate here, Dumézil claims that the three Gallic techniques of human sacrifice, as reported by Lucan and others, represent a tripartite formula and that each technique can be seen as ensuring the social and supernatural effectiveness of one of the three I-E functions. Thus, hanging from a tree related to the first function, burning in a wicker basket related to the second, and drowning in a keg ensured the effectiveness of the third.

Elsewhere among the early I-E speaking communities the evidence is at best much less abundant and in all cases less certain. Among the Greeks, for example, despite the fact that their mythology is perhaps the best known of all the world's mythologies, only a few hints of the tripartite system have as yet been detected.[4] As far as the pantheon is concerned, the Dioscuri, or 'Heavenly Twins,' do indeed seem to correspond to the *twins* . . . and can, in Dumézil's eyes, be reckoned as representing the third function. The other two levels, however, are not clearly defined; e.g. Zeus, like Mithra, exhibits traits characteristic of both the first and second functions. The chief of the Olympians achieves his ends through a combination of magical spells (cf. Varuṇa) and physical force (cf. Indra), and at the same time upholds universal order and the sanctity of oaths and contracts (cf. Mitra).

Perhaps the best single Greek example of mythological tripartition so far uncovered concerns the well-known "judgment of Paris," wherein the Trojan prince must choose between the regal Hera, the warlike Athena, and the voluptuous Aphrodite. So as to influence

---

[4] The difficulty here, it seems, results in large part from the fact that the Greeks, like the Hittites . . . were so profoundly influenced by the non-I-E civilizations of the eastern Mediterranean and that this is reflected throughout their myths and epics; see Dumézil, *L'idéologie tripartie des Indo-Européens*, p. 91. Palmer, working independently, has attempted to demonstrate the presence of a tripartite, feudal social structure in the newly translated Mycenaean texts and has asserted that same pattern was characteristic of the earlier stages of the Hittite Empire as revealed by the texts found at Boghazköy . . . See L. R. Palmer, *Achaeans and Indo-Europeans, an Inaugural Lecture* (Oxford, 1955), pp. 1–21.

him in his choice, each goddess, here seen as a representative of one of the three functions, offers Paris a gift: Hera offers world sovereignty (first function), Athena promises military prowess (second function), and Aphrodite tenders the gift of earthly pleasure (third function). Paris chooses the latter goddess and thus, by alienating Hera and Athena (i.e., the first two functions), ensures Troy's ultimate downfall.[5]

In addition to the gods of the three functions, Dumézil asserts that in most of the I-E pantheons there are certain deities who must be viewed as essentially outside any one level of the tripartite structure; gods (and goddesses) whose function is to support or integrate this structure by summing together in their persons traits characteristic of all three levels. . . .

Finally, as was mentioned earlier, Dumézil claims that this characteristic and uniquely I-E tendency to view phenomena as divided into three hierarchically ranked strata became a deeply ingrained habit of thought; it became, in short, an ideology. As a result, replications of tripartite formulas, including tripartitions within tripartitions, are frequently encountered by Dumézil and his colleagues. For example, it is noted that threefold divisions of the universe, wherein the upper atmosphere is assigned to the first function, the lower atmosphere to the second, and the earth itself to the third, can be found throughout the later Indic literature; and that exhortations, like that found in the famous inscription of Darius at Behistun, to preserve the sanctity of contracts, to defend the society against foreign invasion, and to guard against famine and plague, as well as tripartite divisions of catastrophes into those affecting, respectively, the sovereignty, the military, and the food supply, are found repeatedly—from the Irish *Lebor Gabala* (or "Book of Conquests") to the *Śatapatha Brāhmana*.

Selected Bibliography

Aspects de la fonction querrière chez les Indo-Européens (Paris: Presses Universitaires de France, 1956).

Les dieux des Germains: essai sur la formation de la religion Scandinave (Paris: Presses Universitaires de France, 1959).

---

[5] Dumézil, "Les trois fonctions dans quelques traditions grecques," in *Hommages à Lucien Febvre*, II (Paris, 1953), pp. 25–32. Another important expression of the three functions can be found in Homer's description of the shield of Achilles (*Iliad*, Book 18) wherein the unfolding order of scenes—lawgiving, a city under siege, pastoral activities—seems to conform to the I-E model.

Les dieux des Indo-Européens (Paris: Presses Universitaires de France, 1952).

Le festin d'immortalité: étude de mythologies comparée indo-européen (Paris: P. Geuther, 1924).

L'ideologie tripartie des Indo-Européens (Paris: Presses Universitaires de France, 1948).

La religion romaine archaique avec un appendix sur la religion des Etrusques (Paris: Payot, 1966).

"The Three Last Voyages of Il'ja of Murom," in *Myths and Symbols: Studies in Honor of Mircea Eliade*, eds. Joseph M. Kitagawa and Charles H. Long (Chicago: University of Chicago Press, 1969), pp. 153–162.

For a comprehensive bibliography of Georges Dumézil's works see the appendix to *Hommages à Georges Dumézil*. Collection Latomus XLV (Brussels: Revue d'Etudes Latines, 1966).

On the Morphology of Religious Experience

MIRCEA ELIADE

Perhaps more responsible than any other scholar for the recent upsurge of interest in the history of religions, particularly in America, Mircea Eliade was born in Bucharest, Romania, on March 9, 1907. He received his education in Bucharest, his M.A. degree in 1928 (after doing a treatise on Italian philosophy from Ficino to Bruno), and his Ph.D. (with a dissertation on Yoga) in 1932. From 1928 to 1932 Eliade lived in India, principally in Calcutta, where he traveled extensively and studied both Sanskrit and Indian philosophy under the guidance of Professor Surendranath Dasgupta. He returned to teach in Bucharest in 1933. In 1940 he was sent to the Romanian Legation in London as cultural attaché. Within a year he was transferred to Lisbon where he remained until 1945. In 1945 he went to Paris as a visiting professor at the Ecole des Hautes Etudes of the Sorbonne, then came to the University of Chicago in 1945. Since 1958 he has been Sewell Avery Distinguished Service Professor in the University of Chicago. Technically, Eliade is known as a writer (of both fiction and nonfiction), historian of religion, and orientalist. His interests and talents in these areas, however, have also carried him into a variety of other areas. As one of his biographers has written: "We must also recognize that from his early youth on Eliade has been inclined toward diversified activity. His work is so many-sided that it is precisely this that causes difficulty in approaching it and surveying it. Any single way of considering his work may prove, after a short time, to be too one-sided in comparison with the many-sidedness of his works and endeavors." (Günther Spaltmann, "Authenticity and Experience of Time: Remarks on Mircea Eliade's Literary Works," in Myths and Symbols: Studies in Honor of Mircea Eliade, *Joseph M. Kitagawa and Charles H. Long, eds. (Chicago: University of Chicago Press, 1969, p. 372). Spaltmann goes on to call Eliade a "polymath."*

Man becomes aware of the sacred because it manifests itself, shows itself, as something wholly different from the profane. To designate the *act of manifestation* of the sacred, we have proposed the term *hierophany*. It is a fitting term, because it does not imply anything further; it expresses no more than is implicit in its etymological content, *i.e.*, that *something sacred shows itself to us*.[1] It could be said that the history of religions—from the most primitive to the most highly developed—is constituted by a great number of hierophanies, by manifestations of sacred realities. From the most elementary hierophany —*e.g.*, manifestation of the sacred in some ordinary object, a stone or a tree—to the supreme hierophany (which, for a Christian, is the incarnation of God in Jesus Christ) there is no solution of continuity. In each case we are confronted by the same mysterious act—the manifestation of something of a wholly different order, a reality that does not belong to our world, in objects that are an integral part of our natural "profane" world.

The modern Occidental experiences a certain uneasiness before many manifestations of the sacred. He finds it difficult to accept the fact that, for many human beings, the sacred can be manifested in stones or trees, for example. But as we shall soon see, what is involved is not a veneration of the stone in itself, a cult of the tree in itself. The sacred tree, the sacred stone are not adored as stone or tree; they are worshipped precisely because they are *hierophanies*, because they show something that is no longer stone or tree but the *sacred*, the *ganz andere*.

It is impossible to overemphasize the paradox represented by every hierophany, even the most elementary. By manifesting the sacred, any object becomes *something else*, yet it continues to remain *itself*, for it continues to participate in its surrounding cosmic milieu. A *sacred stone* remains a *stone*; apparently (or, more precisely, from the profane point of view), nothing distinguishes it from all other stones. But for those to whom a stone reveals itself as sacred, its immediate reality is transmuted into a supernatural reality. In other words, for those who have a religious experience all nature is capable of revealing itself as cosmic sacrality. The cosmos in its entirety can become a hierophany.

The man of the archaic societies tends to live as much as possible *in* the sacred or in close proximity to consecrated objects. The tendency is perfectly understandable, because, for primitives as for the

---

[1] Cf. Mircea Eliade, *Patterns in Comparative Religion* (New York: Sheed & Ward, 1958), pp. 7 ff.

man of all premodern societies, the *sacred* is equivalent to a *power*, and, in the last analysis, to *reality*. The sacred is saturated with *being*. Sacred power means reality and at the same time enduringness and efficacy. The polarity sacred-profane is often expressed as an opposition between *real* and *unreal* or pseudoreal. (Naturally, we must not expect to find the archaic languages in possession of this philosophical terminology, *real-unreal*, etc.; but we find the *thing*.) Thus it is easy to understand that religious man deeply desires *to be*, to participate in *reality*, to be saturated with power. . . .

The abyss that divides the two modalities of experience—sacred and profane—will be apparent when we come to describe sacred space and the ritual building of the human habitation, or the varieties of the religious experience of time, or the relations of religious man to nature and the world of tools, or the consecration of human life itself, the sacrility with which man's vital functions (food, sex, work, and so on) can be charged. Simply calling to mind what the city or the house, nature, tools, or work have become for modern and nonreligious man will show with the utmost vividness all that distinguishes such a man from a man belonging to any archaic society, or even from a peasant of Christian Europe. For modern consciousness, a physiological act— eating, sex, and so on—is in sum only an organic phenomenon, however much it may still be encumbered by tabus (imposing, for example, particular rules for "eating properly" or forbidding some sexual behavior disapproved by social morality). But for the primitive, such an act is never simply physiological; it is, or can become, a sacrament, that is, a communion with the sacred.

The reader will very soon realize that *sacred* and *profane* are two modes of being in the world, two existential situations assumed by man in the course of his history. These modes of being in the world are not of concern only to the history of religions or to sociology; they are not the object only of historical, sociological, or ethnological study. In the last analysis, the *sacred* and *profane* modes of being depend upon the different positions that man has conquered in the cosmos; hence they are of concern both to the philosopher and to anyone seeking to discover the possible dimensions of human existence.

It is for this reason that, though he is a historian of religions, the author of this book proposes not to confine himself only to the perspective of his particular science. The man of the traditional societies is admittedly a *homo religiosus*, but his behavior forms part of the general behavior of mankind and hence is of concern to philosophical anthropology, to phenomenology, to psychology. . . .

Our primary concern is to present the specific dimensions of religious experience, to bring out the differences between it and profane experience of the world. I shall not dwell on the variations that religious experience of the world has undergone in the course of time. It is obvious, for example, that the symbolisms and cults of Mother Earth, of human and agricultural fertility, of the sacrality of woman, and the like, could not develop and constitute a complex religious system except through the discovery of agriculture; it is equally obvious that a preagricultural society, devoted to hunting, could not feel the sacrality of Mother Earth in the same way or with the same intensity. Hence there are differences in religious experience explained by differences in economy, culture, and social organization—in short, by history. Nevertheless, between the nomadic hunters and the sedentary cultivators there is a similarity in behavior that seems to us infinitely more important than their differences: *both live in a sacralized cosmos*, both share in a cosmic sacrality manifested equally in the animal world and in the vegetable world. We need only compare their existential situations with that of a man of the modern societies, *living in a desacralized cosmos*, and we shall immediately be aware of all that separates him from them. At the same time we realize the validity of comparisons between religious facts pertaining to different cultures; all these facts arise from a single type of behavior, that of *homo religiosus*.

Selected Bibliography

Cosmos and History (New York: Harper & Row, Publishers, Inc., 1959).

The Forge and the Crucible (New York: Harper & Row, Publishers, Inc., 1962).

Images and Symbols (New York: Sheed & Ward, 1961).

Myth and Reality (New York: Harper & Row, Publishers, Inc., 1963).

Myths, Dreams and Mysteries (New York: Harper & Row, Publishers, Inc., 1960).

Patterns in Comparative Religion (New York: The World Publishing Company, 1958).

The Quest (Chicago: University of Chicago Press, 1969).

Rites and Symbols of Initiation (New York: Harper & Row, Publishers, Inc., 1965).

Shamanism: Archaic Techniques of Ecstasy (New York: Bollingen Foundation, 1964).

The Two and the One (New York: Harper & Row, Publishers, Inc., 1965).

Yoga, Immortality and Freedom (New York: Harper & Row, Publishers, Inc., 1958).

From Primitives to Zen (New York: Harper & Row, Publishers, Inc., 1967).

The History of Religions: Essays in Methodology, with Joseph Kitagawa (Chicago: University of Chicago Press, 1959), and *The History of Religions: Essays in the Problem of Understanding* (Chicago: University of Chicago Press, 1967).

See also the bibliography of works by Mircea Eliade in *Myths and Symbols: Studies in Honor of Mircea Eliade* (Chicago: University of Chicago Press, 1969), pp. 417–433.

The Structures of Human Behavior in Society

Harold W. Scheffler on claude lévi-strauss

Claude Lévi-Strauss was born in Brussels, Belgium, on November 28, 1908. He studied philosophy and law at the University of Paris. From 1935 to 1939 he taught at the University of São Paulo in Brazil, where he did anthropological fieldwork among the natives of the Amazon jungle. From 1939 through 1947 he served in the army, taught in New York City, and worked as a cultural attaché at the French embassy in Washington, D.C. In 1947 he returned to France, and has been professor of social anthropology at the College de France since 1960. Drawing on the methods of contemporary linguistics, Lévi-Strauss has been especially interested in isolating the "structures" of man's cultural experience. Because of this interest and his work on the logic of "the savage mind," he has been able to inspire a veritable school of "structuralists" as well as a popular following. Commenting on the attention given Lévi-Strauss, E. Nelson Hayes and Tanya Hayes have written:

> Some of the reasons for this extreme interest are readily identified. In his seeming rejection of history and humanism, in his refusal to see Western civilization as privileged and unique, in his view of the human mind as programmed, in his emphasis on form over content, and in his insistence that the savage mind is not inferior to the civilized, Lévi-Strauss appeals to the deepest feelings among the alienated and disenchanted intellectuals of our society (in Claude Lévi-Strauss: The Anthropologist as Hero, Cambridge, Mass.: The M.I.T. Press, 1970).

Harold W. Scheffler makes Lévi-Strauss' intentions and accomplishments explicit in the essay that follows.

Most men do not take the universe or their experiences of it, which they confound with it, to be disorderly. Few of us are given even the opportunity to do so, for our societies provide us with ready-made orders which we at first learn as best we can and then later perhaps contribute to or modify, thus sometimes discovering something of the arbitrariness in the relatively serviceable orders we habitually recognize.

These ready-made orders, or sets of "models" of and for experience, we may call a society's *culture,* and the anthropologist assumes, from profitable experience with the assumption, that culture is one of the most powerful constraints on human behavior. This is not to suggest that culture is the sole determinant of human-behavior-in-society. It is simply that men act in accord with their "definitions of situations" and their "rules" for dealing with those situations; in the light of such definitions and rules their behavior may be seen to be rational and therefore comprehensible to us. Most of the supposed "irrational" or "illogical" behavior of so-called primitive people has, on closer inspection, proven to be no more than behavior which differs from what we would expect in a given situation, and the behavior differs because the participants define or conceive of the situation differently than we would.

We have found then that if we can isolate and describe a people's models for perceiving, relating and otherwise interpreting their experiences we have gone a long way towards accounting for their behavior. Such accounts are by no means exhaustive, but they are essential components of any explanation of human social behavior. They invite rather than exclude other modes of explanatory synthesis.

To present such an account is not a simple unproblematic task; the pitfalls are numerous. In order to do so, we must first develop methods for isolating and describing other people's models (ethnographic methods), and these must minimize the danger of foreshortening the process and uncritically imposing alien models. (There is a complementary danger, less well recognized, of refusing to admit that other people's models may at times be very much like our own in some respects.) At the same time, we are confronted with the inherent difficulties of translation. We must avoid distorting other people's models in the process of reporting them in a language different from that in which they are normally expressed. Finally, it would seem that many indigenous models are rather like icebergs, with much of their mass lying below the surface phenomena of language. As Lévi-Strauss would have it, they are in large part "unconscious" or at least "unconsciously structured" and, in the strict sense of the term, not "known" to and certainly not readily verbalizable by those people who live with them. They are then difficult to discover, and validation of our formulations of them is equally problematic.

Linguists are, of course, accustomed to dealing with difficulties like these and it is, therefore, not surprising that many significant contributions to the anthropologist's task have been made by anthropological linguists or anthropologists who have been ready and willing to put the linguist's findings and methods to use. There are, however, several kinds of linguistics, even so-called structural linguistics, as well as several kinds of anthropological structuralism, the latter label now generally signifying a concern for the isolation, description and, ultimately, comparison of the content and *integral* organization of indigenous cultural systems. . . .

Lévi-Strauss' Structural Anthropology

Through their cognitive and intellectual processes and through the exchange of linguistic signs and their meanings, the members of a society produce, maintain, and occasionally modify, elaborate conceptual schemes, plans or models (compare Durkheim's "collective representations") which are logically ordered and which mediate and constrain social transactions in complex ways. Interpersonal transactions may thus be said to "express" such models, just as an utterance expresses the grammar of the language in which it is phrased. But just as a particular utterance does not exhaust the grammar of its language, so any particular transaction between persons is a partial expression of the model or models underlying all transactions between members of a society. Moreover, a particular utterance may be an imperfect (e.g. slurred) realization of the sound units and rules of its language, and similarly a particular social transaction may be a permuted expression of some part or parts of a people's model of social order. Such models are also expressed in verbal behavior, but again only partially, and it must be the anthropologist's task to reconstruct them *in full* (to build his own models of them) from their partial or permuted expressions in verbal and other forms of behavior.

It is possible for the anthropologist to do this because these models are all products of human minds which presumably operate in much the same way as his does. But a naive imaginative apprehension of other people's models will not do as an anthropological method; our apprehension of other people's models must be by means of some systematic, replicable method. Now since these models are all products of human minds, they must, perforce, share the "structure" of the mind, and the anthropologist's task would be facilitated by a knowledge of that structure. Given such knowledge he could proceed to use the "code" or "logic" of the processes of the mind to "decode" any particular product of it, for that same "code" must have been utilized to construct the model in the first place.

The structure of the mind is not, however, given to immediate observation. It must be inferred from empirical observations, and the best place in which to begin to look for this structure, or so Lévi-Strauss argues, is in language. This is because, in most societies, there are no indigenous theories of the language spoken, no "grammars" as "conscious models" or explicit sets of rules, so that linguistic behavior is governed entirely by "unconscious models" or "rules." Linguistic behavior is thus that behavior *par excellence* which is governed by rules and structures which are "unknown" to the actors. When expressed in scientifically constructed grammars, these rules and structures are the more accurate representations of the relatively simple order underlying the diversity of observed behavior (utterances) precisely because they are unknown to the speakers of the languages concerned. As already intimated, Lévi-Strauss supposes that people's models of and for experience have also this property of an unconscious structure (as well as an apparent or phenomenal order) and that it is one of the anthropologist's tasks to construct his own models of these unconsciously structured indigenous models, just as the linguist constructs a grammar.

This task is complicated by the fact that people usually have conscious models ("folk grammars," so to speak) of or for their behavior in society, and anthropologists have sometimes taken these to be the *totality* of their culture. As Lévi-Strauss sees it, these conscious models are often only the products of "reinterpretation" or "secondary rationalization." They may be designed to "perpetuate" an established order rather than to explain it, and, therefore, may be seriously misleading if taken as representations of the order in concrete transactional relations or as representations of an ideal order. Moreover, neither the conscious or unconscious models nor the apparent statistical order in transactional relations may be said to constitute *the* structure of the society concerned. These various forms of order, like the anthropologists' presentations of them, are not *the* structure itself; they are, all of them, only *variant expressions of structure*, which is, again, in Lévi-Strauss' view, the "logic" or "code" whereby the human mind operates. This same structure must underlie and be expressed in not only a people's conscious and unconscious models but also in their concrete social transactions. It must be expressed in the anthropologists' representations of these models, and we shall not be able to make systematic sense of or integrate the different forms and levels of order in human-behavior-in-society until we know and make use of our knowledge of that structure.

Since, in Lévi-Strauss' view, structure, once discovered, must be a tool of analysis, ethnographic analysis is not seen as a procedure for discovering structure. Structural analysis is rather a procedure for sorting out levels of social phenomena, for learning about relations between phenomena at the same or different levels and for relating the conscious and unconscious models of the same or different peoples to one another. In the process of structural analysis the anthropologist will discover unsuspected unconscious models, and his understanding of the phenomenal order in each model, system of models, and system of social transactions should be considerably enhanced. He will discover nothing new about structure itself, but only about the ways in which it may be "expressed."

It should be emphasized that Lévi-Strauss' argument is neither reductionistic nor idealistic (in the philosophical sense), though some have understood it to be. He does not argue that structure is the only "reality" and he is not concerned to reduce sociological facts to psychological facts. He argues: "To derive from language a logical model which, being more accurate and better known, may aid us in understanding the structure of other forms of communication, is in no sense equivalent to treating the former as the origin of the latter" (*Structural Anthropology*, 1963, p. 83).

This passage alludes to a fundamental feature of Lévi-Strauss' approach to the study of human-behavior-in-society. Anthropology, he argues, should seek to become a science of relationships, like economics and linguistics, and these sciences should view themselves as concerned with different forms of *communication*. The consequence would be an ability to relate the findings of these various sciences to one another in terms of the "rules of communication." Thus, it might be possible to demonstrate, for example, that the "rules of kinship and marriage," the "economic rules" and the "linguistic rules" of the same or different societies are all systematically interdependent. To do this, it would not be necessary to reduce each of these types of communication (of women, of goods and services, and of messages, respectively) or their rules to one another. We might instead find that the rules ordering or regulating these different types of communication are best conceived as variant expressions of one another. Though each regulates the circulation or communication of a different kind of "material," the rules for each type of circulation could be at least *formally* similar and perhaps identical. One task would then be to formulate further rules for transforming the rules for one type of communication into the rules for another type. We would also be in a position to discern whether or not the rules regulating a particular type of communication, say "marriage," in different societies are understandable as variants of one another. If all of this could be demonstrated, then, as Merleau-Ponty observed: "It [would be] sound practice to envision at the limit the program of a universal code of structures, which would allow us to deduce them from one another by means of rules of transformation, and to construct possible systems different from the existing ones—if it were only to direct empirical observation, as it has already been directed, toward certain existing institutions which would remain unnoticed without this theoretical anticipation" (*Signs*, 1964, p. 181).

In Lévi-Strauss' views, no society or social system can ever be grasped as a whole. Each society must be seen as composed of diverse and perhaps only more or less interdependent "orders" of relationships between persons, or between persons and objects, or between objects as conceived by persons. These orders differ in the "materials" being interrelated (e.g., women, kinds of objects, events, etc.) or in the ways in which the same materials are conceived as interrelated. Yet each order must have the same ultimate structure as all others. Because of this we may, again, find that each order is but a conditioned variant of some other, the conditioning variables being the kinds of materials involved and the "dialectical" rules governing the number of possible permutations or variations. As noted above, this possibility of viewing "orders" (such as models of and for experience) as conditioned variants of one another applies cross-culturally as well as within the boundaries of a single society.

Cross-cultural comparisons are possible not only because we use the same method (the method of structural analysis)) to analyze models from different societies, but for other reasons as well. The content and organization of any particular model is seldom created wholly anew and is usually but a conditioned variant of the content and organization of another model, perhaps simply one held by the same people at an earlier time. Since societies are historically interrelated it therefore follows that their models may be genetically related, though perhaps via complex chains of transformations or permutations which it is the anthropologist's task to work out.[1] Moreover, it will be found that models from historically unrelated societies will sometimes be quite similar since the nature of the materials being ordered is determinate, if not wholly determinable. Finally, men everywhere face many of the same problems in imputing meaning and order to their experiences, often coming to the same or substantially the same kinds of solutions to such problems.

A fundamental question of interest is then, what does the study of linguistic behavior teach us about the structure of the human mind? A difficulty here is that few linguists have much to say on this matter and what the few have to say is vigorously denied by other linguists. Lévi-Strauss appears, however, to accept as established the position of Roman Jacobson (and others) as expressed in the latter's theory of a universal set of distinctive phonological features.

Linguistics and the Structure of the Mind

For the speakers of most languages, the constituent units of their languages are "words," but the linguist, in his effort to reduce the continuous flow of speech sounds constituting utterances to a few elementary components and their orderly relations, is forced to go further than this. He finds it useful to describe a language in terms of, for example, its morphemes, phonemes and, ultimately, those articulatory "distinctive features" which in various combinations constitute the phonemes.

Jacobson's theory holds that all articulatory distinctive features may be described as the values, or "terms," of two-valued dimensions of opposition. Furthermore, he argues that all phonemic systems may be most economically and, at the same time, satisfactorily described in terms of a single and small set of some twelve or so kinds of binary opposition. In Jacobson's view, this scheme is more than just an economical and fairly satisfactory descriptive device. The fact that it is possible suggests to him, and to others, that it reflects something inherent in the nature of language itself: "a set of binary selections is inherent in the communication process itself as a constraint imposed by the code on the participants in the speech event, who could be spoken of as the *encoder* and *decoder*" (*Preliminaries of Speech Analysis*, 1963 ed. p. 9; with Fant and Halle).

[1] For some examples of this, see *Le Cru et le cuit* and "The Bear and the Barber," *Journal of the Royal Anthropological Institute*, Vol. 93, 1963.

Furthermore, perhaps this situation reflects something inherent in the nature of the "encoder" and "decoder." Halle, for example, suggests: "If it is true that a small set of attributes suffices to describe the phonetic properties of all languages of the world, then it would appear quite likely that these attributes are connected with something fairly basic in man's constitution, something which is quite independent of his cultural background." Halle continues, with proper caution, to venture that "these attributes will prove to be productive parameters for describing man's responses to auditory stimuli in general." [2] Elsewhere, however, Jacobson and Halle are somewhat more expansive in their suggestions. In reply to queries as to whether the "dichotomous scale" is indeed inherent in the structure of language, they reply that it must be. For a system of distinctive features based on binary oppositions is the "optimal code" that can be used, and "it is unwarranted to assume that the speech participants in their encoding and decoding operations use a more complicated and less economic set of differential criteria." Also, they argue, the phonemic code "is acquired in the earliest years of childhood and, as psychology reveals, in a child's mind the pair is anterior to isolated objects. The binary opposition is a child's first logical operation" (*Fundamentals of Language*, 1956, p. 47).

There is, however, room for doubt. It is, first of all, by no means a certainty that all phonemic systems can be satisfactorily described in the terms of Jacobson's distinctive features (though some linguists will contradict me and maintain that it is). Secondly, a scheme admitting only binary discriminations at the elementary level of language structure may be the most economical in the abstract, but it is not necessarily so in practice. Some linguists find that Jacobson's scheme yields relatively uneconomical and formally unsatisfactory results for some languages. While not denying that most dimensions of opposition are indeed best treated as two-valued, they see no reason to rigidly impose this pattern on all dimensions and find that admitting at least some three-valued dimensions of opposition (as Jacobson did at first) may yield the most economical and satisfactory results for some phonemic systems.[3] Also, it would seem that psychology's testimony on the matter of the organization of human thought processes (the

[2] M. Halle, "On the Bases of Phonology," in Fodor and Katz (eds.), *The Structure of Language*, 1964, p. 329.

[3] Curiously, almost all of this discussion has been oral, much of it in the form of papers presented at linguistic professional meetings, and relatively little has appeared in print so far

human mind) is a mixed one. Certainly, Piaget, for example, makes much (and rightly so) of the logical operation of binary opposition, yet other psychologists manage to discuss thinking and linguistic behavior without appeal to any such process, or they relegate it to a less important place as one among several basic processes.[4]

Most importantly, where is the warranty for assuming that *all* levels of language organization—especially those most charged with the duty of carrying meaning—are structured in terms of bipolar oppositions, even if the phonemic level were so structured? Isomorphism of structure (in Lévi-Strauss' sense) at all levels cannot be merely assumed, unless, of course, one is prepared to accept that the structure of phonemic systems most directly reflects the structure of the mind, which is imposed on all its products. But as we have just seen, it is not at all certain that the structure of phonemic systems and the structure of the mind are identical.

Lévi-Strauss' analyses of cultural systems depend, however, on the principle of binary opposition. This principle, he assumes, is not only that which orders human thought processes, it is that which orders all of nature: man's mind and nature have the same structure. Lévi-Strauss' procedure is to search out all binary oppositions relevant to one another in a particular cultural system. He feels that a satisfactory analysis has been achieved when he is able to comprehend and represent a system or sub-system of norms, ideas, ideals (and actions) as one composed of a set of bipolar oppositions, though perhaps a rather elaborate set, and of features not always very obvious. To those familiar with the ethnographic data under analysis, Lévi-Strauss' interpretations frequently appear rather forced and his emphasis on bipolar oppositions too constraining. But even his critics have to admit that his method of analysis may bring out previously unperceived details and, better yet, point to alternate and highly suggestive lines of inquiry.

Selected Bibliography

The Elementary Structures of Kinship (Boston: The Beacon Press, 1969).

Race and History (Paris: UNESCO, 1952).

The Raw and the Cooked (New York: Harper & Row, Publishers, Inc., 1969).

[4] See especially W. Garner, *Uncertainty and Structure as Psychological Concepts*, 1962, and D. Berlyne, *Structure and Direction in Thinking*, 1965.

The Savage Mind (Chicago: University of Chicago Press, 1966).

The Scope of Anthropology (London: Jonathan Cape, 1967).

Structural Anthropology (New York: Doubleday & Company, Inc., 1963).

Totemism (Boston: The Beacon Press, 1963).

World on the Wane (New York: Criteria Books, 1961).

Edmund Leach, *Claude Lévi-Strauss* (New York: Viking Press, 1970).

George Steiner, "A Conversation with Claude Lévi-Strauss," *Encounter*, Vol. XXVI, No. 4 (1966), pp. 32–38.

See also the bibliography of Lévi-Strauss' works in *Claude Lévi-Strauss. The Anthropologist as Hero*, E. Nelson Hayes and Tanya Hayes, eds. (Cambridge, Mass.: The M.I.T. Press, 1970), pp. 247–256.

From Sine Qua Non *to Cultural System*

CLIFFORD GEERTZ

Clifford Geertz was born in San Francisco on August 23, 1926. He received his B.A. degree from Antioch College in 1950, and his Ph.D. degree in anthropology from Harvard in 1956. He began his teaching career at Harvard in 1956, and became a research fellow at the Massachusetts Institute of Technology in 1957 and a fellow of the Center for Advanced Study in the Behavioral Sciences in Palo Alto, California, in 1958. He resumed teaching at the University of California, Berkeley, in 1959, then moved to the University of Chicago where he had been a member of the faculty in anthropology since 1961.

Geertz' interests are many-sided. He has conducted in-depth cultural-anthropological analyses, for example, of the peoples of Javanese villages in Islamic societies. Throughout all of these, he has given special attention to the influences of religious factors on cultural life. From such analyses he has come to be looked upon as the champion of the position that religion can be understood as "cultural system," within which there are also subcultural systems of belief, value, and action. It is on this basis that he reflects about religion in the essay that follows.

There has been a general shift in modern anthropological discussion of culture, and within it of religion as a part of culture, a shift from a concern with thought as an inner mental state or stream of such states to a concern with thought as the utilization by individuals in society of public, historically created vehicles of reasoning, perception, feeling, and understanding—symbols, in the broadest sense of the term. In the study of religion, this shift is in the process of altering our entire view of religious experience and its social and psychological impact. The focus is now neither on subjective life as such nor on outward behavior as such, but on the socially available "systems of

Clifford Geertz, *Islam Observed* (New Haven: Yale University Press, 1968), pp. 95–98. Copyright © 1968 by Yale University.

significance"—beliefs, rites, meaningful objects—in terms of which subjective life is ordered and outward behavior guided.

Such an approach is neither introspectionist nor behaviorist; it is semantic. It is concerned with the collectively created patterns of meaning the individual uses to give form to experience and point to action, with conceptions embodied in symbols and clusters of symbols, and with the directive force of such conceptions in public and private life. So far as religion is concerned, the problem becomes one of a particular sort of perspective, a particular manner of interpreting experience, a certain way of going at the world as opposed to other ways, and the implications such a perspective has for conduct. The aim of the comparative study of religion is (or anyway, ought to be) the scientific characterization of this perspective: the description of the wide variety of forms in which it appears; the uncovering of the forces which bring these forms into existence, alter them, or destroy them; and the assessment of their influences, also various, upon the behavior of men in everyday life.

But how are we to isolate the religious perspective at all? Are we not thrown back once more upon the necessity of defining "religion," adding one more catch phrase—"the belief in spiritual beings," "morality touched with emotion," "ultimate concern"—to what is surely an endless catalog? Must we not go yet once more through the familiar exercise of sorting out "religion" from "superstition," "religion" from "magic," "religion" from "philosophy," "religion" from "custom," from "folklore," from "myth," from "ceremony"? Does not all understanding, or anyway all scientific understanding, depend upon an initial isolation, a laboratory preparation, so to speak, of what it is that one is trying to understand?

Well, no. One can begin in a fog and try to clear it. One can begin, with an assortment of phenomena almost everyone but the professionally contrary will regard as having something vaguely to do with "religion" and seek for what it is that leads us to think so, what it is that leads us to think that these rather singular things certain people do, believe, feel, or say somehow belong together with sufficient intimacy to submit to a common name. This is, I admit, a definitional procedure also, but a definitional procedure of a more inductive sort, rather more comparable to nothing the oblique resemblances in the way in which Dubliners talk or Parisians walk than to filtering out pure substances. We look not for a universal property—"sacredness" or "belief in the supernatural," for example—that divides religious phenomena off from nonreligious ones with Cartesian sharpness, but for a system of concepts that can sum up a set of inexact similarities, which are yet genuine similarities, we sense to inhere in a given body of material. We are attempting to articulate a way of looking at the world, not to describe an unusual object.

The heart of this way of looking at the world, that is, of the religious perspective, is, so I would like to argue, not the theory that beyond the visible world there lies an invisible one (though most religious men have indeed held, with differing degrees of sophistication, to some such theory); not the doctrine that a divine presence broods over the world (though, in an extraordinary variety of forms, from animism to monotheism, that too has been a rather popular idea); not even the more diffident opinion that there are things in heaven and earth undreamt of in our philosophies. Rather, it is the conviction that the values one holds are grounded in the inherent structure of reality, that between the way one ought to live and the way things really are there is an unbreakable inner connection. What sacred symbols do for those to whom they are sacred is to formulate an image of the world's construction and a program for human conduct that are mere reflexes of one another.

In anthropology, it has become customary to refer to the collection of notions a people has of how reality is at base put together as their world view. Their general style of life, the way they do things and like to see things done, we usually call their ethos. It is the office of religious symbols, then, to link these in such a way that they mutually confirm one another. Such symbols render the world view believable and the ethos justifiable, and they do it by invoking each in support of the other. The world view is believable because the ethos, which grows out of it, is felt to be authoritative; the ethos is justifiable because the world view, upon which it rests, is held to be true. Seen from outside the religious perspective, this sort of hanging a picture from a nail driven into its frame appears as a kind of sleight of hand. Seen from inside, it appears as a simple fact.

Religious patterns such as those I have been discussing thus have a double aspect: they are frames of perception, symbolic screens through which experience is interpreted; and they are guides for action, blueprints for conduct. Indonesian illuminationism portrays reality as an aesthetic hierarchy culminating in a void, and it projects a style of life celebrating mental poise. Moroccan maraboutism portrays reality as a field of spiritual energies nucleating in the persons of individual men, and it projects a style of life celebrating moral passion. Kalid-jaga in classical Morocco would not be heroic but unmanly; Lyusi in classical Java would not be a saint but a boor.

The world view side of the religious perspective centers, then, around the problem of belief, the ethos side around the problem of action. As I say, these are, within the confines of faith, not only inseparable, they are reflexes of one another. Yet for analytical purposes, I want to separate them here momentarily and, using the Moroccan and Indonesian cases as reference points, discuss them independently. Having done that, the general relevance of these particular cases for the understanding of religion as such should be more readily apparent, as should the usefulness (I would claim no more for it than that) of this whole approach to the comparative study of it.

The major characteristic of religious beliefs as opposed to other sorts of beliefs, ideological, philosophical, scientific, or commonsensical, is that they are regarded as being not conclusions from experience —from deepened social awareness, from reflective speculation and logical analysis, from empirical observation and hypothesis testing, or from matriculation in the school of hard knocks—but as being prior to it. For those who hold them, religious beliefs are not inductive, they are paradigmatic; the world, to paraphrase a formulation of Alisdair MacIntyre's, provides not evidences for their truth but illustrations of it. They are a light cast upon human life from somewhere outside it.

Selected Bibliography

Agricultural Involution: The Process of Ecological Change in Indonesia (Berkeley: University of California Press, 1963).

The Development of the Javanese Economy (Cambridge: Mass., The M.I.T. Press., 1956).

Islam Observed (New Haven: Yale University Press, 1968).

Person, Time, and Conduct in Bali (New Haven: Yale University Press, 1966).

The Religion of Java (New York: The Free Press, 1960).

Social History of an Indonesian Town (Cambridge: Mass., The M.I.T. Press, 1965).

PART 4

Examining Organic Coordinates: Religions and Religious Traditions

In this section of the anthology the focus is on religions and religious traditions. For men with this focus there is interest in the systematic, wholistic coordination of religious experience, behavior, and reflection. In large scale, this interest can be directed toward the major world religions; in narrower scope, it can be pointed toward the constellations of belief and practice that develop within (or alongside of) the larger religious traditions. In terms of scholarship, this interest has been converted into historical examinations, morphological depictions, and comparative analyses. In every instance, however, the investigation includes a concern for lands, peoples, and customs. There is interest in the way in which a religion is displayed in a given locale and in its influence upon social and cultural habits and practices. There is related interest in the changes that accompany the transportation of a given religion to a cultural setting that is different from its original habitat. In every case, attention focuses on an integral (and sometimes institutionalized) expression of beliefs, ob-

187

servances, and practices. Wherever they are located, such coordinative traditions function not only to prescribe a people's way of life but also as an interpretative framework from which they receive their identity.

The materials in this section of the anthology are included to illustrate the several directions in which a fundamental interest in the religions (and the religious traditions) of the world can take. The essay by Wilfred Cantwell Smith describes the work of a scholar who approaches the religions of the world by distinguishing the historical particularities of a tradition from the religious avowals it makes. Suggesting that his approach is an improvement upon others that seek for the essence of either religion or religions, Smith proposes that attention be given instead to two fundamental factors, the historico-cultural "cumulative tradition," and the personal faith of men and women. His remarks about the function and objectives of the comparative study of religion are regulated by that contention. Despite the fact that both treat the major religions of the world, Ninian Smart's interest differs from Smith's. Although in general a kind of comparativist, Smart is not as much concerned about the historical development of religious traditions as he is about the internal dimensions and characteristics common to several of them. He proceeds, therefore, by distinguishing the mystical strand from the social, the doctrinal from the experiential, the ritual from the mythological, and each from the other, then views the various religions in terms of the number and combination of strands (or dimensions) that they include. Max Weber's outlook, on the other hand, derives from a combination of sociological and religious interests. Looking at religions in terms of their "practical impulses for action," Weber was interested in the correlations that could be stipulated between ethical, economic, and religious concerns. Consequently, the product of his investigations is a series of paradigms by which he charts the ways in which religions become functional systems in socioeconomic life. These three approaches—Smith's, Smart's, and Weber's—are similar in having global perspectives. Each focuses on a complex of religions and then develops techniques for comparing and contrasting those religions. The differences between the three approaches derive primarily from what is pointed to as the content in terms of which religions are constituted.

Two additional works in this section of the anthology look at religions and religious traditions from different perspectives. Both can be regarded as in-depth analyses of a particular subject. The first,

Robert Bellah's essay on civil religion, is consciously nonglobal in scope, and, unlike Smith's and Smart's works, makes no attempt to engage in comparison and contrast. Bellah's intention is to demonstrate that alongside the generally acknowledged religious traditions a more public or civil religious tradition has developed in the United States which, in turn, can also be understood as a coordinated system of experience, belief, behavior, and reflection. In the second article, Thomas F. O'Dea treats the problem of the institutionalization of religion directly. O'Dea provides a sketch of the dynamics of the process of institutionalization and shows how that process works to sustain the fundamental components of corporate religious experience. Although he makes no attempt in the present essay to apply the results of his inquiry to religions other than Christianity, he gives hints of ways in which his analyses might be expanded.

On the Comparative Study of Religion

WILFRED CANTWELL SMITH

Wilfred Cantwell Smith was born on July 21, 1916, in Toronto, Canada. He studied theology, oriental languages, and history at the Universities of Toronto, Cambridge, and Princeton, receiving his doctorate from Princeton in 1948. From 1941 to 1945 he taught Islamic and Indian history in Lahore, then in India, now the capital of West Pakistan, and at the University of Punjab. During this time (and subsequently) he traveled extensively through the major areas of the Muslim world. In 1949 he was appointed the first professor of comparative religion at McGill University in Montreal, and shortly thereafter also became director of the Institute of Islamic Studies at that institution. Since 1964 he has been head of the Center for the Study of World Religions at Harvard University.

In addition to his competence in Islam, particularly in its Indian context, Smith is recognized for his ability to clarify methodological problems in the study of religion. He is particularly sensitive to the necessity and interdependence of empathy and objectivity in the scholarly investigation of given religious traditions. Under the same theme, he has worked to create an awareness and a better understanding of "the religions of other men" as well as of the men of other religions.

The reading selection that follows is taken from Smith's inaugural lecture upon accepting the appointment to the W. M. Birk chair in Religion at McGill University in 1949. Although it was given over twenty years ago—during which time Smith has amplified, expanded, and revised some of his views expressed in 1949—the lecture provided a good indication of the ways in which Smith conceives of the division of labor in his approach to religion.

The comparative study of religion may be viewed as in two parts. One is the history of religion, including the history of the religions. The

Wilfred Cantwell Smith, "The Comparative Study of Religion," in *McGill University Divinity Faculty Inaugural Lectures*, 1949, pp. 39–60.

other, based on the results of the former study, is comparative religion proper: the elucidation by the comparative method of whatever truths may be induced from a survey of that history. At one time it was thought that this second step would consist in the discovery of the essence of religion. Various attempts were made; such as by surveying the whole field of religion's historical development and abstracting therefrom whatever was common to all its multifarious manifestations; or again, by analysing religion's historical origins; and so on. All such attempts may be said by now to have failed. Any competent philosopher of religion can readily pick holes in each of the equally multifarious conclusions arrived at by these and in fact all other methods, whether advanced by scoffer or by saint. The list of definitions of religion is long. But the casualty list is but its carbon copy. The essence of religion has remained elusive. Nor do I contend that a science of religion can at long last contribute a scientific definition. Quite on the contrary: the contribution that it can make is to call off the hunt.

For science is not interested in essences. It seems to me that progress in the study of religion can come when we can bring ourselves to forget about the nature of religion; and attend rather to the process of its contemporary development. It is well known that a physicist cannot define matter. But he can handle it. And he can do so because his predecessors eventually learned that the essence doesn't signify. He can direct the behaviour of matter not because he knows what matter is—he doesn't—; but because he has studied how it behaves.

What does the history of religion teach us, then? Not what religion is—that we do not need to know; but something of much greater import. And yet something so simple that it will sound, at first, tautologous. The history of religion teaches us that religion has a history. This is fundamental; a fact of crucial, even revolutionary, significance. It is not tautologous because religious people have realized it, if at all, in only the most peripheral way. Religious people, like philosophers, have, in general, been interested in essences. And essences do not have a history.

Essences, by nature, do not change. I am suggesting that a science of religion can be founded on the observable fact that religions, in history, do change. The purpose of such a science would be to discover how they change; and to make that knowledge available so that religious people could, if they wished, make them change the way they wanted them to or keep them from changing a way that they do not want them to. It is not the function of the scientist to say what the religions ought to be—that is the part of the prophet. The scientist's job is to elucidate how they can, from what they are, become what they ought to be.

This time I have ventured to use the plural: "religions." Not only is religion as such a vigorous historical process, traceable through human development at least from Mousterian times. Each of the great religions, also, is an historical process; capable of ostensive definition. The essence cannot be grasped; the existence, and the vitality, cannot be denied. Once again, these things can be seen, at least at first, much more clearly in an alien religion, where one's preconceptions are less lively. To an outsider, it can without difficulty be shown that Islam has a history: that it has been modified or expanded at successive stages or areas in its development—in early Arabia; in the cities of the Fertile Crescent under the impact of Greek philosophy and Persian culture and internal advance; later in India; and so on. And there is the difference between Sunni and Shi'ah. Islam is still developing to-day; and my own major interest has been the attempt to observe and interpret the contemporary evolution of this religion in the twentieth century. The Muslim, if pressed, recognizes this history, these variations in the religious life of different generations or groups of Muslims. But to him, the variations are deviations from the 'true' Islam; are successive interpretations, less or more valid, of the essence of his religion. To the historian, on the other hand, these variations, in sum, constitute Islam as an historical process. They *are* the religion.

Similarly the Christian: though he talks of the history of the Church, he has difficulty usually in realizing that there is also, in a most profound sense, a history of Christianity. To the historian, to the student of religion, the variations are not aberrations from a fixed essence; they are the religion. Islam is that empirical process which began in history at a given point and continues to-day. Christianity *is* what it in fact has been, and in fact is, and will in fact be.

The religion of the Early Fathers; the religion of the mediæval Church; the religion of the Reformers; the religion of the late nineteenth-century liberal; the religion of the neo-orthodox to-day; are different. This is a fact. It is possible, I admit, to interpret this fact as a succession of partial or wrong manifestations of a fixed essence; though to do so is not, I submit—at least from our present point of view—useful. Nor is it scientific. It is equally possible, and for the comparative study of religion I believe that it will prove immensely more fruitful, to recognize these 'different' religious data as constituting, in all their fulness, Christianity; constituting it, then, as a vital process, rather than a static idea. The rather momentous implications of this viewpoint for the believer himself will be explored in a moment. Meanwhile we consider the implications for the student of religion.

Religion in any vital sense—or anyway, religion as the subject matter of our study—is not the rites, symbols, doctrines, etc., of the system; but what these mean to a man. What he does with them; and what they do to him. Religion lies somewhere in the interaction between men and their religious material. This is why it has a history. Even when the materials remain fixed, they mean different things to different people: at different times, in different milieus, from different strata of society. Also, through the centuries even the material changes: a little, or (as at the Reformation in Christian history) a lot. And the changes continue to-day, and will continue. To recognize them is not to admit imperfection, but to proclaim vitality. A conservative Muslim said to me, of the highly interesting developments in Islam being proposed to-day in Turkey: "Yes—but it would not be Islam; it would be a new religion." But all religions are new religions, every morning. For religions do not exist up in the sky somewhere, elaborated, finished, and static; they exist in men's hearts. Religions are like living things; and of living thing one does not ask if it can change: it has to be unrelentingly changing, in one sense, in order even to maintain itself, in order even to "stay the same." In spiritual matters, if they are to have any vitality at all, everyone has to start as it were from scratch. A man takes the symbols from his fathers; but he must find out for himself what those symbols mean. To be religious is a personal, and is a creative, act.

If a given religion is transmitted from A to B, it may in one sense be regarded as now the same religion as it was, and we give it the same name. But at the same time, and in a deeper sense, it is not the same; by the very fact of now being B's religion instead of A's. This, quite apart from any subtle variations that may creep in, due to his filling the symbols with new content. Even let us postulate for the sake of argument an ideal case where B attaches exactly the same meaning to the material as does A; if you will, makes the "same" response to God. But even so, it is not the same; just because they are two distinct persons. That is, if we regard religion, as any sensitive student surely must, as an *integral* part of B's person, of his life as a human being; and not merely something external, attached to his life.

Looked at more broadly, we may put it thus. What we call a given religion existing over a period of say a hundred years, is expressing it-

self through, or is carried by or lived by, different generations of believers—or, in my submission, is the dynamic sum of the religion of
those individual believers, each of whom has lived his own personal
life. If the student of the religion is looking for some integral calculus
wherewith to perform that sum, some concept wherewith to make the
synthesis of these many individual instances of the religion in question
and to posit the entity to which we give the name (Christianity,
Islam, Hinduism, or whatever), then I would suggest that, rather than
dealing in essences, he bethink him of the analogy of a living organism. That particular religion is "the same" over those hundred years,
living in the hearts of those thousands or millions of believers, in
somewhat the same sense as that in which a person is the same person over a period of years although through metabolism the material of every cell in his body be replaced. That is what it is to be
alive.

And yet, in quite another sense, the person is not "the same" person year after year at all. He is developing (or degenerating) unceas-
ingly. There is the unity of continuity, integrated into the change of
growth. This, too, is what it is to be alive. Not only does every par-
ticipating part of an organism constantly modify itself, in order to
maintain the totality; more, the totality itself is constantly developing
also, is always new, just because it is alive. The total process may be
very, very slow. But if it should stop altogether the organism as such
would cease to exist. This is true of persons: our life consists in our
ceasing to be what we were yesterday and becoming what we are
to-day and shall or will be to-morrow. It is true also of religions. It is
an historical, observable fact that a religion in one century is not what
it was the century before. The only religions which are not changing
before our eyes are those which have ceased to exist. Mithraism, for
instance. Of other ancient religions, that of Zarathushtra, for example,
is still alive in that it is being *lived*—and one means lived, literally—
by that small but brilliant community of Parsis in Bombay to-day.

If in no other way, each of the historical religions grows by the
sheer fact of every year having that much more history behind it.

An analogy remains, of course, an analogy. A religion is not strictly
an organism. But—if only we could see the fact—it is, quite strictly
and in sober observation, more like an organism than it is like a house.
To be thoroughly precise, the great religions do not exist as such at
all; each is an intellectual abstraction, elicited from a large, and ever
growing, number of personal instances of it, in individual lives. Yet
factors germane to those personal instances do have a certain per-

manence; especially the institutions that emerge and, above all, the developing tradition. These justify our speaking of each religion as a separate object of study, as an historical process, as an ever-growing tradition. For some purposes, however, other levels of abstraction are in order. "Religion" is that abstraction that considers as one integral process in history the whole sweep of this aspect of human activity since the beginning. For other purposes, one must make an abstraction rather at a lower level of generality. For instance, in considering questions of denominationalism (such as the œcumenical movement, to be relevant to practical problems of the day), one abstracts from history those intellectual constructs, the developing processes of Presbyterianism, Methodism, and the like. But whatever the level of abstraction, it remains abstraction. These nouns refer to ideas in the minds of men, not in the mind of God. (This is not to deny that the 'we feeling' engendered by these abstractions and the corresponding institutions gives to the religious processes a *sociological* unity of tremendous consequence. Nor is it to deny that God exists. It is simply to suggest humbly that His mind is not so confused as is the panorama of empirical religion.)

For basically, the student has to deal not with religions but with religious persons.

This may be valid enough, and even useful, for the outside observer. But what about the believer? The *student* may see a given religion as an actual dynamic process, empirical, beginning from a given point in history and continuing therefrom. But must not the believer hold it to be an entity, Platonic idea in heaven? If he sees only the flux, is he not deprived of all stability and norm? To the historian, Islam is the religion of the Muslims; to the Muslim, Islam is the religion of God.

It would delay us too long to explore the ramifications of this weighty question, which adumbrates the general dilemma arising when the mind would treat objectively and scientifically an area of the universe which is in fact not external to us. The existentialists are emphasizing the difference when an activity is looked at, on the one hand, from the outside, and, on the other, by the participant from within. Some other occasion will be more fitting to go into this fascinating problem. In immediate answer to the question above, I must content myself with making two points—apart from calling attention once again to the basic argument about the religious person's believing not primarily in his religion as such but in God—or in God and the Qur'an, God and Christ, God and the local shaman; as the case may be. Of my two points, one is verbal. Some languages—for instance, Arabic—have two distinct terms to express the two senses which I am discriminating of our one word "religion." In these languages, even the believer who did not wish to let go of the essentialist interpretation of his own religion, could none the less concede the steps of my argument, even to the point of the setting up of a comparative study of religion-in-the-empirical-sense so as to arrive at, and perhaps even to apply, a science of religion-in-the-empirical-sense. In other words, the validity of our proposed procedure does not immediately stand or fall with the metaphysics that to me it implies.

My second point tries to answer more specifically the difficulty of the believer who may feel that our description covers the past history of his religion well enough but leaves him at a loss in the face of the immediate present demand. "To be a Christian" has meant in the past what history shows us that it in fact meant. But what, he may well ask, does it then mean for me to-day to be a Christian? If there is no fixed, essential, meaning to the term, what am I to believe?

To begin with, I must point out that such a believer's quandary is peculiar to the dynamic, existential view of Christianity only in theory. In practice, the same quandary faces the essentialist; since in practice he is faced with an ever-growing multiplicity of interpretations as to what Christianity really "is." The Catholic says one thing, the Baptist another; the liberal one thing, the fundamentalist another; and our neo-orthodox friends are busy elaborating one more interpretation. The static viewpoint copes with this multiplicity by assuming that only one of these is "right"; but there is in fact no way of telling which one it is. In effect, each man is free to choose that interpretation which seems to him best, or even to produce a new one; which is why I say that, concerning guidance as to the meaning of Christianity (or Islam, etc.) in fact the essentialist is in no better case than one who takes the historical view. (Normally, each man chooses the interpretation in which he has been brought up; but that does not change the logic of the situation. In practise, most men will doubtless continue to follow their leaders. But it is the leaders who need creative wisdom.)

Yet still the question presses: what does it mean, now, for a man to say, "I am a Christian" (or, "I am a Hindu")? After all this preliminary explication we are now at last in a position to answer such a question; and in giving our answer, and in suggesting one or two of its implications, I shall close. I suggest that a scientific study of comparative religion, based on the history of the religions, leads to a dynamic interpretation of religious processes according to which "to be religious" means: to take one's place in the historical development of religion, which begins as far back as history can trace human development, and continues, through all its changes, until now. "To be a Christian" means: to accept and to enter into the Christian tradition, to participate in the living Church. To be an Anglican, a Presbyterian, a Baptist, etc., means to enter that particular smaller tradition. "To be a Muslim" does not mean to have certain ideas about God, the Prophet, the Qur'an, and so forth: a detailed study of the history of Islam can show that divers Muslims have in fact held diverse views on all these questions. It means to accept membership at the present point in the developing tradition of the Muslim community.

Furthermore, for those who will join me in discarding the essentialist view, to enter the continuing community is to accept the past tradition not as binding, but simply as past tradition. That tradition is open: the future is ours. The future of Christianity lies with Christians; the future of Islam with Muslims. And one is free—free to create. To be a Muslim means to start at the present point of development; but it gives no final indication of where to go from there. And there is no "essence of Islam" for which to search, or which to uphold. The freedom—and therefore the responsibility—of where to go next, of how to continue the development, lies with those who are members of the group. That freedom and that responsibility exist, and have existed, and have been unconsciously exercised in any case; but it becomes conscious only in the modern world, in those whom a scientific study of religious history has emancipated from a misplaced authoritarianism.

When we make this dynamic approach to religion, we do so also to science. Science also is not an essence, a fixed procedure; it too is a tradition, an empirical historical development. 'To be scientific' means to take one's place in an actual on-going process; not slavishly to follow certain fixed rules or to apply certain fixed methods, but creatively to carry further an actual living human activity. As in religion, one has a certain responsibility to the past tradition; for until now it is that past tradition which has constituted science. Yet that past tradition does not contain within itself the final authority for what it shall be now or in the future.

For one's study of religion to be scientific, therefore, means not that it should apply to religious material the methods that have already been elaborated as science in other fields; but rather that it should take its place firmly within the scientific tradition. Each great advance within science has been made by innovators who carried the tradition one step further. The scientists of the older disciplines have no authority to prescribe how a student of religion must proceed in his work; the old procedures can, in fact, readily be shown to be inapplicable. The question at issue is whether man, arising out of the growing process which the established sciences are, can creatively expand that tradition so as to embrace also this newer field.

The relation between science and religion as two ideal systems, two essences, has been explored on the philosophic plane. The hopeful development in the modern world is rather the historical approach which sees them as two developing traditions and asks whether the two can now move into dynamic co-operation. . . .

We have not time here to pursue an interesting speculation, which perhaps has ramifications not only for our own subject but for the social sciences generally, and for all studies of man: namely, as to whether science, in evolving so as to create also a science of religion, might have to recapture an emphasis which in the early Greek phase it had, but has subsequently discarded. Science at that early stage was still rather speculative with regard to the object of inquiry. It was only at the beginning of the modern period that it fully developed the experimental control of the natural sciences, with we might say a sense of the relation between intellectual truth and the severely practical as regards the object. But it meanwhile had lost the Greek sense of a relation between intellectual truth and the practical in the agent —the sense that knowledge is bound up with virtue, and the pursuit of truth is a moral and spiritual discipline. Perhaps to see the kind of truth with which religion deals, or in fact to see any truth about humanity, even the scientific student must somehow and in some measure learn to be a good man. This is a thought that merely increases my own humility in daring to undertake this study when mayhap I have even fewer of the qualifications for it than I at first realized.

Leaving that aside, then, as a monumental issue unexplored, we come back to that dogged question of authority. This, I am convinced, is the crucial point; and it is doubtless here that the proposals that I am outlining will need the most rigorous testing, and perhaps drastic revision. I am disturbed chiefly on two points. One is that I am unable now to satisfy myself with precision concerning the extent to which being a Christian, or a Muslim, means not only what I said just now, accepting for oneself the Christian or the Muslim tradition and community, but also the converse: being accepted by them. This principle operates clearly enough when authority is not merely theoretically postulated but also sociologically organized, as with the Roman Catholic Church. But Luther showed that one can be a Christian without accepting the authority of the Church. The Reformation substituted the authority of the Bible. In the nineteenth century the modernists showed that one can be a Christian without accepting the authority of the Bible. They substituted the authority of the person of Christ. It remains to be seen what will be the historical consequences when one asks if it is possible to be a Muslim without accepting the authority of the Qur'an, or a Protestant without accepting any ostensible authority at all.

My other qualm arises from the historical observation of religious developments in which no outward standards were imposed. These have risen in individual instances to very great heights; but also they have sunk on occasion to depths of degradation out of which they contained no principles to raise themselves. Within Islam, for instance, the distinction between external, formal authority and internal appreciation corresponds by and large to the dichotomy in historical development between Sunni and Sufi; the Law and mysticism. It is true that the greatest Muslims have been Sufis. It is also true that at certain periods the Law, if unenlivened by Sufi warmth and spontaneity, has threatened to become cold, formalistic, and incarceration —and in some ways the twentieth century is one such period. Nonetheless, it is the Law which has kept Islamic society together; moreover, it is only the Law which, religiously, has carried on the tradition by means of which the mystics, or anyone else, could be introduced to that meaning of religion which they, rightly, valued more highly than the outward expression. And it is with some trepidation that one speculates on what would have become of Islam had there been only mystics—with no *shari'ah*, no norm, to call them back to earth from time to time.

On a larger scale, a similar dichotomy can be suggested between, on the one hand, Islam as a whole, with its fixed standard—the Qur'an —and, on the other hand, Hinduism. The welter of Hinduism is perhaps what happens when a religion is not a system, acknowledges no final explicit religious authority. The greatest Hindus have soared to astonishing heights—to heights which attract from time to time brilliant minds from our own society, minds unable to accept the definitions on which Christianity, for good or ill, has insisted. And yet one wonders what those minds can say on the mass of utterly gross and decadent village Hinduism which is perhaps the price that the great Hindus pay for their freedom.

Tentatively—though here I speak with little authority—I rather feel that a similar generalization could be made about China, establishing such a dichotomy between the Confucian and the Tao-ist: the one pedestrian but orderly; the other sometimes magnificently poetic, sometimes merely superstitious.

To come nearer home, there has been the Western Nazi movement, to show us that human freedom exercised without any standards at all can sink to depths more ghastly than a disciplined imagination can well conceive.

As I say, it is here that our approach to religion raises questions most sorely; and it is in this area that inquiry is a prerequisite to further major progress. Meanwhile, may it not be said in defence that we have not created the problem, but merely recognized it? I am not proposing to destroy authority so much as to meet the case of those —Protestants or Buddhists or whatever—for whom, like it or not, religious authority has already broken down. And I feel convinced that it is better squarely to face the situation, than hastily to re-impose some new authority on ourselves or others, in alarm, and against our better judgement.

Perhaps it is necessary to insist here that in finding no authority, we are by no means saying that we find no truth. Quite on the contrary. It is in order to universalize truth that we are freeing it from an authority which is, anyway, breaking down; freeing it also from a religious provincialism which is to-day anachronist. Doctrines that Christians have believed, in so far as they are true, are important not because they are part of Christianity, ideal or empirical, but because they are true. Similarly for other creeds. And it is only in so far as each religious community is consciously seeking Truth that they all can come together. So long as Christians are searching for the real Christianity, and Muslims for the real Islam, they cannot even talk to each other. But immediately when both are looking for truth—for God, as they might well put it—then they can talk very warmly; and of course can learn from each other. The missionary, if he is to escape from being a slightly absurd and slightly pathetic proselytizer, must be a man who feels that his religious community has caught a certain vision of God, has seen an aspect of ultimate truth, which he wants to contribute to the general search for God and truth in which men of other communities are also engaged.

When a man is asked whether he finds any truth in, let us say,

Buddhism, may he not well reply that the question is meaningless? For surely the only truth that matters, the only truth that exists, he must find in the universe itself. It may be the Buddhists who point it out to him. But if it is true, it is true because it is part of the structure of the universe;—not because it is part of the structure of Buddhism. Or, in another context, of the structure of Christianity. This is where metaphysics is married to science, religious truth to my empirical, historical approach to these different faiths. This is why I feel that nothing ultimate is lost in saying that Christianity and Buddhism and the rest have in fact no essential structure. For the scientific observer, there just is no "nature" of Christianity, or of Islam, or of Buddhism; these religions being for him historical constructs. But for the deeply religious man also there is, or need be, no nature of Christianity, or Islam, or Buddhism. For, for the truly religious man the only thing that matters—as for the mystic the only thing that exists—is the nature of God.

What, finally, is our position? We put forward the hypothesis that a scientific, comparative study of religious development can help the religions to take their next great forward step, out of our modern perplexity, by accepting the value, though not the authority, of the religious heritage; the authority, though not the adequacy, of reason; and the example, for emulation though not for imitation, of the scientific tradition. For science is the one field of human endeavour which has so far achieved that balance of freedom and order which we must now attain in religion, lest we or it disintegrate.

Science is dynamic; scientists are free to create. It has been our thesis that religion also, and each particular religion, is dynamic; Christians are free to create. Does that freedom to create not also involve a freedom to bungle? Yes, it does; and that freedom is an awe-inspiring fact, with devastating potentialities. Yet scientists, despite their freedom from authority, have made their astonishing progress in the natural sciences by a most impressive self-disciplined submission to a transcendent standard—let us simplify matters for the moment by calling it that of truth. The existentialists have jeopardized as well as liberated human progress by their insistence on freedom. We, in putting forward our existentialist approach to religion, have arrived at freedom without surrendering all standards; for we are repudiating not the principle of idealism but its misapplications in this area. Although we find no cogent authority within a given religion, our very purpose in freeing ourselves from the search for such authority was expressly to arrive at conceptions which would enable us to devote ourselves, and our religions, without reservation or subterfuge, to those higher standards of truth, of beauty, of goodness. In theological terms, our loyalty is to God; and only to God. This involves also inner standards; we shall return to this in a moment. And our contention is that any lesser final loyalty—even to such an apparently praiseworthy empirical existent as Christianity, say, or Islam—is in the end (and perhaps now is that end) destructive. It is the men whose concern is, not for the absolute transcendent principles, nor for the inner standards, but rather for the historical authorities of a given religion, who are to-day in fact exercising the creative freedom to bungle which threatens to disrupt our heritage and perhaps to devastate our civilization. I do not mean that those new forms of Christianity and the other religions of which we stand in need must be the products of human reason. But surely the vigorous religious innovations of our day which are an affront to human reason and intelligence and a denial of human reliability (and also of human brotherhood, across communal lines) are not going to save either religion or us. I am referring to such movements as, in Arab Islam, the Ikhwan-al-Muslimun; in Hinduism the Mahasabha; in Protestant Christianity, certain tendencies of resurgent irrationalism.

It is on this note that I close. It would seem to me that modern enlightened man, for the sake of his own integrity, intellectual and moral, must, if he is to have any religion at all, have one that is consonant with, and comprehensible in terms of, his developed inner standards of truth (scientific and rational), beauty, and the rest, and that is of universal validity; and that the future of Christianity, or Islam, is assured and to be valued only if its leadership lies in the hands of such men. In looking for the creation of not only new but better, fuller, truer developments of the religious traditions which we know, one must think in terms of loyalty only to universal ideals, and in terms of self-discipline. Again, to transpose the argument into the terms of religion itself, God is both transcendent and immanent; and no form can contain Him. God is greater than any of the religions; and man is potentially great because man is the much-loved child of God. God transcends Islam, but is immanent in Muslims. God transcends Christianity, and yet is immanent in us.

Selected Bibliography

The Faith of Other Men (New York: New American Library, 1963).
Islam in Modern History (Princeton: Princeton University Press, 1957).

"Mankind's Religiously-Divided History Approaches Self-Consciousness," *Harvard Divinity Bulletin.* Vol. XXIX (October 1964), pp. 1–17.

The Meaning and End of Religion (New York: Macmillan, 1963).

Modern Islam in India (Kashmiri Bazar, Lahore: St. M. Ashraf, 1963).

Pakistan as an Islamic State (Kashmiri Bazar, Lahore: St. M. Ashraf, 1963).

"Secularity and the History of Religions," *The Spirit and Power of Christian Secularity*, ed. by A. Schlitzer (Notre Dame: University of Notre Dame Press, 1969), pp. 33–58.

Cross-Religious Comparisons: Introduction

NINIAN SMART

Ninian Smart was born on May 6, 1927, in Cambridge, England. He studied at the Universities of Cambridge and Glasgow before World War II; during the war he studied Chinese and was sent to Ceylon. After the war he returned to Oxford University where he received his Bachelor of Philosophy degree in 1954. He taught in India, at Yale University, the University of Wisconsin, and Birmingham University before being appointed to establish a new Department of Religious Studies at the University of Lancaster in 1967. He is both a philosopher and a historian of religion with special interest in the religions of India. He approaches religions analytically, that is, by separating the various dimensions or strands by which they are composed. Eventually, his goal is a comparison of the religions in terms of their representative dimensions. This is his subject in the second of the two selections that follow. The first selection, prepared for a general reading audience and not for students of the field, provides a more comprehensive introduction to "the comparative study of religion."

The comparative study of religion is rather underdeveloped in this country. The annual meetings of the British Section of the International Association for the History of Religions attract hardly more than twenty or thirty people. The amount of investment in Old and New Testament Studies is far vaster, as is that tied up with theology in general. The reasons are fairly understandable, though in some cases regrettable. A major one is the general underdevelopment of non-European studies, though things have improved with the establishment of centres of Asian and African studies in a number of universities. As often, our educational system lags behind the real shape of the world. The challenge to Christian thinking and feeling

Ninian Smart, "I Recommend You to Read," in *Expository Times*, Vol. LXXIX, No. 7 (1968), pp. 196–200. Reprinted by permission of the publishers, T. & T. Clark, Edinburgh.

constituted by the present knowledge of Asian and other faiths should attract greater interest than it does. Much theology is in this respect done in a parochial context. The situation is not improved by the tendency of many Orientalists in this century to adopt a heavily philological approach to their researches. It is reported of an eminent Sanskritist that he once remarked: 'It is a pity that I do not like anything Indian, except, of course, the languages.' Also, in this century there has been a swing to Barthianism (if not to Barth) and the effect of Hendrik Kraemer's influence on missionary thinking has been to render apparently obsolete any real concern to understand sympathetically the genuine challenge of other faiths: if the Gospel transcends religion, then so much for Hinduism, Buddhism, African religions, and the rest!

It is, nevertheless, a dangerous thing to look at the subject only from the standpoint of Christian faith and theology. The very term 'non-Christian' represents no more rational a way of carving up religions than 'non-Buddhist'; yet the almost inevitable result of looking at the comparative study of religion from a Western angle of vision is to divide the world into Christian and non-Christian (or post-Christian and non-Christian). To some extent I shall in this article adopt this defective or at least partial approach to the subject —having, though, made my protest on behalf of those many folk (whose attitudes, just because they are the attitudes of persons, are vitally important for us to understand) in other cultures and belonging to other persuasions and forms of life who would begin from a different point of departure.

But, of course, even if we are primarily concerned with the Christian interpretation of the world, it is necessary not merely to attend to Scripture and doctrine, but to the world which is to be interpreted. Thus it is important that Christians should enter into other people's experience. The tools for doing this are often provided by those who have no such objective of fashioning a theology of the 'non-Christian' religions.

To complicate the task of nominating half a dozen key books in the comparative study of religion, there is not altogether a clear consensus on what the subject is. For some it is mainly the history of religions; for others it is the comparison of motifs in different religions; for others again speculative and theological concerns enter in. Moreover there is a multiplicity of religions.

To simplify matters, and to treat the phenomena in a way suitable for those who have primarily Christian, theological, and practical concerns, one can divide this multiplicity into three categories of religions. First, there are those which are transcultural or universal, at least in principle, and to this group we can assign the major world religions. Thus Christianity, Islam, and Buddhism are quite clearly not confined to ethnic, tribal or national boundaries; while in principle the doctrines of Judaism and Hinduism are relevant to a wider world than those of the practising Jew and of the born Hindu. These religions in a way represent the greatest theological challenge to Christianity, for they give alternative pictures of the world, of the transcendent and of the destiny of man. These elements are not altogether absent in the next category of religions, though by their nature these have no great incentive to preach outside the communities which nourish them.

I refer here to tribal and national religions—our second category—such as the indigenous religions of sub-Saharan Africa, of the American Indians, and so on. Such religions are bound up even more closely than those of the first category to social institutions, and in fact are coterminous with the tribal and national groups to which they belong. For such societies the distinction between religion and culture is non-existent.

The third category is those religions which are of historical interest, though they are no longer living in the proper sense, however many survivals they may have, for instance the religions of ancient Greece and Rome. For present purposes, then, we can consider the attempt to understand these three groups of religions.

But to understand religions may mean more than to treat each individually, in terms of its own inner dynamics and history. It is often illuminating to search for patterns of similarity and to note dissimilarities. Hence, we must look not just for expositions and treatments of particular religions, but also the comparative study of religion or (to use an overlapping conception) the phenomenology of religion. We have, then, three groups of religions and two modes of approach to them.

In addition, we must note that religions are complex: they contain a variety of aspects—myths, rituals, social teachings, doctrines often, institutions, experiences. Comparisons can concentrate on elements within these aspects, such as mythical motifs, the description of mysticism, comparative theology and so on. To be effective such comparisons must take account of two principles: first, they should see apparent similarities in terms of the organic contexts in which the phenomena compared (it is too easy to pick on superficial resemblances); and second, the phenomena are not to be seen as mere objects of observation. It is necessary to enter into the meanings which religious activities, etc., have for those who perform them.

So already we may look upon the subject in terms of the description of particular religions, including their history; and in terms of comparisons between religions, in respect of elements within special aspects of them. But also the study of non-Christian religions has tended to get mixed up with theological reflections about 'other' religions—notably with Christian reflections. A modified form of this is the enterprise of dialogue with other faiths, where the concern is less to start simply from a Christian position than to engage in a more equal and sympathetic discussion with the other faith. I shall not in this article pay attention to those rather *a priori* ventures in the theology of other religions, mission, etc., which are primarily concerned with expounding the Christian position on these matters. However, it will be useful to refer to the modified theological or dialogical approach to other religions.

Thus for present purposes we can consider the subject as having the following manifestations: descriptions of particular religions or aspects thereof; cross-religious comparisons of a descriptive and diagnostic nature; and dialogical and other theological approaches from the Christian side to other religions. The last strictly is not comparative religion, but readers of this journal will doubtless be interested in it. The three forms of study can be related to the three categories of religions outlined earlier.

Cross-Religious Comparisons: The Dimensions of Religion

NINIAN SMART

The Dimensions of Religion

THE RITUAL DIMENSION If we were asked the use or purpose of such buildings as temples and churches, we would not be far wrong in saying that they are used for ritual or ceremonial purposes. Religion tends in part to express itself through such rituals: through worship, prayers, offerings, and the like. We may call this the *ritual* dimension of religion. About this, some important comments need to be made.

First, when we think of ritual we often think of something very formal and elaborate, like a High Mass or the Liturgy of the Eastern Orthodox Church. But it is worth remarking that even the simplest form of religious service involves ritual, in the sense of some form of outer behavior (such as closing one's eyes in prayer) coordinated to an inner intention to make contact with, or to participate in, the invisible world. I am not concerned here with those who deny the existence of such an "invisible world," however interpreted, whether as God's presence, as nirvana, as a sacred energy pervading nature. Whether or not such an invisible world exists, it forms an aspect of the world seen from the point of view of those who participate in religion. It is believed in. As was said earlier, it is not here our task to pass judgment on the truth or otherwise of religious conceptions. First, then, even the simplest service involves ritual.

Second, since ritual involves both an inner and an outer aspect it is always possible that the latter will come to dominate the former. Ritual then degenerates into a mechanical or conventional process. If people go through the motions of religious observance without accompanying it with the intentions and sentiments which give it human meaning, ritual is merely an empty shell. This is the reason why some religious activities are condemned as "ritualistic." But it would be wrong to conclude that because ritualism in this bad sense exists, therefore ritual is an unimportant or degenerate aspect of religion.

It should not be forgotten that there are secular rituals which we all use, and these can form an integral part of personal and social relationships. Greeting someone with a "Good morning," saying goodbye, saluting the flag—all these in differing ways are secular rituals. Very often in society they are integrated with religious rituals, as when men say "God be with you," which is more than taking leave of someone: it is invoking a blessing upon the other person.

Third, it will prove convenient to extend the meaning of "ritual" beyond its reference to the forms of worship, sacrifice, etc., directed toward God or the gods.

It happens that a crucial part is played in India and elsewhere by yoga and analogous techniques of self-training. The ultimate aim of such methods is the attainment of higher states of consciousness, through which the adept has experience of release from worldly existence, of nirvana, of ultimate reality (the interpretation partly depends on the system of doctrines against which the adept tests his experience). Thus the essence of such religion is contemplative or mystical. Sometimes, it is pursued without reference to God or the gods—for example, in Buddhism, where the rituals of a religion of worship and sacrifice are regarded as largely irrelevant to the pursuit of nirvana. Nevertheless, the techniques of self-training have an analogy to ritual: the adept performs various physical and mental exercises through which he hopes to concentrate the mind on the transcendent, invisible world, or to withdraw his senses from their usual immersion in the flow of empirical experiences. This aspect of religion, then, we shall include in our definition of the ritual dimension. It can be classified as pragmatic (aimed at the attainment of certain experiences) in distinction from sacred ritual (directed toward a holy being, such as God). Sometimes the two forms of ritual are combined, as in Christian mysticism.

The meaning of ritual cannot be understood without reference to the environment of belief in which it is performed. Thus prayer in most ritual is directed toward a divine being. Very often, legends about the gods are used to explain the features of a ceremony or festival; and often the important events of human life, such as birth, marriage, death, are invested with a sacred significance by relating them to the divine world.

All this can happen before a religion has any theology or formal system of doctrines. Theology is an attempt to introduce organization and intellectual power into what is found in less explicit form in the deposit of revelation or traditional mythology of a religion. The collection of myths, images, and stories through which the invisible world is symbolized can suitably be called the *mythological* dimension of religion.

THE MYTHOLOGICAL DIMENSION Some important comments need to be made about this mythological dimension. First, in accordance with modern usage in theology and in the comparative study of religion, the terms "myth," "mythological," etc., are *not* used to mean that the content is false. Perhaps in ordinary English to say "It's a myth" is just a way of saying "It's false." But the use of the term *myth* in relation to religious phenomena is quite neutral as to the truth or falsity of the story enshrined in the myth. In origin, the term "myth" means "story," and in calling something a story we are not thereby saying that it is true or false. We are just reporting on what has been said. Similarly, here we are concerned with reporting on what is believed.

Second, it is convenient to use the term to include not merely stories about God (for instance the story of the creation in Genesis), about the gods (for instance in Homer's *Iliad*), etc., but also the historical events of religious significance in a tradition. For example, the Passover ritual in Judaism reenacts a highly important event that once occurred to the children of Israel; their delivery from bondage in Egypt. The historical event functions as a myth. Thus we shall include stories relating to significant historical events under the head of the mythological dimension—again without prejudice to whether the stories accurately describe what actually occurred in history.

THE DOCTRINAL DIMENSION Third, it is not always easy to differentiate the mythological and the symbolic from what is stated in theology. Doctrines are an attempt to give system, clarity, and intellectual power to what is revealed through the mythological and symbolic language of religious faith and ritual. Naturally, theology must make use of the symbols and myths. For example, when the Christian theologian has to describe the meaning of the Incarnation, he must necessarily make use of Biblical language and history. Thus the dividing line between the mythological and what I shall call the *doctrinal* dimension is not easy to draw. Yet there is clearly a distinction between Aquinas's treatment of creation at the philosophical level and the colorful story of creation in Genesis. The distinction is important, because the world religions owe some of their living power to their success in presenting a total picture of reality, through a coherent system of doctrines.

THE ETHICAL DIMENSION Throughout history we find that religions usually incorporate a code of ethics. Ethics concern the behavior of the individual and, to some extent, the code of ethics of the dominant religion controls the community. Quite obviously, men do not always live up to the standards they profess. And sometimes the standards which are inculcated by the dominant faith in a particular society may not be believed by all sections of that society.

Even so, there is no doubt that religions have been influential in molding the ethical attitudes of the societies they are part of. It is important, however, to distinguish between the moral teaching incorporated in the doctrines and mythology of a religion, and the social facts concerning those who adhere to the faith in question. For instance, Christianity teaches "Love thy neighbor as thyself." As a matter of sociological fact, quite a lot of people in so-called Christian countries, where Christianity is the official, or dominant religion, fail to come anywhere near this ideal. The man who goes to church is not necessarily loving; nor is the man who goes to a Buddhist temple necessarily compassionate. Consequently, we must distinguish between the ethical teachings of a faith, which we shall discuss as the *ethical* dimension of religion, and the actual sociological effects and circumstances of a religion.

Pertinent to this point is the consideration that most religions are institutionalized. This is most obvious in technologically primitive societies, where the priest, soothsayer, or magician is closely integrated into the social structure. Religion is not just a personal matter here: it is part of the life of the community. It is built into the institutions of daily life. But even in sophisticated communities where a line is drawn between religious and secular concerns, as in contemporary America, churches exist as institutions to be reckoned with. They are part of the "establishment." In areas where there is active or latent persecution of religious faith, as in the Soviet Union, there are still organizations for continuing religious activities.

THE SOCIAL DIMENSION Religions are not just systems of *belief*: they are also organizations, or parts of organizations. They have a communal and social significance. This social shape of a religion is, of course, to some extent determined by the religious and ethical ideals and practices that it harbors. Conversely, it often happens that the religious and ethical ideals are adapted to existing social conditions and attitudes. For example, Japanese fishermen reconcile the Buddhist injunction against taking life (even animal or fish life) to their activity as fishermen. The Christian's dedication to brotherly love or his attitude to war may be determined more by patriotism and a national crisis than by the Gospel. Thus, it is important to distinguish between the ethical dimension of religion and the *social* dimension. The latter is the mode in which the religion in question is institutionalized, whereby, through its institutions and teachings, it affects the community in which it finds itself. The doctrinal, mythological, and ethical dimensions express a religion's claims about the nature of the invisible world and its aims about how men's lives ought to be shaped: the social dimension indicates the way in which men's lives are in fact shaped by these claims and the way in which religious institutions operate.

It is, incidentally, clear that the ongoing patterns of ritual are an important element in the institutionalization of religion. For example, if it is believed that certain ceremonies and sacraments can only be properly performed by a priest, then the religious institution will be partly determined by the need to maintain and protect a professional priesthood.

THE EXPERIENTIAL DIMENSION   The dimensions we have so far discussed would indeed be hard to account for were it not for the dimension with which this book is centrally concerned: that of experience, the *experiential* dimension. Although men may hope to have contact with, and participate in, the invisible world through ritual, personal religion normally involves the hope of, or realization of, experience of that world. The Buddhist monk hopes for nirvana, and this includes the contemplative experience of peace and of insight into the transcendent. The Christian who prays to God believes normally that God answers prayers—and this not just "externally" in bringing about certain states of affairs, such as a cure for illness, but more importantly "internally" in the personal relationship that flowers between the man who prays and his Maker. The prayerful Christian believes that God does speak to men in an intimate way and that the individual can and does have an inner experience of God. Hence, personal religion necessarily involves what we have called the experiential dimension.

The factor of religious experience is even more crucial when we consider the events and the human lives from which the great religions have stemmed. The Buddha achieved Enlightenment as he sat in meditation beneath the Bo-Tree. As a consequence of his shattering mystical experience, he believed that he had the secret of the cure for the suffering and dissatisfactions of life in this world. We have records of the inaugural visions of some of the Old Testament prophets, of the experiences that told them something profoundly important about God and that spurred them on to teach men in his name. It was through such experiences that Mohammad began to preach the unity of Allah—a preaching that had an explosive impact upon the world from Central Asia to Spain. One cannot read the Upanishads, the source of so much of Hindu doctrine, without feeling the experience on which their teachings are founded. The most striking passage in the *Bhagavadgita*, perhaps the greatest religious document of Hinduism, is that in which the Lord reveals himself in terrifying splendor to Arjuna. Arjuna is overwhelmed by awe and filled with utter devotion. We have already remarked on the seminal importance of St. Paul's similar experience on the Damascus Road.

The words of Jesus Christ reveal his sense of intimate closeness to the Father; there is little doubt that this rested upon highly significant personal experiences. These and other examples can be given of the crucial part played by religious experience in the genesis of the great faiths.

For this reason, it is unrealistic to treat Marxism as a religion: though it possesses doctrines, symbols, a moral code, and even sometimes rituals, it denies the possibility of an experience of the invisible world. Neither relationship to a personal God nor the hope of an experience of salvation or nirvana can be significant for the Marxist. Likewise Humanism, because it fixes its sights on this-worldly aims, is essentially non-religious. Nevertheless, it is necessary for us to examine the impact of these faiths upon the contemporary world. But the main emphasis will be upon the inner side—what religions mean in personal experience, and how they have been molded by such experience.

There is a special difficulty, however, in undertaking a description of a religious experience. We have to rely upon the testimony of those who have the experience, and their reports must be conveyed to us either by telling or writing. Sometimes accounts of prophetic or mystical experience of important religious leaders have been preserved by oral tradition through many generations before being written down. But for the most part, the individual religious experiences that have influenced large segments of mankind occurred in cultures that knew the art of writing.

This means that the experience occurred in the context of the existing religions which already had a doctrinal dimension. This raises a problem for us in our attempt to understand the unique religious experience of the prophets or founders of religions, for their experiences are likely to be interpreted in the light of existing doctrines, as well as clothed in the mythological and symbolic forms of the age. There is less difficulty when we consider the "lesser" figures of the religions—not the founders, but those saints and visionaries who come after. They interpret their experiences in terms of received doctrines and mythologies.

For these reasons, it is not easy to know about a given report which of the elements in it are based, so to say, purely on the experience itself, and which are due to doctrinal and mythological interpretation. To some extent the problem can be overcome by comparing the reports of men of different cultures—such as India and the West— which had virtually no contact during the periods crucial for the formation and elaboration of the dominant religious beliefs.

Moreover, it is worth noting that there is a *dialectic* between experience and doctrine. Thus, though the Buddha, for example, took over elements from the thought-forms of his own age, he was genuinely a creative teacher, who introduced new elements and transmuted the old. The Old Testament prophets fashioned a genuinely original ethical monotheism from an existent belief in Yahweh. The changes they made in the simple tribal religious teaching they inherited can be understood, to some degree, in terms of the impact of the personal religious experiences that were revelatory for these men. Thus experience and doctrinal interpretation have a dialectical relationship. The latter colors the former, but the former also shapes the latter.

This dialectical interplay also helps us to understand some of the features of personal religion at a humbler level. The Christian, for example, is taught certain doctrines and mythological symbols by his parents. He learns to call God "Our Father"; he is instructed to believe that the world is created by God and sustained by God. These ideas will at first simply be "theoretical" as far as the young Christian is concerned, on a par with other non-observable theories he learns about the world, such as that the earth goes round the sun. But suppose he progresses to a deeper understanding of the Christian faith through a particular personal experience, or through his response to the ritual and ethical demands of the religion. Then he will come to see that in some mysterious way God is a person with whom he can have contact; God is not just like the sun, to be thought of speculatively, or to be looked at. Personally, then, he discovers that he can worship and pray to God. In short, "I believe in God the Father

Almighty, Maker of Heaven and Earth" will come to have a new meaning for him. In a sense, he will now believe something other than what he first believed. In this way, the interplay between doctrine and experiences is fundamental to personal religion. . . .

Religion as an Organism

To sum up our account so far of what religion is: it is a six-dimensional organism, typically containing doctrines, myths, ethical teachings, rituals, and social institutions, and animated by religious experiences of various kinds. To understand the key ideas of religion, such as God and nirvana, one has to understand the pattern of religious life directed toward these goals. God is the focus of worship and praise; nirvana is found by treading the Noble Eightfold Path, culminating in contemplation.

Indeed, one can say something even stronger than this. God is to be *defined* in relation to worship. To say "My God, my God" is to acknowledge that he deserves my loyalty and praise. God and gods are essentially the foci of men's worship and ritual activities. So, when, by a metaphor, we say that a man makes a god of his stomach, we do not mean that he makes a Creator or First Cause of his stomach: but that he "worships" his stomach—eating is his greatest object of loyalty and reverence. To say that there is a God is therefore different from saying that there is a Creator or First Cause. God may be Creator: but primarily he is the object of worship. Thus the understanding of ideas about God requires close attention to their milieu in men's religious life. And the rituals men direct toward God and the gods need to be understood by reference to their inner side, and thus ultimately by reference to a man's religious experience.

This general account of religion which we have given depends on comparing religions as we find them in the world. Comparisons, though, need to be handled carefully. For we are not confronted in fact by some monolithic object, namely religion. We are confronted by *religions*. And each religion has its own style, its own inner dynamic, its own special meanings, its uniqueness. Each religion is an organism, and has to be understood in terms of the interrelation of its different parts. Thus though there are resemblances between religions or between parts of religions, these must not be seen too crudely.

For example, it is correct to say that some religions are monotheistic. They each worship a single God. But the conception of God can vary subtly. For instance, though Islam and Christianity both draw upon the Old Testament heritage, and though Allah has many characteristics of the Christian God, such as being Creator, judge, merciful, providential, nevertheless even the points of resemblance are affected by the rest of the milieu. Thus the Christian idea of the Creator is affected by the fact that creation is not just seen in relation to Genesis but also in relation to the opening verses of John. Belief in Christ seen as the Logos affects belief in God and affects one's view of creation.

It is like a picture. A particular element, such as a patch of yellow, may occur in two different pictures. One can point to the resemblance. Yet the meaning of one patch of yellow can still be very different from the meaning of the other. What it means, how it looks—these depend on what other patches of color surround it. Likewise, elements in a religious organism are affected by the other elements present.

So although we are inevitably drawn to compare religions in order to make sense of the patterns of religious experience found in the history of men's faiths, we also have to recognize that each religion must also be seen essentially in its own terms, from within, as it were. This means that we have to have a sense of the multiplicity of man's religious life, as well as for its points of unity and contact. We are not only concerned with religion: we are concerned also with religions. And we have to see them in the perspective of the world's history.

Selected Bibliography

"The Concept of Heaven," *Talk of God* (Royal Institute of Philosophy Lectures, Vol. II, 1967–68). (New York: St. Martin's Press Inc., 1969), pp. 226–238.

A *Dialogue of Religions* (Baltimore: Penguin Books, Inc., 1960).

Doctrine and Argument in Indian Philosophy (London: Allen and Unwin, Ltd., 1964).

"Interpretation and Mystical Experience," *Religious Studies.* Vol. I, No. 1 (1965), pp. 75–88.

Philosophers and Religious Truth (New York: Collier-Macmillan, 1964).

Reasons and Faiths (London: Routledge and Kegan Paul, Ltd., 1958).

Secular Education and the Logic of Religion (London: Faber & Faber, Ltd., 1968).

The Yogi and the Devotee (London: Allen and Unwin, Ltd., 1968).

On the Social Psychology of the World Religions

MAX WEBER

Recognized for his encyclopedic knowledge as well as for his detailed work in sociology and political economics, Max Weber was born on April 21, 1864, in Erfurt, Germany. He received his education from the Universities of Heidelberg, Berlin, and Göttingen in economics, history, philosophy, and law. He took his bar examination in 1886, and completed his doctoral dissertation on medieval commercial law in 1889. In 1890 Weber was commissioned to investigate the social and economic plight of eastern German farm workers, during which time he also taught law at the University of Berlin. In 1894 he became professor of economics at Freiburg, and in 1896 at Heidelberg. In 1898 Weber suffered a nervous breakdown from which he never fully recovered; he was able to continue with his research and writing, however. In 1903 Weber became associate editor of a leading journal in sociology and politics and in 1904 he began publishing his own works. Late in World War I he resumed his teaching, first on a temporary basis at Vienna, and in 1919 at Munich. He was a consultant to the German armistice commission at Versailles and helped to prepare the first draft of the Weimar Constitution. He died in Munich on June 14, 1920.

Weber's early intellectual interests were inspired by Marxist ideology. He shared an interest in the social origins of capitalism and sought reasons for capitalism's success in the Western world. Similarly, he established correlations between economic interests and ethical ideals, and demonstrated that social status and religious outlook are interdependent. In the selection that follows two of Weber's concerns are illustrated. First, he compares the "salvation interests" of various religions, and secondly, he shows how those religious interests can be correlated with attitudes taken toward secular activities.

By 'world religions,' we understand the five religions or religiously

Max Weber, "The Social Psychology of the World Religions," *From Max Weber: Essays in Sociology*, translated and edited by H. H. Gerth and C. Wright Mills (New York: Oxford University Press, 1946). Reprinted by permission.

determined systems of life-regulation which have known how to gather multitudes of confessors around them. The term is used here in a completely value-neutral sense. The Confucian, Hinduist, Buddhist, Christian, and Islamist religious ethics all belong to the category of world religion. A sixth religion, Judaism, will also be dealt with. It is included because it contains historical preconditions decisive for understanding Christianity and Islamism, and because of its historic and autonomous significance for the development of the modern economic ethic of the Occident—a significance, partly real and partly alleged, which has been discussed several times recently. References to other religions will be made only when they are indispensable for historical connections.[1]

What is meant by the 'economic ethic' of a religion will become increasingly clear during the course of our presentation. This term does not bring into focus the ethical theories of theological compendia; for however important such compendia may be under certain circumstances, they merely serve as tools of knowledge. The term 'economic ethic' points to the practical impulses for action which are founded in the psychological and pragmatic contexts of religions. The following presentation may be sketchy, but it will make obvious how complicated the structures and how many-sided the conditions of a concrete economic ethic usually are. Furthermore, it will show that externally similar forms of economic organization may agree with very different economic ethics and, according to the unique character of their economic ethics, how such forms of economic organization may produce very different historical results. An economic ethic is not a simple 'function' of a form of economic organization; and just as little does the reverse hold, namely, that economic ethics unambiguously stamp the form of the economic organization.

No economic ethic has ever been determined solely by religion. In the face of man's attitudes towards the world—as determined by religious or other (in our sense) 'inner' factors—an economic ethic has, of course, a high measure of autonomy. Given factors of economic geography and history determine this measure of autonomy in the highest degree. The religious determination of life-conduct, however,

---

[1] 'Die Wirtschaftsethik der Weltreligionen,' *Gesammelte Aufsaetze zur Religionssoziologie* (Tübingen, 1922–3), vol. I, pp. 237–68. This is a translation of the Introduction to a series of studies which Weber published as articles in the *Archiv für Sozialforschung* under the title 'Die Wirtschaftsethik der Weltreligionen' (The Economic Ethic of the World Religions). The Introduction and the first parts on Confucianism and Taoism were written in 1913. They were not published until September 1915, in the 41st volume of the *Archiv*.

is also one—note this—only one, of the determinants of the economic ethic. Of course, the religiously determined way of life is itself profoundly influenced by economic and political factors operating within given geographical, political, social, and national boundaries. We should lose ourselves in these discussions if we tried to demonstrate these dependencies in all their singularities. Here we can only attempt to peel off the directive elements in the life-conduct of those social *strata* which have most strongly influenced the practical ethic of their respective religions. These elements have stamped the most characteristic features upon practical ethics, the features that distinguish one ethic from others; *and*, at the same time, they have been important for the respective economic ethics.

By no means must we focus upon only one stratum. Those strata which are decisive in stamping the characteristic features of an economic ethic may change in the course of history. And the influence of a single stratum is never an exclusive one. Nevertheless, as a rule one may determine the strata whose styles of life have been at least predominantly decisive for certain religions. Here are some examples, if one may anticipate:

Confucianism was the status ethic of prebendaries, of men with literary educations who were characterized by a secular rationalism. If one did not belong to this *cultured* stratum he did not count. The religious (or if one wishes, irreligious) status ethic of this stratum has determined the Chinese way of life far beyond the stratum itself.

Earlier Hinduism was borne by a hereditary caste of cultured literati, who, being remote from any office, functioned as a kind of ritualist and spiritual advisers for individuals and communities. They formed a stable center for the orientation of the status stratification, and they placed their stamp upon the social order. Only Brahmans, *educated* in the Veda, formed, as bearers of tradition, the fully recognized religious status group. And only later a non-Brahman status group of ascetics emerged by the side of the Brahmans and competed with them. Still later, during the Indian Middle Ages, Hinduism entered the plain. It represented the ardent sacramental religiosity of the savior, and was borne by the lower strata with their plebeian mystagogues.

Buddhism was propagated by strictly contemplative, mendicant monks, who rejected the world and, having no homes, migrated. Only these were full members of the religious community; all others remained religious laymen of inferior value: objects, not subjects, of religiosity.

During its first period, Islamism was a religion of world-conquering warriors, a knight order of disciplined crusaders. They lacked only the sexual asceticism of their Christian copies of the age of the Crusades. But during the Islamic Middle Ages, contemplative and mystical Sufism attained at least an equal standing under the leadership of plebeian technicians of orgiastics. The brotherhoods of the petty bourgeoisie grew out of Sufism in a manner similar to the Christian Tertiarians, except they were far more universally developed.

Since the Exile, Judaism has been the religion of a civic 'pariah people.' We shall in time become acquainted with the precise meaning of the term. During the Middle Ages Judaism fell under the leadership of a stratum of intellectuals who were trained in literature and ritual, a peculiarity of Judaism. This stratum has represented an increasingly quasi-proletarian and rationalist petty-bourgeois intelligentsia.

Christianity, finally, began its course as a doctrine of itinerant artisan journeymen. During all periods of its mighty external and internal development it has been a quite specifically urban, and above all a civic, religion. This was true during Antiquity, during the Middle Ages, and in Puritanism. The city of the Occident, unique among all other cities of the world—and citizenship, in the sense in which it has emerged only in the Occident—has been the major theatre for Christianity. This holds for the pneumatic piety of the ancient religious community, for the mendicant monk orders of the high Middle Ages, and for the [Protestant] sects of the reformation up to pietism and methodism.

It is not our thesis that the specific nature of a religion is a simple 'function' of the social situation of the stratum which appears as its characteristic bearer, or that it represents the stratum's 'ideology,' or that it is a 'reflection' of a stratum's material or ideal interest-situation. On the contrary, a more basic misunderstanding of the standpoint of these discussions would hardly be possible.

However incisive the social influences, economically and politically determined, may have been upon a religious ethic in a particular case, it receives its stamp primarily from religious sources, and, first of all, from the content of its annunciation and its promise. Frequently the very next generation reinterprets these annunciations and promises in a fundamental fashion. Such reinterpretations adjust the revelations to the needs of the religious community. If this occurs, then it is at least usual that religious doctrines are adjusted to *religious needs*.

Other spheres of interest could have only a secondary influence; often, however, such influence is very obvious and sometimes it is decisive.

For every religion we shall find that a change in the socially decisive strata has usually been of profound importance. On the other hand, the type of a religion, once stamped, has usually exerted a rather far-reaching influence upon the life-conduct of very heterogeneous strata. In various ways people have sought to interpret the connection between religious ethics and interest-situations in such a way that the former appear as mere 'functions' of the latter. Such interpretation occurs in so-called historical materialism—which we shall not here discuss—as well as in a purely psychological sense. . . .

The kind of empirical state of bliss or experience of rebirth that is sought after as the supreme value by a religion has obviously and necessarily varied according to the character of the stratum which was foremost in adopting it. The chivalrous warrior class, peasants, business classes, and intellectuals with literary education have naturally pursued different religious tendencies. As will become evident, these tendencies have not by themselves determined the psychological character of religion; they have, however, exerted a very lasting influence upon it. The contrast between warrior and peasant classes, and intellectual and business classes, is of special importance. Of these groups, the intellectuals have always been the exponents of a rationalism which in their case has been relatively theoretical. The business classes (merchants and artisans) have been at least possible exponents of rationalism of a more practical sort. Rationalism of either kind has borne very different stamps, but has always exerted a great influence upon the religious attitude.

Above all, the peculiarity of the intellectual strata in this matter has been in the past of the greatest importance for religion. At the present time, it matters little in the development of a religion whether or not modern intellectuals feel the need of enjoying a 'religious' state as an 'experience,' in addition to all sorts of other sensations, in order to decorate their internal and stylish furnishings with paraphernalia guaranteed to be genuine and old. A religious revival has never sprung from such a source. In the past, it was the work of the intellectuals to sublimate the possession of sacred values into a belief in 'redemption.' The conception of the idea of redemption, as such, is very old, if one understands by it a liberation from distress, hunger, drought, sickness, and ultimately from suffering and death. Yet redemption attained a specific significance only where it expressed a systematic and rationalized 'image of the world' and represented a stand in the face of the world. For the meaning as well as the intended and actual psychological quality of redemption has depended upon such a world image and such a stand. Not ideas, but material and ideal interests, directly govern men's conduct. Yet very frequently the 'world images' that have been created by 'ideas' have, like switchmen, determined the tracks along which action has been pushed by the dynamic of interest. 'From what' and 'for what' one wished to be redeemed and, let us not forget, 'could be' redeemed, depended upon one's image of the world.

There have been very different possibilities in this connection: One could wish to be saved from political and social servitude and lifted into a Messianic realm in the future of this world; or one could wish to be saved from being defiled by ritual impurity and hope for the pure beauty of psychic and bodily existence. One could wish to escape being incarcerated in an impure body and hope for a purely spiritual existence. One could wish to be saved from the eternal and senseless play of human passions and desires and hope for the quietude of the pure beholding of the divine. One could wish to be saved from radical evil and the servitude of sin and hope for the eternal and free benevolence in the lap of a fatherly god. One could wish to be saved from peonage under the astrologically conceived determination of stellar constellations and long for the dignity of freedom and partaking of the substance of the hidden deity. One could wish to be redeemed from the barriers to the finite, which express themselves in suffering, misery and death, and the threatening punishment of hell, and hope for an eternal bliss in an earthly or paradisical future existence. One could wish to be saved from the cycle of rebirths with their inexorable compensations for the deeds of the times past and hope for eternal rest. One could wish to be saved from senseless brooding and events and long for the dreamless sleep. Many more varieties of belief have, of course, existed. Behind them always lies a stand towards something in the actual world which is experienced as specifically 'senseless.' Thus, the demand has been implied: that the world order in its totality is, could, and should somehow be a meaningful 'cosmos.' This quest, the core of genuine religious rationalism, has been borne precisely by strata of intellectuals. The avenues, the results, and the efficacy of this metaphysical need for a meaningful cosmos have varied widely. Nevertheless, some general comments may be made.

The general result of the modern form of thoroughly rationalizing the conception of the world and of the way of life, theoretically and practically, in a purposive manner, has been that religion has been shifted into the realm of the irrational. This has been the more the case the further the purposive type of rationalization has progressed, if one takes the standpoint of an intellectual articulation of an image of the world. This shift of religion into the irrational realm has occurred for several reasons. On the one hand, the calculation of consistent rationalism has not easily come out even with nothing left over. In music, the Pythagorean 'comma' resisted complete rationalization oriented to tonal physics. The various great systems of music of all peoples and ages have differed in the manner in which they have either covered up or bypassed this inescapable irrationality or, on the other hand, put irrationality into the service of the richness of tonalities. The same has seemed to happen to the theoretical conception of the world, only far more so; and above all, it has seemed to happen to the rationalization of practical life. The various great ways of leading a rational and methodical life have been characterized by irrational presuppositions, which have been accepted simply as 'given' and which have been incorporated into such ways of life. What these presuppositions have been is historically and socially determined, at least to a very large extent, through the peculiarity of those strata that have been the carriers of the ways of life during its formative and decisive period. The *interest* situation of these strata, as determined socially and psychologically, has made for their peculiarity, as we here understand it.

Furthermore, the irrational elements in the rationalization of reality have been the *loci* to which the irrepressible quest of intellectualism for the possession of supernatural values has been compelled to retreat. That is the more so the more denuded of irrationality the world appears to be. The unity of the primitive image of the world, in which everything was concrete magic, has tended to split into rational cognition and mastery of nature, on the one hand, and into 'mystic' experiences, on the other. The inexpressible contents of such experiences remain the only possible 'beyond,' added to the mechanism of a world robbed of gods. In fact, the beyond remains an incorporeal and metaphysical realm in which individuals intimately possess the holy. Where this conclusion has been drawn without any residue, the individual can pursue his quest for salvation only as an individual. This phenomenon appears in some form, with progressive intellectualist rationalism, wherever men have ventured to rationalize the image of the world as being a cosmos governed by impersonal rules. Naturally it has occurred most strongly among religions and religious ethics which have been quite strongly determined by genteel strata of intellectuals devoted to the purely cognitive comprehension of the world and of its 'meaning.' This was the case with Asiatic and, above all, Indian world religions. For all of them, contemplation became the supreme and ultimate religious value accessible to man. Contemplation offered them entrance into the profound and blissful tranquillity and immobility of the All-one. All other forms of religious states, however, have been at best considered a relatively valuable *Ersatz* for contemplation. This has had far-reaching consequences for the relation of religion to life, including economic life, as we shall repeatedly see. Such consequences flow from the general character of 'mystic' experiences, in the contemplative sense, and from the psychological preconditions of the search for them.

The situation in which strata decisive for the development of a religion were active in practical life has been entirely different. Where they were chivalrous warrior heroes, political officials, economically acquisitive classes, or, finally, where an organized hierocracy dominated religion, the results were different than where genteel intellectuals were decisive.

The rationalism of hierocracy grew out of the professional preoccupation with cult and myth or—to a far higher degree—out of the cure of souls, that is, the confession of sin and counsel to sinners. Everywhere hierocracy has sought to monopolize the administration of religious values. They have also sought to bring and to temper the bestowal of religious goods into the form of 'sacramental' or 'corporate grace,' which could be ritually bestowed only by the priesthood and could not be attained by the individual. The individual's quest for salvation or the quest of free communities by means of contemplation, orgies, or asceticism, has been considered highly suspect and has had to be regulated ritually and, above all, controlled hierocratically. From the standpoint of the interests of the priesthood in power, this is only natural.

Every body of *political* officials, on the other hand, has been suspicious of all sorts of individual pursuits of salvation and of the free formation of communities as sources of emancipation from domestication at the hands of the institution of the state. Political officials have distrusted the competing priestly corporation of grace and, above all, at bottom they have despised the very quest for these impractical values lying beyond utilitarian and worldly ends. For all political bureaucracies, religious duties have ultimately been simply official or social obligations of the citizenry and of status groups. Ritual has corresponded to rules and regulations, and, therefore, wherever a bu reaucracy has determined its nature, religion has assumed a ritualist character.

It is also usual for a stratum of *chivalrous* warriors to pursue absolutely worldly interests and to be remote from all 'mysticism.' Such strata, however, have lacked—and this is characteristic of heroism in general—the desire as well as the capacity for a rational mastery of reality. The irrationality of 'fate' and, under certain conditions, the idea of a vague and deterministically conceived 'destiny' (the Homeric *Moira*) has stood above and behind the divinities and demons who were conceived of as passionate and strong heroes, measuring out assistance and hostility, glory and booty, or death to the human heroes.

Peasants have been inclined towards magic. Their whole economic existence has been specifically bound to nature and has made them dependent upon elemental forces. They readily believe in a compelling sorcery directed against spirits who rule over or through natural forces, or they believe in simply buying divine benevolence. Only tremendous transformations of life-orientation have succeeded in tearing them away from this universal and primeval form of religiosity. Such transformations have been derived either from other strata or from mighty prophets, who, through the power of miracles, legitimize themselves as sorcerers. Orgiastic and ecstatic states of 'possession,' produced by means of toxics or by the dance, are strange to the status honor of knights because they are considered undignified. Among the peasants, however, such states have taken the place that 'mysticism' holds among the intellectuals.

Finally, we may consider the strata that in the western European sense are called 'civic,' as well as those which elsewhere correspond to them: artisans, traders, enterprisers engaged in cottage industry, and their derivatives existing only in the modern Occident. Apparently these strata have been the most ambiguous with regard to the religious stands open to them. And this is especially important to us.

Among these 'civic' strata the following religious phenomena have had especially strong roots: the institutional and sacramental grace of the Roman church in the medieval cities—the pillars of the popes; the mystagogic and sacramental grace in the ancient cities and in India; the orgiastic and contemplative Sufi, and Dervish religion of the Middle Eastern Orient; the Taoist magic; the Buddhist contemplation; the ritualist appropriation of grace under the direction of souls by mystagogues in Asia; all the forms of love for a savior; the beliefs in redemption the world over, from the cult of Krishna to the cult of Christ; the rational ritualism of the law and the sermon of the synagogue denuded of all magic among Jewry; the pneumatic and ancient as well as the asceticist medieval sects; the grace of predestination and the ethical regeneration of the Puritan and the Methodist; as well as all sorts of individual pursuits of salvation. All of these have been more firmly rooted among 'civic' strata than among any other. . . .

It is quite understandable that the more weighty the civic strata as such have been, and the more they have been torn from bonds of taboo and from divisions into sibs and castes, the more favorable has been the soil for religions that call for action in this world. Under these conditions, the preferred religious attitude could become the attitude of active asceticism, of God-willed *action* nourished by the sentiment of being God's 'tool,' rather than the possession of the deity or the inward and contemplative surrender to God, which has appeared as the supreme value to religions influenced by strata of genteel intellectuals. In the Occident the attitude of active asceticism has repeatedly retained supremacy over contemplative mysticism and orgiastic or apathetic ecstasy, even though these latter types have been well known in the Occident. Active asceticism, however, has not been confined to civic strata. Such an unambiguous social determination has not in any way existed. The prophecy of Zoroaster was directed at the nobility and the peasantry; the prophecy of Islam was directed to warriors. These prophecies, like the Israelite and the early Christian prophecy and preaching, have had an active character, which stands in contrast with the propaganda of Buddhism, Taoism, Neo-Pythagoreanism, Gnosticism, and Sufism. Certain specific conclusions of emissary prophecies, however, have been drawn precisely on 'eivic' grounds.

In the missionary prophecy the devout have not experienced themselves as vessels of the divine but rather as instruments of a god. This emissary prophecy has had a profound elective affinity to a special conception of God: the conception of a supra-mundane, personal, wrathful, forgiving, loving, demanding, punishing Lord of Creation. Such a conception stands in contrast to the supreme being of exemplary prophecy. As a rule, though by no means without exception, the supreme being of an exemplary prophecy is an impersonal being because, as a static state, he is accessible only by means of contemplation. The conception of an active God, held by emissary prophecy, has dominated the Iranian and Mid-Eastern religions and those Occidental religions which are derived from them. The conception of a supreme and static being, held by exemplary prophecy, has come to dominate Indian and Chinese religiosity.

These differences are not primitive in nature. On the contrary, they have come into existence only by means of a far-reaching sublimation of primitive conceptions of animist spirits and of heroic deities which are everywhere similar in nature. Certainly the connection of conceptions of God with religious states, which are evaluated and desired as sacred values, have also been strongly influential in this process of sublimation. These religious states have simply been interpreted in the direction of a different conception of God, according to whether the holy states, evaluated as supreme, were contemplative mystic experiences or apathetic ecstasy, **or** whether they were the orgiastic possession of god, or visionary inspirations and 'commands.'

Selected Bibliography

Ancient Judaism (New York: The Free Press, 1952).

The City (New York: The Free Press, 1958).

From Max Weber: Essays in Sociology, trans. and ed. by Hans H. Gerth and C. Wright Mills (New York: Oxford University Press, 1946).

Max Weber on the Methodology of the Social Sciences, trans. and ed. by Edward Shils and H. A. Finch (New York: The Free Press, 1949).

The Protestant Ethic and the Spirit of Capitalism, trans. by Talcott Parsons (London: Allen and Unwin, 1930).

The Religion of China: Confucianism and Taoism (New York: The Free Press, 1951).

The Sociology of Religion (Boston: The Beacon Press, 1963).

The Theory of Social and Economic Organization, trans. by A. M. Henderson and Talcott Parsons (New York: The Free Press, 1957).

The Institutionalization of Religion

Thomas F. O'Dea

Thomas F. O'Dea was born on December 1, 1915, in Amesbury, Massachusetts. After serving in the U.S. Army in World War II, he enrolled in Harvard University from which he received his B.A. degree in 1949, his M.A. degree in 1951, and his Ph.D. in 1953. From 1951 to 1953 he was a Carnegie Fellow at Harvard. In 1953 he joined the faculty of the Massachusetts Institute of Technology. From 1955 to 1956 he was a fellow at the Center for Advanced Study in the Behavioral Sciences in Palo Alto, California. From 1956 to 1959 he taught at Fordham University; from 1959 to 1964 at the University of Utah; and from 1964 to 1967 at Columbia University where he was also Chairman of the Department of Religion. In 1967 he joined the faculties of Religious Studies and Sociology at the University of California, Santa Barbara.

   Throughout his career, O'Dea has worked in the fields of both sociology and religious studies, usually simultaneously. In the former he has given stress to two large subject areas, the sociology of knowledge and the problems associated with technology and social change. In religion he has paid particular attention to the ways in which social processes affect religious institutions and to the ways in which religious institutions respond to social processes. Thus, he has been interested in selected religious communities—the Mormons, for example, and contemporary Roman Catholicism—which he has tended to assess in terms of a series of problems presented to such communities by the processes of sociocultural, technological, and ideological change. In the essay that follows, O'Dea has isolated five such "dilemmas" in addressing himself to the subject of the institutionalization of religion.

Five Dilemmas in the Institutionalization of Religion

The dysfunctions of religion, the ambiguities of the relationship between religion and society, and the contribution of religion to the creation and exacerbation of social conflict are all complicated by the fact that the institutionalization of religion is itself the working out of a set of structurally inherent dilemmas. Five such dilemmas may be distinguished as characteristic of the development of specifically religious organizations, and from these derive many of the internal strains and functional problems of such religious bodies. These five paradoxes of institutionalization are discussed below.[1]

THE DILEMMA OF MIXED MOTIVATION   In the first or charismatic period in the development of founded religions, usually to be seen in the relationship between a charismatic leader and his disciples, the motivation of the active participants tends to be characterized by considerable single-mindedness. The religious movement does satisfy complex needs for its adherents, but such needs are focused upon religious values as these are proclaimed and embodied by the charismatic leader. With institutionalization, however, an important innovation is introduced.

Institutionalization involves a stable set of statuses and roles, defined in terms of functions, upon which are encumbent rights and obligations. There arises a structure of offices which involves a stratified set of rewards in terms of prestige, life opportunities, and material compensations.

This process is clearly to be observed in the emergence of specifically religious organizations. The stable structure which thus develops becomes capable of eliciting a wide range of individual motives and of focusing diverse motivations behind the goals of the organization as specified in prescribed role behavior. This process has the strategic functional significance of providing stability, since the organization no longer has to depend upon disinterested motivation. Institutionalization mobilizes behind institutionalized expectations what Parsons has called both disinterested and interested motivation. However, this mobilization of a variety of motives in support of the goals and values of the organization can, and often does, result in the subtle transformation of the goals and values themselves. When a professional clergy emerges in the church, there comes into existence a body of men for whom the clerical life offers not simply the "religious" satisfactions of the earlier charismatic period, but also prestige and respectability,

---

[1] These five dilemmas are treated at somewhat greater length in two articles, "Five Dilemmas in the Institutionalization of Religion," *Journal for the Scientific Study of Religion* (October 1961), No. 1, I:30–39; and "Sociological Dilemmas: Five Paradoxes of Institutionalization," in *Sociological Theory, Values and Sociocultural Change*, Edward A. Tiryakian (ed.) (New York: Free Press of Glencoe, 1963), pp. 71–89.

power and influence, in both church and society, and satisfactions derived from the use of personal talents in teaching, leadership, etc. Moreover, the *maintenance* of the situation in which these rewards are forthcoming tends to become an element in the motivation of the group.

We have already seen numerous examples of the kinds of changes which such developments introduce into the church and the way that they affect the relationship of the church and society. The higher clergy in Christian history became important functionaries and dignitaries in society, with all the rewards and benefits accruing to people in such positions. The higher clergy, in terms of both church office and of non-ecclesiastical governmental functions, became part of the ruling and dominant classes in society, and their interests fused with those of such classes. These new interests of the alienation of symbols. In the Middle Ages, people lost the sense of the original meaning of much of the symbolism involved in the Mass. It then became necessary for churchmen to invent an elaborate secondary allegorization, attributing novel and often extrinsic meanings to the alienated symbols.

A kind of charisma of the obscure may be maintained by the development of archaism, as in the use of a little-understood dead language, special apparel, and a stylization of performance. But such secondary reactions to alienation do not change the basic situation. The embodiment of the sacred in the profane vehicle causes a loss of sacredness. The embodiment of the ultimate in empirical symbols causes a diminution of the sense of ultimacy itself. Repetition robs ritual of its unusual character, so significant for charisma, and routinizes it. The loss of resonance means the loss of the original emotional meaning. The symbolic order thus becomes alienated. Cult, dependent upon symbolism, then is reduced to a routine performance of established formalities, and no longer serves its original purpose.

This alienation of symbolism and the evolution of a charisma of the obscure gives rise to protest. The importance of both to the anti-symbolic reactions of the left-wing of the Reformation can hardly be overestimated. The more extreme Protestant groups attacked the Mass with great bitterness, broke stained-glass windows, removed altars and statues from churches, and violently desecrated the sacrament. Such symbolic expressions of the older church were seen as idols and as barriers in the way of the religious experience, rather than as elements promoting and eliciting it. Thus was religious solidarity weakened and violent protest evoked.

THE DILEMMA OF ADMINISTRATIVE ORDER: ELABORATION AND ALIENA-
TION The routinization of charisma often gives rise to formal
organization with bureaucratic structure. New offices tend to develop
as new functions arise. Moreover, precedents established in action
lead to a transformation of existing offices. The general contours of
the administrative structure tend to reflect the problems and functions in response to which the structure developed. There are several
factors which tend to render such bureaucratic structures dysfunctional. Structures which emerge in one set of conditions and in response to one set of problems may turn out later to be unwieldly
instruments for handling new problems under new conditions. Functional precedents established in handling earlier problems can become
dysfunctional in later situations, and can even become formidable
obstacles blocking any forthright action.

Since it is this structure of offices which becomes the mechanism
for eliciting the mixed motivation we have discussed above, and mobi-
lizing it behind organizational goals, the individuals involved come to
have a vested interest in the structure as it is, and to resist change and
reform, which they tend to see as threatening to themselves. Thus
not only can the structure become overelaborated and alienated from
contemporary problems, but it can contribute to the alienation of
office holders from the rank-and-file members of the group. Such
developments are clearly visible in the history of the clergy often
deviated from the goals and values of the church. The church was
transformed in a subtle way. It became secularized; the clergy became
"worldly." Since it is the clergy who interpret the church's teachings,
these come to be understood and applied in ways which tend to express and maintain the interests of the clerical stratum itself. Thus
while mixed motivation, introduced by institutionalization, enhances
stability and contributes to the survival of the organization, it also
represents a source of serious transformation in the goals and values
of the church.

This development of mixed motivation is most significant with
respect to leadership roles, but it is to be seen in the rank and file as
well. As "born members" replaced people who had been converted, a
different kind of motivation and identification came to prevail in the
church. As the laity became a more passive element in the church, lay
people tended to develop a different kind of identification, and their
motives for participation changed as well. Already in the second century there appears a prophetic literature denouncing the resulting
lukewarmness of many in the church.

THE SYMBOLIC DILEMMA: OBJECTIFICATION VERSUS ALIENATION

We have seen that the cultic re-presentation of the religious experience is central to the life of the religious group, and that it is a symbolic performance. As an embodiment of religious meanings and as the means of acting out religious attitudes, the symbol becomes subject to the strains and dilemmas embodied in religion itself. To retain the original experience, with its supraempirical relation to the ultimate and the sacred, it must be given expression in symbolic forms which are themselves empirical and profane, and which with repetition become prosaic and everyday in character. Hence the use of symbols in order to make possible "a prolongation of hierophanies," [2] or apprehensions of the sacred, can be a first step in routinization.

Susanne Langer has pointed out that ritual is expressive in a logical rather than in a psychological sense. Ritual represents an objectified order of symbols which elicits and articulates attitudes and feelings, molding the personal dispositions of the worshipers after its own model. This objectification is a requisite for continuity, and for sharing within the religious group. Without such objectification and sharing, collective worship would be impossible. Yet a continued use of the same symbolic vehicles has the effect of making them usual and expected—that is, of routinizing them. The necessary objectification tends to remove the symbols from meaningful contact with subjective attitudes. Thus there develops a loss of resonance between the symbol and the attitudes and feelings from which it originally derived. The symbol consequently loses its power to elicit and affect attitudes and emotions. Objectification, necessary for continuity, leads finally to alienation.

The history of religion offers many examples of this process of the church. They were intensified by the rediscovery and appropriation of Roman law, which provided the church with a rational-legal bureaucratic model. The frustration of efforts to reform the church in the two centuries before Luther; the rise of clericalism; the conflict between bishops and bureaucrats of the Roman Curia—all are examples of the effects of this dilemma, as it is complicated by the development of mixed motivation.

THE DILEMMA OF DELIMITATION: CONCRETE DEFINITION VERSUS SUBSTITUTION OF THE LETTER FOR THE SPIRIT

To affect the lives of men, the original religious message must be stated in terms that have

---

[2] Mircea Eliade, *Patterns in Comparative Religion*, trans. by Rosemary Sheed (New York: Sheed & Ward, 1958), p. 448.

relevance to the everyday activities and concerns of people. Moreover, to preserve the import of the message, it must be protected against interpretations which would transform it in ways conflicting with its inner ethos. These needs are characteristic of both the religious message and the ethic implied in it. Both of these needs constitute a strong pressure for definition. Thus in the history of the Christian church we see a continual process in which doctrine is defined in response to interpretations felt to be heretical. Moreover, with respect to the Christian ethic, it was soon found that its implications had to be spelled out in some detail for the new converts made among the gentiles. This involved both the utilization of elements of Hebraic law—the Ten Commandments, especially, which Paul had considered as superseded—and the natural law of Greek philosophy, especially as formulated by the Stoics. Such definition was also a process of concretization, and it was a functional necessity without which the church could hardly have maintained its religious insights and its organizational integrity.

This process of definition and concretization is at the same time a relativization of the religious and ethical message—a rendering of it relevant to the new circumstances of life of the religious group—and therefore involves the risk of making everyday and prosaic what was originally a call to the extraordinary. Moreover, implications drawn in concrete form under particular circumstances may come to be accepted in a literalist manner, in which the original scope of the implications of the religious message may be lost. The problem may be seen quite clearly in the sphere of the religious ethic. The original ethical insight is translated into a set of rules to bring it within the grasp of new converts. These rules give the original ethical insight a kind of "operational definition" comprehensible to the average man. Yet rules, however elaborate they may become, cannot make explicit all that was implied in the original insight itself, and run the risk of losing its spirit. Rules specify, and thereby substitute for the original insight specific items of prescribed or proscribed behavior. Thus there can develop a complicated set of legalistic formulations. In Hinduism this process may be seen in the evolution of elaborate proscriptions to preserve ritual purity. It may also be seen in the Pharisaic rituals in Judaism of the classical period. Both Catholicism and Protestantism show signs of this rigorism in their histories. Here, indeed, as St. Paul put it, "the letter killeth, but the spirit giveth life."

The problem is not, however, limited to the sphere of ethics. The threat and challenge of heresy led to a continual definition of dogma as the required canon of faith in the Roman Catholic Church. This gave rise to a complicated, difficult, and subtle statement of doctrines beyond the competence of those not trained in the theological tradition. Such definitions bear the marks of the conflicts out of which they have arisen and the cultural meanings current at the time. In the Catholic church, once such definitions are made, they are unalterable, and such areas are closed to new thought and definition. This fact has been and will continue to be a serious source of conflict within the church and between the church and other groups in society. Even when the defined precedents may not be of the highest dogmatic status, the importance of definition can cause serious difficulty. This may be seen in the conflict within the church concerning birth control in the light of the church's moral teachings.

While the dangers of distortion of the faith of the church require these definitions of dogma and morals, once established, the definitions themselves pose the possibility of another kind of distortion. They become a vast intellectual structure which serves not to guide the faith of untrained specialists but rather to burden it. Moreover, since such a technically spelled-out content of faith requires the interpretation of specialists, the gulf between clergy and laity is thereby maintained. There is danger that an intellectual assent to authority is substituted for the more holistic act of faith.

Closely related to both this dilemma of delimitation and to the dilemma of the objectification and alienation of symbols is that form of the degeneration of symbols which the great student of religion, Mircea Eliade, calls "a process of infantilization." [3] In this infantilization, the symbol becomes "mechanistic and crude." It is often "taken in a childish way, overconcretely, and apart from the system it belongs to." Eliade points out that this can develop in the "descent" of the symbol "from a scholarly to a popular level." It can also come about by the symbol becoming "a substitute for the sacred object" or "a means of establishing a relationship with it." The symbols, when they are thus converted into means, become magical or quasi-magical in character. Eliade comments that this phenomenon of the infantilization of symbolism is to be found "not only among 'primitives,' but even in the most developed societies." The philosopher, Karl Jaspers, also speaks of magic of this kind as the ever-present perversion in which "the reality of the symbol becomes a purposive and instrumental technique." [4] An example of this infantilism of discursive

[3] Eliade, *op cit.*, pp. 444 and 456.
[4] Karl Jaspers, "Freedom and Authority," *Diogenes* (Winter 1953), 1:33.

symbolism may be seen in biblical fundamentalism in which an over-concrete and extremely literal understanding of biblical texts, outside the context of any historical, theological, or linguistic frame of reference, becomes the rule of religious faith. It is a development that became of considerable importance in American Protestantism. The use of sacred objects as charms, and of prayers as magical rituals, offer other examples of infantilization with presentational as well as verbal symbols.

THE DILEMMA OF POWER: CONVERSION VERSUS COERCION The religious experience exercises a call, and thereby mobilizes the inner dispositions of the person called to a voluntary adherence to religious leaders, beliefs, and movements. It involves that commitment of the individual which may be called the "act of faith." But faith as a commitment to the supraempirical involves the possibility of doubt. When the religious organization becomes institutionalized and accommodates itself to the society and its values, faith is supplemented by public opinion and current ideas of respectability. More precisely, faith is supplemented by consensual validation and by the approval and support of accepted authority. The result is that a specious obviousness tends to develop and render the content of faith commonplace. The content of faith tends to be accepted without examination, but is therefore vulnerable to questions when they do arise. Moreover, the compromise of religion with culture—with the "world" in Troeltsch's sense—tends to make religion the repository of the basic values of the society. Thus not only are religious beliefs made more vulnerable to questioning, but they are also functionally more significant to secular society. Faith and doubt remain closely related, and beneath the institutionalized "self-evidentness," the basic structure of religion and of society's legitimation remains vulnerable to questioning—questioning which dispels the consensually derived but only apparent obviousness of beliefs.

The ever present vulnerability of faith to doubt makes religious leaders tend to rely upon social consensus and even on legal authority to buttress and supplement voluntary adherence. Society's leaders, needing religion to sanctify society's values and support social control, tend to protect religion and religious institutions from threat. Thus there arises the possibility of an alignment of religious and secular authorities. This situation, as may be seen in the history of Christianity, draws religious and secular power together to enforce religious conformity. The heretic and the unbeliever weaken consensus and pose a social threat. Those weak in faith tend to project their own potential and half-conscious doubts onto the unbeliever, and then persecute him. Such "ritualistic" purgings of self have taken place both legally—that is, within the orderly and often careful procedures of courts of inquisition—and illegally, by mob action and other violent forms of attack. Thus intolerance and persecution come to perform two functions. For the society, they reinforce and protect a religion, and through the religion the society and its values, from the undermining of doubt. For individuals, they offer a way of externalizing their own doubts and striking at them in the persons of others. Yet it may be questioned whether indeed these functions are performed without quite negative unintended consequences. The consensus that is built upon or supported by threats of force is one to which genuine adherence is gradually weakened. The reliance upon power to supplement faith violates an important element of the religious experience upon which religious institutions ultimately rest: its spontaneous and voluntary character.

A genuine dilemma is involved. Religion cannot but relate itself to the other institutions of society and to the cultural values. Yet such accommodation tends toward a coalescing of religion and power. The alliance of religion and secular power creates a situation in which apparent religiosity often conceals a deeper cynicism and a growing unbelief. Moreover, by the combination of religious and secular conservatism, a situation is produced in which social unrest and political rebellion necessarily become religious protest, and vice versa. It was only after a long period of religious wars and internal conflicts that Western man discovered that national unity and communal solidarity may be based upon values that are less than ultimate and that religious non-conformity may be permitted. Such a realization dawned only after militant efforts to establish religious conformity proved impossible. In England it was first established among Protestants. It was worked out theoretically in the philosophy of John Locke only after it had been empirically established in English history. Not until much later was the toleration extended to Catholics and Jews.

This tendency toward defensive alliance between religion and political power is related to the tendency we saw earlier for new elites to embrace a religion (or secular ideology, in our day) which gives them a sense of meaning and direction, and which legitimates their efforts and achievements. In later periods, when societies and religions are no longer in the founding and expansion stages, but on the defensive in a hostile or potentially hostile situation, the alliance of religion and power tends to be conservative and defensive.

The five dilemmas we have discussed are inherent in the process of the routinization of religious charisma. They are structural characteristics of the institutionalization process and as such are an important source of strain and conflict. They have been the cause of much protest—which, as we have seen, is a fundamental category of analysis in the study of religious movements. The conflicts of papacy and empire, and of church and state; the rise of anti-clericalism; the Reformation protest against symbolism which reached its furthest extreme in Puritanism and the left sects; the attempt of Reformation communions to return to an older form of church polity; the rejection of scholasticism, with its complex philosophical formulations, and of canon law, with its detailed legal definitions—all these indicate the importance of these dilemmas in the history of Western religion. The use of power by both Catholics and Protestants to force religious assent, and the alignments of throne and altar which followed the Great Reform in both Catholic and Protestant countries, provide examples of the fifth dilemma.

We have now seen that religion performs important functions for societies and individuals, but that these positive functions by no means exhaust the relationship of religion to social structure and to social process. Religion is involved in society in a complex way; it is intricately relation to social structure and to the processes of social change. This relationship may have a positive or a negative functional significance. Often, indeed, it is ambiguous. Moreover, the strains and conflicts inherent in the relation of religion to society are increased and intensified by dilemmas inherent in the process of the institutionalization itself.

Selected Bibliography

Alienation, Atheism, and the Religious Crisis (New York: Sheed & Ward, 1969).

American Catholic Dilemma (New York: Sheed & Ward, 1958).

The Catholic Crisis (Boston: The Beacon Press, 1968).

The Mormons (Chicago: University of Chicago Press, 1957).

Sociology and the Study of Religion (New York: Basic Books, Inc., 1970).

Sociology of Religion (Englewood Cliffs, N.J.: Prentice-Hall, Inc., 1966).

Civil Religion in America

Robert N. Bellah

Robert N. Bellah was born on February 23, 1927, in Altus, Oklahoma. He was educated at Harvard University where he received his doctorate in sociology in 1955. He taught at McGill University in Montreal from 1955 to 1957, and then at Harvard until 1967. Since 1967 he has been professor of sociology at the University of California, Berkeley, and Director of the Institute of International Studies and the Center for Japanese and Korean Studies. His interest in modern religion and social change has been centered in two sociocultural areas, Japan (or Asia more generally) and America. He has written works on particular Japanese religious traditions as well as analyses of the functional role of religion in Asia's movement toward modernization. He has also turned his attention to religion in America, especially to those aspects of America's religious tradition that are not exhausted by "church," in the state-church dichotomy, but which, more representatively, belong to the public domain. A provocative expression of this interest is recorded in Bellah's article "Civil Religion in America" from which the following reading selection was taken.

While some have argued that Christianity is the national faith, and others that church and synagogue celebrate only the generalized religion of "the American Way of Life," few have realized that there actually exists alongside of and rather clearly differentiated from the churches an elaborate and well-institutionalized civil religion in America. This article argues not only that there is such a thing, but also that this religion—or perhaps better, this religious dimension— has its own seriousness and integrity and requires the same care in understanding that any other religion does.[1]

---

[1] Why something so obvious should have escaped serious analytical attention is in itself an interesting problem. Part of the reason is probably the controversial nature of the subject. From the earliest years of the nineteenth century, conservative religious and political groups have argued that Christianity is, in fact, the national religion. Some of them have from time to time and as recently as the 1950's proposed constitutional amendments that would explicitly recognize the sovereignty of Christ. In defending the doctrine of separation of church and state, opponents of such groups have denied that the national polity has, intrinsically, anything

Robert N. Bellah, "Civil Religion in America," in *Daedalus*, Vol. 96, No. 1 (1967), pp. 1–9. Reprinted by permission.

The Kennedy Inaugural

Kennedy's inaugural address of 20 January 1961 serves as an example and a clue with which to introduce this complex subject. That address began:

> We observe today not a victory of party but a celebration of freedom—symbolizing an end as well as a beginning—signifying renewal as well as change. For I have sworn before you and Almighty God the same solemn oath our forebears prescribed nearly a century and three quarters ago.
>
> The world is very different now. For man holds in his mortal hands the power to abolish all forms of human poverty and to abolish all forms of human life. And yet the same revolutionary beliefs for which our forebears fought are still at issue around the globe—the belief that the rights of man come not from the generosity of the state but from the hand of God.

And it concluded:

> Finally, whether you are citizens of America or of the world, ask of us the same high standards of strength and sacrifice that we shall ask of you. With a good conscience our only sure reward, with history the final judge of our deeds, let us go forth to lead the land we love, asking His blessing and His help, but knowing that here on earth God's work must truly be our own.

These are the three places in this brief address in which Kennedy mentioned the name of God. If we could understand why he mentioned God, the way in which he did it, and what he meant to say in those three references, we would understand much about American civil religion. But this is not a simple or obvious task, and American students of religion would probably differ widely in their interpretation of these passages.

---

to do with religion at all. The moderates on this issue have insisted that the American state has taken a permissive and indeed supportive attitude toward religious groups (tax exemption, etc.), thus favoring religion but still missing the positive institutionalization with which I am concerned. But part of the reason this issue has been left in obscurity is certainly due to the peculiarly Western concept of "religion" as denoting a single type of collectivity of which an individual can be a member of one and only one at a time. The Durkheimian notion that every group has a religious dimension, which would be seen as obvious in southern or eastern Asia, is foreign to us. This obscures the recognition of such dimensions in our society.

Let us consider first the placing of the three references. They occur in the two opening paragraphs and in the closing paragraph, thus providing a sort of frame for the more concrete remarks that form the middle part of the speech. Looking beyond this particular speech, we would find that similar references to God are almost invariably to be found in the pronouncements of American presidents on solemn occasions, though usually not in the working messages that the president sends to Congress on various concrete issues. How, then, are we to interpret this placing of references to God?

It might be argued that the passages quoted reveal the essentially irrelevant role of religion in the very secular society that is America. The placing of the references in this speech as well as in public life generally indicates that religion has "only a ceremonial significance"; it gets only a sentimental nod which serves largely to placate the more unenlightened members of the community, before a discussion of the really serious business with which religion has nothing whatever to do. A cynical observer might even say that an American president has to mention God or risk losing votes. A semblance of piety is merely one of the unwritten qualifications for the office, a bit more traditional than but not essentially different from the present-day requirement of a pleasing television personality.

But we know enough about the function of ceremonial and ritual in various societies to make us suspicious of dismissing something as unimportant because it is "only a ritual." What people say on solemn occasions need not be taken at face value, but it is often indicative of deep-seated values and commitments that are not made explicit in the course of everyday life. Following this line of argument, it is worth considering whether the very special placing of the references to God in Kennedy's address may not reveal something rather important and serious about religion in American life.

It might be countered that the very way in which Kennedy made his references reveals the essentially vestigial place of religion today. He did not refer to any religion in particular. He did not refer to Jesus Christ, or to Moses, or to the Christian church; certainly he did not refer to the Catholic Church. In fact, his only reference was to the concept of God, a word which almost all Americans can accept but which means so many different things to so many different people that it is almost an empty sign. Is this not just another indication that in America religion is considered vaguely to be a good thing, but that people care so little about it that it has lost any content whatever? Isn't Eisenhower reported to have said, "Our government makes no sense unless it is founded in a deeply felt religious faith—and I don't care what it is," [2] and isn't that a complete negation of any real religion?

These questions are worth pursuing because they raise the issue of how civil religion relates to the political society, on the one hand, and to private religious organization, on the other. President Kennedy was a Christian, more specifically a Catholic Christian. Thus, his general references to God do not mean that he lacked a specific religious commitment. But why, then, did he not include some remark to the effect that Christ is the Lord of the world or some indication of respect for the Catholic Church? He did not because these are matters of his own private religious belief and of his relation to his own particular church; they are not matters relevant in any direct way to the conduct of his public office. Others with different religious views and commitments to different churches or denominations are equally qualified participants in the political process. The principle of separation of church and state guarantees the freedom of religious belief and association, but at the same time clearly segregates the religious sphere, which is considered to be essentially private, from the political one.

Considering the separation of church and state, how is a president justified in using the word *God* at all? The answer is that the separation of church and state has not denied the political realm a religious dimension. Although matters of personal religious belief, worship, and association are considered to be strictly private affairs, there are, at the same time, certain common elements of religious orientation that the great majority of Americans share. These have played a crucial role in the development of American institutions and still provide a religious dimension for the whole fabric of American life, including the political sphere. This public religious dimension is expressed in a set of beliefs, symbols, and rituals that I am calling the American civil religion. The inauguration of a president is an important ceremonial event in this religion. It reaffirms, among other things, the religious legitimation of the highest political authority.

Let us look more closely at what Kennedy actually said. First he said, "I have sworn before you and Almighty God the same solemn òath our forebears prescribed nearly a century and three quarters ago." The oath is the oath of office, including the acceptance of the obligation to uphold the Constitution. He swears it before the people (you)

---

[2] Quoted in Will Herberg, *Protestant-Catholic-Jew* (New York, 1955), p. 97.

and God. Beyond the Constitution, then, the president's obligation extends not only to the people but to God. In American political theory, sovereignty rests, of course, with the people, but implicitly, and often explicitly, the ultimate sovereignty has been attributed to God. This is the meaning of the motto, "In God we trust," as well as the inclusion of the phrase "under God" in the pledge to the flag. What difference does it make that sovereignty belongs to God? Though the will of the people as expressed in majority vote is carefully institutionalized as the operative source of political authority, it is deprived of an ultimate significance. The will of the people is not itself the criterion of right and wrong. There is a higher criterion in terms of which this will can be judged; it is possible that the people may be wrong. The president's obligation extends to the higher criterion.

When Kennedy says that "the rights of man come not from the generosity of the state but from the hand of God," he is stressing this point again. It does not matter whether the state is the expression of the will of an autocratic monarch or of the "people"; the rights of man are more basic than any political structure and provide a point of revolutionary leverage from which any state structure may be radically altered. That is the basis for his reassertion of the revolutionary significance of America.

But the religious dimension in political life as recognized by Kennedy not only provides a grounding for the rights of man which makes any form of political absolutism illegitimate, it also provides a transcendent goal for the political process. This is implied in his final words that "here on earth God's work must truly be our own." What he means here is, I think, more clearly spelled out in a previous paragraph, the wording of which, incidentally, has a distinctly Biblical ring:

> Now the trumpet summons us again—not as a call to bear arms, though arms we need—not as a call to battle, though embattled we are—but a call to bear the burden of a long twilight struggle, year in and year out, "rejoicing in hope, patient in tribulation"—a struggle against the common enemies of man: tyranny, poverty, disease and war itself.

The whole address can be understood as only the most recent statement of a theme that lies very deep in the American tradition, namely the obligation, both collective and individual, to carry out God's will on earth. This was the motivating spirit of those who founded America, and it has been present in every generation since. Just below the surface throughout Kennedy's inaugural address, it becomes explicit in the closing statement that God's work must be our own. That this very activist and non-contemplative conception of the fundamental religious obligation, which has been historically associated with the Protestant position, should be enunciated so clearly in the first major statement of the first Catholic president seems to underline how deeply established it is in the American outlook. Let us now consider the form and history of the civil religious tradition in which Kennedy was speaking.

The Idea of a Civil Religion

The phrase *civil religion* is, of course, Rousseau's. In Chapter 8, Book 4, of *The Social Contract*, he outlines the simple dogmas of the civil religion: the existence of God, the life to come, the reward of virtue and the punishment of vice, and the exclusion of religious intolerance. All other religious opinions are outside the cognizance of the state and may be freely held by citizens. While the phrase *civil religion* was not used, to the best of my knowledge, by the founding fathers, and I am certainly not arguing for the particular influence of Rousseau, it is clear that similar ideas, as part of the cultural climate of the late-eighteenth century, were to be found among the Americans. For example, Franklin writes in his autobiography,

> I never was without some religious principles. I never doubted, for instance, the existence of the Deity; that he made the world and govern'd it by his Providence; that the most acceptable service of God was the doing of good to men; that our souls are immortal; and that all crime will be punished, and virtue rewarded either here or hereafter. These I esteemed the essentials of every religion; and, being to be found in all the religions we had in our country, I respected them all, tho' with different degrees of respect, as I found them more or less mix'd with other articles, which, without any tendency to inspire, promote or confirm morality, serv'd principally to divide us, and make us unfriendly to one another.

It is easy to dispose of this sort of position as essentially utilitarian in relation to religion. In Washington's Farewell Address (though the words may be Hamilton's) the utilitarian aspect is quite explicit:

> Of all the dispositions and habits which lead to political prosperity, Religion and Morality are indispensable sup-

ports. In vain would that man claim the tribute of Patriotism, who should labour to subvert these great Pillars of human happiness, these firmest props of the duties of men and citizens. The mere politician, equally with the pious man ought to respect and cherish them. A volume could not trace all their connections with private and public felicity. Let it simply be asked where is the security for property, for reputation, for life, if the sense of religious obligation *desert* the oaths, which are the instruments of investigation in Courts of Justice? And let us with caution indulge the supposition, that morality can be maintained without religion. Whatever may be conceded to the influence of refined education on minds of peculiar structure, reason and experience both forbid us to expect that National morality can prevail in exclusion of religious principle.

But there is every reason to believe that religion, particularly the idea of God, played a constitutive role in the thought of the early American statesmen.

Kennedy's inaugural pointed to the religious aspect of the Declaration of Independence, and it might be well to look at that document a bit more closely. There are four references to God. The first speaks of the "Laws of Nature and of Nature's God" which entitle any people to be independent. The second is the famous statement that all men "are endowed by their Creator with certain inalienable Rights." Here Jefferson is locating the fundamental legitimacy of the new nation in a conception of "higher law" that is itself based on both classical natural law and Biblical religion. The third is an appeal to "the Supreme Judge of the world for the rectitude of our intentions," and the last indicates "a firm reliance on the protection of divine Providence." In these last two references, a Biblical God of history who stands in judgment over the world is indicated.

The intimate relation of these religious notions with the self-conception of the new republic is indicated by the frequency of their appearance in early official documents. For example, we find in Washington's first inaugural address of 30 April 1789:

> It would be peculiarly improper to omit in this first official act my fervent supplications to that Almighty Being who rules over the universe, who presides in the councils of nations, and whose providential aids can supply every defect, that His benediction may consecrate to the liberties and happiness of the people of the United States a Government instituted by themselves for these essential purposes,

and may enable every instrument employed in its administration to execute with success the functions allotted to his
charge.

No people can be bound to acknowledge and adore the
Invisible Hand which conducts the affairs of man more
than those of the United States. Every step by which we
have advanced to the character of an independent nation
seems to have been distinguished by some token of providential agency. . . .

The propitious smiles of Heaven can never be expected on
a nation that disregards the eternal rules of order and right
which Heaven itself has ordained. . . . The preservation
of the sacred fire of liberty and the destiny of the republi-
can model of government are justly considered, perhaps, as
deeply, as *finally*, staked on the experiment intrusted to the
hands of the American people.

Nor did these religious sentiments remain merely the personal expression of the president. At the request of both Houses of Congress,
Washington proclaimed on October 3 of that same first year as president that November 26 should be "a day of public thanksgiving and
prayer," the first Thanksgiving Day under the Constitution.

The words and acts of the founding fathers, especially the first few
presidents, shaped the form and tone of the civil religion as it has
been maintained ever since. Though much is selectively derived from
Christianity, this religion is clearly not itself Christianity. For one
thing, neither Washington nor Adams nor Jefferson mentions Christ
in his inaugural address; nor do any of the subsequent presidents,
although not one of them fails to mention God.[3] The God of the
civil religion is not only rather "unitarian," he is also on the austere
side, much more related to order, law, and right than to salvation and
love. Even though he is somewhat deist in cast, he is by no means

[3] God is mentioned or referred to in all inaugural addresses but Washington's
second, which is a very brief (two paragraphs) and perfunctory acknowledgment.
It is not without interest that the actual word *God* does not appear until Monroe's
second inaugural, 5 March 1821. In his first inaugural, Washington refers to God
as "that Almighty Being who rules the universe," "Great Author of every public
and private good," "Invisible Hand," and "benign Parent of the Human Race."
John Adams refers to God as "Providence," "Being who is supreme over all,"
"Patron of Order," "Fountain of Justice," and "Protector in all ages of the world
of virtuous liberty." Jefferson speaks of "that Infinite Power which rules the des-
tinies of the universe," and "that Being in whose hands we are." Madison speaks
of "that Almighty Being whose power regulates the destiny of nations," and
"Heaven." Monroe uses "Providence" and "the Almighty" in his first inaugural
and finally "Almighty God" in his second. See, *Inaugural Addresses of the Presidents of the United States from George Washington 1789 to Harry S. Truman
1949*, 82d Congress, 2d Session, House Document No. 540, 1952.

simply a watchmaker God. He is actively interested and involved in history, with a special concern for America. Here the analogy has much less to do with natural law than with ancient Israel; the equation of America with Israel in the idea of the "American Israel" is not infrequent.[4] What was implicit in the words of Washington already quoted becomes explicit in Jefferson's second inaugural when he said: "I shall need, too, the favor of that Being in whose hands we are, who led our fathers, as Israel of old, from their native land and planted them in a country flowing with all the necessaries and comforts of life." Europe is Egypt; America, the promised land. God has led his people to establish a new sort of social order that shall be a light unto all the nations.[5]

This theme, too, has been a continuous one in the civil religion. We have already alluded to it in the case of the Kennedy inaugural. We find it again in President Johnson's inaugural address:

> They came here—the exile and the stranger, brave but frightened—to find a place where a man could be his own man. They made a covenant with this land. Conceived in justice, written in liberty, bound in union, it was meant one day to inspire the hopes of all mankind; and it binds us still. If we keep its terms, we shall flourish.

What we have, then, from the earliest years of the republic is a collection of beliefs, symbols, and rituals with respect to sacred things and institutionalized in a collectivity. This religion—there seems no other word for it—while not antithetical to and indeed sharing much in common with Christianity, was neither sectarian nor in any specific sense Christian. At a time when the society was overwhelmingly

[4] For example, Adiel Abbot, pastor of the First Church in Haverhill, Massachusetts, delivered a Thanksgiving sermon in 1799, *Traits of Resemblance in the People of the United States of America to Ancient Israel,* in which he said, "It has been often remarked that the people of the United States come nearer to a parallel with Ancient Israel, than any other nation upon the globe. Hence 'Our American Israel' is a term frequently used; and common consent allows it apt and proper." Cited in Hans Kohn, *The Idea of Nationalism* (New York, 1961), p. 665.

[5] That the Mosaic analogy was present in the minds of leaders at the very moment of the birth of the republic is indicated in the designs proposed by Franklin and Jefferson for a seal of the United States of America. Together with Adams, they formed a committee of three delegated by the Continental Congress on July 4, 1776, to draw up the new device. "Franklin proposed as the device Moses lifting up his wand and dividing the Red Sea while Pharaoh was overwhelmed by its waters, with the motto 'Rebellion to tyrants is obedience to God.' Jefferson proposed the children of Israel in the wilderness 'led by a cloud by day and a pillar of fire at night.'" Anson Phelps Stokes, *Church and State in the United States,* Vol. 1 (New York, 1950), pp. 467–68.

Christian, it seems unlikely that this lack of Christian reference was meant to spare the feelings of the tiny non-Christian minority. Rather, the civil religion expressed what those who set the precedents felt was appropriate under the circumstances. It reflected their private as well as public views. Nor was the civil religion simply "religion in general." While generality was undoubtedly seen as a virtue by some, as in the quotation from Franklin above, the civil religion was specific enough when it came to the topic of America. Precisely because of this specificity, the civil religion was saved from empty formalism and served as a genuine vehicle of national religious self-understanding.

But the civil religion was not, in the minds of Franklin, Washington, Jefferson, or other leaders, with the exception of a few radicals like Tom Paine, ever felt to be a substitute for Christianity. There was an implicit but quite clear division of function between the civil religion and Christianity. Under the doctrine of religious liberty, an exceptionally wide sphere of personal piety and voluntary social action was left to the churches. But the churches were neither to control the state nor to be controlled by it. The national magistrate, whatever his private religious views, operates under the rubrics of the civil religion as long as he is in his official capacity, as we have already seen in the case of Kennedy. This accommodation was undoubtedly the product of a particular historical moment and of a cultural background dominated by Protestantism of several varieties and by the Enlightenment, but it has survived despite subsequent changes in the cultural and religious climate. . . .

Selected Bibliography

Beyond Belief: Essays on Religion in a Post-traditional World (New York: Harper & Row, Publishers, 1970).

Changing Japanese Attitudes Toward Modernization, ed. by Marius B. Jansen (Princeton: Princeton University Press, 1965).

Religion and Progress in Modern Asia (New York: The Free Press, 1965).

Religion in America, with William G. McLoughlin (Boston: Houghton Mifflin Company, 1968).

Sociologists at Work, ed. by Philip E. Hammond (New York: Basic Books, Inc., 1964).

Tokugawa Religion (New York: The Free Press, 1957).

PART 5

Sanctionative Criticism: Theological Approaches to Religion

In turning to theological approaches to religion, one must recognize that for many years the objective study of religion was carried forward principally by faculties in divinity schools and theological seminaries. To a large extent, that situation still prevails. Quite understandably, the study of religion is promoted within such settings with theological interests more or less in mind. Consequently, religion has been refracted through a spectrum of pre-established concerns. Matters of faith and belief have frequently served both as the starting point and as the point of principal application for inquiries into religion that have been conducted. In part and in piece, the objective study of religion has been subsumed under a more controlling interest in rightly fixing and interpreting personal and communal belief. This is not to say that theological approaches to religion are always mistaken or misguided, for, indeed, they are not necessarily any more partial than inquiries into religion that are undertaken by sociologists, philosophers, anthropologists, and psychologists. But it is to point out that under such auspices the objective study of religion is not always conducted on its own behalf.

The essays in this section of the anthology are included to provide a representative sampling of theological approaches to religion. The essays by Hendrik Kraemer and Jean Danielou (the first from a Protestant's perspective and the second from that of a Catholic), are attempts to specify the relationship between Christianity and non-Christian religions. Kraemer's view has obviously been colored by missionary interests and the theological outlook of Karl Barth, and it stresses the exclusiveness of Christian revelation. Danielou tends to see Christian and non-Christian religions according to the classic theological formulation of the relation of grace to nature: the first perfects while also confirming the latter. The third essay in this section by Sarvepalli Radhakrishnan offers suggestions for reversing the sequence. Radhakrishnan reflects a set of Indian (or, more precisely, neo-Hindu) attitudes to non-Indian religious traditions; and, according to this view, all religions may be retained without doing violence to any of them. The other essays in this section represent the interests of scholars whose fundamental work has been in the history of religions. The first of these—Joachim Wach's essay on theology vis-à-vis *religionswissenschaft*—attempts to give a proper emphasis to both subjects. In Wach's view, the two fields complement each other. Erwin R. Goodenough's essay, on the contrary, tries to exorcise the study of religion of all residual theological interests. This is necessary, according to Goodenough, if basic confusion is to be overcome and if the issues that properly belong to the field are to be accurately treated.

Taken together, these five essays illustrate a range of opinion, which, in and outside of theological circles, is probably as representative now as it was some years ago. Without doubt, this is a subject on which much attention will continue to be trained. As has already been noted, interest in religion, in large part, has grown up in the schools of theology and will continue to be sustained there. And yet this fact does not make theology a father to religion nor religion the sole father of theology. Neither is it quite accurate to conceive of them as brothers.

Christian Revelation as Critique of Religions

HENDRIK KRAEMER

Hendrik Kraemer, who was born in Holland in 1888, was a missionary-theologian, an advocate of lay leadership within the Christian Church, and a pioneer in establishing ecumenical contact between Protestant denominations. At Leyden University he was trained in Oriental languages and religion, in which fields he received his doctorate. In 1921 he was sent by the Netherlands Bible Society to Java to translate the Bible into the indigenous languages of Indonesia. He became disillusioned with liberal Christian theologies in Asia, and found himself moving closer to the positions made famous by Karl Barth and his followers. Kraemer completed his book, The Christian Message in a Non-Christian World, *in 1938. The book employed aspects of Barthian theology to underscore the differences between Christianity and the religions of other peoples. As the following essay makes evident, Kraemer mistrusts any view that qualifies the truth that belongs exclusively to Christianity. Kraemer died in Holland in 1965.*

As I say, I am a convinced Christian with a long schooling in, and experience of, this field of the study of religions; and the basis and point of view from which I shall approach the subject are by way of being a confession of faith. What it amounts to is briefly this: I propose to set the religions, including Christianity, in the light of the Person of Jesus Christ, who is *the* Revelation of God and alone has the authority to criticize—I mean, to judge discriminately and with complete understanding—every religion and everything that is in man or proceeds from him. I shall give further content to what is here described as the argument develops; but it does seem to me to be concise enough and not liable to be misunderstood. For the present I need only add that by Jesus Christ I mean that Jesus whom we know from the total witness of apostles and evangelists in the New

Testament; the Jesus who says, not: This or that is the truth, but "I am the Truth." So far as I am concerned, therefore, and so far as this book is concerned, He is the criterion of truth, the standard of judgment and evaluation.

I am not suggesting that this is an easy thing—far from it. It is a difficult business and requires a persistent effort of the mind at every step to learn what it means to see light in His light alone, in and over all things and all men. Here then is no yardstick or criterion which one can manipulate; that would be mere sacrilege and self-deception. There is only one thing that one can do and must do: and that is, not to manipulate but to submit oneself to His living, personal actuality and so move forward on a never-ending way, trusting that to each illumination of insight into the religions yet further light may be added.

The Source and Object of Belief

I do believe that I have now put all my cards on the table and that nobody could say that he has been left in the dark about what my position is. On this crucial issue I have made a point of avoiding a lot of unnecessary ratiocination; and I have refused to make qualifications or, to put it less euphemistically, to hedge. I put it fairly and squarely that for me in this book the measure of what is true and what is real, and that not only in a religious context, is Jesus Christ, *the* Truth Himself.

Even so, my cards are not yet quite all on the table. Something remains to be added if the reader is to be kept fully in the picture; and it could not be omitted without a serious danger of underestimating the problematic nature and complexity of the whole subject. The fact is, as appears time and time again, that people may consider themselves earnest Christians, may have studied the religions and know a great deal about them, and yet be at variance in their way of propounding the issue and of dealing with it. Sometimes the differences involved are insubstantial; but in a good many cases they really would appear to be fundamental. I therefore have no right to say that my own adopted criterion is *the* Christian one. I consider that I have every right, however, to say that it is so for me; and, quite frankly, that is exactly what I do, whilst readily admitting that there may be various ways of elaborating the position I have advanced.

None the less, I owe it to the reader to point out at once that there are those who are both experts and sincere Christians, who yet emphatically reject my standpoint and premises in regard to this matter; they follow another path which for them is a validly "Christian" one. It would be interesting to take some obvious examples of the various "Christian" ways of handling the subject and examine them in detail—whether it be the cases which do not differ in *essentials* from the approach I have set forth or those in which one has to speak of really profound differences. However, that would take us too far out of our way. I just want to say something quite briefly, by way of illustration, about one instance of radical disagreement, and one only.

Here is an example. Professor C. J. Bleeker, whose informative book on the religions I can recommend as a useful guide, is both an "expert" and a sincere Christian. Not long ago, *à propos* of the Congress of the History of Religions held in Tokyo in 1958, he wrote an article entitled: "An East-West conversation on religion." In that article he says a number of things which I do not consider to be in every respect wide of the mark—far from it indeed; yet regarding the essential part of what he has to say, I feel that I must take issue with him. One of the things he says is that it is high time we abandoned all our theological misgivings and frankly recognized the truth and the worth of the non-Christian religions. As will appear clearly enough from what follows in this book, I have not the least objection to this statement in itself. When Professor Bleeker explains his meaning in more detail, however, it strikes me that whilst two people may say the same thing, they do not necessarily mean the same thing as well; for the Professor goes on: "Anyone who looks at the world as a whole must realize that these religions are a powerful spiritual force and that there is no getting away from that fact"; and he adds that, at any rate in this discourse with the other religions, the Christian must forego the claim that the entire world has to acknowledge the absolute truth of what he believes.

I make no pretension of having an all-embracing "worldwide outlook" myself; but like Professor Bleeker I am absolutely sure that such an outlook or insight is indeed required by the "discourse between the religions," as it is in other important matters too. I heartily agree with him when he says that the "non-Christian" religions are a powerful spiritual force which is not to be denied. I have been saying that repeatedly over many years now; for it is the formidable and sober truth.

My objection to this passage in Professor Bleeker's article therefore lies elsewhere: in that he deploys these *facts*, which are undeniably part and parcel of the situation today, as *arguments* for an out-and-out recognition of the truth and value of the non-Christian religions. To my mind, this mixing up of what are undeniable facts with arguments in favour of quite another point betrays a kind of thinking which fails to distinguish clearly and pertinently and therefore, so far from serving any useful purpose, actually bedevils the issue. Let me take a single instance to illustrate this.

No one with an eye for what goes on in the world today is going to be so bold as to deny that communism is one of the great spiritual forces of our time, or—to take another, more trivial, example which none the less is not to be made light of—that the Jehovah Witnesses constitute a powerful spiritual factor which can no more be dismissed out of hand than communism itself. Yet few, surely, would consider this fact a cogent argument for a "thorough-going recognition of the truth and value" of communism or the uncompromising creed of the Jehovah Witnesses. In that case, the bare fact that here is an influential force, commanding a great deal of numerical support, would be the criterion of truth.

So also in his second statement, where Professor Bleeker says that Christians should drop their "absolute" claims, I think that he fails to make a clear distinction. I must first of all say once again (although it may seem odd) that when Professor Bleeker insists that "the Christian must forego the claim that the entire world has to acknowledge the absolute truth of what he believes," I fully agree with him. As will become apparent later on in this book, the criterion which I have adopted involves precisely that contention.

For me, therefore, what is wrong with Professor Bleeker's statement is not its insistence that the Christian must surrender the claim to the absolute truth of what he believes, to which the whole world is obliged to submit. That this claim has been in the past, and is still today, very frequently made is an incontrovertible fact; but it is precisely in the light of Christ—*the* critic of all religions as of everything else—that we see it to be an *unwarranted*, a thoroughly unchristian pretension. For it is not Christian belief which is absolute, but the source and object of that belief: namely, God's Self-revelation in Jesus Christ. It is over the matter of recognizing and understanding Jesus Christ in His "absolute-ness" here and now that Christians, and especially theologians, disagree.

This raises another point. The disagreements among Christians as to how one should state the question at issue and how it should be dealt with go back to each individual's "Christology"—that is, to his conception of Christ's being, status and significance; but besides that, there is yet another determining factor. That is the place given to the testimony of the Bible and the store which one sets by that testimony, especially where the New Testament is concerned. Such concepts as "normative" or "deserving to be taken into consideration" and terms like "orthodox" or "liberal"—to describe different ways of looking at the Bible—are beside the point here. The thing is whether one is prepared to take seriously, without reservations, the witness of the Bible regarding the *Person* of Jesus Christ and because of that—and not because of some orthodox or liberal view which one may hold *about* Him—to be guided, corrected and inspired by Him; a very different thing from slavish submission to some dictatorial authority. Confronted with the Person of Jesus Christ, we are lifted way above those disagreements and opposed positions which we describe as "liberal" and "orthodox."

In this first brief chapter I have said what, as it seemed to me, needed to be said, if from the very start the reader is to be on the lookout for all the snares and pitfalls which beset this complex subject. In dealing with the whole problem now before us, it is generally assumed that the meaning of the words, "the relation of Christianity to the other religions"—is plain and straightforward enough. But my remarks also demonstrate, in view of what has been said about Christ as the criterion and standard of judgment, that both these expressions serve rather to conceal the profound and crucial issue involved here than to disclose it. . . .

Selected Bibliography

The Christian Message in a Non-Christian World (Grand Rapids: Kregel Publications, 1963).

Theology of the Laity (Philadelphia: Westminster Press, 1959).

World Cultures and World Religions: The Common Dialogue (Philadelphia: Westminster Press, 1961).

See also Johannes Aagaard, "Revelation and Religion," in *Studia Theologica*, Vol. XIX, No. 2 (1960), pp. 148–158, an analysis of the influence of Barthian theology on Kraemer's understanding of the relationship between Christianity and non-Christian religions.

Theology and the Scientific Study of Religion

JOACHIM WACH

Joachim Wach was born on January 25, 1898, in Saxony, Germany. He studied at the Universities of Leipzig, Munich, and Berlin, specializing in the history of religions, philosophy of religion, and Oriental studies. He received his doctorate from the University of Leipzig, where he also taught until 1935 when the Nazis terminated his appointment. He moved to America, became a professor at Brown University in Rhode Island until 1945, and then was appointed chairman of the history-of-religions field in the Divinity School of the University of Chicago, a position he held until his death on August 27, 1955. Wach's life and thought have been very ably summarized by Joseph M. Kitagawa in the Introduction to Joachim Wach, The Comparative Study of Religions (New York: Columbia University Press, 1958, pp. xiii–xlvii).

Perhaps more than for anything else, Wach was distinguished by the unusual breadth of view that he brought to the study of religion. He was a student of Buddhism and was also generally equipped in the history of religions. A number of his works deal specifically with the philosophical origins of religionswissenschaft. He is also widely recognized for his work in the sociology of religion. Because of his skill in using the techniques of the social sciences in engaging in comparative studies in religion, Wach has also been regarded as a pioneer in the development of methodological self-consciousness in religious studies. Throughout his lifetime he maintained the conviction that the scientific study of religion would aid rather than detract from theology. The selection that follows sketches Wach's attitude in this respect.

If it is the task of theology to investigate, buttress, and teach the faith of a religious community to which it is committed, as well as to kindle zeal and fervor for the defense and spread of this faith, it is the responsibility of a comparative study to guide and to purify it. How

Joachim Wach, *The Comparative Study of Religions*, edited by Joseph M. Kitagawa (New York: Columbia University Press, 1958), pp. 9–21.

can that be brought about? That which I value and cherish and hold dear beyond all else, I also want thoroughly to understand in all its implications. It is true that to love truth you must hate untruth, but it is not true that in order to exalt your own faith you must hate and denigrate those of another faith. A comparative study of religions such as the new era made possible enables us to have a fuller vision of what religious experience can mean, what forms its expression may take, and what it might do for man. It could be argued that this would mean the subjection of one's religious faith to a judgment pronounced in the name of some generalized notions. But does a ruby or an emerald sparkle less if called a jewel? Not only different religious communities but groups within them develop certain emphases and neglect other aspects.

Next to reorientation to the primary norm of religious experience, what better way to understand religions is there than to study the notions and practices of others?

But can you understand a religion other than your own? This question must be analyzed. There seems to be a sense in which the answer would have to be "No," and yet there are indications that in some sense a positive reply is possible. Undoubtedly it is possible to "know the facts" in the sense of gathering and organizing all the available information. As we have seen, that was and is the task of our field according to the positivistically minded scholar. Yet, is that enough? Is it not necessary to be a member of a religious community to understand its religious notions and customs? But what does it mean to be a "member?" Could it be seriously maintained that a great scholar belonging to Group A would be less capable of understanding the religion of Group B than any ignorant and humble person belonging to the latter? Obviously official membership cannot be the criterion for the possibility of understanding. Could not one conceivably participate in the ritual performance of a cultic group, for example, and yet be unaware of the meaning of that which is said and done? Does that in turn signify that even a commitment would not be sufficient in itself, since such could also exist in the case of an ignorant and humble member? And how about the alert skeptic who may be nearer a "conversion" than he or anyone else may know? In all tribal religion the question of membership is a relatively simple one: it is conferred by birth and birth only, though there may be qualifications such as the fulfillment of duties, and so on. It is more complicated in specifically religious communities. Among these there are usually objective criteria of membership—*notae ecclesiac*—but the fideists, mystics, and spiritualists usually insist on additional and often subjective standards. An inner attitude alone can qualify one as a "true" member. It goes without saying that in the latter case it would be more difficult to indicate what "full understanding" would entail than in the former case where participation is regulated in a more automatic or mechanical sense.

There are definite stages of understanding. One stage would be partial, another integral, comprehension. Thus it is conceivable that we could do justice to a particular religious thought or act without being able to grasp others appearing in the same context or to grasp this context as a whole. Religious communities recognize this by stratifying their religious groups, especially those with an esoteric character such as mystery societies in which different grades correspond to varying degrees of "comprehension." In this problem of religious understanding there is also the law of irreversibility, according to which it is possible for the higher to comprehend the lower and the older (master) to perceive what is going on in the younger (disciple) but not vice versa. That brings us to the discussion of the conditions that must prevail if an integral understanding is to be achieved.

Let us turn first to the necessary equipment. We have seen previously that it will in part be of an intellectual nature. There is no hope of understanding a religion or a religious phenomenon without the most extensive information possible. We owe a great debt of gratitude to the painstaking work of the past one hundred and fifty years which has so increased the depth and degree of our knowledge of other religions. The most comprehensive survey of this development has been given by the French Jesuit scholar, Pinard de la Boullaye, in the first volume of his *Étude comparée des religions* (1922). The student of religions is never well enough equipped linguistically. It is now desirable to know many languages and families of languages which were barely known by name fifty years ago. This is especially true with regard to the ancient Near East, Africa, Central Asia, and South America. Yet we agree with Webb when he says: "I do not indeed suppose that it is necessary, in order to enter into the spirit of a religion, that one should be able to read its scriptures and its doctrines in their original languages. A man may be a very good Christian without Greek or Hebrew, and a very bad Christian with both." It may not be necessary, but the chances of an adequate understanding are infinitely better where the interpreter is in a position to at least check on the translation of key terms, if he is not actually competent to read the foreign tongue. Yet this competence in and by itself does not guarantee positive results in the study of religion.

Secondly, a successful venture in understanding a religion different from our own requires an adequate emotional condition. What is required is not indifference, as positivism in its heyday believed—"Grey cold eyes do not know the value of things," objected Nietzsche—but rather an engagement of feeling, interest, *metexis*, or participation. This is not an endorsement of the widespread notion that religion as such is an exclusively emotional affair (a notion held by Schleiermacher and Otto). As we shall see in greater detail, religion is a concern of the total person, engaging intellect, emotion, and will.

The realms of the human personality and human values are often invaded by a scientism which insists upon only one method of knowing and one type of knowledge. One of the weightiest arguments for those who want to preserve the human personality and its values against the imperatives of science is the demonstration that any form of reduction falls short of the aim of a student of religion, which is to do justice to that religion's true nature.

A third form of equipment, the equipment of volition, is therefore required for anyone who wishes to deal adequately with the religion of his fellow man. The will must be directed and oriented toward a constructive purpose. Neither idle curiosity nor a passion for annihilating whatever differs from one's own position is an appropriate motive for this task. Ignorance, uncontrolled passion, and lack of direction are enemies of that state of mind which alone promises success in the venture of understanding. There will never be a lack of those differences (difference in temperament is one example) which make it difficult even for the student of broad concerns and deep sympathies to comprehend various kinds of religiosity, types of religious thought, or devotional practices which differ sharply from his own.

But there is still something else that is essential equipment for the study of religion, and that is experience. We use this term here in a wide sense, leaving the analysis of the nature of religious experience for the next chapter. We should like to define experience in the broadest sense, thus opposing all narrow concepts which separate and even isolate it as a province of life into which only the specialized professional can enter. In all likelihood there is no contact with any aspect of life which would not bear upon the problem of understanding another's religion. As the psychologists and sociologists of religion have told us, there are not only different religious temperaments (beginning with William James's "healthy-minded" and "sick-minded") but also different types of religious institutions. Whoever has had wide experience with human character possesses one more qualification for understanding an alien religion, for such a person has thereby contacted the minds of people in the variety of their acting, feeling, and ways of thinking. It is important for one to realize that there are different ways to be "religious," to know and to worship God; for in the area of expression between man and man even the narrowest religious fellowships show differences. The group as well as the individual will be religious in its own way. We are not talking here about "heresies" but about the legitimate range of psychological and sociological differences. This is not an endorsement of pluralism or relativism. Even if one holds fast to the belief that truth is one it is possible to concede that there are "many mansions" in our Father's house.

After dwelling upon the nature and the task of comparative studies in religion, we can now discuss the method to be followed. Much controversy has been carried on in the last decade between two schools of thought. One has insisted that the method of religious studies is totally *sui generis* and in no way comparable or related to methods in other fields of knowledge. The other school has maintained that, irrespective of the character of the subject matter to be investigated, the only legitimate method is the so-called "scientific" method. The term scientific is used here in a double sense: in the narrower sense it denotes the method used in the so-called natural sciences, and in the wider sense it refers to any procedure which works with logical and coherent discipline from clearly indicated premises. Both these approaches have been found wanting; in the present era of the comparative study of religions a new synthesis is being worked out. Beginning with the second school of thought, we see that there is good reason to oppose an unqualified pluralism or even a dualism in matters of method and of knowledge. Truth is one; the cosmos is one; hence knowledge also must be one. This insight is all important. Although we will not agree with the positivistic interpretation of this principle, we must incorporate it into our methodology, which will be based on a dual demand. The first demand is that the method be unified. Such is the imperative of Aristotle, Aquinas, Leibniz, and Whitehead. All idealism and all naturalism—including materialism—stand or fall with methodological monism. Yet to conceive of one truth is one thing and to possess or comprehend it is another. We should be realistic enough to see the profound wisdom in the apostle's words that here we know only in part, which is to say that only God himself can be aware of the whole. The second demand is that the method be adequate for the subject matter. This qualifies the first principle, that of a unified method.

Many theological and philosophical writers in the first half of this century have demonstrated the insufficiency of the narrowly defined scientific approach to the study of religion. Many distinguished scientists have questioned the applicability of the methods and techniques of experimental, quantitative, causal investigation to the world of the spirit. The philosophical vindication of the freedom of the spirit was ably pursued by Bergson, Dilthey, Balfour, Von Hügel, Troeltsch, Husserl, Scheler, Temple, Otto, Jung, Baillie, Berdyaev, and others. In order that the method be adequate for the subject matter, the phenomenon of individuality, the nature of value, and the meaning of freedom must be recognized. It has been rightly said that the whole realm of the personal, with which the religious quest is so indissolubly connected, must remain closed to the investigator who does not make concession to his method as required by the nature of the subject matter.

A positivistic age could cherish the notion of a universally applicable technique of inquiry. Religion was to be studied exactly as any phenomenon of the inorganic or organic world. With the above-mentioned qualification that the method must fit the subject matter, the new era has shown a growing demand for a metaphysical concept which would do justice to the nature of phenomena of the spiritual as well as of the physical world.

The tremendous success of the philosophy of Alfred North White-head in the Anglo-Saxon world can be explained in terms of this need. It has been widely felt that he has provided a coherent system for understanding nature, mind, and spirit. This is the necessary successor to a prolonged preoccupation with technical problems of a primarily epistemological and somewhat esoteric character. With its appearance the school of emergent evolution has been added to the two major systems, Roman Catholic and Marxian interpretation, which have survived the positivistic era in the West and which have maintained their formidable prestige among many systems of metaphysics. We cannot trace the development and fortunes of emergent evolution here; we can only indicate with a few quotations what its aims and conclusions are. The underlying metaphysical concept is described in the words of its founder, Lloyd Morgan: "Evolution, in the broad sense, is the name we give to the comprehensive plan of sequences in all natural events. But the orderly sequence, historically viewed, appears to present from time to time something genuinely new. . . . Salient examples are afforded in the advent of life, in the advent of mind, and in the advent of reflective thought. If nothing new emerges, if there be only regrouping of pre-existing events and nothing more—then there is no emergent evolution."

Methodologically that meant that "the emergent entity is not to be accounted for in terms of antecedent stages of the process." Hence allowance was made for recognizing the emergence of new and unpredictable properties. "Emergent evolution urges that the more of any given stage, even the highest, involves the 'less' of the stages which preceded it and continues to co-exist with it. It does not interpret the higher in terms of the lower only." It is no accident that Morgan was himself religious. More than the somewhat abstract Alexander, Whitehead himself has pointed out the implications of this philosophy for religion. The final word on this topic has yet to be said. A wholly satisfactory monographic treatment of the role of religion in the thought of Whitehead remains to be written. The best criticism and constructive interpretation from the point of view of Christian thought is still the famous Gifford Lectures of Temple, *Nature, Man and God* (1932–34). Though there is little reference to non-Christian religions and their study, all the implications and consequences of the philosophy of emergent evolution are clearly indicated for the understanding of individuality, values, meaning, and freedom —in short, for the realm of the personal. Thus the demand for a unified method which accords with the exigencies of the subject matter is justified. It is therefore not surprising to see the influence of his thinking on some of the keenest students of these problems in our own day. It will be sufficient to name, besides Thornton, Richardson and Ferré. Richardson's apologetic follows Temple's methodology, particularly in the doctrine of revelation, and D. G. Moses's penetrating analysis of the notion of religious truth proceeds along the same lines. While clearly stating his conviction that "ultimate truth is one," Moses holds that "the different aspects of reality disclose their nature only as we use different methods of knowing." He maintains that "reality" is an identity expressing itself differently in different parts. "Matter, life, mind and self-consciousness represent different levels or orders of reality." Here we agree wholeheartedly with Moses's distinctions, though we shall later take exception to his notion of the criterion of religious truth.

In a very provocative sentence in *Nature, Man and God*, Temple points to the fact that the mind itself emerges in the midst of the process which it apprehends. This means that consciousness is not given priority as that which legislates the principles of possible experience. Rather we must look upon a mind as that which arises out of the background of its given world and progressively constructs its own concept according to the kind of connection which it finds or expects to find in its world. It tries to express this connection in symbolic form. This is a hint as to how we have to understand the old saying (which dates at least from the time of Plato) that there must be a resemblance between the knower and the known. "We come back, therefore, to the Platonic principle that if any rational understanding is to be possible, the *logos* in us must be akin to a *logos* in things." This hermeneutical principle proves to be valid for the understanding of religion, too. A love letter will appear meaningless and silly to anybody not in love, though it may be appreciated aesthetically if it happens to be a work of art. As Richard of St. Victor says, "How then can a man speak about love who does not feel it? Only the one who composes his speech according to what the heart dictates can worthily speak of love." By the same token a religious utterance will bewilder, frustrate, or repel anyone whose religious sensitivities have not been developed.

It is in this context that the Christian doctrine of the Holy Spirit and His inner testimony must be understood. Otto has said, "The mere word, even when it comes as a living voice, is powerless without the 'spirit in the heart' of the hearer to move him to apprehension." It was not by accident that Otto's first written study dealt with this subject. This seems to me to be a more adequate statement than the notion of some "preunderstanding" (*Vor-Verständnis*) tied to the self-analysis with which a certain type of existentialism is so much concerned. It is right to say that "no understanding and no interpretation of sources is possible without the *inter esse* of the scholar. He must engage in a dialogue with the past, but not primarily because it is a part of his own history." Schleiermacher was right in pointing out that the realm of the understandable extends between the utterly foreign and the totally familiar.

Interestingly enough there is a close parallel between the thought of the Anglo-Saxon philosophy of emergence and that of the new theory of ontological stratification of Nicolai Hartmann. His conception of reality as a structure (*Gefüge*—that same mode of being or reality which encompasses everything from matter to spirit) involves four separate levels (*Schichten*). He distinguishes between the material, the organic, the psychic (*seelisch*), and the spiritual (*geistig*) without assuming that they have evolved from each other or from "below" or "above." Each of these strata has its own peculiar onto-logical categories. In every instance some categories characteristic of the lower stage recur in the next one. Certain fundamental ones such as unity, temporality, and so on, apply to all of them. New cat-egories, as in the realm of the mental (psychic) and the spiritual, constitute a superstructure and hence necessitate different methods of approach for study. "The categorical laws teach the dependence of the higher ontological strata on the lower strata, the former being supported and partly determined by the latter." Because the higher depend on the lower and not conversely, the latter are the stronger ones. "Strength and height in the order of strata stand in an inverse relationship." "The center of gravity of the higher stratum is in the laws of novelty and freedom." There is freedom in the "novelty" which the higher level represents in comparison to the lower. "An-thropology has room for the autonomy of spiritual life but it also knows how to unite it with the organic stratum of the human being." Yet Hartmann tends to ascribe the greater power to the "lower" levels as Marx and Scheler did before him.

As is the world, continues Hartmann, so also is man an ordered structure of body, soul, and mind which is reducible neither to the merely biological nor to the spiritual. However, body and spirit do not shade off into each other. There is no continuum between them. The spirit has its own kind of power, but it is a limited one. It is a power different from everything that opposes it; it is based upon the un-paralleled singularity of the categorical novelty of the spirit. It pre-supposes the whole stratification of the lower powers with which it has to deal in life, and at the same time it rests upon them. Body and spirit do have a connection in the third intermediate and distinct ontological stratum called psychic being. "The nature of man can be adequately understood only as the integrated whole of combining strata, and, furthermore, as placed within the totality of the same order of strata which, outside of man, determines the structure of the real world."

We have mentioned the resemblance of the knower and the known and the implication of this principle for the study of religion. We feel that it is here that the Western understanding of religion has a great deal to learn from the East. Until recently at least, there has been little inclination in the East to admit that perception and in-ference are the only legitimate ways of knowing. The Eastern sages have always insisted that there is an immediate awareness of an inclination toward truth, although the sources of religious insight have been differently conceived in different communities of faith. Datta has shown us how knowledge (prama) and the true source of knowledge (pramana) are conceived in different schools of the Vedanta. (True knowledge is defined as cognition of an object neither contradicted nor already known.) In Hinduism the true method of knowing reality must be based upon the revealed texts, and this knowledge is identical with liberation. Metaphysics precedes epistemology. For some the only pramana is perception. Others add inference, comparison, postulation, and "non-perception." "Authority" or "testimony" (sabda) is finally recognized as an independent and ultimate source of knowledge by almost all Indian thinkers except Carvakas, Buddhists, and Vaisesikas. The fact that authorities may disagree does not invalidate this source of knowledge since this may be the case with the other pramanas as well.

The West, however, rightly conceives of knowledge in terms which enable it to incorporate the information acquired into the various departments of scientific pursuits—scientific in the wide sense of the word—for thus it fruitfully relates knowledge and life. This does not put essential and nonessential knowledge on the same level; rather does it attempt to overcome indifference toward all that does not immediately pertain to salvation. It is also an effort to avoid a pluralistic epistemology according to which there is no relationship between different levels of inquiry. The East may profit by pursuing this aim instead of copying Western positivism, for the ancient and noble tradition by which the East has always lived is that the highest goal for man is realization of the truth. In this Western incorporation of knowledge and life, Christianity is not in league with those for whom religion is "a sense of scruples which impede the free exercise of our faculties" (Salomon Reinach). It is not contrary to, but rather in harmony with, the Christian gospel which teaches that truth is God's truth and hence one truth. To know this truth is to be free, yet one can know it here only in part. This truth is that there is an order in man's cosmos of knowledge even as there is order in the universe.

Selected Bibliography

The Comparative Study of Religions (New York: Columbia University Press, 1958).

The History of Religions, ed. by Joseph M. Kitagawa (Chicago: University of Chicago Press, 1967).

"The Place of the History of Religions in the Study of Theology," *The Journal of Religion*, Vol. XXVII, No. 3 (1947), pp. 157–177.

Religionswissenschaft: Prolegomena zu ihre Grundlegung (Leipzig: J. C. Hinrichs, 1924).

Sociology of Religion (Chicago: University of Chicago Press, 1944).

Types of Religious Experience—Christian and Non-Christian (Chicago: University of Chicago Press, 1951).

Das Verstehen: Grundzüge einer Geschichte der hermeneutischen Theorie im 19. Jahrhundert (Tübingen: J. C. B. Mohr, 1926–33).

An Eastern Theological Perspective on Western Faiths

SARVEPALLI RADHAKRISHNAN

Sarvepalli Radhakrishnan, philosopher, statesman, and religious apologist, was born into a Brahmanic family in India on September 5, 1888. Educated in India, he began a distinguished academic career in 1918, holding chairs of philosophy at the Universities of Mysore and Calcutta and at Banaras Hindu University. From 1936 until 1952 he was Spaulding Professor of Eastern Religion and Ethics at Oxford, and from 1953 until 1962 he was chancellor of Delhi University. At the same time, he was active in Indian political life, serving from 1949 to 1952 as Ambassador to the Soviet Union. He was Vice-President of the Republic of India from 1952 to 1962, and was President from 1962 to 1967. Politically, he has always stressed the need to create a classless and casteless society in India. As an interpreter of the Indian religious tradition to the West, he has sought to minimize the influence of world-negating views and has represented that tradition as being committed to technological, social, and political progress. In his own religious teaching, Radhakrishnan has been an exponent of a modernization and reinterpretation of the teachings of Sankara. By means of these views, Radhakrishnan is enabled to argue that the teachings of the major religions of the world are not beyond reconciliation with each other He once stated his views in capsule form: "Religion begins for us with an awareness that our life is not of ourselves alone. There is another, greater life enfolding and sustaining us. Religion as man's search for this greater self will not accept any creeds as final or any laws as perfect. It will be evolutionary, moving ever onward." This view is more fully articulated in the selection that follows

Karl Barth is definite that the glimpses and intuitions of God found in other religions are not a preparation for the full revelation in Christ but are misdirections. In this matter Karl Barth may have the support of rigid minds, but the general Christian tradition is not with him.

S. Radhakrishnan, *Eastern Religions and Western Thought* (London: Oxford University Press, 1939), pp. 343–348, by permission of the Clarendon Press, Oxford.

Even in the Old Testament the local cults were not destroyed, but reformed. The prophets, it is true, repudiated the cult of the Queen of Heaven, but she has returned in the Virgin Mother. Adherents of Trinitarian religions persuade themselves by a jugglery of words that they believe in one God, and the best that has been said on the subject is that it is a mystery of which no rational explanation is possible. It is difficult to know the real distinction between praying to the Madonna, Saints, and Angels and worshipping minor deities as symbols of the Supreme. The Christian doctrine did not grow up in a vacuum, in a straight encounter between God and soul. It arose in a world full of warring sects and rival faiths, and used whatever was at hand. Palestine gave morality and monotheism, Greece art and philosophy, Rome order and organization, and the East mysticism and a gift for worship. The great Church Fathers did not repudiate the non-Christian faiths in the Barthian way. Clement was not only a Christian Father but a learned philosopher, who clothed the new religion in the amenities of Greek thought. Origen said in reply to Celsus' criticism: 'When God sent Jesus to the human race, it was not as though He had just awakened from a long sleep. Jesus has at all times been doing good to the human race. No noble deed amongst men has ever been done without the Divine word visiting the souls of those who even for a brief space were able to receive its operations.' 'That which is called the Christian religion', says Augustine, 'existed among the ancients, and never did not exist, from the beginning of the human race until Christ came in the flesh, at which time the true religion which already existed began to be called Christianity.'

The second view recognizes the divine element in the other religions of the world, but contends that Christianity is the peak of the development of religion. It is the crown and completion of the religion of humanity, the standard by which all others are judged.[1] While on the first view no recognition is given to the workings of the spirit in other religions, here it is conceded that others also sought to know God and do His will, but they are merely preparations for the Christian religion, which is unique.

The difference between Christianity and any other religion is that of the best and the good, and the good is the enemy of the best. 'God, having of old time spoken . . . by divers portions and in divers man-

---

[1] Cf. 'It is the Christian religion which is the perfect religion, the religion which represents the Being of Spirit in a realised form, for itself, the religion in which religion has itself become objective in relation to itself' (Hegel, *The Philosophy of Religion*, E.T. (1895), vol. ii, p. 330).

ners, hath at the end of these days spoken unto us in His son',[2] that is to say, spoken perfectly and finally. 'Christ is indeed the true light, light of light eternal, while all of us children of men, have had kindled within us—just because we are children of men—flickering candles, smoking flax, lit all alike at the first by the divine Hand, but now, poor dim guttering lamps that can only shine again if they are kindled anew, if they can have their oil replenished from the source.'[3] Those, like Dr. Macnicol and the late Dr. Farquhar, who maintain this view would use the scriptures of the Indian people and their rites in their attempts to naturalize Christianity. But at a certain stage in this process they feel that they come up against a rock which they have no right to ignore. 'There is a core of adamant in our Christian faith that is not any one's private property to barter or to buy or to sell.'[4] Truth and falsehood are embattled opposites. While Christianity need not stand solitary apart from other religions, it is not to be regarded as merely relatively excellent, one among many efforts of human beings.

These two attitudes are common to all missionary religions. Each claims with absolute sincerity that it alone is the true light while others are will-o'-the-wisps that blind us to the truth and lure us away from it. When it attempts to be a little more understanding, it affirms that the light of its religion is to that of others as the sun is to the stars, and the minor lights may be tolerated so long as they accept their position of subordination.

An increasing number of Christians adopt a third attitude, the Hindu one, which is definitely against proselytism. The Syrian Christians, who have the longest Christian tradition in India, are opposed to proselytism. Among the later converts to Christianity, this attitude is gaining acceptance.[5] The International Missionary Council at its

[2] Hebrews i. 1, 2.

[3] Macnicol, *Is Christianity Unique?* (1936), p. 166.

[4] Ibid., p. 19. Dr. Frick writes in the *International Review of Missions* (Oct. 1926): 'As long as we claim to be Christians in deed and truth, we must cultivate a certain consciousness of superiority' (p. 10).

[5] Rājkumāri Amrit Kaur writes: 'The conversion or the desire to impel another person to change his faith has always savoured of an arrogance tantamount to a violent attitude of mind which must surely be against that very doctrine of love for which I believe that Christ lived and died. . . . While there has been no conscious effort to purge the Indian Church of the taint of untouchability that exists within its own doors, the untouchability that exists in Hinduism has been exploited to the extent of attempted mass and wholesale conversions to so-called Christianity of the Depressed Classes. I say "so-called Christianity" advisedly, because I know not one of these poor people to whom I have spoken—and I have spoken to many—who has been able to tell me anything of the spiritual implica-

Jerusalem meeting held in 1928 declared: 'We would repudiate any symptoms of a religious imperialism that would desire to impose beliefs and practices on others in order to manage their souls in their supposed interests. We obey a God who respects our wills and we desire to respect those of others.' [6] The Report calls upon non-Christian religion to join forces with Christianity in resisting the attacks of those who deny God and the world of spirit. 'We call on the followers of the non-Christian religions to hold fast to faith in the unseen and eternal, in face of the growing materialism of the world and to co-operate with us against all the evils of secularism.' [7] It has a perception of the desperate need of the world as well as of the fellowship of all believers in God, in the deep places of the spirit. The Report of the American Commission of Laymen affirms that it is unwise to undermine men's faith in their traditions. 'There is a real danger that the sound elements of tradition will be discarded with its abuses and that nothing will be adequate to take the place of the restraints of the older cultures, which, however misconceived, at least maintained a social order.' [8] The task of the missionary would be to pool

---

tions of his change of faith . . . Is there not room for Jesus in Hinduism? There must be. I cannot believe that any who seek to worship God in spirit and in truth are outside the pale of any of the great religions which draw their inspiration from Him who is the fountainhead of all truth. I am sure that I am not the only Indian born in the Christian faith who holds these views' (*The Harijan*, 30 Jan. 1937).

[6] *The World Mission of Christianity*, p. 10. Mr. Bernard Lucas in his book *Our Task in India* draws a distinction between proselytism and evangelism. The former is what Jesus condemned when he said: 'Woe unto you Scribes and Pharisees, hypocrites! for ye compass sea and land to make one proselyte; and when he is become so ye make him twofold more a son of Gehenna than yourselfs' (St. Matthew). The latter is, for Mr. Lucas, what is implied in the words 'But go then and publish abroad the Kingdom of God' (St. Luke). Commenting on the latter, Mr. Lucas writes: 'The standpoint of evangelism recognises the value of the law of heredity in the religious development of the race. There is a distinct type of religious thought and life in India which God has been evolving through the centuries and this must be saved for India and for the world.' He adds that if India loses her distinctive religious genius it would be an irretrievable and incalculable loss to the world. 'The Hindu must be saved as a Hindu.' Dr. D. J. Fleming in his book on *Whither Bound in Missions* (1925) pleads for a 'mutuality in giving and receiving.' He argues that there is a just resentment at the imperialist type of missionary endeavour. He feels that we must be impartial enough to recognize that each race has its special gift and its special contribution to civilization. His first chapter is entitled 'Eradicating a Sense of Superiority.'

[7] *The World Mission of Christianity*, p. 14.

[8] There are Christian missionaries who adopt and advocate this view. Rev. Verrier Elwin says: 'I live among the Gonds and love them. I have never interfered with their religion and when any of them ask me to make them Christian, I refuse. I think myself, that it would be better for all to adopt a similar attitude of detachment and leave their ancestral faith alone' (*Indian Social Reformer*, 2 Nov. 1935, p. 136).

his religion along with others. 'Perhaps the chief hope for an important deepening of self-knowledge on the part of Christendom is by way of a more thorough-going sharing of its life with the life of the Orient. The relations between religions must take increasingly hereafter the form of a common search for truth.' A growing apprehension of truth is effected by the creative interaction of different minds and their insights, by the mutual criticism and enlargement which result from a fuller appreciation of other systems of thought and culture. 'All fences and private properties in truth are futile; the final truth whatever it may be is the New Testament of every existing faith.' There is a common ethical and religious ideal influencing the whole civilized world, and each people tries to find it in its own religion and does find it there. In other words, this Report admits that no religion in its present form is final and every religion is seeking for a better expression. It looks forward to a time when 'the names that now separate men may lose their divisive meaning.' [9] 'Supposing they worship a Being with the same attributes,' Dr. Inge says, 'it does not very much matter whether they call him Buddha or Christ. We must look to things rather than to words.' [10]

There are thus three different attitudes, right, centre, and left, which Christian missionaries adopt towards other religions. Here, as elsewhere, the hopes of the future are under the left wing of liberals and not with the reactionaries or conservatives. If we do not bring together in love those who sincerely believe in God and seek to do His will, if we persist in killing one another theologically, we shall only weaken men's faith in God. If the great religions continue to waste their energies in a fratricidal war instead of looking upon themselves as friendly partners in the supreme task of nourishing the spiritual life of mankind, the swift advance of secular humanism and moral materialism is assured. In a restless and disordered world which is unbelieving to an extent which we have all too little realized, where sinister superstitions are setting forth their rival claims to the allegiance of men, we cannot afford to waver in our determination that the whole of humanity shall remain a united people, where Muslim and Christian, Buddhist and Hindu shall stand together bound by common devotion, not to something behind but to something ahead, not to a racial past or a geographical unit, but to a great dream of a world society with a universal religion of which the historical faiths

[9] (1932) pp. 44, 46, 47, 58.
[10] *Inquirer*, 12 June 1926.

are but branches. We must recognize humbly the partial and defective character of our isolated traditions and seek their source in the generic tradition from which they all have sprung.[11]

Each religion has sat at the feet of teachers that never bowed to its authority, and this process is taking place to-day on a scale unprecedented in the history of humanity and will have most profound effects upon religion. In their wide environment, religions are assisting each other to find their own souls and grow to their full stature. Owing to a cross-fertilization of ideas and insights, behind which lie centuries of racial and cultural tradition and earnest endeavour, a great unification is taking place in the deeper fabric of men's thoughts. Unconsciously perhaps, respect for other points of view, appreciation of the treasures of other cultures, confidence in one another's unselfish motives are growing. We are slowly realizing that believers with different opinions and convictions are necessary to each other to work out the larger synthesis which alone can give the spiritual basis to a world brought together into intimate oneness by man's mechanical ingenuity.

Selected Bibliography

East and West in Religion (London: Allen and Unwin, Ltd., 1953).

Eastern Religions and Western Thought (London: Oxford University Press, 1964).

The Hindu View of Life (New York: Macmillan, 1957).

History of Philosophy, Eastern and Western (London: Allen and Unwin, Ltd., 1952–1953).

Indian Philosophy (New York: Macmillan, 1929–1930).

Mahatma Ghandi (London: Allen and Unwin, Ltd., 1949).

Recovery of Faith (New York: Harper & Row Publishers, 1955).

The Reign of Religion in Contemporary Philosophy (London: Macmillan, 1920).

Religion and Society (London: Allen and Unwin, Ltd., 1959).

Religion in a Changing World (London: Allen and Unwin, Ltd., 1967).

[11] Cf. Professor Hocking: 'We have to recognise that a *world religion exists*. We give religious systems separate names, but they are not separate; they are not closed globules. They merge in the universal human faith in the divine being'— quoted in Basil Mathews, *Roads to the City of God* (1928), p. 43.

Christianity as the Transformation of Religions

JEAN DANIELOU, S. J.

*Jean Cardinal Danielou, one of the leading Roman Catholic theo-
logians in the twentieth century, was born on May 14, 1905, in Paris.
He was educated at the College Sainte Croix de Neuilly, and at the
Sorbonne, University of Paris from which he took the Docteur es
lettres degree in 1927. He received his doctorate in theology from the
University of Lyon in 1944. In 1929 he entered the Society of Jesus,
and was ordained a priest in 1938. After serving in the French army
during World War II, he began teaching. In 1944 he became professor of primitive Christianity in the Institute Catholique in Paris.*

*Through the years, Father Danielou has distinguished himself both
as theologian, historian, and churchman. Although his scholarly activity has centered upon the area of primitive Christianity and the
Church fathers, on which he has written many books and articles, he
has also served as an interpreter of Catholicism to Catholics. Those
auspices are implicit in the essay that follows in which Father Danielou sets forth some proposals regarding the place of Christianity vis-
à-vis the other religions of the world.*

In making a study of the great non-Christian religions—Hinduism,
Islamism, Buddhism—one finds at the same time a problem which
cannot be avoided, that of the confrontation between these religions
and Christianity. It is this decisive question that we should like to
take up here. We do not intend to set forth Christianity as it is in
itself, but to see how we can best represent to ourselves its relation to
the other religions.

The existence of Hindu speculation on three divinities or on the
symbolism of the cross, for example, raises for us the question of the
possible relation of these doctrines to the Christian Trinity or to the
cross of Jesus Christ. The good we derive from reading a certain
Hindu or Moslem mystic makes us think carefully about the specific
character of the Christian mystics and, at times, we might be tempted

Jean Danielou, "The Transcendence of Christianity," chap. 9 of *Introduction to
the Great Religions* (Notre Dame: Fides Publishers, Inc., 1964), pp. 149–159.

to say with Simone Weil: "In fact, the mystics of almost all religious traditions resemble one another, nearly to the point of identity" (*Letter to a Religious,* p. 49).

The two temptations which lie in wait here for the Christian, that of disdain and that of syncretism, are both dangerous and difficult to overcome. It is accordingly necessary to delineate the problem carefully and, while doing justice to the values of the pagan religions, to see how Christianity goes beyond them.

The first trait which characterizes Christianity is that it is faith in an event, that of the Incarnation and Resurrection of Christ. This event constitutes an intervention of God in history which radically changes the human condition and is an absolute novelty. Now this distinguishes Christianity completely from all the other religions. To reduce it, as René Guénon does, to merely one of the forms of the primitive tradition, is precisely to empty it of its original element. The great non-Christian religions affirm the existence of an eternal world opposed to the world of time. They know nothing about an intervention of the eternal in time which gives time consistency and transforms it into history.

This intervention constitutes a thenceforth irrevocable promotion, an irreversible acquisition, so that man shall nevermore be able to turn back. Nothing will be able to separate the union in Jesus Christ of the divine nature and human nature. From that time forward, there is a past and a future in the complete sense of those words. The world becomes organized into a history of which the divine interventions form the decisive acts. From the Creation to the Resurrection of Jesus Christ, passing through the election of Abraham, the Christian Revelation is that of a sacred history, the history of the *"mirabilia Dei,"* the "marvelous deeds of God." The Bible is the documentation of this history. And it is remarkable that, alone of all the sacred Books, that of the Christians is a history and not an exposition of doctrines.

This history does not consist merely of ancient events. The New Testament is continued among us in the sacraments of the Church. The Christian is someone who is aware of living at the heart of sacred history, in a world in which God never ceases to act, to intervene, to perform His admirable actions, those which are fulfilled in the conversion and sanctification of hearts. That is the real history, more real than that of empires or inventions, a history in which the incorruptible Body of Christ is fashioned mysteriously through the activity of supernatural charity.

This history appears as constituting a plan ordered to an end, which is the glorification of God and the sanctification of man. It is accomplished in Jesus Christ. In Him, Creation achieved its goal, the world became successful. In this sense, He is the "novissimus Adam," ever the newest man. It is a characteristic feature of the Christian view of the world that no new event shall ever bring us anything as important as Jesus Christ; thus, the concept of some religion of the future, with Christianity as but a stage leading to it, is excluded. One does not go beyond Jesus Christ.

Nevertheless, while the order of things instituted in Jesus Christ is the final one, it involves interior growth. The Incarnation started it. But it awaits its fulfilment. This fulfilment will be the Parousia, the last event in the history of salvation. It will be characterized by the reverberation throughout the entire cosmos of the Resurrection of Jesus Christ, which heretofore has produced its effects only in the world of souls. And so Christianity, even after the Incarnation, remains an eschatology. It is the expectation of an ultimate intervention by God taking up His work again in order to bring it to its final conclusion.

We have said that Christianity was faith in an intervention by God in the world, in Jesus Christ. Now we come to a second affirmation, namely, that only this action of God's can save man, that is, that there is no salvation outside of Jesus Christ. This is what is overlooked by a position, derived from a kind of syncretism, which believes that the mystiques of all religions "meet one another even to identity." The breadth of this view seduces certain minds, which contrast it with Christian intransigence. But, in affirming that the mystiques of all religions are similar, it is saying in effect that what saves is the ascetical effort at detachment and union with God, and not the efficacy of the Cross in Jesus Christ. Once again, we are faced with a radical opposition.

What we are saying here should not be misunderstood. In no way is it a question of deprecating the examples of interior life and of detachment which we find in non-Christian religions. China, along with the doctrines of Confucius, has brought us some admirable rules of wisdom for relations among men. India offers us the example of a people who have always seen in asceticism and contemplation the highest ideal. Nor can one read its masters, from the author of the Bhaghavad Gita to Aurobindo, without experiencing the feeling of the unreality of worldly goods and of the sovereign reality of the invisible world. It is understandable that, in our modern Western world, which is concerned only with harnessing the energies of the cosmos, and which has absorbed from Marxism the illusion that man can be transformed by changing his material living conditions, the wisdom of India attracts souls thirsting for silence and the interior life.

But the fact remains that this assumes that man is able to reach God by his own powers. Christianity must categorically deny this, for two reasons. The first is the reality of original sin. This consists in a separation between man and God, which man cannot abolish by himself. It is not enough, therefore, to say that man alienated himself by turning toward the exterior world, and that he has only to turn aside from the life of the body to discover the pure spirituality which is his very being. For Christianity, it is not the body which is the principle of sin, but the whole man, soul and body, is the captive of evil and God alone can liberate him from this captivity, through grace.

The second reason is that the Christian God is absolutely inaccessible. He alone can, therefore, introduce man to this participation in His nature which supernatural life is. For Hinduism, in fact, or neo-Platonism, the soul is divine by nature, and it only needs to move away from what is alien to it in order to find God by finding itself. But this concept assumes that there is no radical distinction between the uncreated God and the created spirit. The mystique of India presupposes a certain pantheism. On the other hand, the first article of Christian faith is the doctrine of the Creator-God, that is, the radical distinction between God and man. Accordingly, God alone is able to raise man to this participation in Him which is the supernatural life, the apex of which is the mystical life. It is inaccessible to any human asceticism.

The fundamental reversal of perspectives is clear. For syncretism, the saved are the interior souls, regardless of the religion to which they may belong. For Christianity, the saved are those who believe, regardless of their level of interior life. A little child, a worker weighed down by his labors, if they believe, are superior to the greatest ascetics. "We are not great religious personalities," as Guardini put it so well, "we are servants of the Word." Christ had already said that, while St. John the Baptist might be "the greatest among the sons of men, yet the least of the sons of the kingdom is greater than he." It is possible that there are in the world some great religious personalities outside Christianity; it may even happen that at a given time, the greatest religious personalities will be found outside Christianity. This is of no consequence. What does matter, is obedience to the words of Jesus Christ.

In this light, the difference between non-Christian mystiques and the Christian mystique appears. For the former, union with God is the goal of an asceticism through which the soul, stripping itself of what is alien to it, discovers its pure essence, which is God Himself. The emphasis will therefore be placed on ascetical techniques: exercises of recollection, unification of the soul, etc. It happens that Christian mystics make use of these methods. But they are always secondary, and they are never sufficient. The Christian God is, in fact, a living and transcendent God whom no technique could ever reach. He communicates Himself freely, when and as He wishes. The mystical experience is not conditioned upon any technique. Thus, the grace of God strikes Paul enroute to Damascus, enters the soul of Marie of the Incarnation rolling casks on the Loire docks. It has no other source than the sovereign liberty of the divine love. It is not so much psychological exercises which dispose the soul to receive it as it is the religious attitudes which render the soul pleasing to God.

Up to now, we have stressed primarily Christianity's nature as a divine fact. But its transcendence is also apparent on the level of doctrines. This fact is disregarded by a third type of syncretism which believes it can find the main Christian dogmas, the Trinity, the Redemption, etc., in other religions. Thus, there are a number of comparisons the superficiality of which has been demonstrated many times and which no serious mind should retain, but which continue to be spread, sowing some uncertainty in the minds of many of our contemporaries, which dilutes the faith. It is astonishing that Simone Weil, otherwise gifted with a very sharp critical sense, should have yielded to this temptation. In her *Letter to a Religious*, she repeats a large share of these slogans.

Thus, she compares the words of Christ: "I am the true vine," to the role of the vine in the cult of Dionysos (p. 21). But it has been established that we are dealing here with two different themes: the Palestinian theme of the vine as the figure of the people of God (Isaias 5:1), and the Greek theme in which the vine symbolizes immortality, in connection with drunkenness. The maternity of the Virgin is compared to the mother goddesses of antiquity. Yet it is certain that the cult of the Virgin in Christianity stems from the historical role of Mary in the plan of salvation, and not from a sublimation of femininity, as in the religions of nature. The death of Christ on the Cross is compared to the crucifixion of the soul of the world in Plato's *Timeus* (p. 23). It is clear, however, that the role of the Cross in Christianity derives from the gibbet on which Jesus was sacrificed, which was in the form of a T. In no way does it come from the symbolism of the four dimensions which is found in various religions. The Christian Trinity is compared to the Greek triads (p. 27) and the Hindu triads (p. 33). But it is certain that, far from proceeding from a dialectical requirement, the Trinity constitutes a stumbling block as far as reason is concerned, for it is not a question of a primordial unity and its manifestations, but of Three Persons Who subsist eternally in the unity of one nature.

I cannot take more than a word here to indicate the essential contrast for each of these points. It has often happened that Christianity has utilized in its liturgy symbols borrowed from the religions of nature. Thus, in the third century A.D., Hippolyte of Rome gave the cross a cosmic symbolism. The language of the pagan mysteries was employed for the sacraments beginning in the fourth century. The catacomb paintings show us the vine as a symbol of immortality. And in our own time, Father Monchanin proposes to designate the Trinity by means of the sacred formula *saccidânanda*, which describes the Hindu triad. But those are secondary developments and cultural adaptations. Insofar as their origins are concerned, the Christian dogmas are a new revelation.

Does this mean that the natural religions have not attained certain truths concerning God? Such a statement would be inaccurate. St. Paul himself teaches that "since the creation of the world, the invisible perfections of God are known through visible things." The non-Christian religions have been able to grasp that which human reason left to itself is capable of discovering, that is, God's exterior, His existence and His perfections as they are manifest through His action in the world.

But there is something no reason has ever been able to suspect, a threshold no foot has ever crossed, a darkness where no one enters by stealth: it is the mystery of the inner life of God. The depths of the Trinity are absolutely inaccessible to man and only the Son of God has been able to introduce man thereto: "No one has ever seen God. But the only Son, who is in the bosom of the Father, he has made him known to us." We have reached the heart of what constitutes the irreducible originality of Christianity, namely, the fact that the Son of God, having come among us, has revealed to us these two truths, which are closely joined to one another: the presence of this mysterious life of love in God called the Trinity, and our own calling, in Him and through Him, to participate eternally in this life. It is summed up in one person, the person of Jesus Christ, God made man, in Whom can be found all that we must know. The religions of nature—and this is what is valuable about them—testify to man's movement toward God; Christianity is the movement of God Who, in Jesus Christ, comes to take man in order to lead him to Himself.

Thus, compared with Christianity, the pagan religions seem out of date and distorted. Still, they contain some worthwhile elements. Would not their disappearance then be an impoverishment? Simone Weil feared that it would: "If the other traditions disappear from the surface of the earth," she wrote, "it would be an irreparable loss. As it is, the missionaries have already caused too many to disappear." (p. 35.) Against this accusation, we must set forth the true concept of the Christian mission. Pius XII enunciated it thus in the encyclical *Divini Praecones*: "The Church has never treated the doctrines of the pagans with contempt and disdain; rather, she has freed them from all error, then completed them and crowned them with Christian wisdom."

This formula admirably sums up the attitude of Christianity. It does not treat the religious values of the pagan religions with disdain. But it first purifies them from all error, that is, it destroys the corruption—especially idolatry. This is why conversion will always be a rupture. Progress from paganism to Christianity is never accomplished through homogeneous evolution. Then, Christianity, through Christian wisdom, completes and fulfills the imperfect truths which exist in the pagan religions. It takes up the natural values of the religious man, it recovers them in order to consecrate them. Thus, we find early Christianity integrating the values of Greek philosophy after having purified them. Thus shall we be able to see in the future, Christianity assuming all the values contained in the asceticism of the Hindus or the wisdom of Confucius, after having purified them. The Christian mission, when it is what it is supposed to be, is not destruction, but liberation and transformation of the religious values of paganism. Christ did not come to destroy, but to fulfill.

Selected Bibliography

The Dead Sea Scrolls and Primitive Christianity (New York: The New American Library, Inc., 1962).

Dialogue with Israel (Baltimore: Helicon Press, Inc., 1968).

(Coeditor with Henri Marrou) *The First Six Hundred Years* (New York: McGraw-Hill, Inc., 1964).

The Lord of History (Chicago: Henry Regnery Company, 1960).

"Phenomenology of Religions and Philosophy of Religion," in *The History of Religions: Essays in Methodology*, ed. by Mircea Eliade and Joseph M. Kitagawa (Chicago: University of Chicago Press, 1959), pp. 67–85.

Primitive Christian Symbols (Baltimore: Helicon Press, Inc., 1964).

The Theology of Jewish Christianity (Chicago: Henry Regnery Company, 1964).

On Extricating
Religionswissenschaft
from Theology
ERWIN R. GOODENOUGH

As an historian rather than a philosopher, I must say that no definition of religion I have ever heard, or made (and I have made many)
has any but suggestive and partial value. The most important words,
of course, can never be defined, and deeper understanding of them
usually involves discovering the inadequacy of old definitions. Even
so precise a term as chemistry can no longer be defined. What, today,
is it? Who will now sharply distinguish it from physics or botany?
Certainly not the students of chemistry themselves. Nuclear physics
can be studied apart from chemistry, or biology, or astronomy, to a
point, but only to a point. A fortiori, who can set up any but pretty
verbal barriers between history, science, and philosophy? Similarly
Freudians have come to understand sex better as they have confused
the rest of us by seeing its manifestations everywhere, even in the
conduct of infants. Man is a physiological animal, a sexual animal, a
political animal, an economic animal, a social animal. He is also a
religious animal. He is all of these simultaneously, for beneath the
distinctive terms is man himself. Those who study man from one
point of view rather than another always tend to see their own approach as the one really all-encompassing in human structure. The
function and goal of Religionswissenschaft is to come better to
understand the *homo religiosus*. But all these approaches blend so
inextricably that to define the character and compass of any one
aspect invades the boundaries of every other. If we do not recognize
this we limit to the point of petty distortion the aspect we try to
define. Sociologists and psychologists have no notion of defining their
fields in such a way as to exclude the other, or, in fact, of excluding
man's religous patterns. Religion, in turn, cannot be forced to define
itself in such a way as not to impinge upon, indeed largely to include,
at least sociology and psychology. So, if we are not by verbal calis-
thenics to weaken our understanding of all these fields, we must

Erwin R. Goodenough, "Religionswissenschaft," in *Numen*, Vol. VI (1959), pp.
77–95. Pages 85–91 reprinted by permission.

resort to description which moves from an essential center indefinitely outward, rather than fabricate definitions that work from borders inward.

In brief, then, I see religion arising from the universal phenomenon that we are born and live in an external universe, and with internal depth and emotions, which we neither understand nor control. Man exists largely helpless before the forces of nature and society, and really knows nothing basic about himself, and the meaning and purpose of life, individually or collectively. The conscious mind, and probably even more persistently the unconscious mind, are always confronted by the tremendum, both within oneself and without. By modern science man has to a slight degree mitigated the sense of helplessness and confusion he feels before the tremendum, but now when men collectively know more than ever in history, we call ourselves the Age of Anxiety, because we are freshly, almost pathologically, sensitive to the ignorance and helplessness that characterize us. Such ignorance has always characterized mankind, characterizes all animal life. But if an animal is hungry, while he looks eagerly for food, so far as we know he has no diffused anxiety about the problem of food supply. Or of death, or sex, or security in general. Without debating whether that be true for mice and rabbits, or for rats that have been psychologically tortured, this generalization will stand better than most, that awareness of our helplessness and ignorance, along with the anxiety they produce, generally characterizes human beings.

Religion steps in for all of us at this point. Man has never been able to accept himself on this level as helpless before the tremendum. He must have the illusion, at least, that he can do something to control the apparently uncontrollable, to explain the inexplicable. We may laugh at the savage stories of creation through a cosmic bull, or turtle, or egg, but the understanding most people in this room have of the process of evolution is probably just about as far from reality, and starts from quite as vague a protozoon, or protozoa, as the stories of the savages. It gives us comfort, nevertheless, to believe in evolution. Those least satisfied by the theory of evolution are my friends in biology who know how fragmentary and inadequate the whole theory really is. All great tragedy faces the unintelligibility of life, and terrifies us as it suddenly dangles our helpless ignorance before us. Shakespeare had no answers for Hamlet and Lear. The Oresteia loses its dignity when Athena at the end introduces a divine justice that exists in religion, not reality. For Aeschylus had finally to succumb to his craving for divine consolation, and so he projected its reality, as Socrates did not. But how few men in history have given their lives rather than deny their own ignorance! For one such man there have been untold millions of Athenian citizens who would murder, and not always mercifully by hemlock, a man who doubted the reality of the myths which they hold like curtains to screen themselves from the unintelligibility and uncontrollability of the tremendum.

Here seems the essence of religion, the problem of how man can live over against the great unknown, the tremendum. Traditional religions have given two basic answers. Most commonly man has screened himself off from the tremendum by mythical accounts of the origin and nature of things, by rites which would placate its unpredictable lightnings and whirlwinds, by holy places and seasons, by divinely given codes of laws. In all these ways man has tried to protect himself from what is, to him the chaos of the tremendum. Man has draped curtains about him, with fine paintings in perspective on them. This perspective could give him the illusion that he lives in the tremendum itself while the curtains actually only protect him from its impact. The patterns on other people's curtains are, of course, myths; those on our own are theology. The masses of men must get their myths, their rites, and their codes, their symbols, the designs on their curtains, from the traditions of their social groups. Few can escape them, or make new ones of their own. Since a few can do so, however, our myths of explanation and our rites for controlling nature, or fate, cannot be simply social institutions forced upon all. And those of us who break away are not thereby irreligious, else the Jewish prophets, the Buddha, Socrates, and Jesus were irreligious.

As over against the apotropaic, the second basic formulation is that in which an individual has broken the curtains, or lifted them, to go alone into the Alone, and to face the numenous tremendum in itself. Moses on Sinai, the prophets announcing their new visions, Jesus at Gethsemane, the Buddha as he left his earthly kingdom, many young savage candidates to achieve spiritual leadership in the tribe, these represent an utterly different conception of an adjustment to the universal reality from which most men screen themselves. These men left, or still leave, the formulation about them, to court the very tremendum itself, and be taken over by it. Buddhist monks practise this approach, and train the more intelligent laymen in it, though it has little appeal to the mass of Buddhists who live almost entirely in their apotropaic exercises.

The History of Religions examines this drive of man to adjust himself to the tremendum, the masses by screening themselves from it, others by freshly approaching it. About the tremendum itself as a whole we all come out with myths, of course, whether traditional myths or ones of our own creation, since the tremendum as a whole is utterly too much for us. Practical living is impossible without a skeleton of myths that establish values and meaning. The myths of men have given them their courage both to live and love, and to destroy and kill. It is in the name of myths proclaiming a meaning of life that Hitler and Lenin killed, and Gandhi refused to kill. All decisive action, in the last analysis all action and life, comes from faith, pure faith that the nature of the tremendum is thus, and so, and so, and that we have such or such relation to it.

If true religion be a matter of formal revelation from the tremendum, however, those who assert that science and its methods have no relation to it cannot be disputed. In that case, a Society of the History of Religion would be a group collecting curious information about behavioral aberrations and strange myths, essentially not religious at all, because not a part of what we consider revelation. Its members might have much good information, and practical advice to give diplomats or business men in dealing with peoples of the world, but their work would have no relation to Religionswissenschaft. Perhaps we should assume, on the other hand, in Jungian terms, that religion is a matter of less formal, but no less real, invasion of humanity by the tremendum through the emergence of universally similar rites and myths. In that case, by accepting the Jungian hypothesis that these materials come to man through the Collective Unconscious, we can perhaps get increasing insights into the nature of the tremendum. But, to be brutal, this approach may well be only another method for obscuring from ourselves our ultimate ignorance, and of painting new designs, or a new term, on our curtains. Whether we think this fair to Jungians or not, most of our scientific colleagues would at once answer that the Jungian approach goes too rapidly from data to overall conclusions.

Can a really objective approach to the value of the myths and practices of religions ever be found? Is one myth painted on the curtain as good as any other? Should we believe anything that makes living and dying comfortable, and destroy those who would shake our belief and so disturb our comfort? As one Catholic wrote me: "There are too many things we shall never know. Here it seems to me is the role of the revealed religions, of which there is only one true one, meaning mine, for the simple reason that Catholicism did it so much better than any other religion." This is, indeed the usual pattern of religion, especially in the West, including modern Russia. At this point the Science of Religion, with the History of Religions as one of its chief tools, can step in. For we shall believe that only our cowardice makes the tremendum terrible, and that so long as we admit our ignorance we can step up to the tremendum itself in matters of human value as physics does in matters of material value (if we can use the word material any more). The method of modern science is, unabashed by general ignorance of reality, to go to the great unknown with little questions that inch their way into bits, consistent bits, of knowledge. I believe that in the Science of Religion we must learn to do the same.

Personally, I do not see how in the modern world we have a right to speak of, or look for, a science of religion so long as we ourselves live within apotropaic curtains, or live with the stated purpose of having our personalities and critical faculties blurred out in mysticism. For we can no longer use the word "science" in its original sense of the Latin Scientia, or of Plato's *episteme*. Science now means, as I have said, a method of study in which, by the most exact methods applicable to a given sort of data, we draw up hypotheses from the data, and then verify (or reject) the hypotheses by some fresh return to the data, or by return to fresh data. A cataloguing of data, or a learned collection of information, can no longer pose as scientific knowledge, what the word Wissenschaft often meant a century ago. Scientific study takes empirical data, and tries to see the principles inherent in them. Science proverbially says it can do nothing with an isolated fact. It can do just as little with inherently miscellaneous facts. For what science seeks always is structural, inherent, relationships.

In saying this about science we seem to have begun again describing religion since religion has been man's passionate attempt to adjust himself to the tremendum by understanding its nature and how to use it. It is possible that the rejection of science by religion, and of theology by science, is only the old war of religions on a new front, and that science seems a threat to old formulations of religion precisely because it is a new formulation of man's relation to the tremendum, actually a totally new form of religion itself. I believe that that is precisely the case and that the emergence of this type of thinking, which followers of the old religions continue to mark as irreligious, signifies the emergence of a new religion. The new religion takes a new attitude toward the tremendum: It no longer hides its head, ostrich fashion, in myths asserting that the tremendum is less perilous than it is; it no longer surrenders to the tremendum, and asks to be reabsorbed into it. Instead, refusing either to run away or to surrender, it accepts the tremendum, and the individual's helplessness and insignificance before it. It drops no curtain, but faces the overwhelming within and without, while it seeks to find relationships and meaning as far as it can by its own new method. The new religion of science, and most of the men and women who practise it, have few illusions. Few of them want to discuss the nature of reality, or work from a prioris, except the basic one announced by Einstein, that the only thing unintelligible about the universe is that it should be intelligible. To assert that the universe is universally intelligible would indeed be another painted curtain. Certainly it is not intelligible now. But society finds itself deluged with the apparently limitless flow of dimes from the jackpot of nature which the scientific conception of intelligibility has released upon us. As Theodore Sizer remarked the other day, the new deluge, in the eyes of millions, has been enormously rewarding but depressingly stupefying. In other words, science has released not only gadgets and dimes to engulf us, but has stupefied us with the tremendum itself, and that in a way for which we have formed no protective devices. It has often stupefied even the scientists in their private lives, but does not do so in the lives of those truly dedicated to the new point of view, people whom I may call the saints of science. Many of them have a private logion, such as that of the great astronomer Harlow Shapley, who, as he looks in his telescope, or does his celestial mathematics, mutters to himself: "All nature is God, all God is nature." He approaches this nature-God, however, not by traditional forms of worship, but through his observations and calculations, which have become his sacrament. No one in this room has a conception of the immensity of the universe, or of the smallness of man in it, comparable to Shapley's. But the tremendum has no terror for him. He looks at it with quiet eyes, astonished, reverent, but unafraid. He carried this attitude over to society and politics when McCarthy created fear and trembling. He regarded Senatorial Committees for Hysteria with the same calm eyes, and spoke up to them as, in his mathematics, he speaks up to the universe. Throughout he keeps his integrity, his dignity, as an ignorant but seeking human being. This, gentlemen, is religion pure and undefiled, and we do ourselves, and our subject, small service if we fail to recognize it as such.

PART 6

Modal Parsing:
The Language of Religion

This section of the anthology gives attention to the means, forms, and components of religious expressions. The section itself is divided into two parts, giving place to those whose focal object is symbolization in general and those who pay particular attention to discourse. The first are usually called historians of symbolic forms, or, more generally, cultural historians; the second are usually called language analysts. Although often regarded as strange bedfellows, especially by each other, the representatives of these two occupations are grouped together here on grounds that it would be advantageous to have both present at any forum on "the language of religion."

Representing philosophies of symbolism are three persons who have figured prominently in the development of that discipline, Ernst Cassirer, Susanne K. Langer, and Paul Ricoeur. All can be understood to have been engaged in the morphology of cultural symbolization. Well-known for his three-volume examination of the symbolic forms manifested in human culture, Cassirer sees religion both as an instrument of man's self-consciousness and as evidence of his work. In a similar fashion,

Langer's particular interest is the transformations that occur in the passage of content between language, ritual, myth, music, and pictorial art. Religion is implicit in her portrayals because of its role in the creation of life-symbols. A selection from the writings of Paul Ricoeur is also included to give us an indication of his interest in providing a full-scale hermeneutics of symbols. Ricoeur's effort to trace the transposition from symbolic to discursive language is an aspect of his larger program in which an attempt is made to provide a comprehensive "phenomenology of the will"—a subject that also carries him into analyses of evil, guilt, and human fault.

The language analysts, on the other hand, focus almost exclusively on utterances made in statement form. Consequently, most of them stand not only for particular methodological techniques but also for a set of philosophical theses. First, they understand language to be the means by which men conduct their practical affairs. Next, they assert that words and phrases receive their meaning from the ordinary life situations in which they are used. Thus, men make sense when they employ language according to the customary rules of communication or nonsense when they depart from the rules governing ordinary language usage. Seen from this vantage point, religion is a party to the creation of both sense and nonsense, primarily since religion is also a source of utterances made in statement form. According to the analysts, much of the confusion that occurs in the history of theology and philosophy can be attributed to misconceptions regarding the use of language. Many of these problems simply dissolve upon concerted examination, while others are reduced to forms in which they can be clarified. Taken *in toto*, language analysis (in the form of linguistic philosophy) is designed to play a therapeutic role. Its function is to clarify puzzles and resolve confusion by careful attention to semantics, word usage, and rules of sense.

A variety of kinds of selections are included in this section of the anthology to illustrate the several sides of influence that linguistic philosophy possesses. At the outset is a brief summary-interpretation by Gilbert Ryle of the work of Ludwig Wittgenstein, the principle precipitant of the recent philosophical wave. Although it does not deal directly with religious studies or religious issues, and is inserted here as a kind of extra piece, it is necessary background material. One need only recall that much of the work in this field has been prompted by Wittgenstein's insights. R. B. Braithwaite summarizes some of the prominent, direct implications of language analysis with respect to the statements frequently made in religious circles. At stake in his discussion is the issue, "Do religious statements make truth claims?" Braithwaite's article is followed by an exposition by philosopher-theologian Paul L. Holmer, which employs insights from this approach to distinguish ways in which words are used in religious communication. Peter Winch's essay discusses the use of language analysis as a means of access to the forms of social organization of early man. Winch's work shows a variety of affinities with the objectives of such cultural anthropologists as Claude Lévi-Strauss and E. E. Evans-Pritchard. Since the latter's research has also been tapped to clarify questions about the morphology of tribal religion, it is entirely conceivable that Wittgenstein's suggestions will bear additional fruit in unanticipated ways in religious studies.

Symbolic Forms

Towards a Morphology of Symbolic Expressions

Ernst Cassirer

Ernst Cassirer, philosopher and cultural historian, was born in Breslau on July 28, 1874, and educated at the Universities of Berlin, Leipzig, Heidelberg, and Marburg. He became professor of philosophy in Hamburg in 1919 and rector of that institution in 1930. Cassirer resigned his position in the university when Hitler came to power. He taught at Oxford from 1933 to 1935, in Sweden at Gothenburg from 1935 to 1941, in the United States at Yale University from 1941 to 1945, and at Columbia University until his death on April 13, 1945.

Inheriting a nest of problems from Kantian and Neo-Kantian philosophical traditions—the thought of Hermann Cohen had been highly influential in his educational training—Cassirer sought to trace and describe those prelogical and preconceptual forms of knowledge to which Kant's critiques had no direct access. Consequently, as the following essay illustrates, Cassirer paid particular attention to such cultural manifestations of mental activity as musical, artistic, religious, and, most particularly, mythological expressions. From this standpoint, he touches the source and gives articulation to the mode by which religion gains expression.

The Definition of Man in Terms of Human Culture

It was a turning point in Greek culture and Greek thought when Plato interpreted the maxim "Know thyself" in an entirely new sense. This interpretation introduced a problem which was not only alien to pre-Socratic thought but also went far beyond the limits of the Socratic method. In order to obey the demand of the Delphic god, in order to fulfill the religious duty of self-examination and self-knowledge, Socrates had approached the individual man. Plato recognized the limitations of the Socratic way of inquiry. In order to solve the problem, he declared, we must project it upon a larger plan. The phenomena we encounter in our individual experience are so various, so complicated and contradictory that we can scarcely disentangle them. Man is to be studied not in his individual life but in his political and social life. Human nature, according to Plato, is like a difficult text, the meaning of which has to be deciphered by philosophy. But in our personal experience this text is written in such small characters that it becomes illegible. The first labor of philosophy must be to enlarge these characters. Philosophy cannot give us a satisfactory theory of man until it has developed a theory of the state. The nature of man is written in capital letters in the nature of the state. Here the hidden meaning of the text suddenly emerges, and what seemed obscure and confused becomes clear and legible.

But political life is not the only form of a communal human existence. In the history of mankind the state, in its present form, is a late product of the civilizing process. Long before man had discovered this form of social organization he had made other attempts to organize his feelings, desires, and thoughts. Such organizations and systematizations are contained in language, in myth, in religion, and in art. We must accept this broader basis if we wish to develop a theory of man. The state, however important, is not all. It cannot express or absorb all the other activities of man. To be sure these activities in their historical evolution are closely connected with the development of the state; in many respects they are dependent upon the forms of political life. But, while not possessing a separate historical existence, they have nevertheless a purport and value of their own.

In modern philosophy Comte was one of the first to approach this problem and to formulate it in a clear and systematic way. It is something of a paradox that in this respect we must regard the positivism of Comte as a modern parallel to the Platonic theory of man. Comte was of course never a Platonist. He could not accept the logical and metaphysical presuppositions upon which Plato's theory of ideas is based. Yet, on the other hand, he was strongly opposed to the views of the French ideologists. In his hierarchy of human knowledge two new sciences, the science of social ethics and that of social dynamics, occupy the highest rank. From this sociological viewpoint Comte attacks the psychologism of his age. One of the fundamental maxims of his philosophy is that our method of studying man must, indeed, be subjective, but that it cannot be individual. For the subject we wish to know is not the individual consciousness but the universal subject. If we refer to this subject by the term "humanity," then we must affirm that humanity is not to be explained by man, but man by humanity. The problem must be reformulated and re-examined; it must be put on a broader and sounder basis. Such a basis we have discovered in sociological and historical thought. "To know yourself," says Comte, "know history." Henceforth historical psychology supplements and supersedes all previous forms of individual psychology. "The so-called observations made on the mind, considered in itself and *a priori*," wrote Comte in a letter, "are pure illusions. All that we call *logic, metaphysics, ideology*, is an idle fancy and a dream when it is not an absurdity."[1]

In Comte's *Cours de philosophie positive* we can trace step by step the nineteenth-century transition in methodological ideals. Comte began merely as a scientist, his interest being apparently wholly absorbed in mathematical, physical, and chemical problems. In his hierarchy of human knowledge the scale goes from astronomy through mathematics, physics, and chemistry to biology. Then comes what looks like a sudden reversal of this order. As we approach the human world the principles of mathematics or of the natural sciences do not become invalid, but they are no longer sufficient. Social phenomena are subject to the same rules as physical phenomena, yet they are of a different and much more complicated character. They are not to be described merely in terms of physics, chemistry, and biology. "In all social phenomena," says Comte,

> we perceive the working of the physiological laws of the individual; and moreover something which modifies their effects, and which belongs to the influence of individuals over each other—singularly complicated in the case of the human race by the influence of generations on their successors. Thus it is clear that our social science must issue from that which relates to the life of the individual. On the other hand, there is no occasion to suppose, as some eminent physiologists have done, that Social Physics is only an appendage to Physiology. The phenomena of the two are not identical, though they are homogeneous; and it is of high importance to hold the two sciences separate. As social conditions modify the operation of physiological laws, Social Physics must have a set of observations of its own.[2]

[1] Comte, *Lettres à Valat*, p. 89; cited from L. Lévy-Bruhl, *La philosophie d'Auguste Comte*. For further details see Lévy-Bruhl, *op. cit.* English trans., *The Philosophy of Comte* (New York and London, 1903), pp. 247 ff.

[2] Comte, *Cours de philosophie positive*. English trans. by Harriet Martineau, *Positive Philosophy* (New York, 1855), Intro., chap. ii, 45 f.

The disciples and followers of Comte were not, however, inclined to accept this distinction. They denied the difference between physiology and sociology because they feared that acknowledging it would lead back to a metaphysical dualism. Their ambition was to establish a purely naturalistic theory of the social and cultural world. To this end they found it necessary to negate and destroy all those barriers which seem to separate the human from the animal world. The theory of evolution had evidently effaced all these differences. Even before Darwin the progress of natural history had frustrated all attempts at such differentiation. In the earlier stages of empirical observation it was still possible for the scientist to cherish the hope of finding eventually an anatomical character reserved for man. As late as the eighteenth century it was still a generally accepted theory that there is a marked difference, in some respects a sharp contrast, between the anatomical structure of man and that of the other animals. It was one of Goethe's great merits in the field of comparative anatomy that he vigorously combated this theory. The same homogeneity, not merely in the anatomical and physiological but also in the mental structure of man, remained to be demonstrated. For this purpose all the attacks on the older way of thinking had to be concentrated upon one point. The thing to be proved was that what we call the intelligence of man is by no means a self-dependent, original faculty. Proponents of the naturalistic theories could appeal for proof to the principles of psychology established by the older schools of sensationalism. Taine developed the psychological basis for his general theory of human culture in a work on the intelligence of man.[3] According to Taine, what we call "intelligent behavior" is not a special principle or privilege of human nature; it is only a more refined and complicated play of the same associative mechanism and automatism which we find in all animal reactions. If we accept this explanation the difference between intelligence and instinct becomes negligible; it is a mere difference of degree, not of quality. Intelligence itself becomes a useless and scientifically meaningless term.

The most surprising and paradoxical feature of the theories of this type is the striking contrast between what they promise and what they actually give us. The thinkers who built up these theories were very severe with respect to their methodological principles. They were not content to speak of human nature in terms of our common experience, for they were striving after a much higher ideal, an ideal of absolute scientific exactness. But if we compare their results with this

[3] *De l'intelligence* (Paris, 1870). 2 vols.

standard we cannot help being greatly disappointed. "Instinct" is a very vague term. It may have a certain descriptive value but it has obviously no explanatory value. By reducing some classes of organic or human phenomena to certain fundamental instincts, we have not alleged a new cause; we have only introduced a new name. We have put a question, not answered one. The term "instinct" gives us at best an *idem per idem*, and in most cases it is an *obscurum per obscurius*. Even in the description of animal behavior most modern biologists and psycho-biologists have become very cautious about using it. They warn us against the fallacies which appear to be inextricably connected with it. They try rather to avoid or to abandon "the error-freighted concept of instinct and the oversimple concept of intelligence." In one of his most recent publications Robert M. Yerkes declares that the terms "instinct" and "intelligence" are outmoded and that the concepts for which they stand are sadly in need of redefining.[4] But in the field of anthropological philosophy we are still, apparently, far from any such redefinition. Here these terms are very often accepted quite naïvely without critical analysis. When used in this way the concept of instinct becomes an example of that typical methodological error which was described by William James as the psychologist's fallacy. The word "instinct," which may be useful for the description of animal or human behavior, is hypostatized into a sort of natural power. Curiously enough this error was often committed by thinkers who, in all other respects, felt secure against relapses into scholastic realism or "faculty-psychology." A very clear and impressive criticism of this mode of thinking is contained in John Dewey's *Human Nature and Conduct*. "It is unscientific," writes Dewey,

> to try to restrict original activities to a definite number of sharply demarcated classes of instincts. And the practical result of this attempt is injurious. To classify is, indeed, as useful as it is natural. The indefinite multitude of particular and changing events is met by the mind with acts of defining, inventorying, and listing, reducing to common heads and tying up in bunches. . . . But when we assume that our lists and bunches represent fixed separations and collections *in rerum natura*, we obstruct rather than aid our transactions with things. We are guilty of a presumption which nature promptly punishes. We are rendered incompetent to deal effectively with the delicacies and novelties of nature and life. . . . The tendency to forget the office

[4] *Chimpanzees*, p. 110.

of distinctions and classifications, and to take them as marking things in themselves is the current fallacy of scientific specialism. . . . This attitude which once flourished in physical science now governs theorizing about human nature. Man has been resolved into a definite collection of primary instincts which may be numbered, catalogued and exhaustively described one by one. Theorists differ only or chiefly as to their number and ranking. Some say one, self-love; some two, egoism and altruism; some three, greed, fear and glory; while today writers of a more empirical turn run the number up to fifty and sixty. But in fact there are as many specific reactions to differing stimulating conditions as there is time for, and our lists are only classifications for a purpose.[5]

After this brief survey of the different methods that have hitherto been employed in answering the question: What is man? we now come to our central issue. Are these methods sufficient and exhaustive? Or is there still another approach to an anthropological philosophy? Is any other way left open besides that of psychological introspection, biological observation and experiment, and of historical investigation? I have endeavored to discover such an alternative approach in my *Philosophy of Symbolic Forms*.[6] The method of this work is by no means a radical innovation. It is not designed to abrogate but to complement former views. The philosophy of symbolic forms starts from the presupposition that, if there is any definition of the nature or "essence" of man, this definition can only be understood as a functional one, not a substantial one. We cannot define man by any inherent principle which constitutes his metaphysical essence— nor can we define him by any inborn faculty or instinct that may be ascertained by empirical observation. Man's outstanding characteristic, his distinguishing mark, is not his metaphysical or physical nature—but his work. It is this work, it is the system of human activities, which defines and determines the circle of "humanity." Language, myth, religion, art, science, history are the constituents, the various sectors of this circle. A "philosophy of man" would therefore be a philosophy which would give us insight into the fundamental structure of each of these human activities, and which at the same time would enable us to understand them as an organic whole.

[5] John Dewey, *Human Nature and Conduct* (New York, Holt & Co., 1922), Pt. II, sec. 5 p. 131

[6] *Philosophie der symbolischen Formen.* Vol. I, *Die Sprache* (1923); Vol. II, *Das mythische Denken* (1925); Vol. III, *Phaenomenologie der Erkenntnis* (1929).

Language, art, myth, religion are no isolated, random creations. They are held together by a common bond. But this bond is not a *vinculum substantiale*, as it was conceived and described in scholastic thought; it is rather a *vinculum functionale*. It is the basic function of speech, of myth, of art, of religion that we must seek far behind their innumerable shapes and utterances, and that in the last analysis we must attempt to trace back to a common origin.

It is obvious that in the performance of this task we cannot neglect any possible source of information. We must examine all the available empirical evidence, and utilize all the methods of introspection, biological observation, and historical inquiry. These older methods are not to be eliminated but referred to a new intellectual center, and hence seen from a new angle. In describing the structure of language, myth, religion, art, and science, we feel the constant need of a psychological terminology. We speak of religious "feeling," of artistic or mythical "imagination," of logical or rational thought. And we cannot enter into all these worlds without a sound scientific psychological method. Child psychology gives us valuable clues for the study of the general development of human speech. Even more valuable seems to be the help we get from the study of general sociology. We cannot understand the form of primitive mythical thought without taking into consideration the forms of primitive society. And more urgent still is the use of historical methods. The question as to what language, myth, and religion "are" cannot be answered without a penetrating study of their historical development.

But even if it were possible to answer all these psychological, sociological, and historical questions, we should still be in the precincts of the properly "human" world; we should not have passed its threshold. All human works arise under particular historical and sociological conditions. But we could never understand these special conditions unless we were able to grasp the general structural principles underlying these works. In our study of language, art, and myth the problem of meaning takes precedence over the problem of historical development. And here too we can ascertain a slow and continuous change in the methodological concepts and ideals of empirical science. In linguistics, for instance, the conception that the history of language covers the whole field of linguistic studies was for a long time an accepted dogma. This dogma left its mark upon the whole development of linguistics during the nineteenth century. Nowadays, however, this one-sidedness appears to have been definitely overcome.

The necessity of independent methods of descriptive analysis is generally recognized.[7] We cannot hope to measure the depth of a special branch of human culture unless such measurement is preceded by a descriptive analysis. This structural view of culture must precede the merely historical view. History itself would be lost in the boundless mass of disconnected facts if it did not have a general structural scheme by means of which it can classify, order, and organize these facts. In the field of the history of art such a scheme was developed, for instance, by Heinrich Wölfflin. As Wölfflin insists, the historian of art would be unable to characterize the art of different epochs or of different individual artists if he were not in possession of some fundamental *categories* of artistic description. He finds these categories by studying and analyzing the different modes and possibilities of artistic expression. These possibilities are not unlimited; as a matter of fact they may be reduced to a small number. It was from this point of view that Wölfflin gave his famous description of classic and baroque. Here the terms "classic" and "baroque" were not used as names for definite historical phases. They were intended to designate some general structural patterns not restricted to a particular age. "It is not the art of the sixteenth and seventeenth centuries," says Wölfflin at the end of his *Principles of Art History,*

> which was to be analyzed—only the schema and the visual and creative possibilities within which art remained in both cases. To illustrate this, we could naturally only proceed by referring to the individual work of art, but everything which was said of Raphael and Titian, of Rembrandt and Velasquez, was only intended to elucidate the general course of things. . . . Everything is transition and it is hard to answer the man who regards history as an endless flow. For us, intellectual self-preservation demands that we should classify the infinity of events with reference to a few results.[8]

If the linguist and the historian of art require fundamental structural categories for their "intellectual self-preservation," such categories are even more necessary to a philosophical description of human civilization. Philosophy cannot be content with analyzing the individual forms of human culture. It seeks a universal synthetic view which includes all individual forms. But is not such an all-embracing

[7] For a fuller discussion of the problem see Chap. VIII, pp. 119–121.

[8] Wölfflin, *Kunstgeschichtliche Grundbegriffe.* English trans. by M. D. Hottinger (London, G. Bell & Sons, 1932), pp. 226 f.

view an impossible task, a mere chimera? In human experience we by no means find the various activities which constitute the world of culture existing in harmony. On the contrary, we find the perpetual strife of diverse conflicting forces. Scientific thought contradicts and suppresses mythical thought. Religion in its highest theoretical and ethical development is under the necessity of defending the purity of its own ideal against the extravagant fancies of myth or art. Thus the unity and harmony of human culture appear to be little more than a *pium desiderium*—a pious fraud—which is constantly frustrated by the real course of events.

But here we must make a sharp distinction between a material and a formal point of view. Undoubtedly human culture is divided into various activities proceeding along different lines and pursuing different ends. If we content ourselves with contemplating the results of these activities—the creations of myth, religious rites or creeds, works of art, scientific theories—it seems impossible to reduce them to a common denominator. But a philosophic synthesis means something different. Here we seek not a unity of effects but a unity of action; not a unity of products but a unity of the *creative process*. If the term "humanity" means anything at all it means that, in spite of all the differences and oppositions existing among its various forms, these are, nevertheless, all working toward a common end. In the long run there must be found an outstanding feature, a universal character, in which they all agree and harmonize. If we can determine this character the divergent rays may be assembled and brought into a focus of thought. As has been pointed out, such an organization of the facts of human culture is already getting under way in the particular sciences—in linguistics, in the comparative study of myth and religion, in the history of art. All of these sciences are striving for certain principles, for definite "categories," by virtue of which to bring the phenomena of religion, of art, of language into a systematic order. Were it not for this previous synthesis effected by the sciences themselves philosophy would have no starting point. Philosophy cannot, on the other hand, stop here. It must seek to achieve an even greater condensation and centralization. In the boundless multiplicity and variety of mythical images, of religious dogmas, of linguistic forms, of works of art, philosophic thought reveals the unity of a general function by which all these creations are held together. Myth, religion, art, language, even science, are now looked upon as so many variations on a common theme—and it is the task of philosophy to make this theme audible and understandable.

Selected Bibliography

The Individual and Cosmos in Renaissance Philosophy (New York: Barnes and Noble, Inc., 1963).

Language and Myth, trans. by Susanne K. Langer (New York: Dover Publications, Inc., 1946).

Logic of the Humanities (New Haven: Yale University Press, 1961).

Myth of the State (London: Oxford University Press, 1946).

The Philosophy of Symbolic Forms (New Haven: Yale University Press, 1953–1957), 3 vols.

The Philosophy of the Enlightenment (Boston: The Beacon Press, 1961).

The Problem of Knowledge (New Haven: Yale University Press, 1950).

Rousseau, Kant, Goethe (Princeton: Princeton University Press, 1947).

See also the comprehensive bibliography of Ernst Cassirer's works in Paul Arthur Schilpp, ed. *The Philosophy of Ernst Cassirer* (Evanston: Library of Living Philosophers, 1949), pp. 881–910.

On the Mythological Mode

SUSANNE K. LANGER

Susanne K. Langer was born in New York City on December 20, 1895. She studied at Radcliffe College, from which she received her doctorate in 1926, and at the University of Vienna. She taught philosophy at Radcliffe from 1927 to 1942, and since then has held teaching positions at the Universities of Delaware, New York, Columbia, Northwestern, Ohio State, and Washington. In 1954 she became professor of philosophy at Connecticut College where she taught until her retirement in 1961. Since that time she has continued at Connecticut College as professor emeritus and research scholar.

Mrs. Langer's lifetime interests have been in the fields of philosophy (particularly epistemology and symbolic logic), art, and aesthetics. The chief influences in the early development of these interests were two of her teachers, Henry M. Sheffer and Alfred North Whitehead. Whitehead wrote the preface to her book on the purposes and methods of philosophy, The Practice of Philosophy, *which was published in 1930. Later, she was inspired by Ernst Cassirer, the German pioneer in the philosophy of symbolism. The logic of symbolism has been the controlling focus of her attention. She understands man as a symbol maker, one who recognizes that discursive language is limited in giving expression to human experience. The way in which this basic function and need of man has reference to religion is approached in the essay that follows.*

Myth . . . is a recognition of natural conflicts, of human desire frustrated by non-human powers, hostile oppression, or contrary desires; it is a story of the birth, passion, and defeat by death which is man's common fate. Its ultimate end is not wishful distortion of the world, but serious envisagement of its fundamental truths; moral orientation, not escape. That is why it does not exhaust its whole function in the telling, and why separate myths cannot be left entirely unrelated to any others. Because it presents, however metaphorically,

Reprinted by permission of the publishers from Susanne K. Langer, *Philosophy in a New Key* (Cambridge, Mass.: Harvard University Press, Copyright, 1942, 1951, 1957, by the President and Fellows of Harvard College; 1970 by Susanne K. Langer).

a world-picture, an insight into life generally, not a personal imaginary biography, myth tends to become systematized; figures with the same poetic meaning are blended into one, and characters of quite separate origin enter into definite relations with each other. Moreover, because the mythical hero is not the subject of an egocentric day-dream, but a subject greater than any individual, he is always felt to be superhuman, even if not quite divine. He is at least a descendant of the gods, something more than a man. His sphere of activity is the real world, because what he symbolizes belongs to the real world, no matter how fantastic its expression may be (this is exactly contrary to the fairytale technique, which transports a natural individual to a fairyland outside reality).

The material of myth is, indeed, just the familiar symbolism of dream—image and fantasy. No wonder psychologists have discovered that it is the same material as that of fairytale; that both have symbols for father and son, maiden and wife and mother, possession and passion, birth and death. The difference is in the two respective *uses* of that material; the one, primarily for supplying vicarious experience, the other essentially for understanding actual experience. Both interests may be served in one and the same fiction; their complete separation belongs only to classic cases. Semi-mythical motives occur in sheer day-dream and even night-dream, and an element of compensation-fantasy may persist in the most universalized, perfected myths. That is inevitable, because the latter type has grown at some point out of the former, as all realistic thinking springs from self-centered fancy. There is no clean dividing line. Yet the two are as distinct as summer and winter, night and day, or any other extremes that have no exact zero-point between them.

We do not know just where, in the evolution of human thought, myth-making begins, but it begins somewhere with the recognition of *realistic significance* in a story. In every fantasy, no matter how utopian, there are elements that represent real human relations, real needs and fears, the quandaries and conflicts which the "happy ending" resolves. Even if the real situation is symbolized rather than stated (a shocking condition may well be disguised, or a mysterious one strangely conceived), a certain importance, an emotional interest, attaches to those elements. The ogre, the dragon, the witch, are intriguing figures in fairy-lore. Unlike the hero, they are usually ancient beings, that have troubled the land for many generations. They have their castles or caves or hermitages, their magic cook-pots and sorcerer's wands; they have evil deeds laid up against them, and extremely bad habits, usually of a cannibalistic turn. Their records are merely suggested in the story, which hastens to get on with the fortunes of the hero; but the suggestion is enough to activate a mind which is, after all, committed to some interests besides dream-spinning. Because they represent the realistic setting from which the dream starts its fanciful escape, they command a serious sort of contemplation.

It is significant that people who refuse to tell their children fairy-tales do not fear that the children will believe in princes and princesses, but that they will believe in witches and bogeys. Prince or princess, to whom the wish-fulfilment happens, we find in ourselves, and need not seek in the outer world; their reference is subjective, their history is our dream, and we know well enough that it is "make-believe." But the incidental figures are material for superstition, because their meanings are in the real world. They represent those same powers that are conceived, first perhaps through "dreadful" objects like corpses or skulls or hideous idols, as ghosts, keres, hoodoos, and similar spooks. The ogres of literature and the ghouls of popular conception embody the same mysterious Powers; therefore the fairy-tale, which even most children will not credit as a narrative, may carry with it a whole cargo of ideas, purely secondary to its own purpose, that are most convincing elements for superstition. The awful ancestor in the grave goes abroad as the goblin of story: that is the god of superstition. The world-picture of spook-religion is a reflection of fairytale, a dream whose nightmare elements become attached to visible cult objects and thus taken seriously.

There is nothing cosmological about the being such a symbol can embody. Deities in the classical sense cannot be born of tales whose significance is personal, because the setting of such tales is necessarily a *genre* picture, a local, temporal, human environment, no matter how distorted and disguised. The forces that play into an individual's dream are social forces, not world-powers. So long as the hero is the self, the metaphorical dragons he slays are his elders, his rivals, or his personal enemies; their projection into the real world as sacred beings can yield only ancestors, cave-monsters, manitos, and capricious demigods.

It is noteworthy that when these secondary characters of day-dream or story are incorporated into our picture of the external world as objects of superstition, they represent a generalized, heightened conception of the social forces in question: not a man's father, but his *fathers*, the paternal power in all generations, may be seen in the fabulous animal-ancestor he reveres; not his brother, but a "Great Brother," in the manito-bear that is his familiar of the forest. The process of symbolization, while it often obscures the origin of our ideas, enhances their conceptual form. The demon, therefore, presents to us not a specific person, but the human estate of such a person, by virtue of which we are oppressed, challenged, tempted, or triumphant. Although he is born of a purely self-centered imagination, he is super-personal; a product not only of particular experience, but of social insight. He is the envisagement of a vital factor in life; that is why he is projected into reality by the symbolism of religion.

The great step from fairytale to myth is taken when not only social forces—persons, customs, laws, traditions—but also cosmic forces surrounding mankind, are expressed in the story; when not only relationships of an individual to society, but of mankind to nature, are conceived through the spontaneous metaphor of poetic fantasy.

Perhaps this transition from subjectively oriented stories, separate and self-contained, to the organized and permanent envisagement of a world-drama could never be made if creative thought were not helped by the presence of permanent, obvious symbols, supplied by nature: the heavenly bodies, the changes of day and night, the seasons, and the tides. Just as the social framework of personal life, first conceived in dreamlike, inchoate forms, is gradually given enduring recognition through religious symbols, so the cosmic setting of man's existence is imponderable, or at best a mere nightmare, until the sun and the moon, the procession of stars, the winds and waters of earth, exhibit a divine rule, and define the realm of human activity. When these gods arrive, whose names connote heavenly powers and natural processes, the deities of local caves and groves become mere vassals and lesser lights.

It has often been asked, not without justification, how men of sane observant minds—however unschooled or innocent—can be led to identify sun, moon, or stars with the anthropomorphic agents of sacred story. Yet the interpretation of gods and heroes as nature-symbols is very ancient; it has been variously accepted and rejected, disputed, exploded, and reestablished, by Hellenic philosophers, medieval scholars, modern philologists, archeologists, and theologians, over a period of twenty-five hundred years. Mystifying as it is to psychology, it challenges us as a fact. . . .

It is a peculiar fact that every major advance in thinking, every epoch-making new insight, springs from a new type of symbolic transformation. A higher level of thought is primarily a new activity;

its course is opened up by a new departure in semantic. The step from mere sign-using to symbol-using marked the crossing of the line between animal and man; this initiated the natural growth of language. The birth of symbolic gesture from emotional and practical movement probably begot the whole order of ritual, as well as the discursive mode of pantomime. The recognition of vague, vital meanings in physical forms—perhaps the first dawn of symbolism—gave us our idols, emblems, and totems; the primitive function of dream permits our first envisagement of events. The momentous discovery of nature-symbolism, of the pattern of life reflected in natural phenomena, produced the first universal insights. Every mode of thought is bestowed on us, like a gift, with some new principle of symbolic expression. It has a logical development, which is simply the exploitation of all the uses to which that symbolism lends itself; and when these uses are exhausted, the mental activity in question has found its limit. Either it serves its purpose and becomes truistic, like our orientation in "Euclidean space" or our appreciation of objects and their accidents (on the pattern of language-structure, significantly called "logic"); or it is superseded by some more powerful symbolic mode which opens new avenues of thought.

The origin of myth is dynamic, but its purpose is philosophical. It is the primitive phase of metaphysical thought, the first embodiment of general ideas. It can do no more than initiate and present them; for it is a non-discursive symbolism, it does not lend itself to analytic and genuinely abstractive techniques. The highest development of which myth is capable is the exhibition of human life and cosmic order that epic poetry reveals. We cannot abstract and manipulate its concepts any further *within the mythical mode*. When this mode is exhausted, natural religion is superseded by a discursive and more literal form of thought, namely philosophy.

Language, in its literal capacity, is a stiff and conventional medium, unadapted to the expression of genuinely new ideas, which usually have to break in upon the mind through some great and bewildering metaphor. But bare denotative language is a most excellent instrument of exact reason; it is, in fact, the only general precision instrument the human brain has ever evolved. Ideas first adumbrated in fantastic form become real intellectual property only when discursive language rises to their expression. That is why myth is the indispensable forerunner of metaphysics; and metaphysics is the literal formulation of basic abstractions, on which our comprehension of sober facts is based. All detail of knowledge, all exact distinction, measure, and practical manipulation, are possible only on a basis of truly abstract concepts, and a framework of such concepts constitutes a philosophy of nature, literal, denotative, and sytematic. Only language has the power to effect such an analysis of experience, such a rationalization of knowledge. But it is only where experience is already presented—through some other formative medium, some vehicle of apprehension and memory—that the canons of literal thought have any application. We must have ideas before we can make literal analyses of them; and really new ideas have their own modes of appearance in the unpredictable creative mind.

The first inquiry as to the literal truth of a myth marks the change from poetic to discursive thinking. As soon as the interest in factual values awakes, the mythical mode of world-envisagement is on the wane. But emotional attitudes that have long centered on a myth are not easily broken; the vital ideas embodied in it cannot be repudiated because someone discovers that the myth does not constitute a *fact*. Poetic significance and factual reference, which are two entirely different relations in the general symbol-and-meaning pattern, become identified under the one name of "truth." People who discover the obvious discrepancy between fantasy and fact deny that myths are true; those who recognize the truth of myths claim that they register facts. There is the silly conflict of religion and science, in which science must triumph, not because what it says about religion is just, but because religion rests on a young and provisional form of thought, to which philosophy of nature—proudly called "science," or "knowledge"—must succeed if thinking is to go on. There must be a rationalistic period from this point onward. Some day when the vision is totally rationalized, the ideas exploited and exhausted, there will be another vision, a new mythology.

Selected Bibliography

Feeling and Form: A Theory of Art (New York: Charles Scribner's Sons, 1953).

An Introduction to Symbolic Logic (New York: Dover Publications, Inc., 1967).

Mind: An Essay on Human Feeling (Baltimore: John Hopkins Press, 1967).

Philosophical Sketches (Baltimore: John Hopkins Press, 1962).

Problems of Art (New York: Charles Scribner's Sons, 1957).

Reflections on Art (New York: Oxford University Press, 1962).

The Symbol Gives Rise to Thought

PAUL RICOEUR

Paul Ricoeur was born on February 27, 1913, in Valence, France. He studied in Rennes and Paris, receiving his doctorate in philosophy. He began teaching in 1933; from 1948 to 1956 he was professor of the history of philosophy at Strasbourg. Since 1956 he has been teaching philosophy at the University of Paris and has held a variety of administrative posts within that university.

Ricoeur is part of the phenomenological movement founded by Edmund Husserl. Within that stance, Ricoeur's work has dealt primarily with the hermeneutics, or science of the principles of interpretation, of symbols. In the essay that follows, for example, Ricoeur traces the movement of symbols into thoughts, after first characterizing symbols. His work on symbolization, however, belongs to a larger, more comprehensive interest in providing a "phenomenology of the will." In this regard, Ricoeur has been influenced not only by Husserl but also by Max Scheler, Paul-Ludwig Landsberg, Pierre Thevenaz, Maurice Merleau-Ponty (with whom Ricoeur differs on a number of large issues), Gabriel Marcel, and, to a limited extent, by Martin Heidegger. Opposed to the negations implicit in the existentialism of one such as Jean-Paul Sartre, Ricoeur has attempted to reconcile nature and freedom. But the starting point is the symbols that speak of man's self-consciousness of "brokenness" and "fault," and thus give rise to conceptual thought.

I should like to say a word at the outset about the preoccupation behind this article. At a certain point in reflection a meditation on *symbols* comes up, whether this be done after the fashion of Eliade or Jung or Freud or Bachelard. And this fits in with a particular situation in modern philosophy—perhaps even in that modern culture which we must try to understand.

As M. Bachelard says in his *The Poetics of Space*, such recourse to

From Paul Ricoeur, "The Symbol—Food for Thought," in *Philosophy Today*, Vol. IV (1960), pp. 196–207.

the archaic and nocturnal and oneirotic takes us back to the birthplace of language. I should add that it is also an effort to bypass the thorny problem about the starting point of philosophy. We recall the tiresome backward march of thought seeking the first truth, and, more basically still, seeking a radical starting point which might not be a first truth at all. Perhaps you must actually experience the frustration involved in seeking a philosophy without presuppositions to appreciate the problem we are raising. In contrast to philosophies wrestling with starting points, a meditation on symbols starts right out with language and with the meaning that is always there already. It takes off in the midst of language already existing, where everything has already been said after a fashion; it gladly embraces thought with all its presuppositions. Its big problem is not to get started, but, in the midst of words, to remember once again.

However, contrasting this problem of the symbol with Descartes' and Husserl's search for a starting point unduly ties down our meditation to a precise point in the philosophic dialogue. Probably we ought to take a broader viewpoint. If we raise the problem of the symbol *now*, at *this* period of history, we do so because of certain characteristics of our "modernity"—and as a rejoinder to this "modernity." The historical moment of the philosophy of the symbol is both the moment of forgetting and the moment of restoring. Forgetting hierophanies, forgetting the signs of the Sacred, losing hold of man himself as belonging to the Sacred. This forgetting is of course the counterpart to the awesome task of feeding men and meeting their needs through planetary control of nature. The dim recognition of this forgetting is what bestirs us to restore language in its integrity. In this very age when language is becoming more precise, more univocal, more technical, better suited to those formalizations that are called precisely "symbolic" logic (we shall return to this strange ambiguity of the word "symbol")—it is in this very age that we seek to recharge language, to start out again from language in its *fullness*. And this too comes from "modernity." For we moderns are men of philology, of exegesis of the phenomenology of religion, of the psychoanalysis of language. The very age which develops the possibility of emptying language is also the age for filling it anew.

Our outlook therefore is not the homesickness of Atlas' grieving daughters. Rather, with the bleak sands of criticism behind us, we want a new hearing.

"The symbol provides food for thought." This maxim that I find so intriguing says two things. The symbol provides: it is not I myself, but the symbol, which puts in meaning. And what it provides food for is thought, something to think about. The statement therefore suggests that while, enigmatically, everything has already been said, nonetheless in the dimension of thought you always have to keep starting over and over. It is this articulation between thought and symbol that I want to ferret out and understand.

But by way of preliminary I should like to offer a quick *criteriology of the symbol*: first an enumeration of symbolic categories, and then an essential analysis of symbolic structures.

The Symbol's Various Domains

To mark the boundaries of the symbol's various spheres we must start out with an enumeration. Albert Béguin, in the preface to his *L'Ame romantisue et le rêve,* lines up in a row "the fables of various mythologies, the folk tales of all countries and ages, the dreams that haunt us during night's unconsciousness like the distractions of the day." This passage clearly indicates the three areas where symbols emerge.

Tied in with rites and myths, symbols constitute in the first place the language of the Sacred, the expression of "hierophanies," to use Eliade's term. We would recall merely the first example on which Eliade reflects in his *Patterns of Comparative Religion,* the example of the sky: the symbol of the most high, of the elevated and immense, of the powerful and well-ordered, of the shrewd and wise, of the sovereign and immovable. This symbol is truly inexhaustible; it branches out into cosmic, ethical, and political categories. The sky is but a single example among many that Eliade interprets; the function of all of them, he says, is "to fix the exemplary models for all meaningful human rites and actions." Far from being fanciful projections or puerile allegories on human action, symbols initiate that action, they make it possible by sacralizing it.

The second area is that of the nocturnal and oneirotic. We know that for Freud himself a symbol does not mean just any representation that stands for something else, that covers up and dissembles. Rather, symbols are those oneirotic representations that go beyond individual history—archeology without a subject. They plunge down into the depths of that imagery which is common to every culture, the folklore of mankind as a whole. Jung has shown that these symbols are not so much projections of the infantile and instinctive side of the psyche as themes that foretell our possibilities for evolution and maturation. Discovering them is not just a matter of reducing obstacles; it is a way of exploring our potentialities. Jung's philosophical interpretation, which sees here either the auto-representation of psychic energy or archetypes, is less important than the discovery itself; his psychological Platonism should not bother us any more than Feud's metapsychology. The main point is that in Jung's therapy (addressed no doubt to a different type of person than Freud's) symbols provide those themes for meditation that can open the way to "becoming oneself"—the *Selbstwerden*. It is this forward-looking aspect of symbols that I would retain; and I would connect it with what Eliade calls the cosmo-theogical function of symbols, by which man is reintegrated into his whole sacred past.

The third area of symbols: poetic imagination. M. Bachelard has shown that the problem of the imagination is not the problem of the image, not even of the image in relation to the absence or the annihilation of the real. This representation-image still depends on the thing it makes unreal; it is still a means, as Sartre puts it, for rendering objects in some way present. "The poetic image," M. Bachelard says in his Introduction to *The Poetics of Space*, "brings us to the origin of the being who speaks." And later on: "It becomes a new being in our language; it expresses ourselves by making us into what it expresses." This word-image which is no longer representation-image is what I am here calling symbol. The one difference from the two preceding cases is that the poetic symbol (for instance that of the house, which M. Bachelard explores from every side among the poets) shows up at the moment when it is an emergence from language, when it puts language in a state of emergence. Unlike the case of the history of religions, it is not restored in its hieratic stability in the custody of rite and myth. The basic point is that what is born and reborn in the poetic image is the same symbolic structure that runs through the most prophetic dreams of our inner development and that sustains sacred language in its most archaic and stable forms.

The Symbol's Structure

This enumeration, which offhand looks so disjointed, taken as it is from the history of religions, the psychoanalysis of dreams, and the investigation of the poetic imagination, does however seem to show a certain convergence. It opens up the way to intentional analysis, which alone can furnish a unifying principle for our whole study.

I have in mind an intentional analysis which *distinguishes* the symbol from a series of related structures and which will clear the path for a more or less intuitive grasp of an identical nucleus of meaning. Thus I shall distinguish in turn the symbol from the sign, the allegory, the symbol itself in the sense of symbolic logic, and finally the myth.

1. That symbols are signs is obvious. Signs are expressions that carry a meaning, which is revealed through the intention of signifying that is conveyed by words. Even though symbols are (as Eliade sometimes says) elements of the universe (sky, water, moon) or thing (trees, stones), it is still within the world of discourse that these things take on their symbolic dimension (words of consecration or invocation, myth commentary). As Dumézil says: "Research in the history of religions today is taking place under the sign of logos, not under the sign of mana." (Preface to Eliade's *Patterns*) The same holds for dreams: though they are nocturnal scenes, they are basically close to words, because they can be recounted, communicated. But to say that the symbol is a sign is drawing the circle too big; we now have to narrow it down. Every sign is directed to something beyond itself and stands for this something. But not every sign is a symbol. I would say that the symbol has hidden within its purpose a double intentionality. As an example let us take the pure and impure, which M. Moulinier has studied among the Greeks. There is a first or literal intentionality which, like any signifying intentionality, implies the triumph of the conventional over the natural sign. This would be the stained, the dirty—words which do not resemble the thing signified. But upon this first intentionality a second one is built up, which, through the physically dirty, points to a certain condition of man within the sacred. This condition, pointed to by first meaning, is precisely that of the besmirched, dirty-being. The obvious and literal meaning therefore points beyond itself to something that is *like* a stain. In contrast with completely transparent technical signs that say only what they want to say by indicating the thing signified, symbolic signs are opaque. The first obvious literal meaning itself looks analogically toward a second meaning which is found only in the first meaning (we shall return to this point in distinguishing symbols from allegories). This opaqueness is the symbol's very profundity, an inexhaustible depth.

But let us be clear about the analogical bond between the literal meaning and the symbolic meaning. Analogy itself is a nonconclusive line of reasoning that proceeds by means of a proportional fourth term (A is to B as C is to D). But in the symbol I cannot objectivize the analogical relation that binds the second meaning to the first. When I live the first meaning it sweeps me along beyond itself. The symbolic meaning is constituted in and by the literal meaning, which brings off the analogy by providing the analogue. Maurice Blondel used to say: "Analogies are rooted less in notional resemblances (*similitudines*) than in an inward stimulation, an assimilative attraction (*intentio ad assimilationem*)." Unlike a comparison which we *look at* from the outside, the symbol in fact is the very movement of the primary meaning which makes us share the hidden meaning and thus assimilates us to the thing symbolized, without our being able to get hold of the similarity intellectually. It is in this sense that the symbol "provides"; it provides, because it is a primary intentionality which yields a second meaning.

This brings us close to our second point, the relationship of analogy to symbol. But it is perhaps not useless to insist one last time on this first criterion. We dare not say that the symbol is a return to natural signs. No, it presupposes a conventional language which has broken away from vocal resemblance. It is in the second intentionality of the thing signified that the analogical correspondence resides, and the correspondence is not between signifying word and signified thing, but between first meaning and second meaning.

2. Our second criterion, concerning the distinction between symbol and allegory, simply prolongs our remarks about the analogy effected through the literal meaning itself. M. Pépin (*Mythe et allégorie*) has clarified this problem: in allegory, the first thing signified (the literal meaning) is contingent, and the second thing signified, the symbolic meaning itself, is sufficiently exterior to be directly accessible. Between the two meanings then there is a relation of *translation*. Once the translation is made you can let the symbol fall by the way, since it has become useless. We have to admit that the symbolic dimension has gradually won out over allegory. Historically, allegory was less a literary and rhetorical device for artificially constructing pseudo-symbols than a means for treating myths as allegories. This is the case with the Storic interpretation of the myths of Homer and Hesiod, which consisted in handling myths as philosophy in disguise. Interpretation means tearing off the disguise and by that very fact rendering it useless. In other words, allegory was much more a modality of *hermeneutics* (exegesis of signs, symbols, allegories, and myths) than

a spontaneous creation of signs. It would be much more valid to speak about allegorizing interpretation than about allegory. Symbol and allegory are therefore not on the same level. The symbol precedes hermeneutics, while the allegory is already hermeneutic. This is the case because the symbol makes its meaning become transparent in quite another fashion than by translation. I should rather say that it evokes, it "suggests" (in the sense of the Greek word for suggest, which is the basis for our word "enigma"): the symbol yields its meaning in enigma and not through translation. What the symbol gives transparently contrasts with what the allegory gives by translation.

3. There is no need to point out that the symbols we are treating have nothing in common with what symbolic logic calls by that name. But we have to do more than make the statement; we must understand why. The cases are exactly reversed: for symbolic logic the symbol is the apex of formalism. Formal logic had already replaced the terms of the syllogism by signs that can stand for anything (All B is C, but A is B, hence A is C), but the words "all," "some," "is," "imply," had not yet been removed from ordinary language. In symbolic logic these latter expressions themselves are replaced by letters, by written signs, which need not be spoken and about which it is possible to *calculate*, without asking how they are incorporated into a deontology of reasoning. They are not even abbreviations of known verbal expressions, but "characters," in Leibniz's sense of the word, i.e., elements of calculus. Obviously symbols in our sense are exactly the opposite of "characters." They belong to thought that is *bound up* with content and hence thought that is not formal. Moreover, the analogical bond tying the second meaning to the first and the impossibility of the symbolic meaning yielding itself up except through the very working of that analogy, makes symbolic language a language that is essentially *bound*, bound to its content, and through its primary content bound to its second content. In this sense we have the utter reverse of absolute formalism. That is why, from the very beginning of this essay, I have kept talking about the *fullness* of language. It might seem surprising that symbol is used in two ways that differ so sharply. The reason perhaps should be sought in the structure of signification. On the one hand, signification is related to absence, because it points out things that are absent. But on the other hand, it is related to presence, because it represents, it renders present, that which is absent. In these two differing forms we have been discussing,

the symbol carries each possibility to the extreme. But this is going beyond our subject; we shall no longer speak of symbol in the sense of symbolic logic.

4. The final criterion: how to distinguish myths from symbols? M. Pépin contrasts myth to allegory, but does not clearly distinguish myth from symbol. It seems sometimes that the symbol is a non-allegorical way of getting hold of a myth. Symbol and allegory would thus be two intellectual attitudes or dispositions proper to hermeneutics. Symbolic interpretation and allegorical interpretation would be two directions taken by an interpretation concerned with the same content of myths. I however take symbol in Eliade's more radical meaning of analogical significations spontaneously formed and given, as for instance the meaning of water as threatening in the deluge and purifying in baptism—and so with all the primitive hierophanies. I take myth to be a species of symbol, a symbol developed into narrative form, articulated within a time and space that cannot be coordinated with critical history and geography. The Exile, for instance, is a primary symbol of human alienation, but the story of Adam and Eve being driven from Paradise is a mythical narrative of the second level, bringing into play fabled persons, places, time and episodes. It seems to me that this added depth is essential to the myth—not to mention the attempt at explanation found in the etiological myths. Basically I am pretty much in agreement with the schema of Jaspers, who distinguishes the primitive language of number (what I call symbols), the language of myths, which mediate the primary symbols, and finally the symbols of the third level, which are more speculative, as for instance the representation of evil as "war" in Heraclitus, or "body" in Plato's *Phaedo*, or "hereditary original sin" in Saint Augustine.

Selected Bibliography

"Existence et herméneutique," *Dialogue*, IV (1965–1966), pp. 1–25.
Fallible Man (Chicago: Henry Regnery Company, 1965).
"The Father Image: From Fantasy to Symbol," *Criterion*, Vol. VIII (1968–1969), pp. 1–7.
Freud and Philosophy (New Haven: Yale University Press, 1970).
"Guilt, Ethics and Religion," *Talk of God* (Royal Institute of Philosophy Lectures, Vol. II, 1967–1968). (New York: St. Martin's Press, Inc., 1969), pp. 100–117.
"The Hermeneutics of Symbols and Philosophical Reflection," *In-*

ternational Philosophical Quarterly, Vol. II (May 1962), pp. 191–218.

History and Truth (Evanston: Northwestern University Press, 1965).

Husserl: An Analysis of His Phenomenology (Evanston: Northwestern University Press, 1967).

(Coauthor with Alasdair MacIntyre) *The Religious Significance of Atheism* (New York: Columbia University Press, 1969).

The Symbolism of Evil (Boston: The Beacon Press, 1967).

The Voluntary and the Involuntary (Evanston: Northwestern University Press, 1966).

For a summary of Ricoeur's program, see the helpful analysis by Don Ihde, "From Phenomenology to Hermeneutic," in *Journal of Existentialism*, Vol. VII, No. 30 (Winter 1967–1968), pp. 111–132.

Ricoeur's works prior to 1968 are listed in D. Vansina, "Bibliographie de Paul Ricoeur," in *Revue Philosophique de Louvain*, No. 66 (Fall 1968), pp. 85–101.

Discourse

Ludwig Wittgenstein and the Transition to the Linguistic View

GILBERT RYLE

Ludwig Wittgenstein, who was largely responsible for the development of such philosophical schools as logical positivism and linguistic analysis, was born in Vienna on April 26, 1889, of Jewish descent. He died in Cambridge, England, on April 29, 1951, after a distinguished career as a professor of philosophy. His life and work is recounted and interpreted by Gilbert Ryle, in the essay that follows, as collateral material to the essays that deal directly with the scope of his influence upon the study and conception of religion.

An original and powerful philosopher, Ludwig Wittgenstein, an Austrian who finally became a naturalized British subject, came to England shortly before the first World War to study engineering. In 1912, bitten by logical and philosophical problems about the nature of mathematics, he migrated to Cambridge to work with Bertrand Russell. During that war, he was in the Austrian army and ended up a prisoner of war. In this period he wrote his one book, the famous *Tractatus Logico-Philosophicus*, of which a not quite reliable English translation was published in 1922. He taught in an Austrian village school for some time, during which he came into close philosophical touch with a few of the leading members of the Vienna Circle. In 1929 he came to Cambridge, where the importance of his ideas had been quickly recognized. In 1939 he became Professor. For part of the last war he was a hospital orderly at Guy's Hospital. In 1947 he resigned his Chair. Besides the *Tractatus*, he published only one article.

In the last twenty years, so far as I know, he published nothing; attended no philosophical conferences; gave no lectures outside Cambridge; corresponded on philosophical subjects with nobody and dis-

Gilbert Ryle, "Ludwig Wittgenstein," *Analysis*, Vol. XII, No. 1 (October, 1951), pp. 1–9; reprinted in *Essays on Wittgenstein's Tractatus*, edited by Irving M. Copi and Robert W. Beard (New York: Crowell-Collier and Macmillan, Inc., 1966), pp. 1–8.

couraged the circulation even of notes of his Cambridge lectures and discussions. But with his serious students and a few colleagues, economists, mathematicians, physicists and philosophers, he would discuss philosophical matters unwearyingly. Yet from his jealously preserved little pond, there have spread waves over the philosophical thinking of much of the English-speaking world. Philosophers who never met him—and few of us did meet him—can be heard talking philosophy in his tones of voice; and students who can barely spell his name now wrinkle up their noses at things which had a bad smell for him. So what is the difference that he has made to philosophy?

It is vain to try to forecast the verdict of history upon a contemporary. I have to try to do this for one who has for about 30 years avoided any publication of his ideas. So what I offer is a set of impressions, interpretations, partly, of mere echoes of echoes.

From the time of Locke to that of Bradley philosophers had debated their issues as if they were psychological issues. Certainly their problems were, often, genuine philosophical problems, but they discussed them in psychological terms. And if they asked themselves, as they seldom did ask, what they were investigating, they tended to say that they were investigating the workings of the mind, just as physical scientists investigate the working of bodies. The sorts of "Mental Science" that they talked were sometimes positivistic, sometimes idealistic, according roughly, as they were more impressed by chemistry than by theology or vice versa.

However, fifty years ago philosophers were getting their feet out of these psychological boots. For psychology had now begun to be done in laboratories and clinics, so arm-chair psychology became suspect. But even more influential was the fact that logical quandaries had recently been exposed at the very roots of pure mathematics. The mathematicians needed lifelines, which they could not provide for themselves. Logicians had to work out the logic of mathematics, and they could not base this logic on the findings of any empirical science, especially of so hazy a science as psychology. If logic and philosophy were not psychological inquiries, what were they?

During the first twenty years of this century, many philosophers gave another answer to this question, a Platonic answer. Philosophy studies not the workings of minds or, of course, of bodies either; it studies the denizens of a third domain, the domain of abstract, or conceptual entities, of possibilities, essences, timelessly subsisting universals, numbers, truths, falsities, values and meanings. This idea enabled its holders to continue to say that philosophy was the science of something, while denying that it was the science of any ordinary subject-matter; to champion its autonomy as a discipline, while denying that it was just one science among others; to give it the standing of a science while admitting its unlikeness to the sciences. Thus the question "What are philosophy and logic the sciences of?" received a new answer, though one with a disquietingly dreamlike ring. It was the answer given by Frege and by Russell.

In Vienna thinkers were facing much the same question, though from an opposite angle. Whereas here it had been widely assumed that philosophy was Mental Science, and therefore just a sister-science to physics, chemistry, zoology, etc., in the German-speaking world it was widely assumed that philosophy stood to the other sciences not as sister but as mother—or even governess. Somehow professors of philosophy there enjoyed such a pedagogic domination that they could dictate even to the scientists. *Of course* philosophers were the right people to decide whether the teachings of Darwin, Freud and Einstein were true.

Late in the nineteenth century Mach had mutinied against this view that metaphysics was a governess-science. By the early 1920s this mutiny became a rebellion. The Vienna Circle repudiated the myth that the questions of physics, biology, psychology or mathematics can be decided by metaphysical considerations. Metaphysics is not a governess-science or a sister-science; it is not a science at all. The classic case was that of Einstein's Relativity principle. The claims of professors of philosophy to refute this principle were baseless. Scientific questions are soluble only by scientific methods, and these are not the methods of philosophers.

Thus, in England the question was this. What are the special virtues which the natural and the mathematical sciences lack but logic and philosophy possess, such that these must be invoked when the former find themselves in quandaries? In Vienna the question was this. Given that philosophers cannot decide scientific questions, what are the logical virtues which scientific procedures possess, but philosophical procedures lack? The contrast between philosophy and science was drawn in both places. In Vienna, where the autonomy of the sciences was actually challenged, the object was to expose the pretensions of philosophy as a governess-science. Here, where, save for psychology, the autonomy of the sciences was not seriously challenged, it was drawn in order to extract the positive functions of logic and philosophy was regarded in Vienna as a blood-sucking parasite; in England as a medicinal leech.

To Wittgenstein the question came in its English form. And so he could not be called one of the Logical Positivists. Their polemics were not his; and his quest for the positive function of logic and philosophy was not, until much later, theirs. He was influenced by Frege and Russell, not by Mach. He had not himself felt the dead hand of professional philosophy which cramped, and still cramps, even scientific thought in Germany and Austria. He, conversely, himself helped to fix the logical lifelines for the mathematicians.

I want to show how Wittgenstein transformed and answered what was all the time his master-question, "What can philosophers and logicians do, and how should they do it?"

I have said that after a long imprisonment in psychological idioms, philosophy was, for a time, re-housed in Platonic idioms. But this was only a temporary asylum. For after a short period during which philosophers tried not to mind the dreamlike character of the new asylum, something awoke them from the dream. Russell, in his inquiries into the logical principles underlying mathematics, found that he could not well help constructing statements which had the logically disturbing property that they were true only on condition that they were false, and false only on condition that they were true. Some of these self-subverting statements seemed to be inherent in the very basis which was to make mathematics secure. There was a major leak in the dry dock which Frege and he had built for mathematics.

Russell found a patch for the leak. Underlying the familiar distinction between truth and falsehood, there is a more radical distinction between significance and meaninglessness. True and false statements are both significant, but some forms of words, with the vocabulary and constructions of statements, are neither true nor false, but nonsensical—and nonsensical not for reasons of wording or of grammar, but for logical reasons. The self-subverting statements were of this sort, neither true nor false, but nonsensical simulacra of statements. Notice, it is only of such things as complex verbal expressions that we can ask whether they are significant or nonsense. The question could not be asked of mental processes; or of Platonic entities. So logic is from the start concerned, not with these but rather with what can or cannot be significantly said. Its subject-matter is a linguistic one, though its tasks are not at all those of philology.

In Wittgenstein's *Tractatus* this departmental conclusion is generalized. All logic and all philosophy are enquiries into what makes it significant or nonsensical to say certain things. The sciences aim at saying what is true about the world; philosophy aims at disclosing only the logic of what can be truly or even falsely said about the world. This is why philosophy is not a sister-science or a parent-science; that its business is not to add to the number of scientific statements, but to disclose their logic.

Wittgenstein begins by considering how a sentence, a map, a diagram or a scale-model can represent or even significantly misrepresent the facts. The isolated words 'London' and 'south' are not true or false. Nor can a single dot on a sheet of paper be an accurate or inaccurate map. The sentence 'London is north of Brighton' is true. The same words, differently arranged as 'Brighton is north of London', make a false statement. Arranged as 'South is London of Brighton' they make a farrago which is neither true nor false, but nonsense. For dots on paper to represent or misrepresent the direction of Brighton from London, there must be a dot for each town and they must be set out in accordance with some convention for points of the compass. For a statement, map or diagram to be true or false, there must be a plurality of words or marks; but, more, these bits must be put together in certain ways. And underlying the fact that the truth or falsity of the statement or map partly depends upon the particular way in which its bits are arranged, there lies the fact that whether a significant statement or map results at all, depends wholly on the general way in which the bits are put together. Some ways of jumbling them together are ruled out. What rules rule them out?

In the *Tractatus* Wittgenstein came to the frustrating conclusion that these principles of arrangement inevitably baffle significant statement. To try to tell what makes the difference between significant and nonsensical talk is itself to cross the divide between significant and nonsensical talk. Philosophizing can, indeed, open our eyes to these structural principles, but it cannot issue in significant statements of them. Philosophy is not a science; it cannot yield theories or doctrines. None the less it can be skilful or unskilful, successful or unsuccessful. It is in pursuing the activity itself that we see what we need to see. Rather like learning music or tennis, learning philosophy does not result in our being able to tell what we have learned; though, as in music and tennis, we can show what we have learned.

Now it is true that philosophical clarity is achieved in the acts of appreciating arguments rather than in propounding theorems. But it is false that all philosophical talk is nonsensical talk. Wittgenstein had himself said very effective things, and talking effectively is not talking nonsensically. What had brought him to this frustrating conclusion? When he wrote the *Tractatus,* he was, I think, overinfluenced by his own analogies between saying things and making maps, diagrams and scale-models. Certainly, for marks on paper to constitute a temperature-chart, or for spoken words to constitute a significant statement, the dots and the words must be arranged according to rules and conventions. Only if the zigzag of dots on the nurse's graph paper is systematically correlated with the thermometer-readings taken at successive moments of a day, can it represent or even misrepresent the alterations in the patient's temperature. Only if words are organized according to a number of complex general rules does a true or false statement result.

Suppose we now asked the nurse to depict on a second sheet of graph paper, not the course of the patient's temperature, but the rules for representing his temperature by dots on graph paper, she would be baffled. Nor can the rules and conventions of map-making themselves be mapped. So Wittgenstein argued in the *Tractatus* that the philosopher or logician is debarred from saying what it is that makes things said significant or nonsensical. He can show it, but not tell it. After the *Tractatus* he realized that though saying things does resemble depicting things or mapping things in the respect for which he originally drew the analogy, it does not resemble them in all respects. Just as the nurse can tell, though not depict, how the temperature-chart represents or misrepresents the patient's temperature, so the philosopher can tell why, say, a scientist's statement makes or does not make sense. What alone would be absurd would be a sentence which purported to convey a comment upon its own significance or meaninglessness.

The *Tractatus* has two distinct but connected aims. The first, which I have crudely sketched, is to show both what philosophy is not, namely any sort of a science, and what it is, namely an activity of exploring the internal logic of what is said, for example, in this or that scientific theory. The second, which I shall not even try to sketch, is to show what sort of an inquiry Formal Logic is. This brings me to a general point about the *Tractatus*. Wittgenstein's first interest had been in the logic of mathematics and thence in the logical paradoxes which were the big leak in the dry dock that Frege and Russell had built. He was, therefore, equipped and predisposed to squeeze whatever can be significantly said into the few statement-patterns with which the logic of mathematical statements operates. He used its terminology, its codes, and its abacus-operations in his task of exploring various philosophical issues, and, above all, his own master-issue, that of the nature of philosophizing itself. In consequence, the *Trac-*

tatus is, in large measure, a closed book to those who lack this technical equipment. Few people can read it without feeling that something important is happening; but few experts, even, can say what is happening.

But this is not the end of the story. Maybe it is only the preface. For, after lying fallow for some years, Wittgenstein returned to philosophy. His teaching in this period differs markedly from that of the *Tractatus*; it even repudiates parts of the *Tractatus*.

First, he no longer forces all expressions into the favored few patterns of the logic of mathematics. With this goes a revolt against moulds of any sorts. The rubrics of logical systems and the abstract terms of philosophical schools are like the shoes of Chinese ladies, which deformed their feet and prevented them from walking on them. Philosophical elucidation is still inspection of expressions, but it is no longer inspection through the slots of a logician's stencil or through the prisms of a scholastic classification-system. His diction has reverted from that of a Russell discussing esoteric matters with mathematicians to that of a Socrates discussing everyday ideas with unindoctrinated young men. Nor does he now elucidate only the propositions of the sciences. Like Moore, he explores the logic of all the things that all of us say.

Next, though I think that his master-problem is still that of the nature, tasks and methods of the philosophical activity, he no longer thinks that philosophers are condemned to trying to say the unsayable. But he now avoids any general statement of the nature of philosophy, not because this would be to say the unsayable, but because it would be to say a scholastic and therefore an obscuring thing. In philosophy, generalizations are unclarifications. The nature of philosophy is to be taught by producing concrete specimens of it. As the medical student learns surgery by witnessing and practising operations on dead and on live subjects, so the student of philosophy learns what philosophy is by following and practising operations on particular quandary-generating ways of talking. Thus Wittgenstein would rove, apparently aimlessly because without any statement of aim, from one concrete puzzle to its brothers, its cousins, its parents and its associates, demonstrating both what makes them puzzling and how to resolve them—demonstrating, but not telling; going through the moves, but not compiling a manual of them; teaching a skill, not dictating a doctrine.

One favourite procedure of his might be called the "tea-tasting method". Tea-tasters do not lump their samples into two or three comprehensive types. Rather they savour each sample and try to place it next door to its closest neighbours, and this not in respect of just one discriminable quality, but along the lengths of various lines of qualities. So Wittgenstein would exhibit the characteristic manner of working of a particular expression, by matching it against example after example of expressions progressively diverging from it in various respects and directions. He would show how striking similarities may go with important but ordinarily unremarked differences, and how we are tempted to lean too heavily on their similarities and hence to be tripped up by their latent differences.

For philosophers do not examine expressions at random. The quest for their internal logic is forced upon us by the fact that we find ourselves already caught up in unforeseen entanglements. Why do we slide into quandaries? Let me invent an example. We find ourselves talking as if like a train, so time itself might one day slow down and stop. We divide a train into coaches and coaches into compartments. We divide a month into weeks and weeks into days. When a train is passing me, some coaches are beyond me, some are still to come, and one compartment of one coach is directly abreast of me. I look at its occupants through the window. Surely time is like this. Last week has gone, next week is still to come, but I can exchange glances with the occupants of Now. So, as trains always slow down and stop somewhere, what makes time puff on so tirelessly? Might not Now be the last compartment of the last coach? Yet surely not; there would still be something behind it, if only the empty wind. You see that it is tempting, but also that it smells like nonsense to speak of the last compartment of time. Why may we say some things about time which are very much like some things that we legitimately say about trains, when to some of the proper corollaries of what we say about trains there correspond no proper corollaries about time? To answer this question, we should have to examine the functioning of whole ranges of things that we say about trains, rivers and winds; about moving shadows, rainbows and reflections; about perpetual motion machines, stars, clocks, sundials, and calendars; about the series of numbers, days of the week and minutes of the day. And then we may see why we slid and no longer incline to slide from the proper corollaries of familiar dictions about trains to corresponding corollaries of somewhat similar dictions about time. We see that we had overpressed certain analogies between ways of talking; and that we were so dominated by a favorite model, that we had gone on using it where it could no longer work. And now we know, in a way, what time is, though there is no shorter or better way of saying what time is than by going through again the same sort of process of linguistic tea-tasting.

I must conclude. Wittgenstein has made our generation of philosophers self-conscious about philosophy itself. It is, of course, possible for a person to be very thoughtful about the nature and methods of an activity, without being made any the better at performing it. The centipede of the poem ran well until he began to wonder how he ran. Maybe we have been made a bit neurotic about the nature of our calling. But Wittgenstein's demolition of the idea that philosophy is a sort of science has at least made us vigilant about our tools. We no longer try to use for our problems the methods of arguing which are the right ones for demonstrating theorems or establishing hypotheses. In particular we have learned to pay deliberate attention to what can and cannot be said. What had, since the early days of this century, been the practice of G. E. Moore has received a rationale from Wittgenstein; and I expect that when the curtain is lifted we shall also find that Wittgenstein's concrete methods have increased the power, scope and delicacy of the methods by which Moore has for so long explored in detail the internal logic of what we say.

Truth Claims in Religion

R. B. BRAITHWAITE

Richard B. Braithwaite was born in Banbury, England, in 1900, and was educated at Kings College, Cambridge University, in physics, mathematics, and philosophy. He has had a distinguished career as professor of moral philosophy at Cambridge and as president of both the Mind Association and the Aristotelian Society. His writings include contributions to the fields of scientific methodology, moral philosophy, and the philosophy of religion.

In general, the essay that follows can be described as an attempt to assess the impact that linguistic philosophy has had on religion. More specifically, it tries deliberately to enumerate the issues that are at stake in the conflict between the two interests. It also provides occasion for Braithwaite to set forth some proposals regarding the context within which religious statements make proper truth claims. It is fair to point out that when he enumerates the issues, he is summarizing generally agreed-upon contentions among scholars who have been involved in both fields. In the clarification of those issues, and especially in his push toward normalizing the ethical context, he is speaking more particularly on his own behalf.

There are three classes of statement whose method of truth-value testing is in general outline clear: statements about particular matters of empirical fact, scientific hypotheses and other general empirical statements, and the logically necessary statements of logic and mathematics (and their contradictories). Do religious statements fall into any of these three classes? If they do, the problem of their meaningfulness will be solved: their truth-values will be testable by the methods appropriate to empirical statements, particular or general, or to mathematical statements. It seems to me clear that religious statements, as they are normally used, have no place in this trichotomy. I shall give my reasons very briefly, since I have little to add here to what other empiricist philosophers have said.

R. B. Braithwaite, "An Empiricist's View of the Nature of Religious Belief," in John Hick, ed., *The Existence of God* (New York: Macmillan, 1964), pp. 231–245.

I. Statements about particular empirical facts are testable by direct observation. The only facts that can be directly known by observation are that the things observed have certain observable properties or stand in certain observable relations to one another. If it is maintained that the *existence* of God is known by observation, for example, in the "self-authenticating" experience of "meeting God," the term "God" is being used merely as part of the description of that particular experience. Any interesting theological proposition, e.g. that God is personal, will attribute a property to God which is not an observable one and so cannot be known by direct observation. Comparison with our knowledge of other people is an unreal comparison. I can get to know things about an intimate friend at a glance, but this knowledge is not self-authenticating; it is based upon a great deal of previous knowledge about the connection between facial and bodily expressions and states of mind.

II. The view that would class religious statements with scientific hypotheses must be taken much more seriously. It would be very unplausible if a Baconian methodology of science had to be employed, and scientific hypotheses taken as simple generalizations from particular instances, for then there could be no understanding of a general theological proposition unless particular instances of it could be directly observed. But an advanced science has progressed far beyond its natural history stage; it makes use in its explanatory hypotheses of concepts of a high degree of abstractness and at a far remove from experience. These theoretical concepts are given a meaning by the place they occupy in a deductive system consisting of hypotheses of different degrees of generality in which the least general hypotheses, deducible from the more general ones, are generalizations of observable facts. So it is no valid criticism of the view that would treat God as an empirical concept entering into an explanatory hypothesis to say that God is not directly observable. No more is an electric field of force or a Schrödinger wave-function. There is no prima facie objection to regarding such a proposition as that there is a God who created and sustains the world as an explanatory scientific hypothesis.

But if a set of theological propositions are to be regarded as scientific explanations of facts in the empirical world, they must e refutable by experience. We must be willing to abandon them if the facts prove different from what we think they are. A hypothesis which is consistent with every possible empirical fact is not an empirical one. And though the theoretical concepts in a hypothesis need not be explicitly definable in terms of direct observation—indeed they must not be if the system is to be applicable to novel situations—yet they must be related to some and not to all of the possible facts in the world in order to have a non-vacuous significance. If there is a personal God, how would the world be different if there were not? Unless this question can be answered God's existence cannot be given an empirical meaning.

At earlier times in the history of religion God's personal existence has been treated as a scientific hypothesis subjectable to empirical test. Elijah's contest with the prophets of Baal was an experiment to test the hypothesis that Jehovah and not Baal controlled the physical world. But most educated believers at the present time do not think of God as being detectable in this sort of way, and hence do not think of theological propositions as explanations of facts in the world of nature in the way in which established scientific hypotheses are.

It may be maintained, however, that theological propositions explain facts about the world in another way. Nor perhaps the physical world, for physical science has been so successful with its own explanations; but the facts of biological and psychological development. Now it is certainly the case that a great deal of traditional Christian language—phrases such as "original sin," "the old Adam," "the new man," "growth in holiness"—can be given meanings within statements expressing general hypotheses about human personality. Indeed it is hardly too much to say that almost all statements about God as immanent, as an indwelling spirit, can be interpreted as asserting psychological facts in metaphorical language. But would those interpreting religious statements in this way be prepared to abandon them if the empirical facts were found to be different? Or would they rather re-interpret them to fit the new facts? In the latter case the possibility of interpreting them to fit experience is not enough to give an empirical meaning to the statements. Mere consistency with experience without the possibility of inconsistency does not determine meaning. And a metaphorical description is not in itself an explanation. This criticism also holds against attempts to interpret theism as an explanation of the course of history, unless it is admitted (which few theists would be willing to admit) that, had the course of history been different in some specific way, God would not have existed.

Philosophers of religion who wish to make empirical facts relevant to the meaning of religious statements but at the same time desire to hold on to these statements whatever the empirical facts may be are indulging, I believe, in a sort of "double-think" attitude: they want to hold that religious statements both are about the actual world (i.e.

are empirical statements) and also are not refutable in any possible world, the characteristics of statements which are logically necessary.

III. The view that statements of natural theology resemble the propositions of logic and mathematics in being logically necessary would have as a consequence that they make no assertion of existence. Whatever exactly be the status of logically necessary propositions, Hume and Kant have conclusively shown that they are essentially hypothetical. $2 + 3 = 5$ makes no assertion about there being any things in the world; what it says is that, *if* there is a class of five things in the world, *then* this class is the union of two mutually exclusive sub-classes one comprising two and the other comprising three things. The logical-positivist thesis, due to Wittgenstein, that the truth of this hypothetical proposition is verified not by any logical fact about the world but by the way in which we use numerical symbols in our thinking goes further than Kant did in displacing logic and mathematics from the world of reality. But it is not necessary to accept this more radical thesis in order to agree with Kant that no logically necessary proposition can assert existence; and this excludes the possibility of regarding theological propositions as logically necessary in the way in which the hypothetical propositions of mathematics and logic are necessary.

The traditional arguments for a Necessary God—the ontological and the cosmological—were elaborated by Anselm and the scholastic philosophers before the concurrent and inter-related development of natural science and of mathematics had enabled necessity and contingency to be clearly distinguished. The necessity attributed by these arguments to the being of God may perhaps be different from the logical necessity of mathematical truths; but, if so, no method has been provided for testing the truth-value of the statement that God is necessary being, and consequently no way given for assigning meaning to the terms "necessary being" and "God."

If religious statements cannot be held to fall into any of these three classes, their method of verification cannot be any of the standard methods applicable to statements falling in these classes. Does this imply that religious statements are not verifiable, with the corollary, according to the verificational principle, that they have no meaning and, though they purport to say something, are in fact nonsensical sentences? The earlier logical positivists thought so: they would have echoed the demand of their precursor Hume that a volume ("of divinity or school metaphysics") which contains neither "any abstract reasoning concerning quantity or number" nor "any experimental reasoning concerning matter of fact and existence" should be committed to the flames; though their justification for the holocaust would be even more cogent than Hume's. The volume would not contain even "sophistry and illusion": it would contain nothing but meaningless marks of printer's ink.

Religious statements, however, are not the only statements which are unverifiable by standard methods; moral statements have the same peculiarity. A moral principle, like the utilitarian principle that a man ought to act so as to maximize happiness, does not seem to be either a logically necessary or a logically impossible proposition. But neither does it seem to be an empirical proposition, all the attempts of ethical empiricists to give naturalistic analyses having failed. Though a tough-minded logical positivist might be prepared to say that all religious statements are sound and fury, signifying nothing, he can hardly say that of all moral statements. For moral statements have a use in guiding conduct: and if they have a use they surely have a meaning—in some sense of meaning. So the verificational principle of meaning in the hands of empiricist philosophers in the 1930's became modified either by a glossing of the term "verification" or by a change of the verification principle into the use principle: the meaning of any statement is given by the way in which it is used.

Since I wish to continue to employ verification in the restricted sense of ascertaining truth-value, I shall take the principle of meaning in this new form in which the word "verification" has disappeared. But in removing this term from the statement of the principle, there is no desertion from the spirit of empiricism. The older verificational principle is subsumed under the new use principle: the use of an empirical statement derives from the fact that the statement is empirically verifiable, and the logical-positivist thesis of the "linguistic" character of logical and mathematical statements can be equally well, if not better, expressed in terms of their use than of their method of verification. Moreover the only way of discovering how a statement is used is by an empirical enquiry; a statement need not itself be empirically verifiable, but that it is used in a particular way is always a straightforwardly empirical proposition.

The meaning of any statement, then, will be taken as being given by the way it is used. The kernel for an empiricist of the problem of the nature of religious belief is to explain, in empirical terms, how a religious statement is used by a man who asserts it in order to express his religious conviction.

Since I shall argue that the primary element in this use is that the religious assertion is used as a moral assertion, I must first consider how moral assertions are used. According to the view developed by various moral philosophers since the impossibility of regarding moral statements as verifiable propositions was recognized, a moral assertion is used to express an *attitude* of the man making the assertion. It is not used to assert the proposition that he has the attitude—a verifiable psychological proposition; it is used to show forth or evince his attitude. The attitude is concerned with the action which he asserts to be right or to be his duty, or the state of affairs which he asserts to be good; it is a highly complex state, and contains elements to which various degrees of importance have been attached by moral philosophers who have tried to work out an "ethics without propositions." One element in the attitude is a feeling of approval towards the action; this element was taken as the fundamental one in the first attempts, and views of ethics without propositions are frequently lumped together as "emotive" theories of ethics. But discussion of the subject during the last twenty years has made it clear, I think, that no emotion or feeling of approval is fundamental to the use of moral assertions; it may be the case that the moral asserter has some specific feeling directed on to the course of action said to be right, but this is not the most important element in his "proattitude" towards the course of action: what is primary is his intention to perform the action when the occasion for it arises.

Let us now consider what light this way of regarding moral assertions throws upon assertions of religious conviction. The idealist philosopher McTaggart described religion as "an emotion resting on a conviction of a harmony between ourselves and the universe at large," and many educated people at the present time would agree with him. If religion is essentially concerned with emotion, it is natural to explain the use of religious assertions on the lines of the original emotive theory of ethics and to regard them as primarily evincing religious feelings or emotions. The assertion, for example, that God is our Heavenly Father will be taken to express the asserter's feeling secure in the same way as he would feel secure in his father's presence. But explanations of religion in terms of feeling, and of religious assertions as expressions of such feelings, are usually propounded by people who stand outside any religious system; they rarely satisfy those who speak from inside. Few religious men would be prepared to admit that their religion was a matter merely of feeling: feelings—of joy, of consolation, of being at one with the universe—may enter into their religion, but to evince such feelings is certainly not the primary use of their religious assertions.

This objection, however, does not seem to me to apply to treating religious assertions in the conative way in which recent moral philosophers have treated moral statements—as being primarily declarations of adherence to a policy of action, declarations of commitment to a way of life. That the way of life led by the believer is highly relevant to the sincerity of his religious conviction has been insisted upon by all the moral religions, above all, perhaps, by Christianity. "By their fruits ye shall know them." The view which I put forward for your consideration is that the intention of a Christian to follow a Christian way of life is not only the criterion for the sincerity of his belief in the assertions of Christianity; it is the criterion for the meaningfulness of his assertions. Just as the meaning of a moral assertion is given by its use in expressing the asserter's intention to act, so far as in him lies, in accordance with the moral principle involved, so the meaning of a religious assertion is given by its use in expressing the asserter's intention to follow a specified policy of behavior. To say that it is belief in the dogmas of religion which is the cause of the believer's intending to behave as he does is to put the cart before the horse: it is the intention to behave which constitutes what is known as religious conviction.

The way to find out what are the intentions embodied in a set of religious assertions, and hence what is the meaning of the assertions, is by discovering what principles of conduct the asserter takes the assertions to involve. These may be ascertained both by asking him questions and by seeing how he behaves, each test being supplemental to the other. If what is wanted is not the meaning of the religious assertions made by a particular man but what the set of assertions would mean were they to be made by anyone of the same religion (which I will call their *typical* meaning), all that can be done is to specify the form of behavior which is in accordance with what one takes to be the fundamental moral principles of the religion in question. Since different people will take different views as to what these fundamental moral principles are, the typical meaning of religious assertions will be different for different people. I myself take the typical meaning of the body of Christian assertions as being given by their proclaiming intentions to follow an agapeistic way of life, and for a description of this way of life—a description in general and metaphorical terms, but an empirical description nevertheless—I should quote most of the thirteenth chapter of I Corinthians. Others may think that the Christian way of life should be described somewhat differently, and will therefore take the typical meaning of the assertions of Christianity to correspond to their different view of its fundamental moral teaching.

My contention then is that the primary use of religious assertions is to announce allegiance to a set of moral principles; without such allegiance there is no "true religion." This is borne out by all the accounts of what happens when an unbeliever becomes converted to a religion. The conversion is not only a change in the propositions believed—indeed there may be no specifically intellectual change at all; it is a change in the state of will. An excellent instance is C. S. Lewis's recently published account of his conversion from an idealist metaphysic—"a religion [as he says] that cost nothing"— to a theism where he faced (and he quotes George MacDonald's phrase) "something to be neither more nor less nor other than *done*." There was no intellectual change, for (as he says) "there had long been an ethic (theoretically) attached to my Idealism": it was the recognition that he had to do something about it, that "an attempt at complete virtue must be made." His conversion was a re-orientation of the will.

In assimilating religious assertions to moral assertions I do not wish to deny that there are any important differences. One is the fact already noticed that usually the behavior policy intended is not specified by one religious assertion in isolation. Another difference is that the fundamental moral teaching of the religion is frequently given, not in abstract terms, but by means of concrete examples—of how to behave, for instance, if one meets a man set upon by thieves on the road to Jericho. A resolution to behave like the good Samaritan does not, in itself, specify the behavior to be resolved upon in quite different circumstances. However, absence of explicitly recognized general principles does not prevent a man from acting in accordance with such principles; it only makes it more difficult for a questioner to discover upon what principles he is acting. And the difficulty is not only one way round. If moral principles are stated in the most general form, as most moral philosophers have wished to state them, they tend to become so far removed from particular courses of conduct that it is difficult, if not impossible, to give them any precise content. It may be hard to find out what exactly is involved in the imitation of Christ; but it is not very easy to discover what exactly is meant by the pursuit of Aristotle's *eudaemonia* or of Mill's *happiness*. The tests for what it is to live agapeistically are as empirical as are those for living in quest of happiness; but in each case the tests can best be expounded in terms of examples of particular situations.

A more important difference between religious and purely moral principles is that, in the higher religions at least, the conduct preached by the religion concerns not only external but also internal behavior. The conversion involved in accepting a religion is a conversion, not only of the will, but of the heart. Christianity requires not only that you should behave towards your neighbor as if you loved him as yourself: it requires that you should love him as yourself. And though I have no doubt that the Christian concept of *agape* refers partly to external behavior—the agapeistic behavior for which there are external criteria—yet being filled with *agape* includes more than behaving agapeistically externally: it also includes an agapeistic frame of mind. I have said that I cannot regard the expression of a feeling of any sort as the primary element in religious assertion; but this does not imply that intention to feel in a certain way is not a primary element, nor that it cannot be used to discriminate religious declarations of policy from declarations which are merely moral. Those who say that Confucianism is a code of morals and not, properly speaking, a religion are, I think, making this discrimination.

The resolution proclaimed by a religious assertion may then be taken as referring to inner life as well as to outward conduct. And the superiority of religious conviction over the mere adoption of a moral code in securing conformity to the code arises from a religious conviction changing what the religious man wants. It may be hard enough to love your enemy, but once you have succeeded in doing so it is easy to behave lovingly towards him. But if you continue to hate him, it requires a heroic perseverance continually to behave as if you loved him. Resolutions to feel, even if they are only partly fulfilled, are powerful reinforcements of resolutions to act.

But though these qualifications may be adequate for distinguishing religious assertions from purely moral ones, they are not sufficient to discriminate between assertions belonging to one religious system and those belonging to another system in the case in which the behavior policies, both of inner life and of outward conduct, inculcated by the two systems are identical. For instance, I have said that I take the fundamental moral teaching of Christianity to be the preaching of an agapeistic way of life. But a Jew or a Buddhist may, with considerable plausibility, maintain that the fundamental moral teaching of his religion is to recommend exactly the same way of life. How then can religious assertions be distinguished into those which are Christian, those which are Jewish, those which are Buddhist, by the policies of life which they respectively recommend if, on examination, these policies turn out to be the same?

Many Christians will, no doubt, behave in a specifically Christian manner in that they will follow ritual practices which are Christian and neither Jewish nor Buddhist. But though following certain practices may well be the proper test for membership of a particular religious society, a church, not even the most ecclesiastically-minded Christian will regard participation in a ritual as the fundamental characteristic of a Christian way of life. There must be some more important difference between an agapeistically policed Christian and an agapeistically policed Jew than that the former attends a church and the latter a synagogue.

The really important difference, I think, is to be found in the fact that the intentions to pursue the behavior policies, which may be the same for different religions, are associated with thinking of different *stories* (or sets of stories). By a story I shall here mean a proposition or set of propositions which are straightforwardly empirical propositions capable of empirical test and which are thought of by the religious man in connection with his resolution to follow the way of life advocated by his religion. On the assumption that the ways of life advocated by Christianity and by Buddhism are essentially the same, it will be the fact that the intention to follow this way of life is associated in the mind of a Christian with thinking of one set of stories (the Christian stories) while it is associated in the mind of a Buddhist with thinking of another set of stories (the Buddhist stories) which enables a Christian assertion to be distinguished from a Buddhist one.

A religious assertion will, therefore, have a propositional element which is lacking in a purely moral assertion, in that it will refer to a story as well as to an intention. The reference to the story is not an assertion of the story taken as a matter of empirical fact: it is a telling of the story, or an alluding to the story, in the way in which one can tell, or allude to, the story of a novel with which one is acquainted. To assert the whole set of assertions of the Christian religion is both to tell the Christian doctrinal story and to confess allegiance to the Christian way of life.

The story, I have said, is a set of empirical propositions, and the language expressing the story is given a meaning by the standard method of understanding how the story-statements can be verified.

The empirical story-statements will vary from Christian to Christian: the doctrines of Christianity are capable of different empirical interpretations, and Christians will differ in the interpretations they put upon the doctrines. But the interpretations will all be in terms of empirical propositions.

Selected Bibliography

Scientific Explanation (Cambridge: Cambridge University Press, 1953).

An Empiricist's View of the Nature of Religious Belief (Cambridge: Cambridge University Press, 1955).

Theory of Games as a Tool for the Moral Philosopher (Cambridge: Cambridge University Press, 1955).

"Models in Empirical Science," *Logic, Methodology, and Philosophy of Science*, E. Nagel, P. Suppes, and A. Tarski, eds. (Palo Alto: Stanford University Press, 1962), pp. 224–231.

"Common Action Towards Different Moral Ends," *Proceedings of the Aristotelian Society.* Vol. LIII (1952–1953), pp. 29–46.

"The Theory of Games and Its Relevance to Philosophy," *Philosophy in the Mid-Century*, Raymond Klibansky, ed. Vol. I, Logic and Philosophy of Science (Florence: Nuova Italia, 1958).

The Fittingness of
Religious Language

Paul L. Holmer

Paul L. Holmer was born in Minneapolis, Minnesota, on November 14, 1916. He was educated in Minnesota and at Yale University, where he took his doctorate in philosophy in 1945. After teaching at Gustavus Adolphus College and at the University of Minnesota, he returned to Yale where he has been on the Divinity School faculty since 1960.

Holmer is a recognized authority on the life and thought of Søren Kierkegaard and, at the same time, is one of the leading American figures in initiating dialogue between theology and contemporary analytic philosophy. He has worked tirelessly in both capacities to bring clarity and force to the twin distinctions between the language of religion and the language about religion, and, in Gilbert Ryle's words, the dispositions of knowing-how and knowing-that. For Holmer, knowing-how is in large part a matter of realigning thoughts and beliefs with the religious passions. Meaning and understanding are effected when religious language is fitted to its appropriate context.

The following essay is an excerpt from a larger study on the use of language in religion and theology.

There is no doubt whatsoever that language can be described, for it is being done continually. Furthermore, it is pertinent to remember that phonemes and marks on paper, letters and words, can be distinguished from the meanings. Just how meanings become connected with linguistic forms is an interesting study in itself. The point I wish to make here is that this is not an esoteric and odd business at all, though it is many-sided and complex. Furthermore, most of us have first-hand acquaintance with the processes by which it is done. But the task of describing exhaustively the acquisition of meaning for every form of language has not been done; and in fact it is extremely difficult to see how in principle it could ever be done. For the situations which cause people to speak include everything that happens

Paul L. Holmer, "Language and Theology: Some Critical Notes," in *Harvard Theological Review*, Vol. LVIII, No. 3 (1965), pp. 241–261. Copyright by President and Fellows of Harvard College.

and anything you can see and imagine. In order to have an exhaustive and detailed account of the meanings for every form of speech, we would also need an absolutely exhaustive and accurate account, not only of everything in the talkers' world but also of the speaker too, his whims, desires, cares and so on.

Because we do not have anything like this, our knowledge looks fragmentary; and many students of meaning are inclined to despair of an empirical kind of study. However, this is no cause for leaping to a general philosophical theory, by which we can declare matters in one fell-swoop.

On the contrary, there are ways by which we make meaningful all kinds of language; and we can know the 'ways' well enough. We give meanings to language not by thinking abstract correlatives but rather by putting the language to work as hard and as thoroughly as possible. This is the secret of building a vocabulary, as we probably learned to our dismay when we were young. Because so many words on one's list were simply of no use whatsoever, except to overawe others, it was also easy to forget the definitions and eventually to forget the word altogether. But words, even scientific ones, like the highly artificial and contrived latinized words used in elementary biology, come to life when the occasions for their service are multiple, in laboratories, in reading and in discussions. So, too, with our words of religion. Most of them get their meanings only when their role is pronounced. If there is no role, they too drop away. . . .

We are contending that attention be paid to the actual workings of the speech-forms. When these are put to work in their appropriate contexts, then the meanings simply occur. Therefore, it is a mistake to treat metaphysics and theology as though they actually supplied meanings to more ordinary religious discourse. For if we are despoiled of metaphysical schemes, even grand theological schemes, it may be that this is a symptom and not a cause. Meanings belong to words when uses for them are at hand. The task for theologians, then, if they decry the vacuousness of religious language in the pulpit and the pew is not to sketch a theory that will impart meaning as much as it is to suggest the 'learning how' and all that that involves in the religious life. For the use of religious language, even the Bible and the hymns, liturgy and prayers, is part of the business of learning to be religious. This is part of the 'how' of being religious.

Once the use is gained, words are no longer deprived of their meanings. It might be the case that much of the language of the churches is simply now a coarse kind of custom, quite without justification and point. Also it may be true that certain generalities about it of a sociological sort are justified, namely, that it is trite, a defunct fashion and finally meaningless. But such generalizations do little to suggest the remedy if that is what one seeks. There are all kinds of people who have mastered the use of religious language because they have also learned to be contrite, forgiving, and long-suffering and many more things. It is in that 'how,' that kind of learning, that religious language also begins to acquire a function and role. . . .

One more illustration might suffice. The words "God" and "sin" and others, distinctive to religious people, have definite meanings. Such words have acquired their meanings over a long history. Words were connected with what was being said and done. They changed what was being said and done. These words, then, began to refer to something in virtue of the roles they played in discourse. But it is also true that many people enter the texture of such discourse, in our churches and our common life, without being aware of what is involved. Almost without number, people use these words wrongly or they use them to no point at all. This is because most of them do not know the concepts "God" or "sin" at all. Is this what the critics of supernaturalisms and the older theologies are saying? Maybe so, but there is a small difference that is the point of these remarks. A concept is learned by learning the way the word is used—the tissue of reaction, stimuli and responses. The long-term consensus within which the word has its place is a concept and, therefore, the concept is more like a rule than a thing, a regular practise than an object, an exercise in "concreto" than an essay in "abstracto". . . .

To lose the meaning of the religious words is not like losing their definitions—it is more like losing the practise with which they were associated. To know the meaning of a word supposes keeping with the rule. And concepts are no good—they become just noises or just marks on paper, when they lose that context in which they can be seen to be the rule. But rules are only rules if they are kept. . . .

Selected Bibliography

"Atheism and Theism: A Comment on an Academic Prejudice," *Lutheran World*, Vol. XIII, No. 1 (1966), pp. 14–25.

"Metaphysics and Theology: The Foundation of Theology," *Lutheran Quarterly*, Vol. XVII (November, 1965), pp. 291–315.

"Paul Tillich: 'Language and Meaning,'" *Journal of Religious Thought*, Vol. XXII, No. 2 (1965–1966), pp. 85–106.

Philosophy and the Common Life (Stockton: Philosophical Institute of the College of the Pacific, 1960).

"Scientific Language and the Language of Religion," *Journal for the Scientific Study of Religion*. Vol. I (October, 1961), pp. 42–55.

Theology and the Scientific Study of Religion (Minneapolis: T. S. Denison, 1961).

"Wittgenstein and Theology," *New Essays on Religious Language*, edited by Dallas M. High (New York: Oxford University Press, 1969), pp. 25–35.

Language Games and
Primitive Societies

PETER WINCH

*Peter Winch was born on January 14, 1926, in England, and was
educated at St. Edmund Hall, Oxford. He taught at University College of Swansea from 1951 to 1964, was visiting professor at Rochester
University in New York State in 1961–1962, and, since 1964, has been
professor of philosophy at King's College, London. He has published
in a number of professional journals in philosophy, and is the author
of a book,* The Idea of a Social Science, *published in 1958. Since 1965
he has also been editor of* Analysis. *He is one of the leading figures
in contemporary British philosophy.*

*The essay that follows consists almost entirely of Winch's con-
cluding argument in his criticism of E. E. Evans-Pritchard and Alasdair MacIntyre, both of whom, from slightly different standpoints,
contend that the discrepancies between respective patterns of rationality prevent us from understanding the beliefs and practices of primitive societies. Winch bases his case on the function of language. As
he sees it, conceptions of "reality" are determined by actual language
usage; they are given in the sense that language has. Thus, despite
the fact that its standards of rationality and intelligibility are different
from our own, a primitive culture can be understood when its beliefs
and practices are taken as being instrumental in making sense of
human life.*

In a discussion of Wittgenstein's philosophical use of language
games [1] Mr. Rush Rhees points out that to try to account for the
meaningfulness of language solely in terms of isolated language
games is to omit the important fact that ways of speaking are not
insulated from each other in mutually exclusive systems of rules.
What can be said in one context by the use of a certain expression
depends for its sense on the uses of that expression in other contexts

[1] Rush Rhees, "Wittgenstein's Builders," *Proceedings of the Aristotelian So-
ciety,* vol. 20 (1960), pp. 171–186.
Peter Winch, "Understanding a Primitive Society," *American Philosophical
Quarterly,* Vol. I, No. 4 (October, 1964), pp. 321–324.

(different language games). Language games are played by men who have lives to live—lives involving a wide variety of different interests, which have all kinds of different bearings on each other. Because of this, what a man says or does may make a difference not merely to the performance of the activity upon which he is at present engaged, but to his *life* and to the lives of other people. Whether a man sees point in what he is doing will then depend on whether he is able to see any unity in his multifarious interests, activities, and relations with other men; what sort of sense he sees in his life will depend on the nature of this unity. The ability to see this sort of sense in life depends not merely on the individual concerned, though this is not to say it does not depend on him at all; it depends also on the possibilities for making such sense which the culture in which he lives does, or does not, provide.

What we may learn by studying other cultures are not merely possibilities of different ways of doing things, other techniques. More importantly we may learn different possibilities of making sense of human life, different ideas about the possible importance that the carrying out of certain activities may take on for a man, trying to contemplate the sense of his life as a whole. This dimension of the matter is precisely what [Alasdair] MacIntyre misses in his treatment of Zande magic: he can see in it only a (misguided) technique for producing consumer goods. But a Zande's crops are not just potential objects of consumption: the life he lives, his relations with his fellows, his chances for acting decently or doing evil, may all spring from his relation to his crops. Magical rites constitute a form of expression in which these possibilities and dangers may be contemplated and reflected on—and perhaps also thereby transformed and deepened. The difficulty we find in understanding this is not merely its remoteness from science, but an aspect of the general difficulty we find of thinking about such matters at all except in terms of "efficiency of production"—production, that is, for consumption. This again is a symptom of what Marx called the "alienation" characteristic of man in industrial society, though Marx's own confusions about the relations between production and consumption are further symptoms of that same alienation. Our blindness to the point of primitive modes of life is a corollary of the pointlessness of much of our own life.

[However] my aim is not to engage in moralizing, but to suggest that the concept of *learning from* which is involved in the study of other cultures is closely linked with the concept of *wisdom*. We are confronted not just with different techniques, but with new possibilities of good and evil, in relation to which men may come to terms with life. An investigation into this dimension of a society may indeed require a quite detailed inquiry into alternative techniques (e.g., of production), but an inquiry conducted for the light it throws on those possibilities of good and evil. A very good example of the kind of thing I mean is Simone Weil's analysis of the techniques of modern factory production in *Oppression and Liberty*, which is not a contribution to business management, but part of an inquiry into the peculiar form which the evil of oppression takes in our culture.

In saying this, however, I may seem merely to have lifted to a new level the difficulty raised by [Alasdair] MacIntyre of how to relate our own conceptions of rationality to those of other societies. Here the difficulty concerns the relation betweeen our own conceptions of good an evil and those of other societies. A full investigation would thus require a discussion of ethical relativism at this point. I have tried to show some of the limitations of relativism in an earlier paper.[2] I shall close the present essay with some remarks which are supplementary to that.

I wish to point out that the very conception of human life involves certain fundamental notions—which I shall call "limiting notions"—which have an obvious ethical dimension, and which indeed in a sense determine the "ethical space," within which the possibilities of good and evil in human life can be exercised. The notions which I shall discuss very briefly here correspond closely to those which Vico made the foundation of his idea of natural law, on which he thought the possibility of understanding human history rested: birth, death, sexual relations. Their significance here is that they are inescapably involved in the life of all known human societies in a way which gives us a clue where to look, if we are puzzled about the point of an alien system of institutions. The specific forms which these concepts take, the particular institutions in which they are expressed, vary very considerably from one society to another; but their central position within a society's institutions is and must be a constant factor. In trying to understand the life of an alien society, then, it will be of the utmost importance to be clear about the way in which these notions enter into it. The actual practice of social anthropologists bears this out, although I do not know how many of them would attach the same kind of importance to them as I do.

[2] Peter Winch, "Nature and Convention," *Proceedings of the Aristotelian Society*, Vol. 20 (1960), pp. 231–252.

I speak of a "limit" here because these notions, along no doubt with others, give shape to what we understand by "human life"; and because a concern with questions posed in terms of them seems to me constitutive of what we understand by the "morality" of a society. In saying this, I am of course disagreeing with those moral philosophers who have made attitudes of approval and disapproval, or something similar, fundamental in ethics, and who have held that the *objects* of such attitudes were conceptually irrelevant to the conception of morality. On that view, there might be a society where the sorts of attitude taken up in *our* society to questions about relations between the sexes were reserved, say, for questions about the length people wear their hair, and *vice versa*. This seems to me incoherent. In the first place, there would be a confusion in *calling* a concern of that sort a "moral" concern, however passionately felt. The story of Samson in the Old Testament confirms rather than refutes this point, for the interdict on the cutting of Samson's hair is, of course, connected there with much else: and pre-eminently, it should be noted, with questions about sexual relations. But secondly, if that is thought to be merely verbal quibbling, I will say that it does not seem to me a merely conventional matter that T. S. Eliot's trinity of "birth, copulation and earth" happen to be such deep objects of human concern. I do not mean just that they are made such by fundamental psychological and sociological forces, though that is no doubt true. But I want to say further that the very notion of human life is limited by these conceptions.

Unlike beasts, men do not merely live but also have a conception of life. This is not something that is simply added to their life; rather, it changes the very sense which the word "life" has, when applied to men. It is no longer equivalent to "animate existence." When we are speaking of the life of man, we can ask questions about what is the right way to live, what things are most important in life, whether life has any significance, and if so what.

To have a conception of life is also to have a conception of death. But just as the "life" that is here in question is not the same as animate existence, so the "death" that is here in question is not the same as the end of animate existence. My conception of the death of an animal is of an event that will take place in the world; perhaps I shall observe it—and my life will go on. But when I speak of "my death," I am not speaking of a future event in my life; [3] I am not

---

[3] Cf. Wittgenstein, *Tractatus Logico-Philosophicus*, 6.431–6.4311.

even speaking of an event in anyone else's life. I am speaking of the cessation of my world. That is also a cessation of my ability to do good or evil. It is not just that *as a matter of fact* I shall no longer be able to do good or evil after I am dead; the point is that my very *concept* of what it is to be able to do good or evil is deeply bound up with my concept of my life as ending in death. If ethics is a concern with the right way to live, then clearly the nature of this concern must be deeply affected by the concept of life as ending in death. One's attitude to one's life is at the same time an attitude to one's death.

This point is very well illustrated in an anthropological datum which MacIntyre confesses himself unable to make any sense of.

> According to Spencer and Gillen some aborigines carry about a stick or stone which is treated *as if* it is or embodies the soul of the individual who carries it. If the stick or stone is lost, the individual anoints himself as the dead are anointed. Does the concept of "carrying one's soul about with one" make sense? Of course we can redescribe what the aborigines are doing and transform it into sense, and perhaps Spencer and Gillen (and Durkheim who follows them) misdescribe what occurs. But if their reports are not erroneous, we confront a blank wall here, so far as meaning is concerned, although it is easy to give the rules for the use of the concept.[4]

MacIntyre does not say why he regards the concept of carrying one's soul about with one in a stick "thoroughly incoherent." He is presumably influenced by the fact that it would be hard to make sense of an action like this if performed by a twentieth-century Englishman or American; and by the fact that the soul is not a material object like a piece of paper and cannot, therefore, be carried about in a stick as a piece of paper might be. But it does not seem to me so hard to see sense in the practice, even from the little we are told about it here. Consider that a lover in our society may carry about a picture or lock of hair of the beloved that this may symbolize for him his relation to the beloved and may, indeed, change the relation in all sorts of ways: for example, strengthening it or perverting it. Suppose that when the lover loses the locket he feels guilty and asks his beloved for her forgiveness: there might be a parallel here to the aboriginal's practice of anointing himself when he "loses his soul."

[4] *Is Understanding Religion Compatible with Believing?*

And is there necessarily anything irrational about either of these practices? Why should the lover not regard his carelessness in losing the locket as a sort of betrayal of the beloved? Remember how husbands and wives may feel about the loss of a wedding ring. The aborigine is clearly expressing a concern with his life as a whole in this practice; the anointing shows the close connection between such a concern and contemplation of death. Perhaps it is precisely this practice which makes such a concern possible for him, as religious sacraments make certain sorts of concern possible. The point is that a concern with one's life as a whole, involving as it does the limiting conception of one's death, if it is to be expressed *within* a person's life, can necessarily only be expressed quasi-sacramentally. The form of the concern shows itself in the form of the sacrament.

The sense in which I spoke also of sex as a "limiting concept" again has to do with the concept of a human life. The life of a man is a man's life and the life of a woman is a woman's life: the masculinity or the femininity are not just *components* in the life, they are its *mode*. Adapting Wittgenstein's remark about death, I might say that my masculinity is not an experience in the world, but my way of experiencing the world. Now the concepts of masculinity and femininity obviously require each other. A man is a man in relation to women; and a woman is a woman in relation to men.[5] Thus the form taken by man's relation to women is of quite fundamental importance for the significance he can attach to his own life. The vulgar identification of morality with sexual morality certainly *is* vulgar; but it is a vulgarization of an important truth.

The limiting character of the concept of birth is obviously related to the points I have sketched regarding death and sex. On the one hand, my birth is no more an event in my life than is my death; and through my birth ethical limits are set for my life quite independently of my will: I am, from the outset, in specific relations to other people, from which obligations spring which cannot but be ethically fundamental.[6] On the other hand, the concept of birth is fundamentally linked to that of relations between the sexes. This remains true, however much or little may be known in a society about the

[5] These relations, however, are not simple converses. See Georg Simmel, "Das Relative und das Absolute im Geschlechter-Problem" in *Philosophische Kultur* (Leipzig, Werner Klinkhardt, 1911).

[6] For this reason, among others, I think A. I. Melden is wrong to say that parent-child obligations and rights have nothing directly to do with physical genealogy. Cf. Melden, *Rights and Right Conduct* (Oxford: Basil Blackwell, 1959).

contribution of males and females to procreation; for it remains true that man is born of woman, not of man. This, then, adds a new dimension to the ethical institutions in which relations between the sexes are expressed.

I have tried to do no more, in these last brief remarks, than to focus attention in a certain direction. I have wanted to indicate that forms of these limiting concepts will necessarily be an important feature of any human society and that conceptions of good and evil in human life will necessarily be connected with such concepts. In any attempt to understand the life of another society, therefore, an investigation of the forms taken by such concepts—their role in the life of the society—must always take a central place and provide a basis on which understanding may be built.

> Now since the world of nations has been made by men, let us see in what institutions men agree and always have agreed. For these institutions will be able to give us the universal and eternal principles (such as every science must have) on which all nations were founded and still preserve themselves.
>
> We observe that all nations, barbarous as well as civilized, though separately founded because remote from each other in time and space, keep these three human customs: all have some religion, all contract solemn marriages, all bury their dead. And in no nation, however savage and crude, are any human actions performed with more elaborate ceremonies and more sacred solemnity than the rites of religion, marriage and burial. For by the axiom that "uniform ideas, born among peoples unknown to each other, must have a common ground of truth," it must have been dictated to all nations that from these institutions humanity began among them all, and therefore they must be most devoutly guarded by them all, so that the world should not again become a bestial wilderness. For this reason we have taken these three eternal and universal customs as the first principles of this Science.[7]

Selected Bibliography

The Idea of a Social Science (London: Routledge and Kegan Paul, 1958).

Moral Integrity (Inaugural Lecture in the Chair of Philosophy de-

[7] Giambattista Vico, *The New Science*, pp. 332–333.

livered at King's College, London, May 9, 1968). (Oxford: Basil Blackwell, 1968).

"Social Science," *British Journal of Sociology*, Vol. VII (March, 1956), pp. 18–33.

(ed.) *Studies in the Philosophy of Wittgenstein* (London: Routledge and Kegan Paul, 1969).

"Wittgenstein's Treatment of the Will," *Ratio*, Vol. X (June, 1968), pp. 38–53.

PART 7

Behavioral and Motivational Referents: Religion as Personality Quotient

The final section of the anthology is devoted to studies of the human personality. In every case, religion is approached as a factor in personality development. In some instances, the intention is the isolation of the religious factor; in other instances, a scholar is more interested in the way in which religious factors can be blended with other components of the personality. In some cases, an attempt is made to distinguish the religious personality from those that imply other motivational and attitudinal sets. Then, sometimes, typologies are designed to classify the self-concepts that derive from conscious participation in religious frames of reference. At times, the resources of psychology are drawn upon to track and interpret incidents and patterns of religious behavior. On other occasions, phychological inquiry is pointed toward historical events. But, in every instance, the focus is on the comportment and dimensionality of the human personality.

Once again, the essays included in this section of the anthology are selected to give an indication of the range of interests that belong to this pattern of approach. For example, two of the essays represent the attitudes of the Freudian and Jungian traditions in psychological theory. Erik Erikson represents a modified form of the former position, and C. G. Jung presents his own understanding of some of the ways in which religion and psychology overlap. Although it was written over a decade ago, Erikson's work is already regarded as a classic treatment of the special individual—in this case, Martin Luther—who also qualifies to be called "religious man." Jung's essay contends that archetypes form self-consciousness and religious sensitivity. Two additional essays treat other aspects of the subject. Abraham Maslow illustrates the techniques by which a psychologist can isolate those human experiences that are peculiarly religious. And, the opening selection in the survey consists of a passage from a book, which, in many respects, was the principal factor in inspiring interest in this approach. In that section of his epoch-making *The Varieties of Religious Experience*, William James discusses the differences between "the sick soul" and "healthy-mindedness."

Healthy-Mindedness and World-Sickness

WILLIAM JAMES

William James was born on January 11, 1842, in New York City. His father, Henry James, the elder, was a writer on religious topics and a friend of Thomas Carlyle and Ralph Waldo Emerson; his brother, Henry, was a gifted novelist. William received an intermittent formal education in the United States, England, France, Switzerland, and Germany. In his early years, he vacillated between careers in theology, painting, and medicine. He studied medicine at Harvard, but this was interrupted by an expedition to South America in which James and his party investigated the flora and fauna of Brazil. By this time his interests had shifted to psychology, and he was plagued by illness. Suffering from broken health, James spent 1867–1868 studying psychology in Europe, and despite these obstacles, he received his M.D. degree in 1869. In 1872 he had recovered from illness sufficiently to become an instructor in physiology at Harvard. Four years later he returned to psychology and initiated a revolution by converting that subject into a laboratory science. After publishing his classic textbook, The Principles of Psychology, in 1890, James seems to have lost interest in that field. From there he turned his attention to philosophy, and from 1892 until 1903, his philosophical work focused largely on religious questions. After 1903 he gave much attention to analyses of his own influences upon philosophy; the pragmatism that he championed became a major school in America in the succeeding generation. James died on August 26, 1910, in New Hampshire.

Although James's interests range over a vast sphere of learning, there are certain tendencies and themes that occur repeatedly throughout his works. He was always of an empirical bent, even when doing philosophy. He always recognized the plurality of truth, a position that lies at the heart of the pragmatic philosophy he founded. And, finally, James was always sensitive to the religious dimensions of human experience—whether such experience registers in psychological, physiological, artistic, or philosophical terms.

William James, The Varieties of Religious Experience (New York: Longmans, Green and Company, 1902).

355

The selection that follows is a portion of James' classic, The Varieties of Religious Experience, *originally given as the Gifford Lectures in Edinburgh in 1901–1902. Just as he had divided thinkers into two classes, the "tough-minded" and the "tender-minded," James also categorizes religious believers as "healthy-minded" or "sick-souled." The following excerpt points to the heart of the difference between the two types and speaks about the ways in which both are affected by regeneration or spiritual rebirth.*

The Sick Soul

If we admit that evil is an essential part of our being and the key to the interpretation of our life, we load ourselves down with a difficulty that has always proved burdensome in philosophies of religion. Theism, whenever it has erected itself into a systematic philosophy of the universe, has shown a reluctance to let God be anything less than All-in-All. In other words, philosophic theism has always shown a tendency to become pantheistic and monistic, and to consider the world as one unit of absolute fact; and this has been at variance with popular or practical theism, which latter has ever been more or less frankly pluralistic, not to say polytheistic, and shown itself perfectly well satisfied with a universe composed of many original principles, provided we be only allowed to believe that the divine principle remains supreme, and that the others are subordinate. In this latter case God is not necessarily responsible for the existence of evil; he would only be responsible if it were not finally overcome. But on the monistic or pantheistic view, evil, like everything else, must have its foundation in God; and the difficulty is to see how this can possibly be the case if God be absolutely good. This difficulty faces us in every form of philosophy in which the world appears as one flawless unit of fact. Such a unit is an *Individual,* and in it the worst parts must be as essential as the best, must be as necessary to make the individual what he is; since if any part whatever in an individual were to vanish or alter, it would no longer be *that* individual at all. The philosophy of absolute idealism, so vigorously represented both in Scotland and America to-day, has to struggle with this difficulty quite as much as scholastic theism struggled in its time; and although it would be premature to say that there is no speculative issue whatever from the puzzzle, it is perfectly fair to say that there is no clear or easy issue, and that the only *obvious* escape from paradox here is to cut loose from the monistic assumption altogether, and to allow the world to have existed from its origin in pluralistic form, as an aggregate or collection of higher and lower things and principles, rather than an absolutely unitary fact. For then evil would not need to be essential; it might be, and may always have been, an independent portion that had no rational or absolute right to live with the rest, and which we might conceivably hope to see got rid of at last.

Now the gospel of healthy-mindedness, as we have described it, casts its vote distinctly for this pluralistic view. Whereas the monistic philosopher finds himself more or less bound to say, as Hegel said, that everything actual is rational, and that evil, as an element dialectically required, must be pinned in and kept and consecrated and have a function awarded to it in the final system of truth, healthy-mindedness refuses to say anything of the sort.[1] Evil, it says, is emphatically irrational, and *not* to be pinned in, or preserved, or consecrated in any final system of truth. It is a pure abomination to the Lord, an alien unreality, a waste element, to be sloughed off and negated, and the very memory of it, if possible, wiped out and forgotten. The ideal, so far from being co-extensive with the whole actual, is a mere *extract* from the actual, marked by its deliverance from all contact with this diseased, inferior, and excrementitious stuff.

Here we have the interesting notion fairly and squarely presented to us, of there being elements of the universe which may make no rational whole in conjunction with the other elements, and which, from the point of view of any system which those other elements make up, can only be considered so much irrelevance and accident —so much 'dirt,' as it were, and matter out of place. I ask you now not to forget this notion; for although most philosophers seem either to forget it or to disdain it too much ever to mention it, I believe that we shall have to admit it ourselves in the end as containing an element of truth. The mind-cure gospel thus once more appears to us as having dignity and importance. We have seen it to be a genuine religion, and no mere silly appeal to imagination to cure disease; we have seen its method of experimental verification to be not unlike the method of all science; and now here we find mind-cure as the champion of a perfectly definite conception of the metaphysi-

---

[1] I say this in spite of the monistic utterances of many mind-cure writers; for these utterances are really inconsistent with their attitude towards disease, and can easily be shown not to be logically involved in the experiences of union with a higher Presence with which they connect themselves. The higher Presence, namely, need not be the absolute whole of things, it is quite sufficient for the life of religious experience to regard it as a part, if only it be the most ideal part.

cal structure of the world. I hope that, in view of all this, you will not regret my having pressed it upon your attention at such length.

Let us now say good-by for a while to all this way of thinking, and turn towards those persons who cannot so swiftly throw off the burden of the consciousness of evil, but are congenitally fated to suffer from its presence. Just as we saw that in healthy-mindedness there are shallower and profounder levels, happiness like that of the mere animal, and more regenerate sorts of happiness, so also are there different levels of the morbid mind, and the one is much more formidable than the other. There are people for whom evil means only a mal-adjustment with *things*, a wrong correspondence of one's life with the environment. Such evil as this is curable, in principle at least, upon the natural plane, for merely by modifying either the self or the things, or both at once, the two terms may be made to fit, and all go merry as a marriage bell again. But there are others for whom evil is no mere relation of the subject to particular outer things, but something more radical and general, a wrongness or vice in his essential nature, which no alteration of the environment, or any superficial rearrangement of the inner self, can cure, and which requires a supernatural remedy. On the whole, the Latin races have leaned more towards the former way of looking upon evil, as made up of ills and sins in the plural, removable in detail; while the Germanic races have tended rather to think of Sin in the singular, and with a capital S, as of something ineradicably ingrained in our natural subjectivity, and never to be removed by any superficial piecemeal operations.[2] These comparisons of races are always open to exception, but undoubtedly the northern tone in religion has inclined to the more intimately pessimistic persuasion, and this way of feeling, being the more extreme, we shall find by far the more instructive for our study.

Recent psychology has found great use for the word "threshold" as a symbolic designation for the point at which one state of mind passes into another. Thus we speak of the threshold of a man's consciousness in general, to indicate the amount of noise, pressure, or other outer stimulus which it takes to arouse his attention at all. One with a high threshold will doze through an amount of racket by which one with a low threshold would be immediately waked. Similarly, when one is sensitive to small differences in any order of sensation, we say he has a low "difference-threshold"—his mind easily steps

[2] Cf. J. Milsand, *Luther et le Serf-Arbitre*, 1884, *passim*.

over it into the consciousness of the differences in question. And just so we might speak of a "pain-threshold," a "fear-threshold," a "misery-threshold," and find it quickly overpassed by the consciousness of some individuals, but lying too high in others to be often reached by their consciousness. The sanguine and healthy-minded live habitually on the sunny side of their misery-line, the depressed and melancholy live beyond it, in darkness and apprehension. There are men who seem to have started in life with a bottle or two of champagne inscribed to their credit; whilst others seem to have been born close to the pain-threshold, which the slightest irritants fatally send them over.

Does it not appear as if one who lived more habitually on one side of the pain-threshold might need a different sort of religion from one who habitually lived on the other? This question, of the relativity of different types of religion to different types of need, arises naturally at this point, and will become a serious problem ere we have done. But before we confront it in general terms, we must address ourselves to the unpleasant task of hearing what the sick souls, as we may call them in contrast to the healthy-minded, have to say of the secrets of their prison-house, their own peculiar form of consciousness. Let us then resolutely turn our backs on the once-born and their sky-blue optimistic gospel; let us not simply cry out, in spite of all appearances, "Hurrah for the Universe!—God's in his Heaven, all's right with the world." Let us see rather whether pity, pain, and fear, and the sentiment of human helplessness may not open a profounder view and put into our hands a more complicated key to the meaning of the situation.

To begin with, how *can* things so insecure as the successful experiences of this world afford a stable anchorage? A chain is no stronger than its weakest link, and life is after all a chain. In the healthiest and most prosperous existence, how many links of illness, danger, and disaster are always interposed? Unsuspectedly from the bottom of every fountain of pleasure, as the old poet said, something bitter rises up: a touch of nausea, a falling dead of the delight, a whiff of melancholy, things that sound a knell, for fugitive as they may be, they bring a feeling of coming from a deeper region and often have an appalling convincingness. The buzz of life ceases at their touch as a piano-string stops sounding when the damper falls upon it.

Of course the music can commence again;—and again and again,— at intervals. But with this the healthy-minded consciousness is left with an irremediable sense of precariousness. It is a bell with a crack; it draws its breath on sufferance and by an accident.

Even if we suppose a man so packed with healthy-mindedness as never to have experienced in his own person any of these sobering intervals, still, if he is a reflecting being, he must generalize and class his own lot with that of others; and, doing so, he must see that his escape is just a lucky chance and no essential difference. He might just as well have been born to an entirely different fortune. And then indeed the hollow security! What kind of a frame of things is it of which the best you can say is, "Thank God, it has let me off clear this time!" Is not its blessedness a fragile fiction? Is not your joy in it a very vulgar glee, not much unlike the snicker of any rogue at his success? If indeed it were all success, even on such terms as that! But take the happiest man, the one most envied by the world, and in nine cases out of ten his inmost consciousness is one of failure. Either his ideals in the line of his achievements are pitched far higher than the achievements themselves, or else he has secret ideals of which the world knows nothing, and in regard to which he inwardly knows himself to be found wanting.

When such a conquering optimist as Goethe can express himself in this wise, how must it be with less successful men?

> "I will say nothing," writes Goethe in 1824, "against the course of my existence. But at bottom it has been nothing but pain and burden, and I can affirm that during the whole of my 75 years, I have not had four weeks of genuine well-being. It is but the perpetual rolling of a rock that must be raised up again forever."

What single-handed man was ever on the whole as successful as Luther? yet when he had grown old, he looked back on his life as if it were an absolute failure.

> "I am utterly weary of life. I pray the Lord will come forthwith and carry me hence. Let him come, above all, with his last Judgment: I will stretch out my neck, the thunder will burst forth, and I shall be at rest."—And having a necklace of white agates in his hand at the time he added: "O God, grant that it may come without delay. I would readily eat up this necklace to-day, for the Judgment to come to-morrow."—The Electress Dowager, one day when Luther was dining with her, said to him: "Doctor, I wish you may live forty years to come." "Madam," replied he, "rather than live forty years more, I would give up my chance of Paradise."

Failure, then, failure! so the world stamps us at every turn. We strew it with our blunders, our misdeeds, our lost opportunities, with all the memorials of our inadequacy to our vocation. And with what a damning emphasis does it then blot us out! No easy fine, no mere apology or formal expiation, will satisfy the world's demands, but every pound of flesh exacted is soaked with all its blood. The subtlest forms of suffering known to man are connected with the poisonous humiliations incidental to these results.

And they are pivotal human experiences. A process so ubiquitous and everlasting is evidently an integral part of life. "There is indeed one element in human destiny," Robert Louis Stevenson writes, "that not blindness itself can controvert. Whatever else we are intended to do, we are not intended to succeed; failure is the fate allotted." [3] And our nature being thus rooted in failure, is it any wonder that theologians should have held it to be essential, and thought that only through the personal experience of humiliation which it engenders the deeper sense of life's significance is reached? [4]

But this is only the first stage of the world-sickness. Make the human being's sensitiveness a little greater, carry him a little farther over the misery-threshold, and the good quality of the successful moments themselves when they occur is spoiled and vitiated. All natural goods perish. Riches take wings; fame is a breath; love is a cheat; youth and health and pleasure vanish. Can things whose end is always dust and disappointment be the real goods which our souls require? Back of everything is the great spectre of universal death, the all-encompassing blackness:—

> What profit hath a man of all his labour which he taketh under the Sun? I looked on all the works that my hands had wrought, and behold, all was vanity and vexation of spirit. For that which befalleth the sons of men befalleth beasts; as the one dieth, so dieth the other; all are of the dust, and all turn to dust again. . . . The dead

[3] He adds with characteristic healthy-mindedness: "Our business is to continue to fail in good spirits."

[4] The God of many men is little more than their court of appeal against the damnatory judgment passed on their failures by the opinion of this world. To our own consciousness there is usually a residuum of worth left over after our sins and errors have been told off—our capacity of acknowledging and regretting them is the germ of a better self *in posse* at least. But the world deals with us *in actu* and not *in posse*: and of this hidden germ, not to be guessed at from without, it never takes account. Then we turn to the All-knower, who knows our bad, but knows this good in us also, and who is just. We cast ourselves with our repentance on his mercy: only by an All-knower can we finally be judged. So the need of a God very definitely emerges from this sort of experience of life.

know not anything, neither have they any more a reward; for the memory of them is forgotten. Also their love and their hatred and their envy is now perished; neither have they any more a portion for ever in anything that is done under the Sun. . . . Truly the light is sweet, and a pleasant thing it is for the eyes to behold the Sun: but if a man live many years and rejoice in them all, yet let him remember the days of darkness; for they shall be many.

In short, life and its negation are beaten up inextricably together. But if the life be good, the negation of it must be bad. Yet the two are equally essential facts of existence; and all natural happiness thus seems infected with a contradiction. The breath of the sepulchre surrounds it.

To a mind attentive to this state of things and rightly subject to the joy-destroying chill which such a contemplation engenders, the only relief that healthy-mindedness can give is by saying: 'Stuff and nonsense, get out into the open air!' or 'Cheer up, old fellow, you'll be all right erelong, if you will only drop your morbidness!' But in all seriousness, can such bald animal talk as that be treated as a rational answer? To ascribe religious value to mere happy-go-lucky contentment with one's brief chance at natural good is but the very consecration of forgetfulness and superficiality. Our troubles lie indeed too deep for *that* cure. The fact that we *can* die, that we *can* be ill at all, is what perplexes us; the fact that we now for a moment live and are well is irrelevant to that perplexity. We need a life not correlated with death, a health not liable to illness, a kind of good that will not perish, a good in fact that flies beyond the Goods of nature.

It all depends on how sensitive the soul may become to discords. "The trouble with me is that I believe too much in common happiness and goodness," said a friend of mine whose consciousness was of this sort, "and nothing can console me for their transiency. I am appalled and disconcerted at its being possible." And so with most of us: a little cooling down of animal excitability and instinct, a little loss of animal toughness, a little irritable weakness and descent of the pain-threshold, will bring the worm at the core of all our usual springs of delight into full view, and turn us into melancholy metaphysicians. The pride of life and glory of the world will shrivel. It is after all but the standing quarrel of hot youth and hoary old. Old age has the last word: the purely naturalistic look at life, however enthusiastically it may begin, is sure to end in sadness.

This sadness lies at the heart of every merely positivistic, agnostic, or naturalistic scheme of philosophy. Let sanguine healthy-mindedness do its best with its strange power of living in the moment and ignoring and forgetting, still the evil background is really there to be thought of, and the skull will grin in at the banquet. In the practical life of the individual, we know how his whole gloom or glee about any present fact depends on the remoter schemes and hopes with which it stands related. Its significance and framing give it the chief part of its value. Let it be known to lead nowhere, and however agreeable it may be in its immediacy, its glow and gilding vanish. The old man, sick with an insidious internal disease, may laugh and quaff his wine at first as well as ever, but he knows his fate now, for the doctors have revealed it; and the knowledge knocks the satisfaction out of all these functions. They are partners of death and the worm is their brother, and they turn to a mere flatness.

The lustre of the present hour is always borrowed from the background of possibilities it goes with. Let our common experiences be enveloped in an eternal moral order; let our suffering have an immortal significance; let Heaven smile upon the earth, and deities pay their visits; let faith and hope be the atmosphere which man breathes in;—and his days pass by with zest; they stir with prospects, they thrill with remoter values. Place round them on the contrary the curdling cold and gloom and absence of all permanent meaning which for pure naturalism and the popular science evolutionism of our time are all that is visible ultimately, and the thrill stops short, or turns rather to an anxious trembling.

For naturalism, fed on recent cosmological speculations, mankind is in a position similar to that of a set of people living on a frozen lake, surrounded by cliffs over which there is no escape, yet knowing that little by little the ice is melting, and the inevitable day drawing near when the last film of it will disappear, and to be drowned ignominiously will be the human creature's portion. The merrier the skating, the warmer and more sparkling the sun by day, and the ruddier the bonfires at night, the more poignant the sadness with which one must take in the meaning of the total situation.

The early Greeks are continually held up to us in literary works as models of the healthy-minded joyousness which the religion of nature may engender. There was indeed much joyousness among the Greeks—Homer's flow of enthusiasm for most things that the sun shines upon is steady. But even in Homer the reflective passages are cheerless,[5] and the moment the Greeks grew systematically pensive and thought of ultimates, they became unmitigated pessimists.[6] The jealousy of the gods, the nemesis that follows too much happiness, the all-encompassing death, fate's dark opacity, the ultimate and unintelligible cruelty, were the fixed background of their imagination. The beautiful joyousness of their polytheism is only a poetic modern fiction. They knew no joys comparable in quality of preciousness to those which we shall erelong see that Brahmans, Buddhists, Christians, Mohammedans, twice-born people whose religion is nonnaturalistic, get from their several creeds of mysticism and renunciation.

Selected Bibliography

Essays in Radical Empiricism and a Pluralistic World (New York: Hafner Publishing Company, Inc., 1960).

Essays on Faith and Morals (New York: Longmans Green and Company, 1949).

The Meaning of Truth (Ann Arbor: University of Michigan Press, 1955).

Pragmatism and Other Essays (New York: Meridian Books, 1935).

Principles of Psychology (New York: Dover Publications, Inc., 1962).

Psychology: The Briefer Course (New York: Harper and Row, Publishers, Inc., 1961).

The Varieties of Religious Experience (New York: The New American Library, Inc., 1936).

The Will to Believe (New York: Dover Publications, Inc., 1960).

Talks to Teachers on Psychology and to Students on Some of Life's Ideals (New York: W. W. Norton & Company, Inc., 1939).

[5] E.g., Iliad, XVII. 446: "Nothing then is more wretched anywhere than man of all that breathes and creeps upon this earth."

[6] E.g., Theognis, 425–428: "Best of all for all things upon earth is it not to be born nor to behold the splendors of the Sun; next best to traverse as soon as possible the gates of Hades." See also the almost identical passage in Œdipus in Colonus, 1225.—The Anthology is full of pessimistic utterances: "Naked came I upon the earth, naked I go below the ground—why then do I vainly toil when I see the end naked before me?"—"How did I come to be? Whence am I? Wherefore did I come? To pass away. How can I learn aught when naught I know? Being naught I came to life: once more shall I be what I was. Nothing and nothingness is the whole race of mortals."—"For death we are all cherished and fattened like a herd of hogs that is wantonly butchered."

The Unconscious Mind

CARL G. JUNG

Carl G. Jung was born on July 26, 1875, in Kessuil, Switzerland. His mother was a philologist, and his father, a pastor. His paternal grandfather, raised a Catholic, was converted to Protestantism by Friedrich Schleiermacher in 1813. In addition to the family's strong religious concern, it was also involved in the medical profession. Jung's paternal grandfather founded the first mental hospital in the city of Basel.

Jung studied medicine at the University of Basel, and then concentrated in studies in psychology in Paris under Pierre Janet. From 1900 to 1909 he was a physician in the psychiatric clinic of the University of Zürich, and from 1905 to 1913 was also a lecturer in psychiatry. In 1907 Jung began his association with Sigmund Freud, with whom he broke in 1913, the same year in which Jung engrossed himself in the study of religious myth and symbolism. The next period of his life was one of self-imposed personal and professional exile. After 1921 Jung traveled extensively to the American Indian reservations in Arizona and New Mexico in 1924, to Kenya in 1925, and to Egypt in 1926.

These travels marked the beginning of his professional shift from psychology to cultural analysis. While he continued to be recognized for his contributions to personality theory and psychotherapy, Jung's most enduring contribution has been his investigation of the myths and symbols of both Eastern and Western cultures. In the course of his travels he became increasingly convinced of the spiritual poverty of modern Western man. He discovered that the Pueblo Indian possessed a dignity and tranquil composure missing in modern Western man. He observed that the African, while possessing the same demonic, violent urges as modern Western man, was able to control these urges through his rituals. Jung concluded that Western man had lost the mythical and symbolic means of containing evil. His travels confirmed his impressions based on his analysis of dreams: man in the modern Western world had become disoriented because he had been cut off from his symbolic roots.

Carl Gustav Jung, *Psychology and Religion* (New Haven: Yale University Press, 1938), pp. 1–8, 1423. Reprinted by permission.

In the following essay, Jung discusses the attitude toward religion that has developed from his vocation as a psychologist, psychoanalyst, and comparative cultural analyst.

Notwithstanding the fact that I have often been called a philosopher, I am an empiricist and adhere to the phenomenological standpoint. I trust that it does not collide with the principles of scientific empiricism if one occasionally makes certain reflections which go beyond a mere accumulation and classification of experience. As a matter of fact I believe that an experience is not even possible without reflection, because "experience" is a process of assimilation, without which there could be no understanding. As this statement indicates, I approach psychological matters from a scientific and not from a philosophical standpoint. In as much as religion has a very important psychological aspect, I am dealing with it from a purely empirical point of view, that is, I restrict myself to the observation of phenomena and I refrain from any application of metaphysical or philosophical considerations. I do not deny the validity of other considerations, but I cannot claim to be competent to apply them correctly. I am aware that most people believe they know all there is to be known about psychology, because they think that psychology is nothing but what they know of themselves. But I am afraid psychology is a good deal more than that. While having little to do with philosophy, it has much to do with empirical facts, many of which are not easily accessible to the average experience. It is my intention in this book to give a few glimpses, at least, of the way in which practical psychology becomes confronted with the problem of religion. It is self-evident that the vastness of the problem requires far more than three lectures, as the necessary demonstration of concrete detail needs a great deal of time as well as of explanation. My first chapter will be a sort of introduction to the problem of practical psychology and religion. The second is concerned with facts which bear out the existence of an authentic religious function in the unconscious mind. The third deals with religious symbolism by unconscious processes.

Since I am going to present a rather unusual argument, I cannot assume that my audience is completely aware of the methodological standpoint of that kind of psychology which I represent. This standpoint is exclusively phenomenological, that is, it is concerned with occurrences, events, experiences, in a word, with facts. Its truth is a fact and not a judgment. Speaking for instance of the motive of the virgin birth, psychology is only concerned with the fact that there is such an idea, but it is not concerned with the question whether such an idea is true or false in any other sense. It is psychologically true in as much as it exists. Psychological existence is subjective in so far as an idea occurs in only one individual. But it is objective in so far as it is established by a society—by a consensus gentium.

This point of view is the same as that of natural science. Psychology deals with ideas and other mental contents as zoology for instance deals with different species of animals. An elephant is true because it exists. The elephant, moreover, is neither a conclusion nor a statement nor a subjective judgment of a creator. It is a phenomenon. But we are so used to the idea that psychical events are wilful and arbitrary products, even inventions of the human creator, that we can hardly liberate ourselves from the prejudiced view that the psyche and its contents are nothing but our own arbitrary invention or the more or less illusory product of assumption and judgment. The fact is that certain ideas exist almost everywhere and at all times and they can even spontaneously create themselves quite apart from migration and tradition. They are not made by the individual, but they rather happen—they even force themselves upon the individual's consciousness. This is not platonic philosophy but empirical psychology.

In speaking of religion I must make clear from the start what I mean by that term. Religion, as the Latin word denotes, is a careful and scrupulous observation of what Rudolf Otto aptly termed the "numinosum," that is, a dynamic existence or effect, not caused by an arbitrary act of will. On the contrary, it seizes and controls the human subject, which is always rather its victim than its creator. The numinosum is an involuntary condition of the subject, whatever its cause may be. At all events, religious teaching as well as the consensus gentium always and everywhere explains this condition as being due to a cause external to the individual. The numinosum is either a quality of a visible object or the influence of an invisible presence causing a peculiar alteration of consciousness. This is, at least, the general rule.

There are, however, certain exceptions when it comes to the question of practice or ritual. A great many ritualistic performances are carried out for the sole purpose of producing at will the effect of the numinosum by certain devices of a magic nature, such as invocation, incantation, sacrifice, meditation and other yoga practices, self-inflicted tortures of various descriptions and so forth. But a religious belief in an external and objective divine cause always precedes any such performance. The Catholic church, for instance, administers the sacraments with the purpose of bestowing their spiritual blessings upon the believer; but since this act would amount to enforcing the presence of divine grace by an indubitably magic procedure, it is logically argued that nobody is able to compel divine grace to be present in the sacramental act, but that it is nevertheless inevitably present, the sacrament being a divine institution which God would not have caused to be if he had not had it in mind to support it.

Religion appears to me to be a peculiar attitude of the human mind, which could be formulated in accordance with the original use of the term "religio," that is, a careful consideration and observation of certain dynamic factors, understood to be "powers," spirits, demons, gods, laws, ideas, ideals or whatever name man has given to such factors as he has found in his world powerful, dangerous or helpful enough to be taken into careful consideration, or grand, beautiful and meaningful enough to be devoutly adored and loved. In colloquial language one often says of somebody who is enthusiastically interested in a certain pursuit, that he is almost "religiously devoted" to his cause; William James, for instance, remarks that a scientist often has no creed, but "his temper is devout."

I want to make clear that by the term "religion" I do not mean a creed. It is, however, true that on the one hand every confession is originally based upon the experience of the numinosum and on the other hand upon *Pistis*, the loyalty, trust, and confidence toward a definitely experienced numinous effect and the subsequent alteration of consciousness: the conversion of Paul is a striking example of this. "Religion," it might be said, is the term that designates the attitude peculiar to a consciousness which has been altered by the experience of the numinosum.

Creeds are codified and dogmatized forms of original religious experience. The contents of the experience have become sanctified and usually congealed in a rigid, often elaborate, structure. The practice and the reproduction of the original experience have become a ritual and an unchangeable institution. This does not necessarily mean a lifeless petrification. On the contrary it can become the form of religious experience for ages of time and for millions of people without there being any vital necessity for alterations. Although the Catholic church has often been blamed for a particular rigidity, it admits nevertheless that the dogma has its life and hence is capable of undergoing change and development. Even the number of dogmas is unlimited and can be augmented in the course of time. The same holds true of the ritual. Yet all changes and developments are confined within the frame of the originally experienced facts, thereby involving a particular kind of dogmatic content and emotional value. Even Protestantism—which has surrendered apparently to an almost unlimited liberation from dogmatic tradition and from codified ritual and has thus split into more than four hundred denominations— even Protestantism is bound at least to be Christian and to express itself within the frame of the conviction that God has revealed himself in Christ, who suffered for mankind. This is a definite frame, with definite contents, which cannot be coupled with or amplified by Buddhistic or Islamic ideas and emotions. Yet it is unquestionable that not only Buddha or Mohammed or Confucius or Zarathustra represents religious phenomena, but that Mithras, Attis, Kybele, Mani, Hermes and many exotic cults do so as well. The psychologist, in as much as he assumes a scientific attitude, has to disregard the claim of every creed to be the unique and eternal truth. He must keep his eye on the human side of the religious problem, in that he is concerned with the original religious experience quite apart from what the creeds have made of it.

Being a doctor and a specialist in nervous and mental diseases my point of departure is not any creed, but the psychology of the *homo religiosus*, the man who takes into account and carefully observes certain factors which influence him and, through him, his general condition. It is easy to denominate and define those factors according to historical tradition or anthropological knowledge, but to do the same thing from the standpoint of psychology is an uncommonly difficult task. What I can contribute to the question of religion is derived entirely from my practical experience, both with my patients and with so-called normal beings. . . . In most people there is a sort of primitive *deisidaimonia* [1] concerning the possible contents of the unconscious. Beyond all natural shyness, shame and tact, there is a secret fear of the unknown "perils of the soul." Of course one is reluctant to admit such a ridiculous fear. But one should realize that this fear is by no means unjustifiable; on the contrary, it is only too well founded. We are never sure that a new idea will not seize either upon ourselves or upon our neighbors. We know from modern as well as from ancient history that such ideas can be

[1] Meaning "fear," a "reverence for divinity."

rather strange, so peculiar, indeed, that not everybody can agree with them. The result may be that all dissenters, no matter how well meaning or reasonable they are, get burnt alive or have their heads cut off or are disposed of in masses by the more modern machine gun. We cannot even calm ourselves with the idea that such things belong to a remote past. Unfortunately they seem to belong not only to the present moment, but, quite particularly, to the future. "Homo homini lupus" is a sad, yet eternal truism. There is indeed reason enough why man should be afraid of those nonpersonal forces dwelling in the unconscious mind. We are blissfully unconscious of those forces because they never, or almost never, appear in our personal dealings and under ordinary circumstances. But if, on the other hand, people crowd together and form a mob, then the dynamics of the collective man are set free—beasts or demons which lie dormant in every person till he is part of a mob. Man in the crowd is unconsciously lowered to an inferior moral and intellectual level, to that level which is always there, below the threshold of consciousness, ready to break forth as soon as it is stimulated through the formation of a crowd.

It is, to my mind, a fatal mistake to consider the human psyche as a merely personal affair and to explain it exclusively from a personal point of view. Such a mode of explanation is only applicable to the individual in his ordinary everyday occupations and relationships. If, however, some slight trouble occurs, perhaps in the form of an unforeseen and somewhat extraordinary event, instantly instinctive forces are called up, forces which appear to be wholly unexpected, new, and even strange. They can no longer be explained by personal motives, being comparable rather to certain primitive occurrences like panics at solar eclipses and such things. To explain the murderous outburst of Bolshevistic ideas by a personal father complex appears to me as singularly inadequate.

The change of character that is brought about by the uprush of collective forces is amazing. A gentle and reasonable being can be transformed into a maniac or a savage beast. One is always inclined to lay the blame on external circumstances, but nothing could explode in us if it had not been there. As a matter of fact, we are always living upon a volcano and there is, as far as we know, no human means of protection against a possible outburst which will destroy everybody within its reach. It is certainly a good thing to preach reason and common sense, but what if your audience is a lunatic asylum or a crowd in a collective seizure? There is not much difference either, because the madman as well as the mob is moved by nonpersonal, overwhelming forces.

As a matter of fact, it needs as little as a neurosis to conjure up a force that cannot be dealt with by reasonable means. Our cancer case shows clearly how impotent human reason and intellect are against the most palpable nonsense. I always advise my patients to take such obvious but invincible nonsense as the manifestation of a power and a meaning not yet understood. Experience has taught me that it is a much more effective method of procedure to take such a fact seriously and to seek for a suitable explanation. But an explanation is suitable only when it produces a hypothesis equal to the morbid effect. Our case is confronted with a will power and a suggestion more than equal to anything his consciousness can put against it. In this precarious situation it would be bad strategy to convince the patient that he is somehow, though in a highly incomprehensible way, at the back of his own symptom, secretly inventing and supporting it. Such a suggestion would instantly paralyze his fighting spirit, and he would get demoralized. It is much better if he understands that his complex is an autonomous power directed against his conscious personality. Moreover, such an explanation fits the actual facts much better than a reduction to personal motives. An apparent personal motivation does exist, but it is not made by intention, it just happens to the patient.

When in the Babylonian Epos Gilgamesh's arrogance and *hybris* defy the gods, they invent and create a man equal in strength to Gilgamesh in order to check the hero's unlawful ambition. The very same thing has happened to our patient: he is a thinker who has settled, or is always going to settle, the world by the power of his intellect and reason. His ambition has at least suceeded in carving his own personal fate. He has forced everything under the inexorable law of his reason, but somewhere nature escaped and came back with a vengeance in the form of perfectly unassailable nonsense, the cancer idea. This clever device was formed by the unconscious mind to keep him on a merciless and cruel leash. It was the worst blow which could be given to all his reasonable ideals and above all to his belief in the all-powerful human will. Such an obsession can only occur in a person who makes a habitual misuse of reason and intellect for an egotistical power purpose.

Gilgamesh, however, escaped the revenge of the gods. He had warning dreams to which he paid attention. They showed him how he could overcome his foe. Our patient, living in an age where the gods have become extinct and are even in bad repute, also had such dreams, but he did not listen to them. How could an intelligent man be so superstitious as to take dreams seriously! The very common prejudice against dreams is but one of the symptoms of a far more serious undervaluation of the human soul in general. The marvelous development of science and technics has been counterbalanced on the other side by an appalling lack of wisdom and introspection. It is true that our religious teaching speaks of an immortal soul; but it has very few kind words for the actual human psyche, which would go straight to eternal damnation if it were not for a special act of Divine Grace. Those two important factors are largely responsible for the general undervaluation of the psyche, but not entirely. Much older than those relatively recent developments are the primitive fear of and aversion to everything that borders on the unconscious.

Consciousness must have been a very precarious thing in its beginnings. In relatively primitive societies we can still observe how easily consciousness is lost. One of the "perils of the soul" is, for instance, the loss of a soul. This is a case of a part of the psyche becoming unconscious again. Another example is the amok condition, the equivalent of the berserk condition in the Germanic saga. This is a more or less complete trance, often accompanied by devastating social effects. Even an ordinary emotion can cause a considerable loss of consciousness. Primitives therefore cherish elaborate forms of politeness, speaking with a hushed voice, laying down their weapons, crouching, bowing the head, showing the palms. Even our own forms of politeness still show a "religious" observation of possible psychical dangers. We propitiate the fates by wishing magically a good day. It is not good form to keep the left hand in your pocket or behind your back when shaking hands. If you want to be particularly propitiating you use both hands. Before people of great authority we bow with uncovered head, i.e., we offer our head unprotected, in order to propitiate the powerful one, who might quite easily fall suddenly a prey to a fit of uncontrollable violence. In war dances primitives can become so excited that they may shed blood.

The life of the primitive is filled with constant regard for the ever-lurking possibility of psychical dangers, and the attempts and procedures employed to diminish the risks are very numerous. The creation of tabooed areas is an external evidence of this fact. The innumerable taboos are delimited psychical areas, meticulously and fearfully observed. I made a terrific mistake once when I was with a tribe on the southern slopes of Mt. Elgon. I wanted to inquire about the ghost houses I frequently found in the woods and during a palaver I mentioned the word "seleteni" meaning "ghost." Instantly everybody was silent and painfully embarrassed. They all looked away from me because I had spoken aloud a carefully hushed-up word, and had thus invited most dangerous consequences. I had to change the subject in order to be able to continue the meeting. The same men assured me that they never had dreams; they were the prerogative of the chief and of the medicine man. The medicine man then confessed to me that he no longer had any dreams, for they had the District Commissioner now instead. "Since the English are in the country we have no dreams any more," he said. "The District Commissioner knows everything about war and diseases, and about where we have got to live." This strange statement is based upon the fact that dreams were formerly the supreme political guide, the voice of "mungu." Therefore it would have been unwise for an ordinary man to suggest that he had dreams.

Dreams are the voice of the Unknown, that ever threatens with new schemes, new dangers, sacrifices, warfare and other troublesome things. An African negro once dreamt that his enemies had taken him prisoner and burnt him alive. The next day he called his relatives together and implored them to burn him. They consented to do so to the extent that they bound his feet together and put them in the fire. He was of course badly crippled but had escaped his foes.

There are any amount of creeds and ceremonies that exist for the sole purpose of forming a defense against the unexpected, dangerous tendencies of the unconscious. The peculiar fact that the dream is the divine voice and messenger and yet an unending source of trouble, does not disturb the primitive mind. We still find obvious remnants of this primitive fact in the psychology of the Jewish prophets. Often enough they hesitate to listen to the voice. And it was, we must admit, rather hard on a pious man like Hosea to marry the prostitute in order to obey the Lord's command. Since the dawn of mankind there has been a marked tendency to delimit the unruly and arbitrary "supernatural" influence by definite forms and laws. And this process has gone on in history by the multiplication of rites, institutions and creeds. In the last two thousand years we find the institution of the Christian church assuming a mediating and protective function between these influences and man. It is not denied in medieval ecclesiastical writings that a divine influx could take place in dreams, for instance, but this view is not exactly encouraged and the church reserves the right to decide whether a revelation is to be considered authentic or not. In spite of the fact that the church recognizes the undeniable emanation of certain dreams from God, it is disinclined, even positively averse, to any serious occupation with dreams, while admitting that some might contain an immediate revelation. Thus the change in mental attitudes which has taken place in recent centuries is, from this point of view at least, not wholly unwelcome to the church, because it has effectively discouraged the former introspective attitude which was favorable to a serious consideration of dreams and inner experiences.

Protestantism, having pulled down many a wall which had been carefully erected by the church, began immediately to experience the disintegrating and schismatic effect of individual revelation. As soon as the dogmatic fence was broken down and as soon as the ritual had lost the authority of its efficiency, man was confronted with an inner experience, without the protection and the guidance of a dogma and a ritual which are the unparalleled quintessence of Christian as well as of pagan religious experience. Protestantism has, in the main, lost all the finer shades of the dogma: the mass, the confession, the greater part of the liturgy and the sacrificial importance of priesthood.

I must emphasize the point that this statement is not a judgment of values and has no intention of being one. I merely state the facts. Protestantism has, however, intensified the authority of the Bible as a substitute for the lost authority of the church. But as history has shown, one can interpret certain biblical texts in many ways. Nor has the scientific criticism of the New Testament been very helpful in enhancing the divine character of the holy writings. It is also a fact that under the influence of a so-called scientific enlightenment great masses of educated people have either left the church or have become profoundly indifferent to it. If they were all dull rationalists or neurotic intellectuals the loss would not be regrettable. But many of them are religious people, only incapable of agreeing with the actually existing forms of creed. If this were not so, one could hardly explain the remarkable effect of the Buchman movement on the more or less educated Protestant classes. The Catholic who has turned his back on the church usually develops a secret or manifest inclination toward atheism, whereas the Protestant follows, if possible, a sectarian movement. The absolutism of the Catholic church seems to demand an equally absolute negation, while Protestant relativism permits variations.

Selected Bibliography

Answer to Job (New York: Meridian Books, 1954).

The Collected Works of Carl G. Jung, 15 vols. (New York: Pantheon Books, Inc., 1953–1967).

Essays on the Science of Mythology (New York: Harper and Row, Publishers, Inc., 1963).

The Integration of the Personality (London: Routledge and Kegan Paul, Ltd., 1940).

Man and His Symbols (New York: Doubleday & Co., Inc., 1964).

Memories, Dreams, Reflections (New York: Pantheon Books, Inc., 1963).

The Tibetan Book of the Great Liberation (New York: Oxford University Press, 1954).

The Undiscovered Self (Boston: Little, Brown & Company, Inc., 1958). `

Homo Religiosus as Cultural Worker

Erik Erikson

One of the leading psychoanalysts in the world, Erik H. Erikson was born in Frankfurt, Germany, on June 15, 1902. He graduated from the Vienna Psychological Institute in 1933, and moved to the United States in that same year. Since that time Erikson has both practiced and taught psychoanalysis in this country. Since 1960 he has been Professor of Human Development and Lecturer on Psychology at Harvard. Throughout his life Erikson has been interested in correlating the development of personality with the stages in the human life cycle.

The selection that follows is a portion of Erikson's book Young Man Luther. *From his clinical work with gifted but disturbed young people, Erikson turned to a study of Martin Luther as a paradigmatic instance of "religious genius." Similarly, he has subsequently examined and interpreted the life of Gandhi (in Gandhi's Truth). In treating the development of the personalities of such religious figures, Erikson is interested in pointing to the ways in which their quests for self-identity bear a wider cultural function. He conceives of such men as "cultural workers," men in whom ego and ethos are linked together. In such men, individual aspiration and societal striving are comprehended under the same constructive energy. Thus, the paradigmatic significance of such figures as Luther and Gandhi enable Erikson to design his "psycho-history" with religious subjects in mind.*

The literature on Luther, and by Luther, is stupendous in volume. Yet it adds up to very few reliable data on his childhood and youth. His role in history, and above all his personality, remain ambiguous on a grandiose scale. Luther has been both vilified and sanctified, and both by sincere and proven scholars, who have spent a good portion, if not all, of their lifetimes reconstructing him from the raw data—only to create, whenever they tried to encompass him with a formula, a superhuman or a suprahuman robot, a man who could never have breathed or moved or least of all spoken as Luther spoke. In writing this book, did I intend to do better?

Søren Kierkegaard—the one man who could judge Luther with the compassionate objectivity of a kindred *homo religiosus*—once made a remark which sums up the problem which I felt I could approach with the means at my disposal. He wrote in his diary: "Luther . . . is a patient of exceeding import for Christendom" (*en for Christenheden yderst vigtig Patient*). In quoting this statement out of context, I do not mean to imply that Kierkegaard intended to call Luther a patient in the sense of a clinical "case"; rather, he saw in him a religious attitude (patienthood) exemplified in an archetypal and immensely influential way. In taking this statement as a kind of motto for this book, we do not narrow our perspective to the clinical; we expand our clinical perspective to include a life style of patienthood as a sense of imposed suffering, of an intense need for cure, and (as Kierkegaard adds) a "passion for expressing and describing one's suffering."

Kierkegaard's point was that Luther overdid this subjective, this "patient," side of life, and in his old age failed to reach "a doctor's commanding view" (*Laegen's Overskuelse*). The last question we must leave open for the present.

"A patient". . . . I expected to have access to this wider meaning of patienthood from my work with gifted but acutely disturbed young people. I did not wish merely to reduce young Luther to his diagnosis (which, within limits, could be done rather convincingly); I wished to delineate in his life (as I had done in the lives of young contemporaries) one of those life crises which make conscious or unconscious, diagnosed or unofficial, patients out of people until they find a cure—and this often means a cause.

I have called the major crisis of adolescence the *identity crisis*; it occurs in that period of the life cycle when each youth must forge for himself some central perspective and direction, some working unity, out of the effective remnants of his childhood and the hopes of his anticipated adulthood; he must detect some meaningful resemblance between what he has come to see in himself and what his sharpened awareness tells him others judge and expect him to be. This sounds dangerously like common sense; like all health, however, it is a matter of course only to those who possess it, and appears as a most complex achievement to those who have tasted its absence. Only in ill health does one realize the intricacy of the body; and only in a crisis, individual or historical, does it become obvious what a sensitive combination of interrelated factors the human personality is—a combination of capacities created in the distant past and of opportunities divined in the present; a combination of totally unconscious preconditions developed in individual growth and of social conditions created and recreated in the precarious interplay of generations. In some young people, in some classes, at some periods in history, this crisis will be minimal; in other people, classes, and periods, the crisis will be clearly marked off as a critical period, a kind of "second birth," apt to be aggravated either by widespread neuroticisms or by pervasive ideological unrest. Some young individuals will succumb to this crisis in all manner of neurotic, psychotic, or delinquent behavior; others will resolve it through participation in ideological movements passionately concerned with religion or politics, nature or art. Still others, although suffering and deviating dangerously through what appears to be a prolonged adolescence, eventually come to contribute an original bit to an emerging style of life: the very danger which they have sensed has forced them to mobilize capacities to see and say, to dream and plan, to design and construct, in new ways.

Luther, so it seems, at one time was a rather endangered young man, beset with a syndrome of conflicts whose outline we have learned to recognize, and whose components to analyse. He found a spiritual solution, not without the well-timed help of a therapeutically clever superior in the Augustinian order. His solution roughly bridged a political and psychological vacuum which history had created in a significant portion of Western Christendom. Such coincidence, if further coinciding with the deployment of highly specific personal gifts, makes for historical "greatness." We will follow Luther through the crisis of his youth, and the unfolding of his gifts, to the first manifestation of his originality as a thinker, namely, to the emergence of a new theology, apparently not immediately perceived as a radical innovation either by him or his listeners, in his first Lectures on the Psalms (1513). What happened to him after he had acquired a historical identity is more than another chapter; for even half of the man is too much for one book. The difference between the young and the old Luther is so marked, and the second, the sturdy orator, so exclusive a Luther-image to most readers, that I will speak of "Martin" when I report on Luther's early years, which according to common usage in the Luther literature include his twenties; and of "Luther" where and when he has become the leader of Lutherans, seduced by history into looking back on his past as upon a mythological autobiography.

Kierkegaard's remark has a second part: ". . . of very great import for Christendom." This calls for an investigation of how the individual "case" became an important, an historic "event," and for formulations concerning the spiritual and political identity crisis of Northern Christendom in Luther's time. True, I could have avoided those methodological uncertainties and impurities which will undoubtedly occur by sticking to my accustomed job of writing a case history, and leaving the historical event to those who, in turn, would consider the case a mere accessory to the event. But we clinicians have learned in recent years that we cannot lift a case history out of history, even as we suspect that historians, when they try to separate the logic of the historic event from that of the life histories which intersect in it, leave a number of vital historical problems unattended. So we may have to risk that bit of impurity which is inherent in the hyphen of the psycho-historical as well as of all other hyphenated approaches. They are the compost heap of today's interdisciplinary efforts, which may help to fertilize new fields, and to produce future flowers of new methodological clarity.

Human nature can best be studied in the state of conflict; and human conflict comes to the detailed attention of interested recorders mainly under special circumstances. One such circumstance is the clinical encounter, in which the suffering, for the sake of securing help, have no other choice than to become case histories; and another special circumstance is history, where extraordinary beings, by their own self-centered maneuvers and through the prodding of the charismatic hunger of mankind, become (auto)biographies. Clinical as well as historical scholars have much to learn by going back and forth between these two kinds of recorded history. Luther, always instructive, forces on the workers in both fields a special awareness. He indulged himself as he grew older in florid self-revelations of a kind which can make a clinical biographer feel that he is dealing with a client. If the clinician should indulge himself in this feeling, however, he will soon find out that the imaginary client has been dealing with him: for Luther is one of those autobiographers with a histrionic flair who can make enthusiastic use even of their neurotic suffering, matching selected memories with the clues given to them by their avid public to create their own official identities.

I intend to take my subtitle seriously. This "Study in Psychoanalysis and History" will re-evaluate a segment of history (here the youth of a great reformer) by using psychoanalysis as a historical tool; but it will also, here and there, throw light on psychoanalysis as a tool of history. At this point I must digress for a few pages from the subject of my main title in order to attend to the methodological subtitle.

Psychoanalysis, like alll systems, has its own inner history of development. As a method of observation it takes history; as a system of ideas it makes history.

I indicated in the preface that whenever a psychoanalyst shifts the focus of his interest to a new class of patients—be they of the same age, of similar background, or the victims of the same clinical syndrome—he is forced not only to modify his therapeutic technique, but also to explain the theoretical rationale of his modification. Thus, from a gradual refinement of therapeutic technique, the perfection of a theory of the mind is expected to result. This is the historical idea psychoanalysis lives by.

The treatment of young patients who are neither children, adolescents, nor adults is characterized by a specific exaggeration of trends met with in all therapies. Young patients (as well as extraordinary young people) make rather total demands on themselves and on their environment. They insist on daily confirming themselves and on being confirmed either in their meaningful future or in their senseless past; in some absolute virtue or in a radical state of vice; in the growth of their uniqueness or in abysmal self-loss. Young people in severe trouble are not fit for the couch: they want to face you, and they want you to face them, not as a facsimile of a parent, or wearing the mask of a professional helper, but as the kind of over-all individual a young person can live by or will despair of. When suddenly confronted with such a conflicted young person the psychoanalyst may learn for the first time what facing a face, rather than facing a problem, really means—and I daresay, Dr. Staupitz, Martin's spiritual mentor, would know what I have in mind.

In the treatment of young people, furthermore, it is impossible to ignore what they are busy doing or not doing in their work life or in their unofficial avocations. Probably the most neglected problem in psychoanalysis is the problem of work, in theory as well as in practice: as if the dialectic of the history of ideas had ordered a system of psychological thought which would as resolutely ignore the way in which the individual and his group make a living as Marxism ignores introspective psychology and makes a man's economic position the fulcrum of his acts and thoughts. Decades of case histories have omitted the work histories of the patients or have treated their occupation as a seemingly irrelevant area of life in which data could be disguised with the greatest impunity. Yet, therapeutic experiments with the work life of hospitalized young patients indicate that patients in a climate of self-help, of planful work, and of communal association can display an adaptive resourcefulness which seemed absent only because our theories and beliefs decreed that it be absent.

This is part of the wider problem, now being discussed in a large part of the psychiatric and sociological literature, of how much psychiatry has tended to make patienthood a self-defining, self-limiting role prison, within which the development of the patient's stunted capacities is as clearly prevented, by the mere absence of systematic stimulation and opportunity, as if it were professly forbidden.

Such discoveries make it obvious that clinical methods are subject to a refinement of technique and a clarification of theory only to a point; beyond this point they are subject to ideological influences. The emergence in different countries and cities of intensely divergent schools of clinical thought corroborates the idea that an evolving clinical science of the mind is colored and often darkened by ideological trends even as it inadvertently influences the intellectual and literary climate, if and when and where history makes use of it. Maybe, then, a clinical science of the human mind will eventually demand a special historical self-awareness on the part of the clinical worker and scholar. As the historian Collingwood put it: "History is the life of mind itself which is not mind except so far as it both lives in the historical process and knows itself as so living."

Of all the habits of thought which the historically self-conscious psychoanalyst is apt to detect in his work, one is most important for our book. In its determination to be sparing with teleological assumption, psychoanalysis has gone to the opposite extreme and developed a kind of *originology*—a term which I hope is sufficiently awkward to make a point without suggesting itself for general use. I mean by it a habit of thinking which reduces every human situation to an analogy with an earlier one, and most of all to that earliest, simplest, and most infantile precursor which is assumed to be its "origin."

Psychoanalysis has tended to subordinate the later stages of life to those of childhood. It has lifted to the rank of a cosmology the undeniable fact that man's adulthood contains a persistent childishness: that vistas of the future always reflect the mirages of a missed past, that apparent progression can harbor partial regressions, and firm accomplishment, hidden childish fulfillment. In exclusively studying what is repetition and regression and perseveration in human life, we have learned more about the infantile in the adult than was ever before known. We have thus prepared an ethical reorientation in human life which centers on the preservation of those early energies which man, in the very service of his higher values, is apt to suppress, exploit, or waste. In each treatment, and in all our applications, this reorientation governs our conscious intentions. To formulate them on an historically valid scale, however, it is necessary to realize that the psychopathologist, called upon to treat in theory and practice the passions, anxieties, and rages of the race, will always have to make some kind of convincing philosophy out of a state of partial knowledge; while neurotic patients and panicky people in general are so starved for beliefs that they will fanatically spread among the unbelievers what are often as yet quite shaky convictions.

Because we did not include this fact in our awareness, we were shocked at being called pansexualists when our interest (that is, the affects of curiosity and confirmation) was selectively aroused by the minutest references to sexual symbolism. We were distressed when we saw ourselves caricatured in patients who, in social life, spread a compulsive attitude of mutual mental denuding under the guise of being alert to the defensive tricks of the ego. And we were dismayed when we saw our purpose of enlightenment perverted into a widespread fatalism, according to which man is nothing but a multiplication of his parents' faults and an accumulation of his own earlier selves. We must grudgingly admit that even as we were trying to devise, with scientific determinism, a therapy for the few, we were led to promote an ethical disease among the many.

The existence and the multiplicity of defensive regressive mechanisms in adolescence were systematically demonstrated in Anna Freud's *The Ego and the Mechanisms of Defence*. Her book defines inner defense in the widest sense; but it does not foreclose the psychoanalysis of adolescent development. When she states: "The abstract intellectual discussions and speculations in which young people delight are not genuine attempts at solving the tasks set by reality. Their mental activity is rather an indication of a tense alertness for the instinctual processes and the translation into abstract thought of that which they perceive," she presents the defensive half of the story of adolescent rumination, the other half being its adaptive function, and its function in the history of changing ideas. In this book we will add to this formulation the historical concomitance which teaches us how, in the period between puberty and adulthood, the resources of tradition fuse with new inner resources to create something potentially new: a new person; and with this new person a new generation, and with that, a new era. The question of what happens to persons, generations, and eras because guiding ideologies are of postadolescent origin, will be discussed in conclusion, although it transcends the frame of this study, which is dedicated rather to the proposition that what we have learned as pathologists must become part of an ecology of the mind before we can take full responsibility for the ideological implications of our knowledge.

We cannot even begin to encompass the human life cycle without learning to account for the fact that a human being under observation has grown stage by stage into a social world; this world, always for worse *and* for better, has step by step prepared for him an outer reality made up of human traditions and institutions which utilize and thus nourish his developing capacities, attract and modulate his drives, respond to and delimit his fears and phantasies, and assign to him a position in life appropriate to his psychosocial powers. We cannot even begin to encompass a human being without indicating for each of the stages of his life cycle the framework of social influences and of traditional institutions which determine his perspectives on his more infantile past and on his more adult future. In this sense, we can learn from patients only to the extent that we realize (and the patient realizes) that what is said and done in treatment is based on a formal contract between healer and patient and must be carefully transposed before being applied to the general human condition. This is the reason why the fragments of case histories or psychoanalytic interpretations which flutter around in increasing numbers in our newspapers and magazines seem lost like bats in the daytime.

On the other hand, we cannot leave history entirely to nonclinical observers and to professional historians who often all too nobly immerse themselves into the very disguises, rationalizations, and idealizations of the historical process from which it should be their business to separate themselves. Only when the relation of historical forces to the basic functions and stages of the mind has been jointly charted and understood can we begin a psychoanalytic critique of society as such without falling back into mystical or moralistic philosophizing.

Freud warned against the possible misuse of his work as an ideology, a *"Weltanschauung"*; but as we shall see in Luther's life and work, a man who inspires new ideas has little power to restrict them to the area of his original intentions. And Freud himself did not refrain from interpreting other total approaches to man's condition, such as religion, as consequences of man's inability to shake off the bonds of his prolonged childhood, and thus comparable to collective neuroses. The psychological and historical study of the religious crisis of a young great man renews the opportunity to review this assertion in the light of ego-psychology and of theories of psychosocial development.

As to the dichotomy of psychoanalysis and religion, I will not approach it like a man with a chip on each shoulder. Psychology endeavors to establish what is demonstrably true in human behavior, including such behavior as expresses what to human beings seems true and feels true. I will interpret in psychological terms whatever phenomena clinical experience and psychoanalytic thought have made me recognize are dependent on man's demonstrable psychic structure. This is my job, as a clinician and as a teacher—a job which (as I have pointed out) includes the awareness that psychoanalysis for historical reasons often occupies a position on the borderline of what is demonstrably true and of what demonstrably *feels* true. The fact that each new vital focus of psychoanalytic research inadvertently leads to a new implied value system obliges us to ask ourselves whether or not we mean what we seem to be saying. It obligates us, as well as our critics, to differentiate psychoanalysism from psychoanalysis, and to realize that ours is not only a profession recognized among professions, but also a system of thought subject to fashionable manipulation by molders of public opinion. Our very success suggests that our partisanship be judicial.

Religion, on the other hand, elaborates on what feels profoundly true even though it is not demonstrable: it translates into significant words, images, and codes the exceeding darkness which surrounds man's existence, and the light which pervades it beyond all desert or comprehension. This being a historical book, however, religion will occupy our attention primarily as a source of ideologies for those who seek identities. In depicting the identity struggle of a *young* great man I am not as concerned with the validity of the dogmas which laid claim to him, or of the philosophies which influenced his systematic thought, as I am with the spiritual and intellectual milieu which the isms of his time—and these isms *had* to be religious —offered to his passionate search.

My focus, then, is on the "ideological." In modern history, this word has assumed a specifically political connotation, referring to totalitarian systems of thought which distort historical truth by methods ranging from fanatic self-deception to shrewd falsification and cold propaganda. Karl Mannheim has analyzed this word and the processes for which it stands from the sociological point of view. In this book, *ideology* will mean an unconscious tendency underlying religious and scientific as well as political thought: the tendency at a given time to make facts amenable to ideas, and ideas to facts, in order to create a world image convincing enough to support the collective and the individual sense of identity. Far from being arbitrary or consciously manageable (although it is as exploitable as all of man's unconscious strivings), the total perspective created by ideological simplification reveals its strength by the dominance it exerts on the seeming logic of historical events, and by its influence on the identity formation of individuals (and thus on their "ego-strength"). In this sense, this is a book on identity and ideology.

In some periods of his history, and in some phases of his life cycle, man needs (until we invent something better) a new ideological orientation as surely and as sorely as he must have air and food. I will not be ashamed then, even as I analyze what is analyzable, to display sympathy and empathy with a young man who (by no means lovable all of the time) faced the problems of human *existence* in the most forward terms of his era. I will use the word *existential* in this simplest connotation, mindful that no school of thought has any monopoly on it.

Selected Bibliography

Childhood and Society (New York: W. W. Norton & Company, Inc., 1963).

Gandhi's Truth (New York: W. W. Norton & Company, Inc., 1969).

Identity and the Life Cycle (New York: International Universities Press, 1959).

Identity, Youth and Crisis (New York: W. W. Norton & Company, Inc., 1968).

Insight and Responsibility (New York: W. W. Norton & Company, Inc., 1964).

Young Man Luther (New York: W. W. Norton & Company, Inc., 1958).

Youth: Change and Challenge (New York: Basic Books, Inc., 1963).

The Peak-Experience

Abraham H. Maslow

Born on April 1, 1908, Abraham Maslow was trained at the University of Wisconsin, from which he took his doctorate in 1934. From 1929 to 1934 he was on the faculty at Wisconsin; in 1935, he moved to Columbia University where he was a Carnegie research fellow. He moved to Brooklyn College in 1937, remaining there until 1951. In 1951 he went to the Psychology Department of Brandeis University, where he remained until his death in 1970. The essay that follows was given as a public lecture June 30, 1961, at La Jolla, California. It exhibits Maslow's interest in giving a description in psychological terminology to those experiences that are sometimes denominated as "religious" or "mystical."

What I'm going to talk about tonight is an excursion into the psychology of health, or of the human being at his best. It's a report from the road, of a job not yet done—a kind of commando raid into the unknown in which I have left my scientific flanks very much exposed. This is a warning to those of you who like neatly finished tasks. This is far from finished.

When I started to explore the psychology of health, I picked out the finest, healthiest people, the best specimens of mankind I could find, and studied them to see what they were like. They were *very* different, startlingly different in some ways from the average. The biologist was right who announced that he had found the missing link between the anthropoid apes and civilized man. "It's *us!*"

I learned many lessons from these people. But one in particular is our concern now. I found that these individuals tended to report having had something like mystic experiences, moments of great awe, moments of the most intense happiness or even rapture, ecstasy or bliss (because the word happiness can be too weak to describe this experience).

These moments were of pure, positive happiness when all doubts, all fears, all inhibitions, all tensions, all weaknesses, were left behind.

Abraham H. Maslow, "Lessons from the Peak-Experiences," in *Journal of Humanistic Psychology*, Vol. II, No. 1 (1962), pp. 9–18. Reprinted by permission.

Now self consciousness was lost. All separateness and distance from the world disappeared as they felt *one* with the world, fused with it, really belonging in it and to it, instead of being outside looking in. (One subject said, for instance, "I felt like a member of a family, not like an orphan.")

Perhaps most important of all, however, was the report in these experiences of the feeling that they had really seen the ultimate truth, the essence of things, the secret of life, as if veils had been pulled aside. Alan Watts has described this feeling as, "This is *it!*", as if you had finally gotten there, as if ordinary life was a striving and a straining to get someplace and this was the arrival, this was *Being There!*; the end of straining and of striving, the achievement of the desire and the hope, the fulfillment of the longing and the yearning. Everyone knows how it feels to want something and not know what. These mystic experiences feel like the ultimate satisfaction of vague, unsatisfied yearnings. They are like a sudden stepping into heaven; like the miracle achieved, like perfection finally attained.[1]

But here I had already learned something new. The little that I had ever read about mystic experiences tied them in with religion, with visions of the supernatural. And, like most scientists, I had sniffed at them in disbelief and considered it all nonsense, maybe hallucinations, maybe hysteria—almost surely pathological.

But the people telling me or writing about these experiences were not such people—they were the healthiest people! That was one thing learned! And I may add that it taught me something about the limitations of the small (not the big) orthodox scientist who won't recognize as knowledge, or as reality, any information that doesn't fit into the already existent science. ("I am the master of this college; what I know not is not knowledge.")

These experiences mostly had nothing to do with religion—at least in the ordinary supernaturalistic sense. They came from the great moments of love and sex, from the great esthetic moments (particularly of music), from the bursts of creativeness and the creative furore (the great inspiration), from great moments of insight and of discovery, from women giving natural birth to babies—or just from loving them, from moments of fusion with nature (in a forest, on a seashore, mountains, etc.), from certain athletic experiences, e.g., skindiving, from dancing, etc.

---

[1] "If a man could pass through paradise in a dream, and have a flower presented to him as a pledge that his soul had really been there, and if he found that flower in his hand when he awoke, ay, what then!" Coleridge.

The second big lesson learned was that this was a *natural,* not a *supernatural* experience; and I gave up the name "mystic" experience and started calling them peak-experiences. They can be studied scientifically. (I have started to do this.) They are within reach of human knowledge, not eternal mysteries. They are in the world, not *out* of the world. They belong not only to priests but to all mankind. They are no longer questions of faith but are wide open to human inquisitiveness and to human knowledge. Observe also the implication of naturalistic usages for the words "revelation," "heaven," "salvation," etc. The history of the sciences has been of one science after another carving a chunk for itself out of the jurisdiction of religion. It seems to be happening again here. Or to put this all another way, peak-experiences can be considered to be truly religious experiences in the best and most profound, most universal, and most humanistic sense of that word. It may turn out that pulling religion into the realm of science will have been the most important consequence of this line of work.

The next big lesson learned was that peak-experiences are far more common than I had ever expected: they were *not* confined to healthy people. These peak-experiences occurred also in average and even in psychologically sick people. As a matter of fact, I now suspect they occur in practically everybody although without being recognized or accepted for what they are.

Think for a minute how crazy this is in its implications. It's taken a long time for it to soak in on me. *Practically everybody reports peak-experiences if approached and questioned and encouraged in the right way. Also I've learned that just talking about it, as I'm doing now, seems to release from the depths all sorts of secret memories of peaks never revealed to anyone before, not even to oneself perhaps.* Why are we so shy about them? If something wonderful happens to us, why do we conceal it? Someone pointed out once, "Some people are scared to die; but some are scared to live." Maybe this is it.

There is considerable overlap between the characteristics of peak-experiences and the characteristics of psychological health (more integrated, more alive, more individual, less inhibited, less anxious, etc.) so I have been tempted to call the peak-experience a transient or temporary episode of self-actualization or health. If this *guess* turns out to be correct, it is like saying almost everyone, even the sickest people, can be psychologically healthy part of the time.

Still another lesson that by now I'm very sure of: peak-experiences come from many, many sources and to every kind of person. My list of sources seems to keep on getting longer and longer as I go on with these explorations. Sometimes I am tempted to think that almost any situation where perfection can be attained, or hope fulfilled, or perfect gratification reached, or where everything has gone smoothly, can produce in some people, at some times, a peak-experience. These can be very humble areas of life or of the workaday world; or the situation may have been repeated a thousand times before without producing a peak-experience.

"If your everyday life seems poor to you," wrote Rilke in his *Letters to a Young Poet*, "do not accuse it; accuse yourself, tell yourself you are not poet enough to summon up its riches, since for the creator there is no poverty and no poor or unimportant place."

For instance, a young mother scurrying around her kitchen and getting breakfast for her husband and young children. The sun was streaming in, the children clean and nicely dressed, were chattering as they ate. The husband was casually playing with the children; but as she looked at them she was suddenly so overwhelmed with their beauty and her great love for them, and her feeling of good fortune, that she went into a peak-experience. (This reminds me of my surprise at getting such reports from women. The surprise taught me how much we had masculinized all this.)

A young man working his way through medical school by drumming in a jazz band reported years later, that in all his drumming he had three peaks when he suddenly felt like a great drummer and his performance was perfect.

A hostess after a dinner party where everything had gone perfectly and it had been a fine evening, said good-bye to her last guest, sat down in a chair, looked around at the mess, and went into a peak of great happiness and exhilaration.

Milder peaks have come after a good dinner with good friends as a man sat smoking a fine cigar, or in a woman after she had done a really good cleaning up in her kitchen and it shone and sparkled and looked perfect.

Thus it is clear that there are many paths to these experiences of rapture. They are not necessarily fancy or occult or arcane or esoteric. They don't necessarily take years of training or study. They are not restricted to far-out people, i.e., to monks, saints, or yogis, Zen Buddhists, orientals, or people in any special state of grace. It is not something that happens in the Far East, in special places, or to specially trained or chosen people. It's available in the midst of life to everyday people in everyday occupations. This is a clear support for the writers on Zen and their concept of "nothing special."

Now another generalization which I'm fairly sure of by now. No matter what the source of the peak-experience, all peak-experiences seem to overlap, to tend to be alike. I can't say they're identical—they're not. But they're much closer to being identical than I had ever dreamed. It was a startling thing for me to hear a mother describing her ecstatic feelings during the birth of her one child and using some of the same words and phrases that I had read in the writings of St. Theresa of Avila, or Meister Eckhardt, or in Japanese or Hindu descriptions of *satori* or *samadhi* experiences. (Aldous Huxley makes this same point in his "Perennial Philosophy.")

I haven't done this very carefully yet—these are so far only pilot or preliminary explorations—but I do feel safe in generalizing all peak-experiences to some extent. *The stimuli are very different: the subjective experience tends to be similar.* Or to say it in another way: our *kicks* are the same; we just get them from different paths, perhaps even from rock and roll, drug addiction and alcohol in less strong people. I feel more sure of this after reading in the literatures of mystic experiences, cosmic consciousness, oceanic experiences, esthetic experiences, creative experiences, love experiences, parental experiences, sexual experiences, and insight experiences. They all overlap; they approach similarity and even identity.

One main benefit I've gotten from this discovery, and that we all may get, is that it will help us to understand each other better. If a mathematician and a poet use similar words in describing their peak-experiences from a successful poem and a successful mathematical proof, maybe they're more alike subjectively than we have thought. I can make such parallels between a high school athlete running to a touchdown, a business man describing his feelings over plans for a perfect fig canning factory, a college student catching on to the Adagio movements of Beethoven's Ninth Symphony. I feel men can learn more about women's inner life (and vice versa) if they learn about the things that give them their highest satisfaction and feelings of creativeness. For instance, college girls significantly more often than college boys report their high moments to come from *being* loved. The boys significantly more often get their happiest moments from success, conquest, achievement, winning. This finding conforms both to common sense knowledge and to clinical experience.

If our inner experiences of happiness are very similar no matter what stimulates them and no matter how different the people these experiences happen to (that is, if our insides are more like each other than our outside) then this may furnish us a way of being more sympathetic and understanding with people who are very different from ourselves; athletes and intellectuals, women and men, adults and children, etc. An artist and a housewife are not 1000 miles apart. In some moments they speak a common language, have common experiences, and live in the same world.

Can you bring about these experiences at will? No! Or almost entirely no! In general we are "Surprised by Joy," to use the title of C. S. Lewis's book on just this question. Peaks come unexpectedly, suddenly they *happen* to us. You can't count on them. And, hunting them is a little like hunting happiness. It's best not done directly. It comes as a by-product—an epiphenomenon, for instance, of doing a fine job at a worthy task you can identify with.

Of course we can make it more likely, or less likely, out of our experiences in the past. Some fortunate people can almost always have a peak-experience in sex. Some can count on certain pieces of music, or certain favorite activities like dancing or skindiving. But none of these is ever *guaranteed* to bring on a peak-experience. The most propitious frame of mind for "receiving" them is one of receptivity, almost a kind of passivity, or trust, or surrender, a Taoistic attitude of letting things happen without interfering or butting in. You have to be able to give up pride, will, dominance, being at the wheel, being in charge. You have to be able to relax and let it happen.

I think this will do for you what it did for me—renew my interest in Taoism and the lessons it has to teach. So also for Zen. (On the whole, I can say that my findings conform more with the Zen and Tao philosophies than with any of the religious mysticisms.) . . .

. . . It must by now be obvious to those who are familiar with the literature of mystical experiences that these peak-experiences are very much like them, and overlap them but are not identical with them. What their true relationship is, I do not know. My best guess is that they are different in degree but not in kind. The total mystical experience, as classically described, is more or less approached by greater or lesser peak-experiences.

Selected Bibliography

Goals in Humanistic Education (Big Sur, California: Esalen Institute, 1968).

The Healthy Personality (New York: Van Nostrand Reinhold Company, 1969).

Motivation and Personality (New York: Harper and Row, Publishers. Inc., 1954).

New Knowledge in Human Values (New York: Harper and Row, Publishers, Inc., 1959).

Principles of Abnormal Psychology: The Dynamics of Psychic Illness (New York: Harper and Row, Publishers, Inc., 1951).

Religion, Values, and Peak-Experiences (Columbus: Ohio State University Press, 1964).

Toward a Psychology of Being (New York: Van Nostrand Reinhold Company, 1968).

Index

Cohen, Hermann, 293
Collective representations, 92, 175
Communication, structuralism and, 177–78; *see also* Language
Comparative religion, 188, 190–216, 260, 267–72, 273–80
   evolutionism and, 120–26; *see also* Evolutionism
   function of theology and, 257
Comte, Auguste, 3, 56, 85, 294–96
Confucianism, 29, 31, 200, 218–19, 275
   social psychology of, 218, 219
Confucius, 29, 369
Conscience collective, 92, 175
Conscious models, 176–77
Consciousness
   Buddhist, 39n
   structure of, 138–40
   unconscious mind and, 365–75
Cook, S. A., 127
Creative process, unity of, 301
Culture
   conceptions of, 49–53, 75, 79, 299–300
   man defined in terms of human, 293–302
   matriarchal, 58–69
   religion as, 183–86
   structuralism and, 175
   symbolism in, 287

Danielou, Jean Cardinal, 250, 273–80
Darwin, Charles, 76, 104, 130, 296, 323
Dasgupta, Surendranath, 168
Death, 348–49, 361–62
Delimitation, 232–35
Depth dimension, 49–53
Descartes, René, 310
Dewey, John, 297–98
Dimensions of religions, 208–16
Doctrinal dimension, 210–11
Dreams, 373
Dumézil, Georges, 10, 56, 136, 144n, 150, 161–66, 313
Durkheim, Emile, 10, 11, 56, 85, 93–103, 127, 128, 175, 239n, 349
Dynamic religion, 104–109
Dysfunctions, 228–29

Eckhardt, Meister, 390
Economic ethic, 217–18
Eidós principle, 144

Einstein, Albert, 286, 323
Élan vital, defined, 104
Eliade, Mircea, 136. 168–71
   Cioran on, 10–11
   influence of, 146, 161, 234
   symbols and, 309, 311, 313, 316
Emerson, Ralph Waldo, 33, 355
Engnell, Ivan, 119
Enlightenment (Buddhist principle), 15, 33–44
Enlightenment, the, 18–19, 48
"Entelecheia," 152–60
Epoché, defined, 143, 144
Erikson, Erik H., 354, 376–85
Essence, 124–26, 191–93, 282–83
Evans-Pritchard, E. E., 57, 127–33, 289, 345
"Everyday mind," 39n
Evolutionism, 57, 111–26, 129, 160
   defined, 261–62
   as interpretive principle, 119–26
   as obsolete, 154
   origin of men and, 76
   survival of fittest and, 73
Experimental dimension, 212–14

Failure, 360–62
Fairytales, 304–306
Farrar, Frederic W., 130
Fichte, Johann C., 20
First principles, 13–53
Focal objects in methodological approach to religion, 4
Franklin, Benjamin, 243, 247
Frazer, Sir James G., 10, 56, 57, 78–84, 119, 122, 127, 131
   concept of magic of, criticized, 124–26
Freedom, effects of, 199–202
Freud, Anna, 382
Freud, Sigmund, 209, 211, 213, 309, 311, 323, 365, 383–84
Frick, H., 156, 157

Galton, F., 130
Gandhi, Mohandas K., 284, 376
Geertz, Clifford, 136, 183-86
Gilgamesh epic, 371–72
Gilson, Etienne, 137
Gjerstad, Einar, 111
Gnosticism, 112–13, 226
God
   as appeal from failures, 361n
   in civil religion, 238–47

Christian and Islamic, 215–16
basis of belief in, 46; *see also* Belief
emissary prophecy and concept of, 226–27
as explanatory hypothesis, 331–32
myth-making function and concept of, 108–109
as necessary, 333
omniscience of, 147–48
origin of concept, of, 56, 78–84
problem of evil and, 356–57
religion and concept of, 97
social origin of belief in, 222, 226–27
truth of one religion and nature of, 201
world religions and new concept of, 143–44
See also High God
Goethe, Johann Wolfgang von, 360
Goodenough, Erwin R., 10, 11, 13, 14n, 45–48, 250, 281–86
Greek mythology, 61–65, 165–66
Greek religion, 31, 164–65
Guénon, René, 274

Halle, M., 180
Hamilton, Alexander, 243–47
Hartmann, Nicolai, 263–64
Hayes, E. Nelson, 173
Hayes, Tanya, 173
Health, psychology of, 386–92
Healthy-mindedness, world-sickness and, 355–64
Heavenly Father, 148; *see also* God
Heidegger, Martin, 309
Heiler, F., 142, 146
Henotheism, concept of, 160
Herberg, Will, 241n
Herz, Henrietta, 20
Herz, Marcus, 20
Hidding, K. A. H., 150
Hierophany, 169
High God, 14, 119
concept of, 25–32
Nilsson on, 112
prevalence of, in primitive religion, 153–54
as primary datum of religion, 4
primitive man and concept of, 147–49
Hinduism, 2, 161-64, 194, 202, 273
authority and, 199–200
proselytism and, 269
social psychology of, 217–27

ritual purity and, 233
Historical logic of development of religions, 155
History, 149
comparative religion and, 190–203
of religion, function of, 284
religion precedes, 55
Hocking, William, 27n
Holmer, Paul L., 289, 341–44
Holy, concept of, 46; *see also* Sacred, the
Homo religiosus, 170–71, 190, 281, 369
as cultural worker, 376–85
Hubert, Henri, 89, 101n, 125
Humanism, 213
Hume, David, 333–34
Husserl, Edmund, 137, 138, 261, 309, 310
Huxley, Aldous, 390

Identity crisis, 377
Ideology, 383–85
Illusion, religious, 47–48
Indo-European culture, 161–65
Intellectualism, 221–24
Intelligence
of archaic man, 86–91, 112–14, 116–18, 120–33, 168–71, 345–52, 372
constitution of, 114–17, 139
evolution of, 104–11, 296–97, 304–305
Institutionalization of religion, 189, 228–37, 373
Islam, 2, 150, 156, 190, 364
development of, 192–95
God of, 215–16
as major religion, 28–32
religious person as, 193–203
social psychology of, 217–27
transformation of, 273–80

Jacobson, Roman, 179–82
James, E. O., 146n
James, Henry (brother of William), 355
James, Henry (father of William), 355
James, William, 297, 308, 354–64, 368
Jaspers, Karl, 42n, 234, 316
Jefferson, Thomas, 243–46
Jesus Christ, 156, 274–77, 283
as ultimate revelation, 251–53, 274–75
Judaism, 2, 338–39

Mysticism, 86–88, 131, 388–91
    Christian and non-Christian, 274–80
    defined, 107–109
    revelation through, 212–13
Myth-making function, religion as con-
        trived by, 105–106, 108–109
"Myth and Ritual School," 3
Mythological dimension, 210
Mythology, 301
    comparative, 70
    importance of, 98, 102–103
    language of, 307–308
    mother right in Greek, 61–65
    nature of, 303–308
    religious ties to, 55
    symbols distinguished from, 316
    as translations of needs, 94
    theology and, 256–66
    tremendum and, 283
    tripartitism in Indo-European,
        161–66

National religions, 28–32, 206
Naturalism, 363
Neo-Pythagoreanism, 226
New religion, emergence of, 285–86
Newton, Sir Isaac, 117
Nietzsche, Friedrich, 259
Nilsson, Martin, P., 10, 11, 57, 111–
    18
Non-Christian religions, 267–80
Nonliving religions, 206
Novalis, 20
Numinal experience, 16–24
Numinosum, ritual and, 367–68
Nygren, Anders, 13

O'Dea, Thomas F., 189, 228–37
Omniscience, phenomenology of reli-
        gion and divine, 147–48
Orders, societies as system of, 178–79
Organism, religion as, 215–16
Original monotheism, defined, 28
Otto, Rudolf, 13, 16–24, 142, 156, 259,
    261, 263, 367

Parsons, Talcott, 10, 227n, 229
Paternal powers, 305–306
Patriarchy, ascendency of, 63–64, 68
Paul, St., 213, 233, 277, 278
Peak-experience, 386–92
Pederson, Johs., 144n
Personality, religion and, 353–92
Pépin, M., 314

Pettazzoni, R., 10, 14, 15, 28–32, 119,
    144, 146–49, 153
Phenomenology, 3, 135–60, 288
Philosophy, 77, 137–41, 300–301, 307,
    329
    Wittgenstein and, 321–29
Piaget, Jean, 181
Pietism, history of, 16
Piety, defined, 21–24
Pius XII (Pope), 279
Politics, religion and, 224–25, 235–47
Polytheism, High God and, 153
Power, dilemma of, in religion, 235–37
Primitive civilization, as privileged cases,
    96–97
Primitive man, 70–77
    cause and effect and, 89–90
    High God and, 147–49
    sacred and, 169–71
    search for primordium and, 127–33
Primitive mentality, 56, 85–91
    associations in, 113–17
    lack of a special, 121–23
Primitive religion, defined, 120–21
Primitive religious system, defined,
    92–93
Primitive societies, 26–27, 173–82,
    345–52
Profane, as mode of being, 169–71
Primordium, 55–133
Proselytism, 269
Protestantism, 369
    alienation of symbolism in, 230
    civil religion and, 247
    delimitation dilemma in, 233
    individual revelation and, 374
    influence on modern, 17
    power dilemma for, 235–37
Psychoanalysis, 379–85
Psychological origin of religion, 282–83
Psychology, 353–92
Purification of religion, 159–60

Radhakrishnan, Sarvepalli, 250, 267–72
Radin, P., 122, 123, 129
Rationalism, 17–20, 222–26
Reality, 262–65, 345–50
Redemption, 221–22
Reductionism, 13–53
Regeneration, power of, 155–56
Reinach, Salomon, 265
Religion
    belief in God and, 25–27, 37, 46–47,
        80–81, 108–109, 143, 208–209,